ALL GLORY TO ŚRĪ GURU AND GAURĀṄGA

ŚRĪMAD BHĀGAVATAM

of

KṚṢṆA-DVAIPĀYANA VYĀSA

निष्किञ्चना मय्यनुरक्तचेतसः
शान्ता महान्तोऽखिलजीववत्सलाः ।
कामैरनालब्धधियो जुषन्ति ते
यन्नैरपेक्ष्यं न विदुः सुखं मम ॥१७॥

niṣkiñcanā mayy anurakta-cetasaḥ
śāntā mahānto 'khila-jīva-vatsalāḥ
kāmair anālabdha-dhiyo juṣanti te
yan nairapekṣyaṁ na viduḥ sukhaṁ mama

(p. 222)

BOOKS by His Divine Grace A. C. Bhaktivedanta Swami Prabhupāda

Bhagavad-gītā As It Is
Śrīmad-Bhāgavatam, cantos 1–10 (30 vols.)
Śrī Caitanya-caritāmṛta (17 vols.)
Teachings of Lord Caitanya
The Nectar of Devotion
The Nectar of Instruction
Śrī Īśopaniṣad
Easy Journey to Other Planets
Kṛṣṇa Consciousness: The Topmost Yoga System
Kṛṣṇa, the Supreme Personality of Godhead (3 vols.)
Perfect Questions, Perfect Answers
Dialectical Spiritualism—A Vedic View of Western Philosophy
Teachings of Lord Kapila, the Son of Devahūti
Transcendental Teachings of Prahlād Mahārāja
Teachings of Queen Kuntī
Kṛṣṇa, the Reservoir of Pleasure
The Science of Self-Realization
The Path of Perfection
Search for Liberation
Life Comes From Life
The Perfection of Yoga
Beyond Birth and Death
On the Way to Kṛṣṇa
Geetār-gan (Bengali)
Vairāgya-vidyā (Bengali)
Buddhi-yoga (Bengali)
Bhakti-ratna-bolī (Bengali)
Rāja-vidyā: The King of Knowledge
Elevation to Kṛṣṇa Consciousness
Kṛṣṇa Consciousness: The Matchless Gift
Back to Godhead magazine (founder)

A complete catalog is available upon request.

Bhaktivedanta Book Trust
3764 Watseka Avenue
Los Angeles, California 90034

ŚRĪMAD BHĀGAVATAM

Eleventh Canto

"General History"

(Part Three—Chapters 10–17)

With the Original Sanskrit Text,
Its Roman Transliteration, Synonyms,
Translation and Elaborate Purports

The Great Work of

His Divine Grace
A. C. Bhaktivedanta Swami Prabhupāda
Founder-*Ācārya* of the International Society for Krishna Consciousness

Continued by

His Divine Grace
Hridayananda dāsa Goswami Ācāryadeva

Sanskrit Editing by

Gopīparāṇadhana dāsa Adhikārī

THE BHAKTIVEDANTA BOOK TRUST
Los Angeles · London · Paris · Bombay · Sydney

Readers interested in the subject matter of this book are invited by the International Society for Krishna Consciousness to correspond with its Secretary:

International Society for Krishna Consciousness
3764 Watseka Avenue
Los Angeles, California 90034

First Printing, 1982: 5,000 copies

Library of Congress Cataloging in Publication Data (Revised)

Puranas. Bhāgavatapurāna. English & Sanskrit.
Śrīmad-Bhāgavatam.

Includes bibliographical references and indexes.
Contents: Canto 1. Creation (3 v)— Canto 2. The cosmic manifestation (2 v)— Canto 3. The status quo (4 v)— Canto 4. The creation of the fourth order (4 v)— Canto 5. The creative impetus (2 v)— Canto 6. Prescribed duties for mankind (3 v)— Canto 7. The science of God (3 v)— Canto 8. Withdrawal of the cosmic creations (3 v)— Canto 9. Liberation (3 v)— Canto 10. The summum bonum (3 v)— Canto 11. General history (5 v)

Canto 11- by Hridayananda Goswami Ācāryadeva, completing the great work of His Divine Grace A.C. Bhaktivedanta Swami Prabhupāda; Sanskrit editing by Gopīparāṇadhana Dāsa Adhikārī.

1. Puranas. Bhāgavatapurāṇa—Criticism, interpretation, etc. 2. Chaitanya, 1486–1534. 3. Vaishnavites—India—Biography.
I. Bhaktivedanta Swami, A. C., 1896–1977.
II. Hridayananda Goswami, 1948–
III. Gopīparāṇadhana Dāsa Adhikārī.
IV. Title.
BL1140.4.B432E5 1972 294.5'925 73-169353
ISBN 0-89213-116-0 (Canto 11,v.3) AACR2

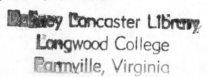

Table of Contents

CHAPTER TWELVE

Beyond Renunciation and Knowledge

CHAPTER THIRTEEN

The Haṁsa-avatāra Answers the Questions of the Sons of Brahmā

CHAPTER FOURTEEN

Lord Kṛṣṇa Explains the Yoga System to Śrī Uddhava

CHAPTER FIFTEEN

Lord Kṛṣṇa's Description of Mystic Yoga Perfections

CHAPTER SIXTEEN

The Lord's Opulence

CHAPTER SEVENTEEN

Lord Kṛṣṇa's Description of the Varṇāśrama System

Appendixes

Preface

nama oṁ viṣṇu-pādāya kṛṣṇa-preṣṭhāya bhū-tale
śrīmate bhaktivedānta-svāmin iti nāmine

I offer my most respectful obeisances at the lotus feet of His Divine Grace A. C. Bhaktivedanta Swami Prabhupāda, who is very dear to Lord Kṛṣṇa on this earth, having taken shelter at His lotus feet.

namas te sārasvate deve gaura-vāṇī-pracāriṇe
nirviśeṣa-śūnyavādi-pāścātya-deśa-tāriṇe

I offer my most respectful obeisances unto the lotus feet of His Divine Grace A. C. Bhaktivedanta Swami Prabhupāda, who is the disciple of Śrīla Bhaktisiddhānta Sarasvatī Ṭhākura and who is powerfully distributing the message of Caitanya Mahāprabhu and thus saving the fallen Western countries from impersonalism and voidism.

Śrīmad-Bhāgavatam, with authorized translation and elaborate purports in the English language, is the great work of His Divine Grace Oṁ Viṣṇupāda Paramahaṁsa Parivrājakācārya Aṣṭottara-śata Śrī Śrīmad A. C. Bhaktivedanta Swami Prabhupāda, our beloved spiritual master. Our present publication is a humble attempt by his servants to complete his most cherished work of *Śrīmad-Bhāgavatam.* Just as one may worship the holy Ganges River by offering Ganges water unto the Ganges, similarly, in our attempt to serve our spiritual master, we are offering to him that which he has given to us.

Śrīla Prabhupāda came to America in 1965 at a critical moment in the history of America and the world in general. The story of Śrīla Prabhupāda's arrival and his specific impact on world civilization, and especially

Western civilization, has been brilliantly documented by His Divine Grace Satsvarūpa dāsa Goswami. In Śrīla Satsvarūpa's authorized biography of Śrīla Prabhupāda, called *Śrīla Prabhupāda-līlāmṛta*, the reader can fully understand Śrīla Prabhupāda's purpose, desire and mission in presenting *Śrīmad-Bhāgavatam.* Further, in Śrīla Prabhupāda's own preface to the *Bhāgavatam* (reprinted as the Foreword in this volume), he clearly states that this transcendental literature will provoke a cultural revolution in the world, and that is now underway. I do not wish to be redundant in repeating what Śrīla Prabhupāda has so eloquently stated in his preface, nor that which has been so abundantly documented by Śrīla Satsvarūpa in his authorized biography.

It is necessary to mention, however, that *Śrīmad-Bhāgavatam* is a completely transcendental, liberated sound vibration coming from the spiritual world. And, being absolute, it is not different from the Absolute Truth Himself, Lord Śrī Kṛṣṇa. By understanding *Śrīmad-Bhāgavatam,* consisting of twelve cantos, the reader acquires perfect knowledge by which he or she may live peacefully and progressively on the earth, attending to all material necessities and achieving simultaneously supreme spiritual liberation. In preparing this and other volumes of *Śrīmad-Bhāgavatam,* our intention and methodology has been always to serve faithfully the lotus feet of our spiritual master, carefully trying to translate and comment exactly as he would have, thus preserving the unity and spiritual potency of this edition of *Śrīmad-Bhāgavatam.* In other words, by strictly following the disciplic succession, called in Sanskrit *guru-paramparā,* this edition of the *Bhāgavatam* will continue to be throughout its volumes a liberated work, free from material contamination and capable of elevating the reader to the kingdom of God.

The purport is that we have faithfully followed the commentaries of previous *ācāryas* and exercised a calculated selectivity of material based on the example and mood of Śrīla Prabhupāda. One may write transcendental literature only by the mercy of the Supreme Personality of Godhead, Śrī Kṛṣṇa, and the authorized, liberated spiritual masters coming in disciplic succession. Thus, we humbly fall at the lotus feet of the previous *ācāryas,* offering special gratitude to the great commentators on the *Bhāgavatam,* namely Śrīla Śrīdhara Svāmī, Śrīla Jīva Gosvāmī, Śrīla Viśvanātha Cakravartī Ṭhākura and Śrīla Bhaktisiddhānta Sarasvatī Gosvāmī, the spiritual master of Śrīla Prabhupāda. We also offer our obeisances at the lotus feet of Śrīla Vīrarāghavācārya, Śrīla Vijayadhvaja Ṭhākura and Śrīla Vaṁśīdhara Ṭhākura, whose commentaries have also helped in this work. Additionally, we offer our humble obeisances at the lotus feet of the great *ācārya* Śrīla Madhva, who has made innumerable learned comments on *Śrīmad-Bhāgavatam.* We further offer our humble obeisances at the lotus feet of the Supreme Personality of Godhead, Śrī Kṛṣṇa Caitanya Mahāprabhu, and to all of His eternally liberated followers, headed by Śrīla Nityānanda Prabhu, Advaita Prabhu, Gadādhara Prabhu and Śrīvāsa Ṭhākura, and to the six Gosvāmīs, Śrīla Rūpa Gosvāmī, Śrīla Sanātana Gosvāmī, Śrīla Raghunātha dāsa Gosvāmī, Śrīla Raghunātha Bhaṭṭa Gosvāmī, Śrīla Jīva Gosvāmī and Śrīla Gopāla Bhaṭṭa Gosvāmī. Finally we offer our most respectful obeisances at the lotus feet of the Absolute Truth, Śrī Śrī Rādhā and Kṛṣṇa, and humbly beg for Their mercy so that this great work of *Śrīmad-Bhāgavatam* can be quickly finished. *Śrīmad-Bhāgavatam* is undoubtedly the most important book within the universe, and the sincere readers of *Śrīmad-Bhāgavatam* will undoubtedly achieve the highest perfection of life, Kṛṣṇa consciousness.

In conclusion, I again remind the reader that *Śrīmad-Bhāgavatam* is the great work of His Divine Grace A. C. Bhaktivedanta Swami Prabhupāda, and that the present volume is the humble attempt of his devoted servants.

Hare Kṛṣṇa

Hridayananda dāsa Goswami

Foreword

We must know the present need of human society. And what is that need? Human society is no longer bounded by geographical limits to particular countries or communities. Human society is broader than in the Middle Ages, and the world tendency is toward one state or one human society. The ideals of spiritual communism, according to *Śrīmad-Bhāgavatam,* are based more or less on the oneness of the entire human society, nay, of the entire energy of living beings. The need is felt by great thinkers to make this a successful ideology. *Śrīmad-Bhāgavatam* will fill this need in human society. It begins, therefore, with the aphorism of Vedānta philosophy *janmādy asya yataḥ* to establish the ideal of a common cause.

Human society, at the present moment, is not in the darkness of oblivion. It has made rapid progress in the field of material comforts, education and economic development throughout the entire world. But there is a pinprick somewhere in the social body at large, and therefore there are large-scale quarrels, even over less important issues. There is need of a clue as to how humanity can become one in peace, friendship and prosperity with a common cause. *Śrīmad-Bhāgavatam* will fill this need, for it is a cultural presentation for the respiritualization of the entire human society.

Śrīmad-Bhāgavatam should be introduced also in the schools and colleges, for it is recommended by the great student-devotee Prahlāda Mahārāja in order to change the demoniac face of society.

kaumāra ācaret prājño
dharmān bhāgavatān iha
durlabhaṁ mānuṣaṁ janma
tad apy adhruvam arthadam
(*Bhāg.* 7.6.1)

Disparity in human society is due to lack of principles in a godless civilization. There is God, or the Almighty One, from whom everything emanates, by whom everything is maintained and in whom everything is merged to rest. Material science has tried to find the ultimate source of creation very insufficiently, but it is a fact that there is one ultimate source of everything that be. This ultimate source is explained rationally and authoritatively in the beautiful *Bhāgavatam*, or *Śrīmad-Bhāgavatam.*

Śrīmad-Bhāgavatam is the transcendental science not only for knowing the ultimate source of everything but also for knowing our relation with Him and our duty toward perfection of the human society on the basis of this perfect knowledge. It is powerful reading matter in the Sanskrit language, and it is now rendered into English elaborately so that simply by a careful reading one will know God perfectly well, so much so that the reader will be sufficiently educated to defend himself from the onslaught of atheists. Over and above this, the reader will be able to convert others to accept God as a concrete principle.

Śrīmad-Bhāgavatam begins with the definition of the ultimate source. It is a bona fide commentary on the *Vedānta-sūtra* by the same author, Śrīla Vyāsadeva, and gradually it develops into nine cantos up to the highest state of God realization. The only qualification one needs to study this great book of transcendental knowledge is to proceed step by step cautiously and not jump forward haphazardly as with an ordinary book. It should be gone through chapter by chapter, one after another. The reading matter is so arranged with its original Sanskrit text, its English transliteration, synonyms, translation and purports so that one is sure to become a God-realized soul at the end of finishing the first nine cantos.

The Tenth Canto is distinct from the first nine cantos because it deals directly with the transcendental activities of the Personality of Godhead, Śrī Kṛṣṇa. One will be unable to capture the effects of the Tenth Canto without going through the first nine cantos. The book is complete in twelve cantos, each independent, but it is good for all to read them in small installments one after another.

I must admit my frailties in presenting *Śrīmad-Bhāgavatam*, but still I am hopeful of its good reception by the thinkers and leaders of society on the strength of the following statement of *Śrīmad-Bhāgavatam* (1.5.11):

tad-vāg-visargo janatāgha-viplavo
yasmin prati-ślokam abaddhavaty api

nāmāny anantasya yaśo 'ṅkitāni yac
chṛṇvanti gāyanti gṛṇanti sādhavaḥ

"On the other hand, that literature which is full with descriptions of the transcendental glories of the name, fame, form and pastimes of the unlimited Supreme Lord is a transcendental creation meant to bring about a revolution in the impious life of a misdirected civilization. Such transcendental literatures, even though irregularly composed, are heard, sung and accepted by purified men who are thoroughly honest."

Oṁ tat sat

A. C. Bhaktivedanta Swami

Introduction

"This *Bhāgavata Purāṇa* is as brilliant as the sun, and it has arisen just after the departure of Lord Kṛṣṇa to His own abode, accompanied by religion, knowledge, etc. Persons who have lost their vision due to the dense darkness of ignorance in the age of Kali shall get light from this *Purāṇa*." (*Śrīmad-Bhāgavatam* 1.3.43)

The timeless wisdom of India is expressed in the *Vedas*, ancient Sanskrit texts that touch upon all fields of human knowledge. Originally preserved through oral tradition, the *Vedas* were first put into writing five thousand years ago by Śrīla Vyāsadeva, the "literary incarnation of God." After compiling the *Vedas*, Vyāsadeva set forth their essence in the aphorisms known as *Vedānta-sūtras*. *Śrīmad-Bhāgavatam* (*Bhāgavata Purāṇa*) is Vyāsadeva's commentary on his own *Vedānta-sūtras*. It was written in the maturity of his spiritual life under the direction of Nārada Muni, his spiritual master. Referred to as "the ripened fruit of the tree of Vedic literature," *Śrīmad-Bhāgavatam* is the most complete and authoritative exposition of Vedic knowledge.

After compiling the *Bhāgavatam*, Vyāsa impressed the synopsis of it upon his son, the sage Śukadeva Gosvāmī. Śukadeva Gosvāmī subsequently recited the entire *Bhāgavatam* to Mahārāja Parīkṣit in an assembly of learned saints on the bank of the Ganges at Hastināpura (now Delhi). Mahārāja Parīkṣit was the emperor of the world and was a great *rājarṣi* (saintly king). Having received a warning that he would die within a week, he renounced his entire kingdom and retired to the bank of the Ganges to fast until death and receive spiritual enlightenment. The *Bhāgavatam* begins with Emperor Parīkṣit's sober inquiry to Śukadeva Gosvāmī: "You are the spiritual master of great saints and devotees. I am therefore begging you to show the way of perfection for all persons, and especially for one who is about to die. Please let me know what a man should hear, chant, remember and worship, and also what he should not do. Please explain all this to me."

Śukadeva Gosvāmī's answer to this question, and numerous other questions posed by Mahārāja Parīkṣit, concerning everything from the nature of the self to the origin of the universe, held the assembled sages in rapt attention continuously for the seven days leading to the King's death. The sage Sūta Gosvāmī, who was present on the bank of the Ganges when Śukadeva Gosvāmī first recited *Śrīmad-Bhāgavatam*, later repeated the *Bhāgavatam* before a gathering of sages in the forest of Naimiṣāraṇya. Those sages, concerned about the spiritual welfare of the people in general, had gathered to perform a long, continuous chain of sacrifices to counteract the degrading influence of the incipient age of Kali. In response to the sages' request that he speak the essence of Vedic wisdom, Sūta Gosvāmī repeated from memory the entire eighteen thousand verses of *Śrīmad-Bhāgavatam*, as spoken by Śukadeva Gosvāmī to Mahārāja Parīkṣit.

The reader of *Śrīmad-Bhāgavatam* hears Sūta Gosvāmī relate the questions of Mahārāja Parīkṣit and the answers of Śukadeva Gosvāmī. Also, Sūta Gosvāmī sometimes responds directly to questions put by Śaunaka Ṛṣi, the spokesman for the sages gathered at Naimiṣāraṇya. One therefore simultaneously hears two dialogues: one between Mahārāja Parīkṣit and Śukadeva Gosvāmī on the bank of the Ganges, and another at Naimiṣāraṇya between Sūta Gosvāmī and the sages at Naimiṣāraṇya Forest, headed by Śaunaka Ṛṣi. Furthermore, while instructing King Parīkṣit, Śukadeva Gosvāmī often relates historical episodes and gives accounts of lengthy philosophical discussions between such great souls as Nārada Muni and Vasudeva. With this understanding of the history of the *Bhāgavatam*, the reader will easily be able to follow its intermingling of dialogues and events from various sources. Since philosophical wisdom, not chronological order, is most important in the text, one need only be attentive to the subject matter of *Śrīmad-Bhāgavatam* to appreciate fully its profound message.

The translator of this edition compares the *Bhāgavatam* to sugar candy—wherever you taste it, you will find it equally sweet and relishable. Therefore, to taste the sweetness of the *Bhāgavatam*, one may begin by reading any of its volumes. After such an introductory taste, however, the serious reader is best advised to go back to Volume One of the First Canto and then proceed through the *Bhāgavatam*, volume after volume, in its natural order.

This edition of the *Bhāgavatam* is the first complete English translation of this important text with an elaborate commentary, and it is the first widely available to the English-speaking public. The first thirty volumes (Canto One through Canto Ten, Volume Three) are the product of the scholarly and devotional effort of His Divine Grace A. C. Bhaktivedanta Swami Prabhupāda, the world's most distinguished teacher of Indian religious and philosophical thought. His consummate Sanskrit scholarship and intimate familiarity with Vedic culture and thought as well as the modern way of life combine to reveal to the West a magnificent exposition of this important classic. Śrīla Prabhupāda departed from this world in 1977, and his monumental work of translating *Śrīmad-Bhāgavatam* is being continued by his disciple His Divine Grace Hridayananda Goswami Ācāryadeva.

Readers will find this work of value for many reasons. For those interested in the classical roots of Indian civilization, it serves as a vast reservoir of detailed information on virtually every one of its aspects. For students of comparative philosophy and religion, the *Bhāgavatam* offers a penetrating view into the meaning of India's profound spiritual heritage. To sociologists and anthropologists, the *Bhāgavatam* reveals the practical workings of a peaceful and scientifically organized Vedic culture, whose institutions were integrated on the basis of a highly developed spiritual world view. Students of literature will discover the *Bhāgavatam* to be a masterpiece of majestic poetry. For students of psychology, the text provides important perspectives on the nature of consciousness, human behavior and the philosophical study of identity. Finally, to those seeking spiritual insight, the *Bhāgavatam* offers simple and practical guidance for attainment of the highest self-knowledge and realization of the Absolute Truth. The entire multivolume text, presented by the Bhaktivedanta Book Trust, promises to occupy a significant place in the intellectual, cultural and spiritual life of modern man for a long time to come.

—The Publishers

CHAPTER TEN

The Nature of Fruitive Activity

In this chapter Lord Śrī Kṛṣṇa refutes the philosophy of the followers of Jaimini and describes to Uddhava how the spirit soul bound within the material body can develop pure transcendental knowledge.

The Vaiṣṇava, or one who has taken shelter of the Supreme Personality of Godhead, Viṣṇu, should observe the rules and regulations found in the *Pañcarātra* and other revealed scriptures. According to his own natural qualities and work, he should follow the code of *varṇāśrama* in a spirit free from motivation. The so-called knowledge received through one's material senses, mind and intelligence is as useless as the dreams experienced by a sleeping person attached to sense gratification. Therefore, one should give up work performed for sense gratification and accept work as a matter of duty. When one has come to understand something of the truth of the self, he should give up material work performed out of duty and simply engage himself in the service of the bona fide spiritual master, who is the manifest representative of the Personality of Godhead. The servant of the spiritual master should have very firm affection for his *guru,* should be anxious to receive from him knowledge of the Absolute Truth, and should be devoid of envy and the tendency to talk nonsense. The soul is distinct from the gross and subtle material bodies. The spirit soul who has entered into the material body accepts bodily functions according to the reactions of his own past activities. Therefore, only the bona fide, transcendental spiritual master is capable of demonstrating pure knowledge of the self.

The followers of Jaimini and other atheistic philosophers accept regulated material work as the purpose of life. But Kṛṣṇa refutes this by explaining that the embodied soul who has come into contact with segmented material time takes upon himself a perpetual chain of births and deaths and is therefore forced to suffer the consequent happiness and distress. In this way there is no possibility that one who is attached to the fruits of his material work can achieve any substantial goal in life. The pleasures of heaven and other destinations, which are achieved by sacrificial rituals, can be experienced for only a short time. After one's enjoyment is finished, one must return to this mortal sphere to partake of lamentation and suffering. On the path of materialism there is certainly no uninterrupted or natural happiness.

TEXT 1

श्रीभगवानुवाच

मयोदितेष्ववहितः स्वधर्मेषु मदाश्रयः ।
वर्णाश्रमकुलाचारमकामात्मा समाचरेत् ॥ १ ॥

śrī-bhagavān uvāca
mayoditeṣv avahitaḥ
sva-dharmeṣu mad-āśrayaḥ
varṇāśrama-kulācāram
akāmātmā samācaret

śrī-bhagavān uvāca—the Supreme Personality of Godhead said; *mayā*—by Me; *uditeṣu*—spoken; *avahitaḥ*—with great care; *sva-dharmeṣu*—in the duties of devotional service to the Lord; *mat-āśrayaḥ*—one who accepts Me as shelter; *varṇa-āśrama*—the Vedic system of social and occupational divisions; *kula*—of the society; *ācāram*—conduct; *akāma*—devoid of material desires; *ātmā*—such a person; *samācaret*—should practice.

TRANSLATION

The Supreme Personality of Godhead said: Taking full shelter in Me, with the mind carefully fixed in the devotional service of the Lord as spoken by Me, one should live without personal desire and practice the social and occupational system called varṇāśrama.

PURPORT

In the previous chapters Lord Kṛṣṇa described through the story of an *avadhūta brāhmaṇa* the qualities and character of a saintly person. Now the Lord describes the practical means for achieving such a saintly position. In the *Pañcarātra* and other scriptures the Personality of Godhead gives instructions for executing devotional service. Similarly, in *Bhagavad-gītā* (4.13) the Lord says, *cātur-varṇyaṁ mayā sṛṣṭaṁ guṇa-karma-vibhāgaśaḥ:* "I have personally created the *varṇāśrama* system." There are innumerable rules and regulations in the *varṇāśrama* system, and the devotee should execute those which do not contradict the process of devotional service. The term *varṇa* indicates different classes of human beings, some in the mode of ignorance, some in the mode of passion and some in the mode of goodness. Devotional service to the Lord is executed on the liberated platform, and therefore some injunctions for those persons in passion and ignorance may be contradictory to the regulative principles for those on the liberated platform. Therefore, under the guidance of a bona fide spiritual master who is nondifferent from the Lord, one should execute the basic principles of *varṇāśrama* in a way favorable for advancement in Kṛṣṇa consciousness.

TEXT 2

अन्वीक्षेत विशुद्धात्मा देहिनां विषयात्मनाम् ।
गुणेषु तत्त्वध्यानेन सर्वारम्भविपर्ययम् ॥ २ ॥

anvīkṣeta viśuddhātmā
dehināṁ viṣayātmanām
guṇeṣu tattva-dhyānena
sarvārambha-viparyayam

anvīkṣeta—one should see; *viśuddha*—purified; *ātmā*—soul; *dehinām*—of the embodied beings; *viṣaya-ātmanām*—of those who are dedicated to sense gratification; *guṇeṣu*—in the material objects of pleasure; *tattva*—as truth; *dhyānena*—by conceiving; *sarva*—of all; *ārambha*—endeavors; *viparyayam*—the inevitable failure.

TRANSLATION

A purified soul should see that because the conditioned souls who are dedicated to sense gratification have falsely accepted the objects of sense pleasure as truth, all of their endeavors are doomed to failure.

PURPORT

In this verse the Lord describes the process of becoming desireless. All material sense objects, including those perceived by their form, taste, flavor, touch or sound, are temporary. We now see our family and nation, but ultimately they will disappear. Even our own body, by which we perceive them, will disappear. Thus, the inevitable result of material enjoyment is *viparyaya*, or great suffering. The word *viśuddhātmā* indicates those who have purified themselves by executing the regulative duties of devotional service. They can clearly see the hopeless frustration of material life, and thus they become *akāmātmā*, or great souls free from material desire.

TEXT 3

सुप्तस्य विषयालोको ध्यायतो वा मनोरथः ।
नानात्मकत्वाद् विफलस्तथा भेदात्मधीर्गुणैः ॥ ३ ॥

suptasya viṣayāloko
dhyāyato vā manorathaḥ
nānātmakatvād viphalas
tathā bhedātma-dhīr guṇaiḥ

suptasya—of one who is sleeping; *viṣaya*—sense gratification; *ālokaḥ*—seeing; *dhyāyataḥ*—of one who is meditating; *vā*—or; *manaḥ-rathaḥ*—merely a creation of the mind; *nānā*—a large variety; *ātmaka-tvāt*—due to having the nature of; *viphalaḥ*—bereft of the real perfection; *tathā*—in that way; *bheda-ātma*—in that which is separately constituted; *dhīḥ*—intelligence; *guṇaiḥ*—by the material senses.

TRANSLATION

One who is sleeping may see many objects of sense gratification in a dream, but such pleasurable things are merely creations of the mind and are thus ultimately useless. Similarly, the living entity who is asleep to his spiritual identity also sees many sense objects, but these innumerable objects of temporary gratification are creations of the Lord's illusory potency and have no permanent exis-

tence. One who meditates upon them, impelled by the senses, uselessly engages his intelligence.

PURPORT

Because the fruits of material work are temporary, it ultimately does not matter whether or not one obtains them; the final result is the same. Materialistic activities can never award the highest perfection of life, Kṛṣṇa consciousness. The material intelligence, impelled by the senses, strongly desires sense gratification. As stated here (*bhedātma-dhīḥ*), such intelligence actually separates one from one's real self-interest. Thus the intelligence, absorbed in that which is materially favorable and unfavorable, becomes divided in pursuit of innumerable categories of material advancement. Such divided intelligence is impotent and cannot understand the Absolute Truth, the Personality of Godhead, Śrī Kṛṣṇa. The devotees of the Lord, however, have their intelligence fixed on one point—Lord Kṛṣṇa. They meditate upon the Lord's form, qualities, pastimes and devotees, and thus their intelligence is never separated from the Absolute Truth. As stated in *Bhagavad-gītā* (2.41):

vyavasāyātmikā buddhir
ekeha kuru-nandana
bahu-śākhā hy anantāś ca
buddhayo 'vyavasāyinām

"Those who are on this path are resolute in purpose, and their aim is one. O beloved child of the Kurus, the intelligence of those who are irresolute is many branched."

If one is not Kṛṣṇa conscious, he is uselessly dreaming without any understanding of his eternal situation. The material intelligence will always devise novel means of achieving happiness, and therefore one bounces from one fruitless program of sense gratification to another, ignoring the simple fact that all material things are temporary and will disappear. In this way one's intelligence becomes infected with material lust and greed, and such infected intelligence cannot bring one to the true goal of life. One should hear from the bona fide spiritual master whose intelligence is pure, and then one will come to Kṛṣṇa consciousness, the highest perfection of life.

TEXT 4

निवृत्तं कर्म सेवेत प्रवृत्तं मत्परस्त्यजेत् ।
जिज्ञासायां संप्रवृत्तो नाद्रियेत् कर्मचोदनाम् ॥ ४ ॥

nivṛttaṁ karma seveta
pravṛttaṁ mat-paras tyajet
jijñāsāyāṁ sampravṛtto
nādriyet karma-codanām

nivṛttam—regulative duties; *karma*—such work; *seveta*—one should perform; *pravṛttam*—activities for sense gratification; *mat-paraḥ*—one who is dedicated to Me; *tyajet*—should give up; *jijñāsāyām*—in searching for spiritual truth; *sampravṛttaḥ*—being perfectly engaged; *na*—not; *ādriyet*—one should accept; *karma*—any material activity; *codanām*—injunctions governing.

TRANSLATION

One who has fixed Me within his mind as the goal of life should give up activities based on sense gratification and should instead execute work governed by the regulative principles for advancement. When, however, one is fully engaged in searching out the ultimate truth of the soul, one should not accept the scriptural injunctions governing fruitive activities.

PURPORT

Śrīla Viśvanātha Cakravartī Ṭhākura explains that the words *jijñāsāyāṁ sampravṛttaḥ* refer to one who is *yoga-ārūḍha*, or advanced in the *yoga* process. In *Bhagavad-gītā* (6.3–4) it is stated:

ārurukṣor muner yogaṁ
karma kāraṇam ucyate
yogārūḍhasya tasyaiva
śamaḥ kāraṇam ucyate

yadā hi nendriyārtheṣu
na karmasv anuṣajjate

sarva-saṅkalpa-sannyāsī
yogārūḍhas tadocyate

"For one who is a neophyte in the eightfold *yoga* system, work is said to be the means; and for one who has already attained to *yoga*, cessation of all material activities is said to be the means. A person is said to have attained to *yoga* when, having renounced all material desires, he neither acts for sense gratification nor engages in fruitive activities." The example may be given that an ordinary man will try to enjoy the company of women for material sense pleasure. This is called *pravṛtta-karma*, or the path of sense gratification. A religious person will also enjoy the company of a woman, but under the regulative principles of the *varṇāśrama* system. However, one who is fully absorbed in spiritual advancement will ultimately give up all sense gratification derived from sexual association, either regulated or illicit. Similarly, in the stage of *pravṛtta-karma*, or ordinary sense gratification, one will eat whatever pleases his tongue. On the other hand, a materialistic devotee will sometimes cook sumptuous preparations and offer them to the Deity, not in order to satisfy the Lord but rather with the intention of satisfying his own tongue and belly. However, one who is *sampravṛtta*, or fully engaged in spiritual consciousness, is never interested in simply gratifying his tongue. He avoids ordinary foods prepared by materialistic persons, and just for the purpose of keeping his body fit for serving Kṛṣṇa he eats moderate quantities of food that has first been offered to the Deity for the Deity's pleasure.

The process of spiritual realization gradually brings a conditioned soul from the lowest point of materialistic consciousness to total absorption in loving service to the Personality of Godhead. In the beginning one is taught to dovetail one's enjoying propensities by first offering to the Lord the fruit of one's work. In the advanced stage, however, the impulse to execute fruitive activities (*karma-codanām*) is absent, and one simply engages in the loving service of the Lord without any selfish motive. For example, a renounced *sannyāsī* preaching Kṛṣṇa consciousness, or even a renounced householder preaching Kṛṣṇa consciousness, is not required to execute all of the injunctions governing sense gratification in family life. Ultimately, every human being should take to the transcendental duties of Kṛṣṇa consciousness. Rather than working to fulfill one's own desires and then offering the results to Kṛṣṇa, one should fully engage in pleasing the Lord directly according to His own intimate desires.

According to Śrīla Bhaktisiddhānta Sarasvatī Ṭhākura, any attempt to enjoy the material world, either religiously or irreligiously, ultimately will be full of contradictions. One should come to the true platform of desirelessness, pure love of Godhead, and thus solve all of the problems of life.

TEXT 5

यमानभीक्ष्णं सेवेत नियमान् मत्परः क्वचित् ।
मदभिज्ञं गुरुं शान्तमुपासीत मदात्मकम् ॥ ५ ॥

yamān abhīkṣṇaṁ seveta
niyamān mat-paraḥ kvacit
mad-abhijñaṁ guruṁ śāntam
upāsīta mad-ātmakam

yamān—major regulative principles, such as not to kill; *abhīkṣṇam*—always; *seveta*—one should observe; *niyamān*—minor regulations, such as cleansing the body; *mat-paraḥ*—one who is devoted to Me; *kvacit*—as far as possible; *mat-abhijñam*—one who knows Me as I am in My personal form; *gurum*—the spiritual master; *śāntam*—peaceful; *upāsīta*—one should serve; *mat-ātmakam*—who is not different from Me.

TRANSLATION

One who has accepted Me as the supreme goal of life should strictly observe the scriptural injunctions forbidding sinful activities and, as far as possible, should execute the injunctions prescribing minor regulative duties such as cleanliness. Ultimately, however, one should approach a bona fide spiritual master who is as full in knowledge of Me as I am, who is peaceful and who by spiritual elevation is not different from Me.

PURPORT

The word *yamān* refers to major regulative injunctions necessary for preserving one's purity. In the Kṛṣṇa consciousness movement all bona fide members must give up eating meat, fish and eggs, and they must also avoid intoxication, gambling and illicit sex. The word *abhijñam* indicates that one cannot at any time perform such forbidden activities, even in difficult circumstances. The word *niyamān* refers to less obligatory injunctions, such as bathing three times daily. In certain difficult situations one may not bathe three times daily yet may still maintain one's spiritual position. But if one engages in sinful, forbidden activities, even in difficult circumstances, there undoubtedly will be a spiritual falldown. Ultimately, as explained in *Upadeśāmṛta*, mere adherence to rules and regulations cannot give one spiritual perfection. One must approach a bona fide spiritual master who is *mad-abhijñam*, or in full knowledge of the personal form of Godhead. The word *mat* ("Me") negates the possibility of a bona fide spiritual master having an impersonal conception of the Absolute Truth. Furthermore, the *guru* must be in complete control of his senses; therefore he is called *śānta*, or peaceful. Because of being completely surrendered to the mission of the Lord, such a spiritual master is *mad-ātmakam*, or nondifferent from the Personality of Godhead.

TEXT 6

अमान्यमत्सरो दक्षो निर्ममो दृढसौहृदः ।
असत्वरोऽर्थजिज्ञासुरनसूयुरमोघवाक् ॥ ६ ॥

amāny amatsaro dakṣo
nirmamo dṛḍha-sauhṛdaḥ
asatvaro 'rtha-jijñāsur
anasūyur amogha-vāk

amānī—without false ego; *amatsaraḥ*—not considering oneself to be the doer; *dakṣaḥ*—without laziness; *nirmamaḥ*—without any sense of proprietorship over one's wife, children, home, society, etc.; *dṛḍha-sauhṛdaḥ*—being fixed in the mood of loving friendship with the spiritual master, who is one's worshipable deity; *asatvaraḥ*—without becoming bewildered due to material passion; *artha-jijñāsuḥ*—desiring knowledge of the Absolute Truth; *anasūyuḥ*—free from envy; *amogha-vāk*—completely free from useless conversation.

TRANSLATION

The servant or disciple of the spiritual master should be free from false prestige, never considering himself to be the doer. He should be active and never lazy and should give up all sense of proprietorship over the objects of the senses, including his wife, children, home and society. He should be endowed with feelings of loving friendship toward the spiritual master and should never become deviated or bewildered. The servant or disciple should always desire advancement in spiritual understanding, should not envy anyone and should always avoid useless conversation.

PURPORT

No one can claim to be the permanent proprietor of his so-called wife, family, home, society, and so on. Such material relationships appear and disappear like bubbles on the surface of the ocean. No one can claim to be the creator of the material elements that produced one's home, society and family. If it were a fact that parents were the ultimate creators of the bodies of their children, children would never die before their parents; the parents would simply create new bodies for the children. Similarly, parents would also not die, because they would create new bodies for themselves to replace the old ones. Actually, God creates everyone's bodies as well as the material elements with which we build our material societies. Therefore, before death drags these things out of our grasp, we should voluntarily engage them in the loving service of the spiritual master, who is the bona fide representative of Lord Kṛṣṇa. Then such material objects, instead of causing lamentation, will be the cause of happiness.

TEXT 7

जायापत्यगृहक्षेत्रस्वजनद्रविणादिषु ।
उदासीनः समं पश्यन् सर्वेष्वर्थमिवात्मनः ॥ ७ ॥

jāyāpatya-gṛha-kṣetra-
svajana-draviṇādiṣu
udāsīnaḥ samaṁ paśyan
sarveṣv artham ivātmanaḥ

jāyā—to wife; *apatya*—children; *gṛha*—home; *kṣetra*—land; *sva-jana*—relatives and friends; *draviṇa*—bank account; *ādiṣu*—and so on; *udāsīnaḥ*—remaining indifferent; *samam*—equally; *paśyan*—seeing; *sarveṣu*—in all of these; *artham*—purpose; *iva*—like; *ātmanaḥ*—of oneself.

TRANSLATION

One should see one's real self-interest in life in all circumstances and should therefore remain detached from wife, children, home, land, relatives, friends, wealth, and so on.

PURPORT

A devotee of the Lord recognizes that his wife, children, home, land, friends and money are meant to be engaged in the loving service of the Supreme Lord. Therefore, he does not frantically make arrangements for the sense gratification of his family and friends. He is not eager to enjoy the false prestige of being the master of his wife and the lord of his children, nor is he anxious to gain prestige from his friends and society. Thus he does not envy anyone and is not lazy in the matter of self-realization. He is free from the false sense of proprietorship and is always eager to develop his understanding of the Supreme Personality of Godhead. He is free from false egotism and automatically turns away from useless materialistic conversation. Thus he is steady and not whimsical, and he is always firmly situated in loving friendship at the lotus feet of the spiritual master.

The question may be raised as to how one can develop freedom from false proprietorship. Śrīla Viśvanātha Cakravartī Ṭhākura has given the following example. An ordinary man is very eager to accumulate more and more money, and he maintains his wealth in the form of stocks, bonds, securities, bank accounts, properties, gold, and so on. As long as these different assets are contributing to his financial well-being, he sees them equally and considers that they belong to him. But if some of his assets are taken by the government for taxes, or if they are lost in an unfortunate business arrangment, then he is forced to give up his sense of proprietorship. In the same way, everyone should be intelligent enough to observe that one's sense of ownership over innumerable material objects is not permanent; therefore one should develop detachment from these things. If one does not cultivate a loving feeling of friendship for the Supreme Personality of Godhead and His pure devotee, the spiritual master, one will undoubtedly be entangled by the network of material society, friendship and love. One will then remain bound up on the material platform with no hope of permanent happiness.

TEXT 8

विलक्षणः स्थूलसूक्ष्माद् देहादात्मेक्षिता स्वदृक् ।
यथाग्निर्दारुणो दाह्याद् दाहकोऽन्यः प्रकाशकः ॥८॥

vilakṣaṇaḥ sthūla-sūkṣmād
dehād ātmekṣitā sva-dṛk
yathāgnir dāruṇo dāhyād
dāhako 'nyaḥ prakāśakaḥ

vilakṣaṇaḥ—having different characteristics; *sthūla*—from the gross; *sūkṣmāt*—and the subtle; *dehāt*—from the body; *ātmā*—the spirit soul; *īkṣitā*—the seer; *sva-dṛk*—self-enlightened; *yathā*—just as; *agniḥ*—fire; *dāruṇaḥ*—from firewood; *dāhyāt*—from that which is to be burned; *dāhakaḥ*—that which burns; *anyaḥ*—other; *prakāśakaḥ*—that which illuminates.

TRANSLATION

Just as fire, which burns and illuminates, is different from firewood, which is to be burned to give illumination, similarly the seer within the body, the self-enlightened spirit soul, is different from the material body, which is to be illuminated by consciousness. Thus the spirit soul and the body possess different characteristics and are separate entities.

PURPORT

It is analytically demonstrated in this verse that one should never falsely identify the ego with the material body. Such misidentification is called false ego, or material illusion. The following question may be raised. Since it is commonly known that the Supreme Personality of Godhead enlightens the conditioned soul, why is the term *sva-dṛk*, or "self-

His Divine Grace
A. C. Bhaktivedanta Swami Prabhupāda
Founder-Ācārya of the International Society for Krishna Consciousness

PLATE ONE: **The Evolution of the Soul**

Lord Kṛṣṇa, the Supreme Personality of Godhead, said to His friend and disciple Uddhava, "Just as fire may appear as dormant, manifest, weak, brilliant, and so on, according to the condition of the fuel, similarly, the spirit soul enters a material body and accepts particular bodily characteristics." The Vedic literatures inform us that there are 8,400,000 species of life, including aquatic, plant, insect, bird, animal

and human varieties. The conditioned soul, having fallen from its original position as a loving servant of the Supreme Lord in the spiritual world, enters these different bodies. In the human form the original nature of the soul is most brilliantly displayed. The human form of life is especially intended for qualifying oneself to return back home, back to Godhead, but if the conditioned soul misuses this opportunity, he may descend once more into the lower species. (*p. 14*)

PLATE TWO: **The Saintly Person Sees the Spiritual Identity of the Living Beings**

The sufferings of the living beings are caused by their identification with the temporary material body. In actuality, the living beings are eternal fragmental parts of the Supreme Personality of Godhead, sharing in His qualities of eternity, knowledge and bliss, but under the spell of false identification with the material body, the conditioned soul undergoes suffering and lamentation. The miseries he experiences, however, are, like those experienced in a dream, merely illusory. The self-realized sage, who sees the true spiritual identity of the living beings and their eternal relationship with Lord Kṛṣṇa, is therefore never bewildered by material happiness or distress. He knows they are caused by a lack of transcendental knowledge. Lord Kṛṣṇa explains to Uddhava, "Just as a dream is merely a creation of one's intelligence but has no actual substance, similarly, material lamentation, illusion, happiness, distress and the acceptance of the material body under the influence of *māyā* are all creations of My illusory energy. In other words, material existence has no essential reality." (*pp. 54–55*)

PLATE THREE: **The Allegory of Two Birds in a Tree**

Lord Kṛṣṇa said, "By chance, two birds have made a nest together in the same tree. The two birds are friends and are of similar nature. One of them, however, is eating the fruits of the tree, whereas the other, who does not eat the fruits, is in a superior position, due to His potency. The bird who does not eat the fruits of the tree is the Supreme Personality of Godhead, who by His omniscience perfectly understands His own position and that of the conditioned living entity, represented by the eating bird. That living entity, on the other hand, does not understand himself or the Lord. He is covered by ignorance and is thus called eternally conditioned, whereas the Personality of Godhead, being full of perfect knowledge, is eternally liberated." (*pp. 61–64*)

PLATE FOUR: **The Perfect Yogī Meditating Upon the Supersoul**

The Supreme Personality of Godhead said, "Sitting on a level seat that is not too high or too low, keeping the body straight and erect yet comfortable, placing the two hands on one's lap and focusing the eyes on the tip of one's nose, one should purify the pathways of breathing. Beginning from the *mūlādhāra-cakra*, one should move the life air continuously upward like the fibers in the lotus stalk until one reaches the heart, where the sacred syllable *oṁ* is situated like the sound of a bell. One should thus continue raising the sacred syllable upward. Keeping the eyes half closed and fixed on the tip of one's nose, being enlivened and alert, one should meditate on the lotus flower situated within the heart. One should meditate on the sun, moon and fire, placing them one after the other within the whorl of that lotus flower. Placing My transcendental form within the fire, one should meditate upon it as the auspicious goal of all meditation." (*pp. 138–43*)

PLATE FIVE: **The Supreme Lord's Swan Incarnation (Haṁsa)**

Lord Kṛṣṇa said, "Lord Brahmā desired to attain the answer to the question that was puzzling him, and thus he fixed his mind in Me, the Supreme Lord. At that time, in My form of Haṁsa, I became visible to Lord Brahmā." *Haṁsa* means "swan," and the specific ability of the swan is to separate a mixture of milk and water, extracting the rich, milky portion. Similarly, Lord Kṛṣṇa appeared as Haṁsa, or the swan, in order to separate the pure consciousness of Lord Brahmā from the modes of material nature. (*p. 176*)

PLATE SIX: **The Supersoul Within the Heart**

"That form is perfectly proportioned, gentle and cheerful. It possesses four beautiful long arms, a charming beautiful neck, a handsome forehead, a pure smile and glowing, shark-shaped earrings suspended from two identical ears. That spiritual form is the color of a dark raincloud and is garbed in golden yellowish silk. The chest of that form is the abode of Śrīvatsa and the goddess of fortune, and that form is also decorated with a conchshell, disc, club, lotus flower and garland of forest flowers. The two brilliant lotus feet are decorated with ankle bells and bracelets, and that form exhibits the Kaustubha gem along with an effulgent crown. The upper hips are beautified by a golden belt, and the arms are decorated with valuable bracelets. All of the limbs of that beautiful form capture the heart, and the face is beautified by merciful glancing." (*pp. 243–44*)

PLATE SEVEN: **The Mystic Yogī Leaves His Body**

Lord Kṛṣṇa said, "The *yogī* who has achieved the mystic perfection called *svacchanda-mṛtyu* (dying at will) blocks the anus with the heel of the foot and then lifts the soul from the heart to the chest, to the neck and finally to the head. Situated within the *brahma-randhra*, the *yogī* then gives up his material body and guides the spirit soul to the selected destination." After describing this and other mystic perfections, the Lord said, "Learned experts in devotional service state that the mystic perfections of *yoga* that I have mentioned are actually impediments and are a waste of time for one who is practicing the supreme *yoga*, by which one achieves all perfection of life directly from Me. Whatever mystic perfections can be achieved by good birth, herbs, austerities and *mantras* can all be achieved by devotional service to Me; indeed, one cannot achieve the actual perfection of *yoga* by any other means." (*pp. 269–79*)

enlightened," used in this verse? Śrīla Viśvanātha Cakravartī Ṭhākura explains that although the Supreme Personality of Godhead certainly furnishes consciousness to the living entity, the living entity, being endowed with the potency of the Lord, has himself the capacity to revive and expand his pure consciousness. He may therefore be considered, in a secondary sense, self-enlightened. The example may be given that gold or silver domes brilliantly reflect the rays of the sun. Although the light comes from the sun, the inherent properties of gold and silver can also be considered causes for the brilliant reflection, since other substances do not possess suitable properties to reflect the sun's light. Similarly, the spirit soul can be considered *sva-dṛk,* or self-enlightened, because he possesses characteristics by which he can brilliantly reflect the potency of the Personality of Godhead, thus illuminating his existential situation, just as a gold or silver dome shines due to its reflective properties.

A nice example is given in this verse to illustrate the different characteristics of the body and soul. Fire, which burns and illuminates, is always different from that which is burned for illumination. It may be said, however, that fire is present in an unmanifest form within wood. Similarly, in the conditioned life of ignorance, the spirit soul is present, though unmanifest, within the body. The enlightened condition of the living entity can be compared to the act of arousing fire within wood. Just as fire quickly burns wood to ashes, similarly the spirit soul, when enlightened, burns to ashes the darkness of ignorance. We are conscious of the body; therefore it may be said that the body is illuminated by consciousness, which is the energy, or symptom, of the spirit soul. Identifying the body and soul as one is just as foolish as considering fire and wood to be the same. In both cases, the intimate circumstantial connection between fire and wood or between the soul and the body does not alter the fact that fire is different from wood or that the soul is always different from the body.

TEXT 9

निरोधोत्पत्त्यणुबृहन्नानात्वं तत्कृतान् गुणान् ।
अन्तःप्रविष्ट आधत्त एवं देहगुणान् परः ॥ ९ ॥

nirodhotpatty-aṇu-bṛhan-
nānātvaṁ tat-kṛtān guṇān

antaḥ praviṣṭa ādhatta
evaṁ deha-guṇān paraḥ

nirodha—dormancy; *utpatti*—manifestation; *aṇu*—tiny; *bṛhat*—large; *nānātvam*—the variety of characteristics; *tat-kṛtān*—produced by that; *guṇān*—qualities; *antaḥ*—within; *praviṣṭaḥ*—having entered; *ādhatte*—accepts; *evam*—thus; *deha*—of the material body; *guṇān*—qualities; *paraḥ*—the transcendental entity.

TRANSLATION

Just as fire may appear differently as dormant, manifest, weak, brilliant, and so on, according to the condition of the fuel, similarly, the spirit soul enters a material body and accepts particular bodily characteristics.

PURPORT

Although fire may appear and disappear within a particular object, the element fire always exists. Similarly, the eternal soul appears within a suitable body and then disappears from that body, but the soul always exists. Just as fire is different from its fuel, the soul is different from the body. A match makes a tiny fire, whereas the explosion of a huge gasoline tank will send flames shooting up into the sky. But still, fire is one. Similarly, one spirit soul may appear in the body of Brahmā and another in the body of an ant, but the spirit soul is qualitatively the same in every body. Because of ignorance we impose the bodily characteristics upon the soul, and thus we say that a particular person is American, Russian, Chinese, African or Mexican or that he is old or young. Although such designations certainly apply to the body, they do not apply to the spirit soul, which is described here as *paraḥ*, or a transcendental entity. As long as the bewildered spirit soul remains inimical to the Supreme Personality of Godhead, the designations of the gross and subtle bodies will wrap themselves around him, keeping him in darkness. If one intellectually identifies oneself with various materialistic philosophies of life, he becomes covered by the subtle mind. Ultimately everything that exists is part and parcel of the Absolute Truth, Lord Kṛṣṇa. When the living entity realizes this, he becomes *nirupādhi*, or free from material designations. This is his constitutional position.

TEXT 10

योऽसौ गुणैर्विरचितो देहोऽयं पुरुषस्य हि ।
संसारस्तन्निबन्धोऽयं पुंसो विद्याच्छिदात्मनः ॥१०॥

yo 'sau guṇair viracito
deho 'yaṁ puruṣasya hi
saṁsāras tan-nibandho 'yaṁ
puṁso vidyā cchid ātmanaḥ

yaḥ—which; *asau*—that (subtle body); *guṇaiḥ*—by the material modes; *viracitaḥ*—constructed; *dehaḥ*—the body; *ayam*—this (gross body); *puruṣasya*—of the Supreme Personality of Godhead; *hi*—certainly; *saṁsāraḥ*—material existence; *tat-nibandhaḥ*—tied to that; *ayam*—this; *puṁsaḥ*—of the living entity; *vidyā*—knowledge; *chit*—that which cuts apart; *ātmanaḥ*—of the soul.

TRANSLATION

The subtle and gross material bodies are created by the material modes of nature, which expand from the potency of the Supreme Personality of Godhead. Material existence occurs when the living entity falsely accepts the qualities of the gross and subtle bodies as being his own factual nature. This illusory state, however, can be destroyed by real knowledge.

PURPORT

Regarding the analogy comparing fire and its fuel to the soul and the body, one may argue that to some extent fire is dependent upon its fuel and cannot exist without it. Since we do not experience the existence of fire independent of fuel, one may therefore still question how it is possible for the living entity to exist separately from the body, become covered by it and eventually become free from it. Only through the Supreme Personality of Godhead's knowledge potency (*vidyā*) can one clearly understand the nature of the living entity. By *vidyā*, or real knowledge, one may cut material existence to pieces and even in this lifetime experience spiritual reality. According to Śrīla Viśvanātha Cakravartī Ṭhākura, our material existence is an artificial imposition. By the Lord's inconceivable potency of nescience, the qualities of gross and subtle material forms are psychologically imposed upon the living being, and because of misidentification with the body, the living entity initiates a series of illusory activities. As explained in the previous chapter, the present material body is like a tree that produces the karmic seed of the next body. However, this cycle of ignorance can be cut to pieces by the transcendental knowledge explained by the Lord.

Unfortunately, the conditioned souls, being inimical to the Supreme Personality of Godhead, do not accept the perfect knowledge spoken by the Lord. Instead they remain absorbed in gross and subtle illusion. But if the living entity accepts the Lord's knowledge, his whole situation can be rectified, and he can return to his original, eternal, blissful life of perfect knowledge in the direct association of the Lord.

TEXT 11

तस्माज्जिज्ञासयात्मानमात्मस्थं केवलं परम् ।
सङ्गम्य निरसेदेतद्वस्तुबुद्धिं यथाक्रमम् ॥११॥

tasmāj jijñāsayātmānam
ātma-sthaṁ kevalaṁ param
saṅgamya nirased etad
vastu-buddhiṁ yathā-kramam

tasmāt—therefore; *jijñāsayā*—by the cultivation of knowledge; *ātmānam*—the Supreme Personality of Godhead; *ātma*—within oneself; *stham*—situated; *kevalam*—pure; *param*—transcendental and supreme; *saṅgamya*—approaching by realized knowledge; *niraset*—one should give up; *etat*—this; *vastu*—within material objects; *buddhim*—concept of reality; *yathā-kramam*—gradually, step by step.

TRANSLATION

Therefore, by the cultivation of knowledge one should approach the Supreme Personality of Godhead situated within oneself. By understanding the Lord's pure, transcendental existence, one should gradually give up the false vision of the material world as independent reality.

PURPORT

The word *yathā-kramam* ("step by step") means that after first realizing oneself to be different from the gross material body one should then progressively detach oneself from material mental activities. In this verse *etad vastu-buddhim* means seeing the material world as existing independently rather than correctly seeing all things as emanations of the Absolute Truth.

When one correctly identifies oneself as eternal spiritual form, one achieves the real fruit of knowledge. The Lord is eternally manifest in His eternal form, and the living entity is similarly manifest in his eternal form as the loving servitor of the Lord. When we falsely assume that temporary, illusory material objects are real, knowledge of our eternal spiritual form is covered by ignorance. If, however, one meditates upon the Lord's supreme presence within everything, one can return to the normal, blissful state of spiritual life. Every human being should seriously endeavor to understand the Absolute Truth, as indicated in this verse by the word *jijñāsayā.*

TEXT 12

आचार्योऽरणिराद्यः स्यादन्तेवास्युत्तरारणिः ।
तत्सन्धानं प्रवचनं विद्यासन्धिः सुखावहः ॥१२॥

ācāryo 'raṇir ādyaḥ syād
ante-vāsy uttarāraṇiḥ
tat-sandhānaṁ pravacanaṁ
vidyā-sandhiḥ sukhāvahaḥ

ācāryaḥ—the spiritual master; *araṇiḥ*—sacred kindling wood used in the sacrificial fire; *ādyaḥ*—held beneath; *syāt*—is to be considered; *ante-vāsī*—the disciple; *uttara*—at the top; *araṇiḥ*—kindling wood; *tat-sandhānam*—the stick in the middle, which connects the upper and lower wood; *pravacanam*—instructions; *vidyā*—transcendental knowledge; *sandhiḥ*—like the fire, arising from the friction, that spreads throughout the firewood; *sukha*—happiness; *āvahaḥ*—bringing.

TRANSLATION

The spiritual master can be compared to the lower kindling stick, the disciple to the upper kindling stick, and the instruction

given by the guru to the third stick placed in between. The transcendental knowledge communicated from guru to disciple is compared to the fire arising from the contact of these, which burns the darkness of ignorance to ashes, bringing great happiness both to guru and disciple.

PURPORT

When the darkness of ignorance is burned to ashes, the dangerous life of ignorance is also eradicated, and one can work for his true self-interest in full knowledge. In this verse the word *ādyaḥ* means "original," and it indicates the spiritual master, who is compared to the sacred kindling stick held below. From the spiritual master transcendental knowledge, like fire, is spread to the disciple. Just as friction between two sticks of firewood produces fire, similarly, bona fide contact between the spiritual master, who is the representative of Kṛṣṇa, and a sincere disciple produces the fire of knowledge. When the disciple takes shelter of the lotus feet of the spiritual master, he automatically acquires perfect knowledge of his original, spiritual form.

TEXT 13

वैशारदी सातिविशुद्धबुद्धि-
धुनोति मायां गुणसम्प्रसूताम् ।
गुणांश्च सन्दह्य यदात्ममेतत्
स्वयं च शाम्यत्यसमिद् यथाग्निः ॥१३॥

vaiśāradī sāti-viśuddha-buddhir
dhunoti māyāṁ guṇa-samprasūtām
guṇāṁś ca sandahya yad-ātmam etat
svayaṁ ca śāṁyaty asamid yathāgniḥ

vaiśāradī—available from the expert; *sā*—this; *ati-viśuddha*—most pure; *buddhiḥ*—intelligence or knowledge; *dhunoti*—repels; *māyām*—illusion; *guṇa*—from the modes of material nature; *samprasūtām*—produced; *guṇān*—the modes of nature themselves; *ca*—also; *sandahya*—completely burning up; *yat*—from which modes; *ātmam*—

constituted; *etat*—this (material existence); *svayam*—itself; *ca*—also; *śāmyati*—is pacified; *asamit*—without fuel; *yathā*—just as; *agniḥ*—fire.

TRANSLATION

By submissively hearing from an expert spiritual master, the expert disciple develops pure knowledge, which repels the onslaught of material illusion arising from the three modes of material nature. Finally this pure knowledge itself ceases, just as fire ceases when the stock of fuel has been consumed.

PURPORT

The Sanskrit word *vaiśāradī* means "that which is derived from the expert [*viśārada*]." Perfect transcendental knowledge comes from the expert spiritual master, and when such knowledge is heard by the expert disciple, it curbs the waves of material illusion. Since the Lord's illusory energy acts eternally within the material world, there is no possibility of destroying illusion. One may, however, destroy the presence of illusion within one's own heart. To accomplish this the disciple must become expert in pleasing the expert spiritual master. As one advances to the perfectional stage of Kṛṣṇa consciousness, experiencing the presence of the Lord everywhere, one's attention shifts to the transcendental platform. At that time, pure knowledge itself, one's constant technical awareness of illusion, diminishes, just as fire diminishes and is extinguished after consuming its stock of fuel.

Śrīla Madhvācārya has quoted from several Vedic scriptures to show that *māyā,* or material illusion, is just like a witch who always haunts the conditioned souls. *Māyā* offers the conditioned souls whatever they like within the three modes of nature, but such offerings are all just like fire that burns the heart to ashes. Therefore, one must understand that the material world is a hellish place, offering a permanent situation to no one. Externally we experience many things, and internally we contemplate our experience, formulating plans for future action. Thus internally and externally we are victims of ignorance. Real knowledge comes from the *Vedas,* or the Supreme Personality of Godhead in His form of perfect wisdom. If we become fully Kṛṣṇa conscious, taking complete shelter of the Lord, there will be no scarcity of pleasure, because the Lord is the reservoir of all pleasure, and His devotees freely move within that reservoir.

TEXTS 14–16

अथैषां कर्मकर्तॄणां भोक्तॄणां सुखदुःखयोः ।
नानात्वमथ नित्यत्वं लोककालागमात्मनाम् ॥१४॥
मन्यसे सर्वभावानां संस्था ह्यौत्पत्तिकी यथा ।
तत्तदाकृतिभेदेन जायते भिद्यते च धीः ॥१५ ॥
एवमप्यङ्ग सर्वेषां देहिनां देहयोगतः ।
कालावयवतः सन्ति भावा जन्मादयोऽसकृत्॥१६॥

athaiṣām karma-kartṝṇāṁ
bhoktṝṇāṁ sukha-duḥkhayoḥ
nānātvam atha nityatvaṁ
loka-kālāgamātmanām

manyase sarva-bhāvānāṁ
saṁsthā hy autpattikī yathā
tat-tad-ākṛti-bhedena
jāyate bhidyate ca dhīḥ

evam apy aṅga sarveṣāṁ
dehināṁ deha-yogataḥ
kālāvayavataḥ santi
bhāvā janmādayo 'sakṛt

atha—thus; *eṣām*—of those; *karma*—fruitive activities; *kartṝṇām*—of the performers; *bhoktṝṇām*—of the enjoyers; *sukha-duḥkhayoḥ*—of happiness and distress; *nānātvam*—variegatedness; *atha*—moreover; *nityatvam*—perpetual existence; *loka*—of the materialistic world; *kāla*—material time; *āgama*—Vedic literatures recommending fruitive activities; *ātmanām*—and the self; *manyase*—if you think; *sarva*—of all; *bhāvānām*—material objects; *saṁsthā*—the actual situation; *hi*—certainly; *autpattikī*—original; *yathā*—as; *tat-tat*—of all different objects; *ākṛti*—of their forms; *bhedena*—by the difference; *jāyate*—is born; *bhidyate*—and changes; *ca*—also; *dhīḥ*—intelligence or knowledge; *evam*—thus; *api*—even though; *aṅga*—O Uddhava; *sarveṣām*—of all; *dehinām*—embodied beings; *deha-yogataḥ*—by contact with a material body; *kāla*—of time; *avayavataḥ*—by the portions or limbs; *santi*—there are; *bhāvāḥ*—states of existence; *janma*—birth; *ādayaḥ*—and so on; *asakṛt*—constantly.

TRANSLATION

My dear Uddhava, I have thus explained to you perfect knowledge. There are philosophers, however, who challenge My conclusion. They state that the natural position of the living entity is to engage in fruitive activities, and they see him as the enjoyer of the happiness and unhappiness that accrue from his own work. According to this materialistic philosophy, the world, time, the revealed scriptures and the self are all variegated and eternal, existing as a perpetual flow of transformations. Knowledge, moreover, cannot be one or eternal, because it arises from the different and changing forms of objects; thus knowledge itself is always subject to change. Even if you accept such a philosophy, My dear Uddhava, there will still be perpetual birth, death, old age and disease, since all living entities must accept a material body subject to the influence of time.

PURPORT

In this verse, according to Śrīla Viśvanātha Cakravartī Ṭhākura, Lord Kṛṣṇa speaks the following to Uddhava. "My dear Uddhava, I have clearly established the actual goal of life in the instructions I have just imparted to you. There are those, however, who challenge My conclusion, especially the followers of Jaimini Kavi. If you are favorable to their understanding and thus do not accept My instructions, then kindly hear the following explanation.

"According to the followers of Jaimini, the living entity is originally and naturally a performer of fruitive activities, and his happiness and distress are derived from the fruits of his own work. The world in which the living entities find their enjoyment, the time during which they enjoy, the revealed scriptures that explain the means for achieving enjoyment, and the subtle bodies through which the living entities experience enjoyment all exist not only in manifold variety but also eternally.

"The living entity need not develop detachment from material sense gratification, either by seeing the temporariness of individual material objects and situations or by seeing the material world as an illusory creation (*māyā*). According to such materialistic philosophy, material objects such as garlands, sandalwood or beautiful women are temporary in specific manifestations but perpetually exist through the natural flow of creation and destruction. In other words, although a particular woman's form is temporary, there will eternally be beautiful women within the material world. Thus, by carefully executing fruitive rituals according to religious scriptures, one can maintain enjoyable contact with women and wealth life after life. In this way one's sense gratification will be eternal.

"The Jaimini philosophers further say that there never was a time when the world did not exist as it does today, which implies that there is no supreme controller who has created it. They claim that the arrangement of this world is real and appropriate and thus is not illusory. Moreover, they say that there is no eternal knowledge of an original perpetual form of the soul. In fact, they say, knowledge arises not from some absolute truth but from the differences among material objects. Knowledge therefore is not eternal and is subject to change. The assumption hidden in this statement is that there is no spirit soul who possesses eternal, constant knowledge of a single, unchanging reality. Rather, the nature of consciousness or knowledge is that it undergoes constant transformation. They state, however, that eternality is not refuted by the perpetually transforming nature of consciousness. Consciousness perpetually exists, they say, but not in the same form.

"Thus, the followers of Jaimini conclude that the transformation of knowledge does not negate its eternality; rather, they state that knowledge eternally exists within the perpetual nature of its transformation. They therefore naturally come to the path of regulated sense gratification rather than the path of renunciation, for in the state of *mukti*, or liberation, the living entity would not have any material senses, and thus the transformation of material understanding would not be possible. Such philosophers consider that the achievement of an unchanging state of *mukti* would stunt or paralyze the natural activity of the living entity and thus would not be in his self-interest. The path of *nivṛtti* (aiming toward renunciation and transcendence of the material world) is naturally not interesting to such materialistic philosophers. Accepting for argument's sake the validity of such materialistic philosophy, one can easily demonstrate that the path of regulated sense gratification brings many unwanted and miserable results to the living entity. Therefore even from a materialistic viewpoint, detachment is desirable. Material time is divided into different sections such as days, weeks, months and years, and by material time the living entity is repeatedly forced to undergo the miseries of birth, death, old age and disease. That such real miseries occur everywhere throughout the universe is well known." In this way, states Śrīla Viśvanātha Cakravartī Ṭhākura, Lord Kṛṣṇa has pointed out the defect of materialistic philosophy to Uddhava.

We may further elaborate that if one falsely accepts the atheistic philosophy of Jaimini and his innumerable modern followers, then the living entity perpetually remains entangled in the anguish of birth, death, old age and disease. This bogus, atheistic philosophy encourages material gratification as the only logical goal of life, but the living entity will inevitably commit mistakes in the execution of regulated sense gratification and eventually go to hell. The Supreme Personality of Godhead, Lord Kṛṣṇa, personally tells Uddhava that this materialistic philosophy is false and irrelevant to the actual self-interest of the living entity.

TEXT 17

तत्रापि कर्मणां कर्तुरस्वातन्त्र्यं च लक्ष्यते ।
भोक्तुश्च दुःखसुखयोः को न्वर्थो विवशं भजेत् ॥१७॥

tatrāpi karmaṇāṁ kartur
asvātantryaṁ ca lakṣyate
bhoktuś ca duḥkha-sukhayoḥ
ko nv artho vivaśaṁ bhajet

tatra—in the matter of one's ability to obtain happiness; *api*—furthermore; *karmaṇām*—of fruitive activities; *kartuḥ*—of the performer; *asvātantryam*—the lack of independence; *ca*—also; *lakṣyate*—is clearly seen; *bhoktuḥ*—of the one who is trying to enjoy; *ca*—also; *duḥkha-sukhayoḥ*—happiness and unhappiness; *kaḥ*—what; *nu*—indeed; *arthaḥ*—value; *vivaśam*—for one who is not in control; *bhajet*—can be derived.

TRANSLATION

Although the performer of fruitive activities desires perpetual happiness, it is clearly observed that materialistic workers are often unhappy and only occasionally satisfied, thus proving that they are not independent or in control of their destiny. When a person is always under the superior control of another, how can he expect any valuable results from his own fruitive actions?

PURPORT

Although materialistic persons reject Kṛṣṇa consciousness and instead pursue temporary sense gratification, even that sense gratification is often beyond their reach. If a person could really control his destiny, why would he create problems for himself? No intelligent person would impose death, old age or disease upon himself or his loved ones. One should recognize that these unwanted miseries are forced upon one by a higher power. Since we are all obviously under superior control, the atheistic philosophy advising one to simply perform fruitive activities and create a happy life is most imperfect.

Due to the influence of time, happiness and misery are created. When a woman becomes pregnant, her husband, relatives and friends eagerly await the birth of the child. As time passes and the child is born, everyone feels great happiness. But as the child grows into old age and eventually dies, that same passage of time is a cause of suffering. Ignorant persons vainly seek help from scientists who work feverishly and fruitlessly in their laboratories to stop death. In modern times, inventions have been created to eliminate the inconveniences of life, but the maintenance and production of such conveniences has proven to be unbearably inconvenient for hundreds of millions of people throughout the world. Only the most foolish person will propose that there is no superior controller and that one can achieve favorable results by expert performance of material activities. Ultimately all material activities are useless because they end in annihilation. If one is driving a car but has only limited control, the situation is most dangerous and must lead inevitably to disaster. Similarly, although we are trying to direct the material body to happiness, we are not in full control of the bodily demands, and therefore there will inevitably be disaster. As stated in *Bhagavad-gītā* (9.3),

aśraddadhānāḥ puruṣā
dharmasyāsya parantapa
aprāpya māṁ nivartante
mṛtyu-saṁsāra-vartmani

"Those who are not faithful on the path of devotional service cannot attain Me, O conqueror of foes, but return to birth and death in this material world." If one is not a devotee of Lord Kṛṣṇa, the eventual result of his activities is simply *mṛtyu-saṁsāra*—repeated birth and death.

TEXT 18

न देहिनां सुखं किञ्चिद् विद्यते विदुषामपि ।
तथा च दुःखं मूढानां वृथाहङ्करणं परम् ॥१८॥

na dehināṁ sukhaṁ kiñcid
vidyate viduṣām api
tathā ca duḥkhaṁ mūḍhānāṁ
vṛthāhaṅkaraṇaṁ param

na—not; *dehinām*—of embodied beings; *sukham*—happiness; *kiñcit*—some; *vidyate*—there is; *viduṣām*—of those who are intelligent; *api*—even; *tathā*—similarly; *ca*—also; *duḥkham*—unhappiness; *mūḍhānām*—of the big fools; *vṛthā*—useless; *ahaṅkaraṇam*—false ego; *param*—only, or completely.

TRANSLATION

It is observed within the material world that sometimes even an intelligent person is not happy. Similarly, sometimes even a great fool is happy. The concept of becoming happy through expertly performing material activities is simply a useless exhibition of false egotism.

PURPORT

It may be argued that an intelligent person can expertly perform pious activities within the material world and thus never experience suffering, since unhappiness is caused by sinful or impious activities. However, we often observe great suffering even among pious, intelligent persons, because they sometimes fail in the execution of their duty and sometimes consciously or unconsciously perform a forbidden activity. With this argument the Lord refutes the theory that simply on the strength of material piety one may remain perpetually happy without Kṛṣṇa consciousness.

On the other hand, we observe that even the most foolish or sinful persons sometimes experience happiness, because even those completely dedicated to sin sometimes accidentally perform pious activities by inadvertently traveling through a holy place or helping a saintly person. The material creation of God is so complex and bewildering that even those dedicated to piety sometimes commit sins, and even those dedicated to sinful life sometimes perform pious actions. Therefore, within the material world we do not find absolute happiness or unhappiness. Rather, every conditioned soul is hovering in confusion, without perfect knowledge. Piety and sin are relative material ideas that bestow relative happiness and unhappiness. Absolute happiness is experienced on the spiritual platform in full Kṛṣṇa consciousness, or love of God. Thus material life is always ambiguous and relative, whereas Kṛṣṇa consciousness is the actual platform of perfect happiness.

TEXT 19

यदि प्राप्तिं विघातं च जानन्ति सुखदुःखयोः ।
तेऽप्यद्धा न विदुर्योगं मृत्युर्न प्रभवेद् यथा ॥१९॥

yadi prāptiṁ vighātaṁ ca
jānanti sukha-duḥkhayoḥ
te 'py addhā na vidur yogaṁ
mṛtyur na prabhaved yathā

yadi—if; *prāptim*—achievement; *vighātam*—removal; *ca*—also; *jānanti*—they know; *sukha*—of happiness; *duḥkhayoḥ*—and of distress; *te*—they; *api*—still; *addhā*—directly; *na*—not; *viduḥ*—do know; *yogam*—the process; *mṛtyuḥ*—death; *na*—not; *prabhavet*—would exert its power; *yathā*—by which.

TRANSLATION

Even if people know how to achieve happiness and avoid unhappiness, they still do not know the process by which death will not be able to exert its power over them.

PURPORT

If the so-called intelligent materialists know the means of achieving happiness and destroying unhappiness, then they should deliver people from inevitable death. The scientists are busily working to solve this problem, but since they have completely failed, it is understood that they are not actually intelligent and that they do not know the means of achieving happiness and eliminating misery. It is most foolish to think that one can be happy with an ax hanging over one's neck. Lord Kṛṣṇa says in *Bhagavad-gītā, mṛtyuḥ sarva-haraś cāham:* "I Myself come before you as death and take everything away." We should not blindly ignore the disaster of material life, but should instead accept the Lord's causeless mercy, which He so magnanimously offers in His incarnation as Caitanya Mahāprabhu. We should surrender to the lotus feet of Lord Caitanya, who offers the real means for achieving unqualified happiness: the chanting of the holy names of the Lord. This is the Lord's desire, and it is in our own self-interest to take up this process.

TEXT 20

को न्वर्थः सुखयत्येनं कामो वा मृत्युरन्तिके ।
आघातं नीयमानस्य वध्यस्येव न तुष्टिदः ॥२०॥

ko 'nv arthaḥ sukhayaty enaṁ
kāmo vā mṛtyur antike
āghātaṁ nīyamānasya
vadhyasyeva na tuṣṭi-daḥ

kaḥ—what; *nu*—certainly; *arthaḥ*—material object; *sukhayati*—gives happiness; *enam*—to a person; *kāmaḥ*—sense gratification derived from material things; *vā*—or; *mṛtyuḥ*—death; *antike*—standing nearby; *āghātam*—to the place of execution; *nīyamānasya*—of one who is being led; *vadhyasya*—of one who is to be killed; *iva*—like; *na*—not at all; *tuṣṭi-daḥ*—gives satisfaction.

TRANSLATION

Death is not at all pleasing, and since everyone is exactly like a condemned man being led to the place of execution, what possible happiness can people derive from material objects or the gratification they provide?

PURPORT

It is customary throughout the world that a condemned man is offered a sumptuous last meal. For the condemned man, however, such a feast is a chilling reminder of his imminent death, and therefore he cannot enjoy it. Similarly, no sane human being can be satisfied in material life, because death is standing near and may strike at any moment. If one is sitting in one's living room with a deadly snake at one's side, knowing that at any moment the poisonous fangs might pierce the flesh, how can one sit peacefully and watch television or read a book? Similarly, unless one is more or less crazy, one cannot be enthusiastic or even peaceful in material life. Knowledge of the inevitability of death should encourage one to become determined in spiritual life.

TEXT 21

श्रुतं च दृष्टवद् दुष्टं स्पर्धासूयात्ययव्ययैः ।
बह्वन्तरायकामत्वात् कृषिवच्चापि निष्फलम् ॥२१॥

śrutaṁ ca dṛṣṭa-vad duṣṭaṁ
spardhāsūyātyaya-vyayaiḥ
bahv-antarāya-kāmatvāt
kṛṣi-vac cāpi niṣphalam

śrutam—material happiness which is heard of; *ca*—also; *dṛṣṭa-vat*—just like that which we have already seen; *duṣṭam*—is contaminated; *spardhā*—by jealousy; *asūyā*—by envy; *atyaya*—by death; *vyayaiḥ*—and by decay; *bahu*—many; *antarāya*—obstacles; *kāmatvāt*—because of accepting happiness with such characteristics; *kṛṣi-vat*—like agriculture; *ca*—also; *api*—even; *niṣphalam*—fruitless.

TRANSLATION

That material happiness of which we hear, such as promotion to heavenly planets for celestial enjoyment, is just like that material happiness we have already experienced. Both are polluted by jealousy, envy, decay and death. Therefore, just as an attempt to raise crops becomes fruitless if there are many problems like crop disease, insect plague or drought, similarly, the attempt to attain material happiness, either on earth or on the heavenly planets, is always fruitless because of innumerable obstacles.

PURPORT

Śrīla Bhaktisiddhānta Sarasvatī Ṭhākura comments as follows on this verse. "Ordinarily, if there is no specific impediment, agricultural endeavors will yield their fruits. If, however, there is a defect in the seed, or if the soil is too salty or barren, or if there is drought, plague, excessive rain or heat out of season, or if there are disturbances caused by animals, birds or insects, then agricultural activities will not yield the desired harvest. Similarly, those who are expert in analyzing the material world see that the heavenly situations offered in the *Vedas* are not basically different from life on the earth. By the interaction of conditioned souls there will inevitably be jealousy as one becomes distinguished as superior and another as inferior. By the power of time these positions are reversed, and therefore violence and intrigue disturb life even on the heavenly planets. In fact, the attempt to promote oneself to the heavenly planets is itself full of problems and disturbances. One should therefore understand that the kingdom of God, Vaikuṇṭha, is transcendental to the limitations and disturbances imposed by the laws of material nature in this world. If one wrongly concludes that such imperfections are also present in the kingdom of God, then one will be polluted by material contamination."

TEXT 22

अन्तरायैरविहितो यदि धर्मः स्वनुष्ठितः ।
तेनापि निर्जितं स्थानं यथा गच्छति तच्छृणु ॥२२॥

antarāyair avihito
yadi dharmaḥ sv-anuṣṭhitaḥ

tenāpi nirjitaṁ sthānaṁ
yathā gacchati tac chṛṇu

antarāyaiḥ—by obstacles and discrepancies; *avihitaḥ*—not affected; *yadi*—if; *dharmaḥ*—one's execution of regulated duties according to Vedic injunctions; *sv-anuṣṭhitaḥ*—excellently performed; *tena*—by that; *api*—even; *nirjitam*—accomplished; *sthānam*—status; *yathā*—the manner in which; *gacchati*—it perishes; *tat*—that; *śṛṇu*—please hear.

TRANSLATION

If one performs Vedic sacrifices and fruitive rituals without any mistake or contamination, one will achieve a heavenly situation in the next life. But even this result, which is only achieved by perfect performance of fruitive rituals, will be vanquished by time. Now hear of this.

PURPORT

The word *gacchati* means "going." In *Bhagavad-gītā* Lord Kṛṣṇa states, *āgamāpāyino 'nityāḥ:* all material experiences, good or bad, come and go. Therefore the word *gacchati* refers to the disappearance of the results of even the most meticulously performed fruitive sacrifices. Any material situation, from the worst to the best, is imperfect. Thus one should strive only for pure Kṛṣṇa consciousness.

TEXT 23

इष्ट्वेह देवता यज्ञैः स्वर्लोकं याति याज्ञिकः ।
भुञ्जीत देववत्तत्र भोगान् दिव्यान् निजार्जितान् ॥२३॥

iṣṭveha devatā yajñaiḥ
svar-lokaṁ yāti yājñikaḥ
bhuñjīta deva-vat tatra
bhogān divyān nijārjitān

iṣṭvā—having worshiped; *iha*—in this world; *devatāḥ*—the demigods; *yajñaiḥ*—with sacrifices; *svaḥ-lokam*—to the heavenly planets; *yāti*—goes; *yājñikaḥ*—the performer of sacrifice; *bhuñjīta*—he may enjoy; *deva-vat*—like a god; *tatra*—therein; *bhogān*—pleasures; *divyān*—celestial; *nija*—by himself; *arjitān*—achieved.

TRANSLATION

If on earth one performs sacrifices for the satisfaction of the demigods, he goes to the heavenly planets where, just like a demigod, he enjoys all of the heavenly pleasures he has earned by his performances.

TEXT 24

स्वपुण्योपचिते शुभ्रे विमान उपगीयते ।
गन्धर्वैर्विहरन् मध्ये देवीनां हृद्यवेषधृक् ॥२४॥

sva-puṇyopacite śubhre
vimāna upagīyate
gandharvair viharan madhye
devīnāṁ hṛdya-veṣa-dhṛk

sva—his own; *puṇya*—by the pious activities; *upacite*—accumulated; *śubhre*—shining; *vimāne*—in an airplane; *upagīyate*—is glorified by songs; *gandharvaiḥ*—by the heavenly Gandharvas; *viharan*—enjoying life; *madhye*—in the middle; *devīnām*—of heavenly goddesses; *hṛdya*—charming; *veṣa*—clothes; *dhṛk*—wearing.

TRANSLATION

Having achieved the heavenly planets, the performer of ritualistic sacrifices travels in a glowing airplane, which he obtains as the result of his piety on earth. Being glorified by songs sung by the Gandharvas and dressed in wonderfully charming clothes, he enjoys life surrounded by heavenly goddesses.

TEXT 25

स्त्रीभिः कामगयानेन किङ्किणीजालमालिना ।
क्रीडन् न वेदात्मपातं सुराक्रीडेषु निर्वृतः ॥२५॥

strībhiḥ kāmaga-yānena
kiṅkiṇī-jāla-mālinā
krīḍan na vedātma-pātaṁ
surākrīḍeṣu nirvṛtaḥ

strībhiḥ—with heavenly women; *kāma-ga*—going wherever one desires; *yānena*—with such an airplane; *kiṅkiṇī-jāla-mālinā*—decorated with circles of bells; *krīḍan*—having a good time; *na*—not; *veda*—does consider; *ātma*—his own; *pātam*—falldown; *sura*—of the demigods; *ākrīḍeṣu*—in the pleasure gardens; *nirvṛtaḥ*—being comfortable, relaxed and happy.

TRANSLATION

Accompanied by heavenly women, the enjoyer of the fruits of sacrifice goes on pleasure rides in a wonderful airplane, decorated with circles of tinkling bells, that flies wherever he desires. Being relaxed, comfortable and happy in the heavenly pleasure gardens, he does not consider that he is exhausting the fruits of his piety and will soon fall down to the mortal world.

TEXT 26

तावत् स मोदते स्वर्गे यावत् पुण्यं समाप्यते ।
क्षीणपुण्यः पतत्यर्वागनिच्छन् कालचालितः ॥२६॥

tāvat sa modate svarge
yāvat puṇyaṁ samāpyate
kṣīṇa-puṇyaḥ pataty arvāg
anicchan kāla-cālitaḥ

tāvat—that long; *saḥ*—he; *modate*—enjoys life; *svarge*—in the heavenly planets; *yāvat*—until; *puṇyam*—his pious results; *samāpyate*—are used up; *kṣīṇa*—exhausted; *puṇyaḥ*—his piety; *patati*—he falls; *arvāk*—down from heaven; *anicchan*—not desiring to fall; *kāla*—by time; *cālitaḥ*—pushed down.

TRANSLATION

Until his pious results are used up, the performer of sacrifice enjoys life in the heavenly planets. When the pious results are exhausted, however, he falls down from the pleasure gardens of heaven, being moved against his desire by the force of eternal time.

TEXTS 27–29

यद्यधर्मरतः सङ्गादसतां वाजितेन्द्रियः ।
कामात्मा कृपणो लुब्धः स्त्रैणो भूतविहिंसकः ॥२७॥
पशूनविधिनालभ्य प्रेतभूतगणान् यजन् ।
नरकानवशो जन्तुर्गत्वा यात्युल्बणं तमः ॥२८॥
कर्माणि दुःखोदर्काणि कुर्वन् देहेन तैः पुनः ।
देहमाभजते तत्र किं सुखं मर्त्यधर्मिणः ॥२९॥

yady adharma-rataḥ saṅgād
asatāṁ vājitendriyaḥ
kāmātmā kṛpaṇo lubdhaḥ
straiṇo bhūta-vihiṁsakaḥ

paśūn avidhinālabhya
preta-bhūta-gaṇān yajan
narakān avaśo jantur
gatvā yāty ulbaṇaṁ tamaḥ

karmāṇi duḥkhodarkāṇi
kurvan dehena taiḥ punaḥ
deham ābhajate tatra
kiṁ sukhaṁ martya-dharmiṇaḥ

yadi—if; *adharma*—in irreligion; *rataḥ*—he is engaged; *saṅgāt*—due to association; *asatām*—of materialistic people; *vā*—or; *ajita*—due to not conquering; *indriyaḥ*—the senses; *kāma*—material lusty desires; *ātmā*—living for; *kṛpaṇaḥ*—miserly; *lubdhaḥ*—greedy; *straiṇaḥ*—a woman-hunter; *bhūta*—against other living beings; *vihiṁsakaḥ*—committing violence; *paśūn*—animals; *avidhinā*—without the authority of Vedic injunctions; *ālabhya*—killing; *preta-bhūta*—ghosts and spirits; *gaṇān*—the groups of; *yajan*—worshiping; *narakān*—to hells; *ava-śaḥ*—helplessly, being under the control of fruitive activities; *jantuḥ*—a living being; *gatvā*—having gone; *yāti*—approaches; *ulbaṇam*—extreme; *tamaḥ*—darkness; *karmāṇi*—activities; *duḥkha*—great unhappiness; *udarkāṇi*—bringing in the future; *kurvan*—performing;

dehena—with such a body; *taiḥ*—by such activities; *punaḥ*—again; *deham*—a material body; *ābhajate*—accepts; *tatra*—therein; *kim*—what; *sukham*—happiness; *martya*—always leading to death; *dharmiṇaḥ*—of one sworn to activities.

TRANSLATION

If a human being is engaged in sinful, irreligious activities, either because of bad association or because of his failure to control his senses, then such a person will certainly develop a personality full of material desires. He thus becomes miserly toward others, greedy and always anxious to exploit the bodies of women. When the mind is so polluted one becomes violent and aggressive and without the authority of Vedic injunctions slaughters innocent animals for sense gratification. Worshiping ghosts and spirits, the bewildered person falls fully into the grip of unauthorized activities and thus goes to hell, where he receives a material body infected by the darkest modes of nature. In such a degraded body, he unfortunately continues to perform inauspicious activities that greatly increase his future unhappiness, and therefore he again accepts a similar material body. What possible happiness can there be for one who engages in activities inevitably terminating in death?

PURPORT

In the Vedic analysis of civilized life there are two paths. One who takes to the path of *nivṛtti-mārga* immediately renounces material sense gratification and purifies his existence by performance of austerity and devotional activities. On the path of *pravṛtti-mārga* one furnishes a steady supply of sense objects to the senses, but one consumes such sense objects under strict regulations and through ritualistic ceremonies, thus gradually purifying the heart and satiating the material senses. Unfortunately, as explained in this and the previous verse, the path of *pravṛtti-mārga* is extremely volatile because rather than becoming detached, the living entity often becomes uncontrolled and fully addicted to further sense gratification. In the previous verse the path of regulated, authorized sense gratification was described, and in this verse the path of unauthorized, demoniac sense gratification is described.

In this verse, the words *saṅgād asatāṁ vājitendriyaḥ* are very significant. One may fall down into sinful life by bad association, or even in good association one may fail to control his senses. Ultimately each living entity is responsible for his existential situation. The word *adharma-rataḥ* in this verse indicates those engaged in excessive sex life, meat-eating, drinking and other inauspicious activities that transgress the codes of civilized human life. Being in the mode of ignorance, these persons develop such a cruel mentality that they do not consider any festive occasion complete without the consumption of large quantities of meat obtained by slaughtering helpless animals. Eventually such persons become influenced by ghosts and spirits, who deprive them of all ability to discriminate between right and wrong. Losing all sense of decency, they become fit candidates for entrance into the darkest modes of material existence. Sometimes these lusty, intoxicated carnivores, considering themselves pious, pray to God in a useless way. Afflicted by innumerable material desires, they rotate from one material body to another without experiencing true happiness. Śrīla Bhaktisiddhānta Sarasvatī Ṭhākura has noted that material life is so disturbing that even if one is allowed to live for an entire day of Brahmā—approximately 8,640,000,000 years—one will eventually be afflicted by the fear of death. In fact, Brahmā himself is disturbed by fear of death, what to speak of tiny human beings who live a paltry seventy or eighty years at most. Thus, as stated here, *kiṁ sukhaṁ martya-dharmiṇaḥ:* what possible happiness can one find within the painful grip of material illusion?

TEXT 30

लोकानां लोकपालानां मद् भयं कल्पजीविनाम् ।
ब्रह्मणोऽपि भयं मत्तो द्विपरार्धपरायुषः ॥३०॥

lokānāṁ loka-pālānāṁ
mad bhayaṁ kalpa-jīvinām
brahmaṇo 'pi bhayaṁ matto
dvi-parārdha-parāyuṣaḥ

lokānām—in all the planetary systems; *loka-pālānām*—and for all the planetary leaders, such as the demigods; *mat*—of Me; *bhayam*—

there is fear; *kalpa-jīvinām*—for those who live for a *kalpa*, or a day of Brahmā; *brahmaṇaḥ*—of Lord Brahmā; *api*—even; *bhayam*—there is fear; *mattaḥ*—from Me; *dvi-parārdha*—two *parārdhas*, totalling 311,-040,000,000,000 years; *para*—supreme; *āyuṣaḥ*—whose duration of life.

TRANSLATION

In all the planetary systems from the heavenly to the hellish, and for all of the great demigods who live for one thousand yuga cycles, there is fear of Me in My form of time. Even Brahmā, who possesses the supreme life span of 311,040,000,000,000 years, is also afraid of Me.

PURPORT

There are many statements throughout Vedic literature proving that even the great demigods fear the time potency of the Supreme Personality of Godhead. Even in the heavenly planets there is no relief from the miseries of material life. No conditioned soul can live eternally, as clearly demonstrated by the deaths of Hiraṇyakaśipu and other demons. Since even the demigods fear the time potency of the Personality of Godhead, one may easily conclude that Kṛṣṇa is the Absolute Truth and that He is eternally the supreme controller of everything and everyone. Lord Kṛṣṇa is the only real shelter.

TEXT 31

गुणाः सृजन्ति कर्माणि गुणोऽनुसृजते गुणान् ।
जीवस्तु गुणसंयुक्तो भुङ्क्ते कर्मफलान्यसौ ॥३१॥

guṇāḥ sṛjanti karmāṇi
guṇo 'nusṛjate guṇān
jīvas tu guṇa-saṁyukto
bhuṅkte karma-phalāny asau

guṇāḥ—the material senses; *sṛjanti*—create; *karmāṇi*—pious and impious material activities; *guṇaḥ*—the three modes of nature; *anusṛjate*—set into motion; *guṇān*—the material senses; *jīvaḥ*—the minute living entity; *tu*—indeed; *guṇa*—the material senses or the material modes of nature; *saṁyuktaḥ*—fully engaged in; *bhuṅkte*—experiences; *karma*—of activities; *phalāni*—the various results; *asau*—the spirit soul.

TRANSLATION

The material senses create material activities, either pious or sinful, and the modes of nature set the material senses into motion. The living entity, being fully engaged by the material senses and modes of nature, experiences the various results of fruitive work.

PURPORT

It has been explained in the previous verses that the living entity under the control of fruitive activities is pushed down into a hellish condition of life. In this verse the exact nature of the living entity's dependence on fruitive activities is described. One can observe that one's activities are performed by the material senses and that the living entity himself is merely conscious of such activities. One may be worshiping the demigods, enjoying sex or performing agricultural or intellectual activities, but in all cases the material senses are performing the work.

One may argue that the spirit soul initiates the activities of the senses and thus is the ultimate doer, but such false egotism is negated in this verse by the statement *guṇāḥ sṛjanti karmāṇi guṇo 'nusṛjate guṇān.* The three modes of nature—goodness, passion and ignorance—stimulate the functions of the material senses, and the living entity, coming under the control of a particular mode of nature, merely experiences the good and bad results of his work. This does not negate the concept of free will, since the living entity chooses to associate with different modes of nature. By one's eating, speaking, sexual activities, occupation, etc., one associates with various modes of nature and acquires a particular mentality. But in all cases the modes of nature themselves are acting, not the living entity. The word *asau* in this verse indicates that the living entity falsely considers himself to be the performer of work carried out by nature. As stated in *Bhagavad-gītā* (3.27):

prakṛteḥ kriyamāṇāni
guṇaiḥ karmāṇi sarvaśaḥ

ahaṅkāra-vimūḍhātmā
kartāham iti manyate

"The bewildered spirit soul, under the influence of the three modes of material nature, thinks himself to be the doer of activities, which are in actuality carried out by nature." The conditioned soul can be liberated simply by giving up this false egoistic conception of life and taking to the devotional service of the Lord, by which the living entity, or marginal potency of the Supreme Personality of Godhead, escapes the disturbing influence of the external potency called *māyā*. In the devotional service of the Lord the liberated entity realizes his actual form of eternity, knowledge and bliss.

It is natural to perform activities with a desire to achieve a good result. The best results, however, can be attained by one who engages in the devotional service of the Lord with a desire to be reinstated in his constitutional position as the Lord's loving servant. In this way the tendency to exploit one's own activities for a particular result can be purified; then the modes of nature and the material senses will no longer engage the living entity in illusion. The living entity is by nature blissful, and when his illusion ceases, all suffering comes to an end. The liberated soul is then fit to reside in Vaikuṇṭha, the kingdom of God.

TEXT 32

यावत् स्याद् गुणवैषम्यं तावन्नानात्वमात्मनः ।
नानात्वमात्मनो यावत् पारतन्त्र्यं तदैव हि ॥३२॥

yāvat syād guṇa-vaiṣamyaṁ
tāvan nānātvam ātmanaḥ
nānātvam ātmano yāvat
pāratantryaṁ tadaiva hi

yāvat—as long as; *syāt*—there is; *guṇa*—of the modes of material nature; *vaiṣamyam*—separate existences; *tāvat*—then there will be; *nānātvam*—different states of existence; *ātmanaḥ*—of the soul; *nānātvam*—different states of existence; *ātmanaḥ*—of the soul; *yāvat*—as long as there are; *pāratantryam*—dependence; *tadā*—then there will be; *eva*—certainly; *hi*—indeed.

TRANSLATION

As long as the living entity thinks that the modes of material nature have separate existences, he will be obliged to take birth in many different forms and will experience varieties of material existence. Therefore, the living entity remains completely dependent on fruitive activities under the modes of nature.

PURPORT

The word *guṇa-vaiṣamyam* indicates forgetfulness of Lord Kṛṣṇa, which causes one to see material varieties as separate states of existence. The living entity, being attracted to material varieties and having faith in them, is forced to experience these varieties in different material bodies, such as those of demigods, pigs, businessmen, insects, and so on. According to the *karma-mīmāṁsā* philosophers, there is no transcendental living entity who is the background of all existence. They accept material variety as the final reality. However, the Supreme Personality of Godhead, Lord Kṛṣṇa, is the actual basis of everything. Everything is within Him, and He is within everything. A pure devotee of the Lord sees Kṛṣṇa everywhere and sees all of the variegated modes of nature as the potency of Lord Kṛṣṇa. One who does not see Lord Kṛṣṇa will certainly see material variegatedness as the supreme reality. Such vision is called *māyā*, or gross illusion, and is similar to the vision of an animal. *Pāratantryam* means one will remain caught in the web of fruitive activities unless one gives up this superficial, separatist vision.

TEXT 33

यावदस्यास्वतन्त्रत्वं तावदीश्वरतो भयम् ।
य एतत् समुपासीरंस्ते मुह्यन्ति शुचार्पिताः ॥३३॥

yāvad asyāsvatantratvaṁ
tāvad īśvarato bhayam
ya etat samupāsīraṁs
te muhyanti śucārpitāḥ

yāvat—as long as; *asya*—of the living being; *asvatantratvam*—there is no freedom from dependence on the modes of nature; *tāvat*—then there will be; *īśvarataḥ*—from the supreme controller; *bhayam*—fear; *ye*—those who; *etat*—to this material concept of life; *samupāsīran*—devote themselves; *te*—they; *muhyanti*—are bewildered; *śucā*—in lamentation; *arpitāḥ*—always absorbed.

TRANSLATION

The conditioned soul who remains dependent on fruitive activities under the material modes of nature will continue to fear Me, the Supreme Personality of Godhead, since I impose the results of one's fruitive activities. Those who accept the material concept of life, taking the variegatedness of the modes of nature to be factual, devote themselves to material enjoyment and are therefore always absorbed in lamentation and grief.

PURPORT

The living entity is bound in the network of illusion, but although he can understand that he is dependent upon superior powers, he does not want to serve the Supreme Lord. He thus becomes filled with fear of life itself. Desiring material sense gratification, the living entity, like the demon Kaṁsa, always fears destruction of his material arrangement. Remaining addicted to the flavors of material nature, one gradually sinks down into an irrational form of life.

Māyā has two potencies—the first covers the living entity, and the second throws him down into a hellish condition of life. When one is covered by *māyā*, one loses all power of discrimination, and *māyā* then throws such a fool into the darkness of ignorance. When one wrongly considers oneself to be independent of the Supreme Personality of Godhead, Lord Kṛṣṇa, one becomes a worshiper of temporary material objects, hoping to enjoy material sense gratification, and as one grows older, one's life becomes filled with fear and anxiety. A conditioned soul considers himself to be in control of his life, but since he does not have any actual controlling potency, his situation is contradictory and not at all pleasing. As all of one's material possessions are taken away by time, one becomes filled with lamentation. All in all, material life is truly abominable, and it is only because of dense illusion that we accept it as satisfactory.

TEXT 34

काल आत्मागमो लोकः स्वभावो धर्म एव च ।
इति मां बहुधा प्राहुर्गुणव्यतिकरे सति ॥३४॥

kāla ātmāgamo lokaḥ
svabhāvo dharma eva ca
iti māṁ bahudhā prāhur
guṇa-vyatikare sati

kālaḥ—time; *ātmā*—the self; *āgamaḥ*—Vedic knowledge; *lokaḥ*—the universe; *svabhāvaḥ*—different natures of different living entities; *dharmaḥ*—religious principles; *eva*—certainly; *ca*—also; *iti*—thus; *mām*—Me; *bahudhā*—in many ways; *prāhuḥ*—they call; *guṇa*—of the modes of nature; *vyatikare*—agitation; *sati*—when there is.

TRANSLATION

When there is agitation and interaction of the material modes of nature, the living entities then describe Me in various ways such as all-powerful time, the Self, Vedic knowledge, the universe, one's own nature, religious ceremonies, and so on.

PURPORT

One can experience the potency of the Personality of Godhead by observing how different species of life—demigods, human beings, animals, fish, birds, insects, plants, etc.—gradually evolve their natures and activities. Each species of life executes a particular process of sense gratification, and this function is called the *dharma* of the species. Lacking knowledge of the Personality of Godhead, ordinary persons catch a glimpse of the Lord's potencies in the above-mentioned manifestations. Śrīla Madhvācārya has cited the following information from the *Tantra-bhāgavata.* The Lord is called *kāla,* or time, because He is the mover and controller of all material qualities. Because He is complete and perfect, He is called *ātmā,* or the Self; and He is the personification of all knowledge. The word *svabhāva* indicates that the Lord fully controls His own destiny; and as the maintainer of everyone He is called *dharma.* One on the liberated platform can achieve unlimited bliss by worshiping the Personality of Godhead, whereas those who are ignorant of the Lord try to find meaning by concocting other objects of worship. If one stubbornly imagines that anything is independent of the Lord, one will remain in the grip of the illusory network of the Lord's potency. Seeing the inevitability of the destruction of material things, one is constantly fearful and perpetually laments in the darkness of ignorance. In such darkness there is no question of happiness. Therefore, one should never think that anything is independent of the Personality of Godhead. As soon as one considers anything to be independent of the Lord, one is immediately gripped by the Lord's illusory network, called *māyā.* One should always remain humble and obedient to the Personality of Godhead, even when one is liberated, and thus one will achieve the supreme spiritual happiness.

TEXT 35

श्रीउद्धव उवाच

गुणेषु वर्तमानोऽपि देहजेष्वनपावृतः ।
गुणैर्न बद्ध्यते देही बद्ध्यते वा कथं विभो ॥३५॥

śrī-uddhava uvāca
guṇeṣu vartamāno 'pi
deha-jeṣv anapāvṛtaḥ
guṇair na badhyate dehī
badhyate vā kathaṁ vibho

śrī-uddhavaḥ uvāca—Śrī Uddhava said; *guṇeṣu*—in the modes of material nature; *vartamānaḥ*—being situated; *api*—although; *deha*—from the material body; *jeṣu*—born; *anapāvṛtaḥ*—being uncovered; *guṇaiḥ*—by the modes of nature; *na*—not; *badhyate*—is bound; *dehī*—the living entity within the material body; *badhyate*—is bound; *vā*—or; *katham*—how does it happen; *vibho*—O my Lord.

TRANSLATION

Śrī Uddhava said: O my Lord, a living entity situated within the material body is surrounded by the modes of nature and the happiness and distress that are born of activities caused by these modes.

How is it possible that he is not bound by this material encirclement? It may also be said that the living entity is ultimately transcendental and has nothing to do with the material world. Then how is he ever bound by material nature?

PURPORT

Due to the influence of the modes of nature the material body generates fruitive activities, which in turn generate material happiness and distress. This material chain reaction is indicated by the word *deha-jeṣu.* The Personality of Godhead has shown Uddhava that the actual goal of life is liberation, not sense gratification. Although the Lord has indicated that the living entity is liberated by devotional service performed with knowledge and renunciation, Uddhava apparently does not understand the specific means of perfection. According to Śrīla Viśvanātha Cakravartī Ṭhākura, Uddhava's question implies that we observe even in the activities of liberated souls such external activities as eating, sleeping, walking, hearing, speaking, etc., which are functions of the gross and subtle bodies. Thus, if even liberated souls are situated within the gross and subtle material bodies, then how are they not bound by the material modes of nature? If it is argued that the living entity is like the sky, which never mixes with any other object and therefore is not bound, then one may ask how such a transcendental living entity can ever be bound by material nature. In other words, how would material existence be possible? In order to completely clarify the path of Kṛṣṇa consciousness, Uddhava presents this question to the supreme spiritual authority, Lord Kṛṣṇa.

In the kingdom of *māyā* there are innumerable speculations about the Supreme Lord, who is variously described as nonexistent, or as possessing material qualities, or as being devoid of all qualities, or as being a neuter object like a eunuch. But through mundane speculation it is not possible to understand the nature of the Supreme Personality of Godhead. Therefore Uddhava wants to clear the path of spiritual liberation so that people can actually understand that Kṛṣṇa is the Supreme Personality of Godhead. As long as one is affected by the modes of nature, perfect understanding is not possible. Lord Kṛṣṇa will now describe to Uddhava further details of spiritual emancipation on the road back home, back to Kṛṣṇa.

TEXTS 36–37

कथं वर्तेत विहरेत् कैर्वा ज्ञायेत लक्षणैः ।
किं भुञ्जीतोत विसृजेच्छयीतासीत याति वा ॥३६॥
एतदच्युत मे ब्रूहि प्रश्नं प्रश्नविदां वर ।
नित्यबद्धो नित्यमुक्त एक एवेति मे भ्रमः ॥३७॥

katham varteta viharet
kair vā jñāyeta lakṣaṇaiḥ
kiṁ bhuñjītota visṛjec
chayītāsīta yāti vā

etad acyuta me brūhi
praśnaṁ praśna-vidāṁ vara
nitya-baddho nitya-mukta
eka eveti me bhramaḥ

katham—in what way; *varteta*—he is situated; *viharet*—he enjoys; *kaiḥ*—by which; *vā*—or; *jñāyeta*—would be known; *lakṣaṇaiḥ*—by symptoms; *kim*—what; *bhuñjīta*—he would eat; *uta*—and; *visṛjet*—would evacuate; *śayīta*—would lie down; *āsīta*—would sit; *yāti*—goes; *vā*—or; *etat*—this; *acyuta*—O Acyuta; *me*—to me; *brūhi*—explain; *praśnam*—the question; *praśna-vidām*—of all those who know how to answer questions; *vara*—O the best; *nitya-baddhaḥ*—eternally conditioned; *nitya-muktaḥ*—eternally liberated; *ekaḥ*—singular; *eva*—certainly; *iti*—thus; *me*—my; *bhramaḥ*—confusion.

TRANSLATION

O my Lord, Acyuta, the same living entity is sometimes described as eternally conditioned and at other times as eternally liberated. I am not able to understand, therefore, the actual situation of the living entity. You, my Lord, are the best of those who are expert in answering philosophical questions. Please explain to me the symptoms by which one can tell the difference between a living entity who is eternally liberated and one who is eternally conditioned. In what various ways would they remain situated, enjoy life, eat, evacuate, lie down, sit or move about?

PURPORT

In previous verses Lord Kṛṣṇa has explained to Uddhava that an eternally liberated soul is beyond the three modes of material nature. Since a liberated soul is considered to be beyond even the superior mode of goodness, how can he be recognized? By false identification with the modes of nature, which produce one's own material body, one is bound by illusion. On the other hand, by transcending the modes of nature, one is liberated. However, in ordinary activities—such as eating, evacuating, relaxing, sitting and sleeping—a liberated soul and a conditioned soul appear to be the same. Therefore Uddhava is inquiring, "By what symptoms can I recognize that one living entity is performing such external activities without false ego, and by what symptoms can I recognize one who is working under the illusory bondage of material identification? This is difficult, because the ordinary bodily functions of liberated and conditioned personalities appear similar." Uddhava has approached the Supreme Personality of Godhead, taking Him as his personal spiritual master, and wants to be enlightened about how to understand the differences between material and spiritual life.

Since the living entity is sometimes called eternally conditioned, how could he ever be considered eternally liberated, or vice versa? This is an apparent contradiction, which will be cleared up by the Supreme Personality of Godhead.

Thus end the purports of the humble servants of His Divine Grace A. C. Bhaktivedanta Swami Prabhupāda, to the Eleventh Canto, Tenth Chapter, of the Śrīmad-Bhāgavatam, *entitled "The Nature of Fruitive Activity."*

CHAPTER ELEVEN

The Symptoms of Conditioned and Liberated Living Entities

In this chapter, Lord Śrī Kṛṣṇa describes to Uddhava the difference between conditioned and liberated living entities, the characteristics of a saintly person and the different aspects of the practice of devotional service.

In the previous chapter Uddhava had presented questions regarding conditioned and liberated souls. In His replies, the almighty Lord Śrī Kṛṣṇa states that although the spirit soul is part and parcel of the Supreme Personality of Godhead, on account of his infinitesimal nature, he falls into contact with the material energy, which causes him to accept the covering designations of the modes of goodness, passion and ignorance. Thus the soul has been bound up since time immemorial. But when he achieves the shelter of pure devotional service, he becomes designated as eternally liberated. Transcendental knowledge is therefore the cause of the living entity's liberation, and ignorance is the cause of his bondage. Both knowledge and ignorance are produced by the *māyā* energy of Lord Śrī Kṛṣṇa and are His eternal potencies. The living entities who become attracted to the modes of nature are bewildered by false ego, which causes them to see themselves as the enjoyers of misery, confusion, happiness, distress, danger, and so on. In this way, they meditate upon such states of being, although in the real, or spiritual, world these things do not exist. Both the *jīva* (individual soul) and the Supersoul reside within the same body. The difference between them is that the almighty Supersoul, being fully cognizant, does not indulge in enjoying the fruits of material work but remains simply as a witness, whereas the infinitesimal conditioned *jīva*, being ignorant, suffers the consequences of his own work. The liberated *jīva*, in spite of being within a material body because of the remaining reactions of his past activities, does not become disturbed by the happiness and suffering of the body.

He sees such bodily experiences in the same way that a person who has just awakened from a dream sees his dream experiences. On the other hand, although the conditioned living entity is by nature not the enjoyer of the happiness and misery of the body, he imagines himself to be the enjoyer of his bodily experiences, just as a person in a dream imagines his dream experiences to be real. Just as the sun reflected upon water is not actually bound up in the water, and just as the air is not confined to some particular segment of the sky, similarly a detached person takes advantage of his broad outlook on the world to cut off all his doubts with the sword of appropriate renunciation, *yukta-vairāgya.* Since his life force, senses, mind and intelligence have no tendency to fix themselves on sense objects, he remains liberated even while situated within the material body. Regardless of whether he is harassed or worshiped, he remains equipoised. He is therefore considered liberated even in this life. A liberated person has nothing to do with the piety and sin of this world, but rather sees everything equally. A self-satisfied sage does not praise or condemn anyone. He does not speak uselessly to anyone and does not fix his mind on material things. Rather, he is always merged in meditation upon the Supreme Personality of Godhead, so in the eyes of fools he seems to be a speechless, crazy person.

Even if someone has studied or even taught all the different Vedic literatures, if he has not developed pure attraction to the service of the Personality of Godhead, he has accomplished nothing beyond his own labor. One should study only those scriptures in which the nature of the Supreme Personality of Godhead, His enchanting pastimes and the nectarean topics of His various incarnations are scientifically discussed; thus one gains the highest good fortune. However, by studying scriptures other than these, one simply acquires misfortune.

With full determination one should properly understand the identity of the soul and give up false identification with this material body. He may then offer his heart at the lotus feet of the Supreme Lord, Śrī Kṛṣṇa, the reservoir of all love, and attain real peace. When the mind is carried away by the three modes of nature, it can no longer meditate properly on the transcendental Supreme Truth. After many lifetimes, faithful persons who have performed Vedic sacrifices for acquiring religiosity, economic development and sense gratification finally engage in hearing, chanting and constantly thinking of the Supreme Lord's all-auspicious pastimes, which purify the entire universe. Such persons then achieve the association of a bona fide spiritual master and the saintly devotees. After that, by the mercy of the spiritual master they begin to follow the paths set out by the standard authorities of spiritual life, the *mahājanas*, and become actually perfect in realization of their own true identity.

Having heard these instructions from Lord Kṛṣṇa, Uddhava further desired to understand the characteristics of a factually saintly person and the different aspects of devotional practice. Lord Kṛṣṇa replied that a real *sādhu*, or Vaiṣṇava, is qualified with the following characteristics. He is merciful, nonenvious, always truthful, self-controlled, faultless, magnanimous, gentle, clean, nonpossessive, helpful to all, peaceful, *dependent on Kṛṣṇa alone*, free from lust, devoid of material endeavor, steady, in control of the six enemies of the mind, moderate in eating, never bewildered, always respectful to others, never desirous of respect for himself, sober, compassionate, friendly, poetic, expert and silent. The principal characteristic of a *sādhu* is that he takes shelter of Kṛṣṇa alone. One who engages exclusively in Kṛṣṇa's service and understands Him as the limitless, indwelling Lord who comprises eternity, knowledge and bliss, is the topmost devotee. The practice of devotional service includes sixty-four kinds of activities. Among these are: (1–6) seeing, touching, worshiping, serving, glorifying and offering obeisances to the Deity of the Lord and His pure devotees; (7) developing attachment for hearing the chanting of the Lord's qualities, pastimes, and so on; (8) remaining always in meditation upon the Lord; (9) offering everything one acquires to the Lord; (10) accepting oneself to be the Lord's servant; (11) offering the Lord one's heart and soul; (12) engaging in glorification of the Lord's birth and activities; (13) observing holidays related to the Lord; (14) performing festivals in the Lord's temple in the company of other devotees, and with music, singing and dancing; (15) celebrating all varieties of yearly functions; (16) offering foodstuffs to the Lord; (17) taking initiation according to the *Vedas* and *tantras;* (18)taking vows related to the Lord; (19) being eager to establish Deities of the Lord; (20) endeavoring either alone or in association with others in constructing, for the service of the Lord, vegetable and flower gardens, temples, cities, and so on; (21) humbly cleansing the temple of the Lord; and (22) rendering service to the Lord's house by painting it, washing it with water and decorating it with auspicious designs.

After this, the process of worshiping the Deity of the Supreme Lord is described in brief.

TEXT 1

श्रीभगवानुवाच
बद्धो मुक्त इति व्याख्या गुणतो मे न वस्तुतः।
गुणस्य मायामूलत्वान्न मे मोक्षो न बन्धनम् ॥ १ ॥

śrī-bhagavān uvāca
baddho mukta iti vyākhyā
guṇato me na vastutaḥ
guṇasya māyā-mūlatvān
na me mokṣo na bandhanam

śrī-bhagavān uvāca—the Supreme Personality of Godhead said; *baddhaḥ*—in bondage; *muktaḥ*—liberated; *iti*—thus; *vyākhyā*—the explanation of the living entity; *guṇataḥ*—due to the modes of material nature; *me*—which are My potency; *na*—not; *vastutaḥ*—in reality; *guṇasya*—of the modes of material nature; *māyā*—My illusory energy; *mūlatvāt*—because of being the cause; *na*—not; *me*—of Me; *mokṣaḥ*—liberation; *na*—nor; *bandhanam*—bondage.

TRANSLATION

The Supreme Personality of Godhead said: My dear Uddhava, due to the influence of the material modes of nature, which are under My control, the living entity is sometimes designated as conditioned and sometimes as liberated. In fact, however, the soul is never really bound up or liberated, and since I am the supreme Lord of māyā, which is the cause of the modes of nature, I also am never to be considered liberated or in bondage.

PURPORT

In this chapter the Supreme Personality of Godhead, Kṛṣṇa, explains the different characteristics of conditioned and liberated life, the symptoms by which one can recognize saintly persons, and the various processes of devotional service to the Lord. In the previous chapter, Uddhava inquired from the Lord how conditioned and liberated life are possible. The Lord now replies that Uddhava's question is somewhat superficial, since the pure spirit soul is never entangled in the material energy of the Lord. The living entity imagines a false connection with the three modes of nature and accepts the material body as the self. The living entity therefore suffers the consequences of his own imagination, just as one suffers the illusory activities of a dream. This does not indicate that the material world is illusory in the sense that it is nonexistent. The material world is certainly real, being the potency of the Personality of Godhead, and the living entity, being the superior potency of God, is also real. But the living entity's dream of being part and parcel of the material world is an illusion that drags him into the contradictory state called material conditioned life. The living entity is never actually *baddha*, or bound up, since he merely imagines a false connection with the material world.

Because there is ultimately no permanent connection between the living entity and matter, there is no actual liberation. The living entity, being eternally transcendental to the inferior material energy of the Lord, is eternally liberated. Lord Kṛṣṇa reveals that in one sense the living entity is factually not bound up and thus cannot be liberated. But in another sense, the terms *bondage* and *liberation* can be conveniently applied to indicate the particular situation of the individual soul, who is the marginal potency of the Lord. Although the individual soul is never actually bound to matter, he suffers the reactions of material nature because of false identification, and thus the term *baddha*, or "bound up," may be used to indicate the nature of a living entity's experience within the inferior energy of the Lord. Since *baddha* describes a false situation, freedom from such a false situation may also be described as *mokṣa*, or liberation. Therefore the terms *bondage* and *liberation* are acceptable if one understands that such terms only refer to temporary situations created by illusion and do not refer to the ultimate nature of the living entity. In this verse Lord Kṛṣṇa states, *guṇasya māyā-mūlatvān na me mokṣo na bandhanam:* the terms *liberation* and *bondage* can never be applied to the Supreme Personality of Godhead, since He is the Absolute Truth and the supreme controller of everything. Lord Kṛṣṇa is eternally the supreme transcendental entity, and He can never be bound by illusion. It is the duty of the illusory potency of the Personality of Godhead to attract the living entities to ignorance by creating the false impression of a blissful existence separate from Lord Kṛṣṇa. The illusory conception of existence apart from the Personality of Godhead is called *māyā*, or material illusion. Since Lord Kṛṣṇa is the supreme absolute controller of *māyā*, there is no possibility that *māyā* could have any influence over the Personality of Godhead. Thus the term *bandhanam*, or "bondage," cannot be applied to the eternal, blissful and omniscient Personality of Godhead. The term *mokṣa*, or "liberation," indicating freedom from *bandhana*, is equally irrelevant to the Lord.

Śrīla Bhaktisiddhānta Sarasvatī Ṭhākura has commented on this verse as follows. The Supreme Personality of Godhead is endowed with great spiritual potencies. Because of mundane concoction, the conditioned soul imagines that the Absolute Truth is devoid of variegated spiritual potencies by which He may enjoy blissful life. Although the living entity is the spiritual potency of the Lord, he is presently situated in the inferior, illusory potency, and by engaging in mental speculation he becomes bound in conditioned life. Liberation means that the living entity should transfer himself to the spiritual potency of the Lord, which can be divided into three categories—*hlādinī*, the potency of bliss; *sandhinī*, the potency of eternal existence; and *saṁvit*, the potency of omniscience. Since the Personality of Godhead is eternally endowed with a pure existence of bliss and knowledge, He is never conditioned or liberated. The living entity, however, being entangled in the Lord's material potency, is sometimes conditioned and sometimes liberated.

The neutral, original state of the three modes of nature is called *māyā*. When the three modes of nature interact, one of them will become powerful, subordinating the other two modes until another mode becomes prominent. In this way, the three can be distinguished in their variety of manifestation. Although the threefold material potency expands from the Personality of Godhead, the Lord Himself in His personal form is the actual abode of the three spiritual potencies, namely eternality, bliss and knowledge. If one desires to become free from the entanglement of conditioned life within the material sky, called the kingdom of *māyā*, one must come to the spiritual sky, wherein the living entities are filled with bliss, possess eternal spiritual bodies and engage in the loving devotional service of the Lord. By developing one's eternal, spiritual form in the loving service of the Lord, one immediately transcends the duality of conditioned life and impersonal liberation and can directly experience the spiritual potencies of the Lord. At that time there is no possibility of false identification with the material world.

Realizing oneself to be eternal spirit soul, the living entity can understand that he is never truly connected to matter, because he is part of the superior energy of the Lord. Therefore, both material bondage and liberation are ultimately meaningless within the reality of the spiritual sky. The living entity is the marginal potency of the Lord and should exercise his free will to engage in the pure devotional service of the Lord. By reviving one's eternal, spiritual body one can understand oneself to be a minute particle of the spiritual potency of the Lord. In other words, the living entity is a minute particle of eternity, bliss and omniscience, and thus in full Kṛṣṇa consciousness there is no possibility of his being carried away by the illusion of the three modes of nature. In conclusion, it may be stated that the individual living entity is never actually entangled in matter and is thus not liberated, although his illusory state may be accurately described as entangled and liberated. On the other hand, the Supreme Personality of Godhead is eternally situated in His own spiritual potencies and can never be described as being bound up, and thus there is no meaning to the concept of the Lord's freeing Himself from such a nonexistent condition.

TEXT 2

शोकमोहौ सुखं दुःखं देहापत्तिश्च मायया ।
स्वप्नो यथात्मनः ख्यातिः संसृतिर्न तु वास्तवी ॥२॥

śoka-mohau sukhaṁ duḥkhaṁ
dehāpattiś ca māyayā
svapno yathātmanaḥ khyātiḥ
saṁsṛtir na tu vāstavī

śoka—lamentation; *mohau*—and illusion; *sukham*—happiness; *duḥkham*—distress; *deha-āpattiḥ*—accepting a material body; *ca*—also; *māyayā*—by the influence of *māyā; svapnaḥ*—a dream; *yathā*—just as; *ātmanaḥ*—of the intelligence; *khyātiḥ*—merely an idea; *saṁsṛtiḥ*—material existence; *na*—is not; *tu*—indeed; *vāstavī*—real.

TRANSLATION

Just as a dream is merely a creation of one's intelligence but has no actual substance, similarly, material lamentation, illusion,

happiness, distress and the acceptance of the material body under the influence of māyā are all creations of My illusory energy. In other words, material existence has no essential reality.

PURPORT

The word *deha-āpattiḥ* indicates that the living entity falsely identifies himself with the external material body and thus transmigrates from one body to another. *Āpatti* also indicates great suffering or misfortune. Because of such false identification under the influence of illusion, the living entity experiences the miserable symptoms described here. *Māyā* means the false concept that anything can exist without Lord Kṛṣṇa or for any purpose other than the pleasure of the Supreme Lord. Although the conditioned living entities are trying to enjoy material sense gratification, the result is always painful, and such painful experiences turn the conditioned soul back toward the Supreme Personality of Godhead. In other words, the ultimate purpose of the material creation is to bring the living entity back to the loving devotional service of the Lord. Therefore, even the sufferings of the material world may be seen as the transcendental mercy of the Personality of Godhead. The conditioned soul, imagining that material objects are meant for his personal enjoyment, bitterly laments the loss of such objects. In this verse, the example is given of a dream in which the material intelligence creates many illusory objects. Similarly, our polluted material consciousness creates the false impression of material sense gratification, but this phantasmagoria, being devoid of Kṛṣṇa consciousness, has no real existence. By surrendering to polluted material consciousness, the living entity is afflicted with innumerable troubles. The only solution is to see Lord Kṛṣṇa within everything and everything within Lord Kṛṣṇa. Thus, one understands that Lord Kṛṣṇa is the supreme enjoyer, the proprietor of everything and the well-wishing friend of all living beings.

In material illusion there is no understanding of one's eternal, spiritual body, nor is there knowledge of the Absolute Truth. Therefore, material existence, even in its most sophisticated or pious form, is always foolishness. One should not misunderstand the example of the dream to mean that the material world has no real existence. Material nature is the manifestation of the Lord's external potency, just as the spiritual sky is the manifestation of the Lord's internal potency. Although material objects are subject to transformation and thus have no permanent existence, the material energy is real because it comes from the supreme reality, Lord Kṛṣṇa. It is only our false acceptance of the material body as the factual self and our foolish dream that the material world is meant for our pleasure that have no real existence. They are merely mental concoctions. One should cleanse oneself of material designations and wake up to the all-pervading reality of the Personality of Godhead, Lord Kṛṣṇa.

TEXT 3

विद्याविद्ये मम तनू विद्ध्युद्धव शरीरिणाम् ।
मोक्षबन्धकरी आद्ये मायया मे विनिर्मिते ॥ ३ ॥

vidyāvidye mama tanū
viddhy uddhava śarīriṇām
mokṣa-bandha-karī ādye
māyayā me vinirmite

vidyā—knowledge; *avidye*—and ignorance; *mama*—My; *tanū*—manifested energies; *viddhi*—please understand; *uddhava*—O Uddhava; *śarīriṇām*—of the embodied living entities; *mokṣa*—liberation; *bandha*—bondage; *karī*—causing; *ādye*—original, eternal; *māyayā*—by the potency; *me*—My; *vinirmite*—produced.

TRANSLATION

O Uddhava, both knowledge and ignorance, being products of māyā, are expansions of My potency. Both knowledge and ignorance are beginningless and perpetually award liberation and bondage to embodied living beings.

PURPORT

By the expansion of *vidyā*, or knowledge, a conditioned soul is liberated from the clutches of *māyā*, and similarly, by the expansion of *avidyā*, or ignorance, the conditioned soul is driven further into illusion and bondage. Both knowledge and ignorance are products of the mighty potency of the Personality of Godhead. The living being is bound by illusion when he considers himself the proprietor of the subtle and gross material bodies. According to Śrīla Jīva Gosvāmī the living entity may be designated as *jīva-māyā*, whereas matter is called *guṇa-māyā*. The living entity places his living potency (*jīva-māyā*) in the grip of the mundane qualitative potency (*guṇa-māyā*) and falsely dreams that he is part and parcel of the material world. Such an artificial mixture is called illusion or ignorance. When all of the Lord's potencies are correctly perceived in their proper categories, the living entity is liberated from material bondage and returns to his blissful eternal residence in the spiritual sky.

The Supreme Personality of Godhead is not different from His potencies, yet He is always above them as the supreme controller. The Supreme Personality of Godhead may be designated as *mukta*, or liberated, only to indicate that He is eternally free from material contamination and never to indicate that the Lord has been freed from actual entanglement in a material situation. According to Śrīla Madhvācārya, *vidyā* indicates the goddess of fortune, the internal potency of the Lord, whereas *avidyā* indicates Durgā, the external potency of the Lord. Ultimately, however, the Personality of Godhead can transform His potencies according to His own desire, as explained by Śrīla Prabhupāda in his commentary on *Śrīmad-Bhāgavatam* (1.3.34), "Because the Lord is the absolute Transcendence, all of His forms, names, pastimes, attributes, associates and energies are identical with Him. His transcendental energy acts according to His omnipotency. The same energy acts as His external, internal and marginal energies, and by His omnipotency He can perform anything and everything through the agency of any of the above energies. He can turn the external energy into internal by His will."

Śrīla Śrīdhara Svāmī notes in this regard that although the Lord has explained in the first verse of this chapter that the living entity is never actually in bondage, and therefore never actually liberated, one may apply the terms *bondage* and *liberation* if one remembers that the living entity is eternally a transcendental fragment of the Personality of Godhead. Further, one should not misinterpret the words *māyayā me vinirmite* to indicate that both material bondage and liberation are temporary states, being creations of the potency of the Lord. Therefore, the term *ādye*, or "primeval and eternal," is used in this verse. The *vidyā* and *avidyā* potencies of the Lord are stated to be creations of *māyā* because they carry out the functions of the Lord's potencies. The *vidyā* potency engages the living entities in the Lord's pastimes, whereas the *avidyā* potency engages the living entities in forgetting the Lord and merging into darkness. Actually, both knowledge and ignorance are eternal alternatives of the marginal potency of the Lord, and in this sense it is not incorrect to state that the living entity is either eternally conditioned or eternally liberated. The term *vinirmite*, or "produced," in this case indicates that the Lord expands His own energy as knowledge and ignorance, which display the functions of the Lord's internal and external potencies. Such potential exhibitions may appear and disappear in different times, places and circumstances, but material bondage and spiritual freedom are eternal options of the marginal potency of the Lord.

TEXT 4

एकस्यैव ममांशस्य जीवस्यैव महामते ।
बन्धोऽस्याविद्ययानादिर्विद्यया च तथेतरः ॥ ४ ॥

ekasyaiva mamāṁśasya
jīvasyaiva mahā-mate
bandho 'syāvidyayānādir
vidyayā ca tathetaraḥ

ekasya—of the one; *eva*—certainly; *mama*—My; *aṁśasya*—part and parcel; *jīvasya*—of the living entity; *eva*—certainly; *mahā-mate*—O most intelligent one; *bandhaḥ*—bondage; *asya*—of him; *avidyayā*—by ignorance; *anādiḥ*—beginningless; *vidyayā*—by knowledge; *ca*—and; *tathā*—similarly; *itaraḥ*—the opposite of bondage, liberation.

TRANSLATION

O most intelligent Uddhava, the living entity, called jīva, is part and parcel of Me, but due to ignorance has been suffering in material bondage since time immemorial. By knowledge, however, he can be liberated.

PURPORT

Just as the sun reveals itself through its own light or covers itself by creating clouds, the Personality of Godhead reveals and covers Himself by knowledge and ignorance, which are expansions of His potency. As stated in *Bhagavad-gītā* (7.5):

apareyam itas tv anyāṁ
prakṛtiṁ viddhi me parām
jīva-bhūtāṁ mahā-bāho
yayedaṁ dhāryate jagat

"Besides this inferior nature, O mighty-armed Arjuna, there is a superior energy of Mine, consisting of all living entities who are struggling with material nature and are sustaining the universe." Śrīla Prabhupāda states in connection with this verse: "The Supreme Lord Kṛṣṇa is the only controller, and all living entities are controlled by Him. These living entities are His superior energy because the quality of their existence is one and the same with the Supreme, but they are never equal to the Lord in quantity of power."

Because of quantitative inferiority of potency, the living entity becomes covered by *māyā* and is again liberated by surrendering to the Lord. The word *aṁśa*, or "part and parcel," is also mentioned in *Bhagavad-gītā* (15.7): *mamaivāṁśo jīva-loke jīva-bhūtaḥ sanātanaḥ.* The living entity is *aṁśa*, or a minute particle, and therefore subject to liberation and bondage. As stated in the *Viṣṇu Purāṇa:*

viṣṇu-śaktiḥ parā proktā
kṣetrajñākhyā tathā parā
avidyā-karma-saṁjñānyā
tṛtīyā śaktir iṣyate

"The Supreme Personality of Godhead, Viṣṇu, possesses His superior internal potency as well as the potency called *kṣetrajñā śakti.* This *ksetrajñā śakti* is also spiritual potency, but it is sometimes covered by the third, or material, potency called ignorance. Thus because of the various stages of covering, the second, or marginal, potency is manifested in different evolutionary phases."

Śrīla Bhaktivinoda Ṭhākura has written that the living entity has been executing fruitive activities since time immemorial. Thus his conditioned life may be called beginningless. Such conditioned life, however, is not endless, since the living entity may achieve liberation through the loving devotional service of the Lord. Since the living entity may acquire liberation, Śrīla Bhaktivinoda Ṭhākura states that his liberated life begins at a certain point but is endless, because liberated life is understood to be eternal. In any case, one who has achieved the shelter of the Supreme Personality of Godhead, Kṛṣṇa, may be understood to be eternally liberated, since such a person has entered into the eternal atmosphere of the spiritual sky. Since there is no material time in the spiritual sky, one who has achieved his eternal spiritual body on Lord Kṛṣṇa's planet is not subject to the influence of time. His eternal blissful life with Kṛṣṇa is not designated in terms of material past, present and future and is therefore called eternal liberation. Material time is conspicuous by its absence in the spiritual sky, and every living entity there is eternally liberated, having attained the supreme situation. Such liberation can be achieved by *vidyā*, or perfect knowledge, which is understood in three phases called Brahman, Paramātmā and Bhagavān, as described in *Śrīmad-Bhāgavatam.* The ultimate phase of *vidyā*, or knowledge, is to understand the Supreme Personality of Godhead. In *Bhagavad-gītā* such knowledge is called *rāja-vidyā*, or the king of all knowledge, and it awards the supreme liberation.

TEXT 5

अथ बद्धस्य मुक्तस्य वैलक्षण्यं वदामि ते ।
विरुद्धधर्मिणोस्तात स्थितयोरेकधर्मिणि ॥ ५ ॥

atha baddhasya muktasya
vailakṣaṇyaṁ vadāmi te
viruddha-dharmiṇos tāta
sthitayor eka-dharmiṇi

atha—thus; *baddhasya*—of the conditioned soul; *muktasya*—of the liberated Personality of Godhead; *vailakṣaṇyam*—different characteristics; *vadāmi*—I will now speak; *te*—unto you; *viruddha*—opposing; *dharmiṇoḥ*—whose two natures; *tāta*—My dear Uddhava; *sthitayoḥ*—of the two who are situated; *eka-dharmiṇi*—in the one body which manifests their different characteristics.

TRANSLATION

Thus, My dear Uddhava, in the same material body we find opposing characteristics, such as great happiness and misery. That is because both the Supreme Personality of Godhead, who is eternally liberated, as well as the conditioned soul are within the body. I shall now speak to you about their different characteristics.

PURPORT

In verse 36 of the previous chapter, Uddhava inquired about the different symptoms of liberated and conditioned life. Śrīla Śrīdhara Svāmī explains that the characteristics of bondage and liberation may be understood in two divisions—as the difference between the ordinary conditioned soul and the eternally liberated Personality of Godhead, or as the difference between conditioned and liberated living entities in the *jīva* category. The Lord will first explain the difference between the ordinary living entity and the Supreme Personality of Godhead, which may be understood as the difference between the controlled and the controller.

TEXT 6

सुपर्णावेतौ सदृशौ सखायौ
यदृच्छयैतौ कृतनीडौ च वृक्षे ।
एकस्तयोः खादति पिप्पलान्न-
मन्यो निरन्नोऽपि बलेन भूयान् ॥ ६ ॥

suparṇāv etau sadṛśau sakhāyau
yadṛcchayaitau kṛta-nīḍau ca vṛkṣe
ekas tayoḥ khādati pippalānnam
anyo niranno 'pi balena bhūyān

suparṇau—two birds; *etau*—these; *sadṛśau*—similar; *sakhāyau*—friends; *yadṛcchayā*—by chance; *etau*—these two; *kṛta*—made; *nīḍau*—a nest; *ca*—and; *vṛkṣe*—in a tree; *ekaḥ*—one; *tayoḥ*—of the two; *khādati*—is eating; *pippala*—of the tree; *annam*—the fruits; *anyaḥ*—the other; *nirannaḥ*—not eating; *api*—although; *balena*—by strength; *bhūyān*—He is superior.

TRANSLATION

By chance, two birds have made a nest together in the same tree. The two birds are friends and are of similar nature. One of them, however, is eating the fruits of the tree, whereas the other, who does not eat the fruits, is in a superior position, due to His potency.

PURPORT

The example of two birds in the same tree is given to illustrate the presence within the heart of the material body of both the individual soul and the Supersoul, the Personality of Godhead. Just as a bird makes a nest in a tree, the living entity sits within the heart. The example is appropriate because the bird is always distinct from the tree. Similarly, both the individual soul and the Supersoul are distinct entities, separate from the temporary material body. The word *balena* indicates that the Supreme Personality of Godhead is satisfied by His own internal potency, which consists of eternality, omniscience and bliss. As indicated by the word *bhūyān*, or "having superior existence," the Supreme Lord is always in a superior position, whereas the living entity is sometimes in illusion and sometimes enlightened. The word *balena* indicates that the Lord is never in darkness or ignorance, but is always full in His perfect, blissful consciousness.

Thus, the Lord is *niranna*, or uninterested in the bitter fruits of material activities, whereas the ordinary conditioned soul busily consumes such bitter fruits, thinking them to be sweet. Ultimately, the fruit of all material endeavor is death, but the living entity foolishly thinks material things will bring him pleasure. The word *sakhāyau*, or "two friends," is also significant. Our real friend is Lord Kṛṣṇa, who is situated within our heart. Only He knows our actual needs, and only He can give us real happiness.

Lord Kṛṣṇa is so kind that He patiently sits in the heart, trying to guide the conditioned soul back home, back to Godhead. Certainly no material friend would remain with his foolish companion for millions of years, especially if his companion were to ignore him or even curse him. But Lord Kṛṣṇa is such a faithful, loving friend that He accompanies even the most demoniac living entity and is also in the heart of the insect, pig and dog. That is because Lord Kṛṣṇa is supremely Kṛṣṇa conscious and sees every living entity as part and parcel of Himself. Every living being should give up the bitter fruits of the tree of material existence. One should turn one's face to the Lord within the heart and revive one's eternal loving relationship with one's real friend, Lord Kṛṣṇa. The word *sadṛśau,* or "of similar nature," indicates that both the living entity and the Personality of Godhead are conscious entities. As part and parcel of the Lord we share the Lord's nature, but in infinitesimal quantity. Thus the Lord and the living entity are *sadṛśau.* A similar statement is found in the *Śvetāśvatara Upaniṣad* (4.6):

dvā suparṇā sayujā sakhāyā
samānaṁ vṛkṣaṁ pariṣasvajāte
tayor anyaḥ pippalaṁ svādv atty
anaśnann anyo 'bhicākaśīti

"There are two birds in one tree. One of them is eating the fruits of the tree, while the other is witnessing the actions. The witness is the Lord, and the fruit-eater is the living entity."

TEXT 7

आत्मानमन्यं च स वेद विद्वा-
नपिप्पलादो न तु पिप्पलादः ।
योऽविद्यया युक् स तु नित्यबद्धो
विद्यामयो यः स तु नित्यमुक्तः ॥ ७ ॥

ātmānam anyaṁ ca sa veda vidvān
apippalādo na tu pippalādaḥ
yo 'vidyayā yuk sa tu nitya-baddho
vidyā-mayo yaḥ sa tu nitya-muktaḥ

ātmānam—Himself; *anyam*—the other; *ca*—also; *saḥ*—He; *veda*—knows; *vidvān*—being omniscient; *apippala-adaḥ*—not eating the fruits of the tree; *na*—not; *tu*—but; *pippala-adaḥ*—the one who is eating the fruits of the tree; *yaḥ*—who; *avidyayā*—with ignorance; *yuk*—filled; *saḥ*—he; *tu*—indeed; *nitya*—eternally; *baddhaḥ*—conditioned; *vidyā-*

mayaḥ—full of perfect knowledge; *yaḥ*—who; *saḥ*—he; *tu*—indeed; *nitya*—eternally; *muktaḥ*—liberated.

TRANSLATION

The bird who does not eat the fruits of the tree is the Supreme Personality of Godhead, who by His omniscience perfectly understands His own position and that of the conditioned living entity, represented by the eating bird. That living entity, on the other hand, does not understand himself or the Lord. He is covered by ignorance and is thus called eternally conditioned, whereas the Personality of Godhead, being full of perfect knowledge, is eternally liberated.

PURPORT

The word *vidyā-maya* in this verse indicates the internal potency of the Lord and not the external potency, *mahā-māyā.* Within the material world there is *vidyā,* or material science, and *avidyā,* or material ignorance, but in this verse *vidyā* means the internal spiritual knowledge by which the Personality of Godhead is fixed in omniscience. The example of two birds in a tree, which is given in many Vedic literatures, demonstrates the statement *nityo nityānām:* there are two categories of eternal living entities, namely the Supreme Lord and the minute *jīva* soul. The conditioned *jīva* soul, forgetting his identity as an eternal servant of the Lord, tries to enjoy the fruits of his own activities and thus comes under the spell of ignorance. This bondage of ignorance has existed since time immemorial and can be rectified only by one's taking to the loving devotional service of the Lord, which is full of spiritual knowledge. In conditioned life the living entity is forced by the laws of nature to engage in pious and impious fruitive activities, but the liberated position of every living entity is to offer the fruits of his work to the Lord, the supreme enjoyer. It should be understood that even when the living entity is in a liberated condition, his knowledge is never equal in quantity to that of the Personality of Godhead. Even Lord Brahmā, the supreme living entity within this universe, acquires only partial knowledge of the Personality of Godhead and His potencies. In *Bhagavad-gītā* (4.5), the Lord explains His superior knowledge to Arjuna:

bahūni me vyatītāni
janmāni tava cārjuna
tāny ahaṁ veda sarvāṇi
na tvaṁ vettha parantapa

"The Blessed Lord said: Many, many births both you and I have passed. I can remember all of them, but you cannot, O subduer of the enemy!"

The term *baddha*, or "bound," is also understood to refer to the living entity's eternal dependence upon the Lord, either in the conditioned or liberated state. In the kingdom of *māyā* the living entity is bound to the cruel laws of birth and death, whereas in the spiritual sky the living entity is fixed in a bond of love to the Lord. Liberation means freedom from the miseries of life, but never freedom from one's loving relationship with Lord Kṛṣṇa, which is the essence of one's eternal existence. According to Śrīla Madhvācārya, the Lord is the only eternally free living entity, and all other living entities are eternally dependent and bound to the Lord, either through blissful loving service or through the bondage of *māyā*. The conditioned soul should give up tasting the bitter fruits of the tree of material existence and turn to his dearmost friend, Lord Kṛṣṇa, who is sitting within his heart. There is no pleasure equal to or greater than the pleasure of pure devotional service to Lord Kṛṣṇa, and by tasting the fruit of love of Kṛṣṇa, the liberated living entity enters the ocean of happiness.

TEXT 8

देहस्थोऽपि न देहस्थो विद्वान् स्वप्नाद् यथोत्थितः।
अदेहस्थोऽपि देहस्थः कुमतिः स्वप्नदृग् यथा ॥ ८॥

deha-stho 'pi na deha-stho
vidvān svapnād yathotthitaḥ
adeha-stho 'pi deha-sthaḥ
kumatiḥ svapna-dṛg yathā

deha—in the material body; *sthaḥ*—situated; *api*—although; *na*—not; *deha*—in the body; *sthaḥ*—situated; *vidvān*—an enlightened person; *svapnāt*—from a dream; *yathā*—just as; *utthitaḥ*—having risen; *adeha*—not in the body; *sthaḥ*—situated; *api*—although; *deha*—in the body; *sthaḥ*—situated; *ku-matiḥ*—a foolish person; *svapna*—a dream; *dṛk*—seeing; *yathā*—just as.

TRANSLATION

One who is enlightened in self-realization, although living within the material body, sees himself as transcendental to the body, just as one who has arisen from a dream gives up identification with the dream body. A foolish person, however, although not identical with his material body but transcendental to it, thinks himself to be situated in the body, just as one who is dreaming sees himself as situated in an imaginary body.

PURPORT

In Lord Kṛṣṇa's discussion of the different characteristics of liberated and conditioned souls, the Lord first clarified the distinction between the eternally liberated Personality of Godhead and the marginal potency, the innumerable *jīvas,* who are sometimes conditioned and sometimes liberated. In this and the next nine verses, the Lord describes the different symptoms of liberated and conditioned *jīva* souls. In a dream one sees oneself in an imaginary body, but upon waking one gives up all identification with that body. Similarly, one who has awakened to Kṛṣṇa consciousness no longer identifies with the gross or subtle material bodies, nor does he become affected by the happiness and distress of material life. On the other hand, a foolish person (*kumati*) does not awaken from the dream of material existence and is afflicted with innumerable problems due to false identification with the gross and subtle material bodies. One should become situated in one's eternal spiritual identity (*nitya-svarūpa*). By properly identifying oneself as the eternal servant of Kṛṣṇa, one becomes relieved of his false material identity, and therefore the miseries of illusory existence immediately cease, just as the anxiety of a troublesome dream ceases as soon as one awakens to his normal, pleasant surroundings. It should be understood, however, that the analogy of awakening from a dream can never be applied to the Supreme Personality of Godhead, who is never in illusion. The Lord is eternally awake and enlightened in His own unique category called *viṣṇu-tattva.* Such knowledge is easily understood by one who is *vidvān,* or enlightened in Kṛṣṇa consciousness.

TEXT 9

इन्द्रियैरिन्द्रियार्थेषु गुणैरपि गुणेषु च ।
गृह्यमाणेष्वहंकुर्यान्न विद्वान् यस्त्वविक्रियः ॥ ९ ॥

indriyair indriyārtheṣu
guṇair api guṇeṣu ca
gṛhyamāṇeṣv ahaṁ kuryān
na vidvān yas tv avikriyaḥ

indriyaiḥ—by the senses; *indriya*—of the senses; *artheṣu*—in the objects; *guṇaiḥ*—by those generated from the modes of nature; *api*—even; *guṇeṣu*—in those generated by the same modes; *ca*—also; *gṛhyamāṇeṣu*—as they are being accepted; *aham*—false ego; *kuryāt*—should create; *na*—not; *vidvān*—one who is enlightened; *yaḥ*—who; *tu*—indeed; *avikriyaḥ*—is not affected by material desire.

TRANSLATION

An enlightened person who is free from the contamination of material desire does not consider himself to be the performer of bodily activities; rather, he knows that in all such activities it is only the senses, born of the modes of nature, that are contacting sense objects born of the same modes of nature.

PURPORT

Lord Kṛṣṇa makes a similar statement in *Bhagavad-gītā* (3.28):

tattva-vit tu mahā-bāho
guṇa-karma-vibhāgayoḥ
guṇā guṇeṣu vartanta
iti matvā na sajjate

"One who is in knowledge of the Absolute Truth, O mighty-armed, does not engage himself in the senses and sense gratification, knowing well the difference between work in devotion and work for fruitive results."

The material body always interacts with the sense objects, for in order to survive the body must eat, drink, speak, sleep, and so on, but an enlightened person who knows the science of Kṛṣṇa consciousness never thinks, "I am accepting these sense objects as my property. They are meant for my pleasure." Similarly, if the body performs a wonderful activity, a Kṛṣṇa conscious person does not become proud, nor is he depressed by the failure of the body to function in a particular way. In other words, Kṛṣṇa consciousness means giving up identification with the gross and subtle material bodies. One should see them as the external energy of the Lord, working under the direction of the Lord's empowered representative *māyā.* One absorbed in fruitive activities works under the jurisdiction of *mahā-māyā,* or the external illusory potency, and experiences the miseries of material existence. On the other hand, a devotee works under the internal potency, called *yoga-māyā,* and remains satisfied by offering his loving service to the Lord. In either case, the Lord Himself, by His multifarious potencies, is the ultimate performer of action.

According to Śrīla Viśvanātha Cakravartī Ṭhākura, one who claims to be transcendental to the bodily concept of life, but at the same time remains under the influence of material desire and mental transformation, is understood to be a cheater and the lowest type of conditioned soul.

TEXT 10

दैवाधीने शरीरेऽस्मिन् गुणभाव्येन कर्मणा ।
वर्तमानोऽबुधस्तत्र कर्तास्मीति निबद्ध्यते ॥१०॥

daivādhīne śarīre 'smin
guṇa-bhāvyena karmaṇā
vartamāno 'budhas tatra
kartāsmīti nibadhyate

daiva—of one's previous fruitive activities; *adhīne*—which is under the influence; *śarīre*—in the material body; *asmin*—in this; *guṇa*—by the modes of nature; *bhāvyena*—which are produced; *karmaṇā*—by fruitive activities; *vartamānaḥ*—being situated; *abudhaḥ*—one who is foolish; *tatra*—within the bodily functions; *kartā*—the doer; *asmi*—I am; *iti*—thus; *nibadhyate*—is bound up.

TRANSLATION

An unintelligent person situated within the body created by his previous fruitive activities thinks, "I am the performer of action." Bewildered by false ego, such a foolish person is therefore bound up by fruitive activities, which are in fact carried out by the modes of nature.

PURPORT

As stated in *Bhagavad-gītā* (3.27):

prakṛteḥ kriyamāṇāni
guṇaiḥ karmāṇi sarvaśaḥ
ahaṅkāra-vimūḍhātmā
kartāham iti manyate

The living entity is dependent on the supreme entity, Lord Kṛṣṇa, but because of false pride he ignores the Supreme Personality of Godhead and considers himself to be the performer of action and enjoyer of everything. Śrīla Madhvācārya states that just as a king punishes a rebellious subject, the Supreme Lord punishes the sinful living entity by forcing him to transmigrate from one body to another in the network of the illusory energy.

TEXT 11

एवं विरक्तः शयन आसनाटनमज्जने ।
दर्शनस्पर्शनघ्राणभोजनश्रवणादिषु
न तथा बद्ध्यते विद्वन्तत्र तत्रादयन् गुणान् ॥११॥

evaṁ viraktaḥ śayana
āsanāṭana-majjane
darśana-sparśana-ghrāṇa-
bhojana-śravaṇādiṣu
na tathā badhyate vidvān
tatra tatrādayan guṇān

evam—thus; *viraktaḥ*—detached from material enjoyment; *śayane*—in lying or sleeping; *āsana*—in sitting; *aṭana*—walking; *majjane*—or in bathing; *darśana*—in seeing; *sparśana*—touching; *ghrāṇa*—smelling; *bhojana*—eating; *śravaṇa*—hearing; *ādiṣu*—and so on; *na*—not; *tathā*—in that way; *badhyate*—is bound; *vidvān*—an intelligent person; *tatra tatra*—wherever he goes; *ādayan*—causing to experience; *guṇān*—the senses, born of the modes of nature.

TRANSLATION

An enlightened person fixed in detachment engages his body in lying down, sitting, walking, bathing, seeing, touching, smelling, eating, hearing, and so on, but is never entangled by such activities. Indeed, remaining as a witness to all bodily functions, he merely engages his bodily senses with their objects and does not become entangled like an unintelligent person.

PURPORT

In the previous chapter, Uddhava asked Lord Kṛṣṇa why an enlightened person, just like a conditioned soul, engages in external bodily functions. Here is the Lord's answer. While engaged in bodily functions, an unintelligent person is attached to both the means and end of material life and therefore experiences intense lamentation and jubilation on the material platform. A self-realized soul, however, studies the inevitable defeat and suffering of ordinary persons and does not make the mistake of trying to enjoy the bodily functions even slightly. He instead remains a detached witness, merely engaging his senses in the normal functions of bodily maintenance. As indicated here by the word *ādayan*, he engages something other than his actual self in material experience.

TEXTS 12–13

प्रकृतिस्थोऽप्यसंसक्तो यथा खं सवितानिलः ।
वैशारद्येक्षयासङ्गशितया छिन्नसंशयः ॥१२॥
प्रतिबुद्ध इव स्वप्नान्नानात्वाद् विनिवर्तते ॥१३॥

prakṛti-stho 'py asaṁsakto
yathā khaṁ savitānilaḥ

vaiśāradyekṣayāsaṅga-
śitayā chinna-saṁśayaḥ
pratibuddha iva svapnān
nānātvād vinivartate

prakṛti—in the material world; *sthaḥ*—situated; *api*—even though; *asaṁsaktaḥ*—completely detached from sense gratification; *yathā*—just as; *kham*—the sky; *savitā*—the sun; *anilaḥ*—the wind; *vaiśāradyā*—by most expert; *īkṣayā*—vision; *asaṅga*—through detachment; *śitayā*—sharpened; *chinna*—cut to pieces; *saṁśayaḥ*—doubts; *pratibuddhaḥ*—awakened; *iva*—like; *svapnāt*—from a dream; *nānātvāt*—from the duality of variety of the material world; *vinivartate*—one turns away or renounces.

TRANSLATION

Although the sky, or space, is the resting place of everything, the sky does not mix with anything, nor is it entangled. Similarly, the sun is not at all attached to the water in which it is reflected within innumerable reservoirs, and the mighty wind blowing everywhere is not affected by the innumerable aromas and atmospheres through which it passes. In the same way, a self-realized soul is completely detached from the material body and the material world around it. He is like a person who has awakened and arisen from a dream. With expert vision sharpened by detachment, the self-realized soul cuts all doubts to pieces through knowledge of the self and completely withdraws his consciousness from the expansion of material variety.

PURPORT

According to Śrīla Bhaktisiddhānta Sarasvatī Ṭhākura, a self-realized soul cuts all doubts to pieces by direct experience of his true spiritual identity. The Supreme Personality of Godhead is Lord Kṛṣṇa, and there is no possibility of any existence separate from Lord Kṛṣṇa. Such expert knowledge cuts all doubts to pieces. As stated here, *prakṛti-stho 'py asaṁsaktaḥ:* like the sky, the sun or the wind, one who is self-realized is not entangled, though situated within the material creation of the Lord. *Nānātva,* or "material variety," refers to one's material body, the bodies of others and the unlimited paraphernalia for bodily sense gratification, both physical and mental. By awakening to Kṛṣṇa consciousness, one completely retires from illusory sense gratification and becomes absorbed in the progressive realization of the soul situated within the body. As revealed in the example of the two birds in a tree, both the individual soul and the Personality of Godhead are completely separate from the gross and subtle material bodies. If one turns one's face to the Lord, recognizing one's eternal dependence on Him, there will be no further suffering or anxiety, even though one is still situated within the material world. The unlimited experiences of material objects only increase one's anxiety, whereas perception of the Absolute Truth, Śrī Kṛṣṇa, immediately brings one to the platform of peace. Thus one who is intelligent retires from the world of matter and becomes a fully self-realized Kṛṣṇa conscious person.

TEXT 14

यस्य स्युर्वीतसङ्कल्पाः प्राणेन्द्रियमनोधियाम् ।
वृत्तयः स विनिर्मुक्तो देहस्थोऽपि हि तद्गुणैः ॥१४॥

yasya syur vīta-saṅkalpāḥ
prāṇendriya-mano-dhiyām
vṛttayaḥ sa vinirmukto
deha-stho 'pi hi tad-guṇaiḥ

yasya—of whom; *syuḥ*—they are; *vīta*—freed from; *saṅkalpāḥ*—material desire; *prāṇa*—of the vital energy; *indriya*—the senses; *manaḥ*—the mind; *dhiyām*—and of intelligence; *vṛttayaḥ*—the functions; *saḥ*—such a person; *vinirmuktaḥ*—completely freed; *deha*—in the body; *sthaḥ*—situated; *api*—even though; *hi*—certainly; *tat*—of the body; *guṇaiḥ*—from all of the qualities.

TRANSLATION

A person is considered to be completely liberated from the gross and subtle material bodies when all the functions of his vital energy, senses, mind and intelligence are performed without material desire. Such a person, although situated within the body, is not entangled.

PURPORT

The material body and mind are subject to lamentation, illusion, hunger, lust, greed, insanity, frustration, etc., but one who remains active in this world without attachment is considered *vinirmukta*, or completely liberated. The vital energy, senses, mind and intelligence are purified when engaged in the devotional service of Lord Kṛṣṇa, as confirmed throughout *Śrīmad-Bhāgavatam.*

TEXT 15

यस्यात्मा हिंस्यते हिंस्रैर्येन किञ्चिद् यदृच्छया ।
अर्च्यते वा क्वचित्तत्र न व्यतिक्रियते बुधः ॥१५॥

yasyātmā hiṁsyate hiṁsrair
yena kiñcid yadṛcchayā
arcyate vā kvacit tatra
na vyatikriyate budhaḥ

yasya—of whom; *ātmā*—the body; *hiṁsyate*—is attacked; *hiṁsraiḥ*—by sinful people or violent animals; *yena*—by someone; *kiñcit*—somewhat; *yadṛcchayā*—somehow or other; *arcyate*—is worshiped; *vā*—or; *kvacit*—somewhere; *tatra*—therein; *na*—not; *vyatikriyate*—is transformed or affected; *budhaḥ*—one who is intelligent.

TRANSLATION

Sometimes for no apparent reason one's body is attacked by cruel people or violent animals. At other times and in other places, one will suddenly be offered great respect or worship. One who does not become angry when attacked nor satisfied when worshiped is actually intelligent.

PURPORT

If one does not become angry when attacked for no apparent reason, and if one does not become enlivened when glorified or worshiped, then one has passed the test of self-realization and is considered fixed in spiritual intelligence. Uddhava asked Lord Kṛṣṇa, *kair vā jñāyeta lakṣaṇaiḥ:* by what symptoms can a self-realized person be recognized? Just as Lord

Kṛṣṇa enlightened Arjuna, He now explains the same subject matter to Uddhava. In this verse the Lord describes symptoms by which it is very easy to recognize a saintly person, for a normal person becomes furious when criticized or attacked and overwhelmed with joy when glorified by others. There is a similar statement by Yājñavalkya to the effect that one who is actually intelligent does not become angry though pricked with thorns and does not become satisfied at heart merely by being worshiped with auspicious paraphernalia such as sandalwood.

TEXT 16

न स्तुवीत न निन्देत कुर्वतः साध्वसाधु वा ।
वदतो गुणदोषाभ्यां वर्जितः समदृङ् मुनिः ॥१६॥

na stuvīta na nindeta
kurvataḥ sādhv asādhu vā
vadato guṇa-doṣābhyāṁ
varjitaḥ sama-dṛṅ muniḥ

na stuvīta—does not praise; *na nindeta*—does not criticize; *kurvataḥ*—those who are working; *sādhu*—very nicely; *asādhu*—very badly; *vā*—or; *vadataḥ*—those who are speaking; *guṇa-doṣābhyām*—from good and bad qualities; *varjitaḥ*—freed; *sama-dṛk*—seeing things equally; *muniḥ*—a saintly sage.

TRANSLATION

A saintly sage sees with equal vision and therefore is not affected by that which is materially good or bad. Indeed, although he observes others performing good and bad work and speaking properly and improperly, the sage does not praise or criticize anyone.

TEXT 17

न कुर्यान्न वदेत् किञ्चिन्न ध्यायेत् साध्वसाधु वा ।
आत्मारामोऽनया वृत्त्या विचरेज्जडवन्मुनिः ॥१७॥

na kuryān na vadet kiñcin
na dhyāyet sādhv asādhu vā

ātmārāmo 'nayā vṛttyā
vicarej jaḍa-van muniḥ

na kuryāt—should not do; *na vadet*—should not speak; *kiñcit*—anything; *na dhyāyet*—should not contemplate; *sādhu asādhu vā*—either good or bad things; *ātma-ārāmaḥ*—one who is taking pleasure in self-realization; *anayā*—with this; *vṛttyā*—life-style; *vicaret*—he should wander; *jaḍa-vat*—just like a stunted person; *muniḥ*—a saintly sage.

TRANSLATION

For the purpose of maintaining his body, a liberated sage should not act, speak or contemplate in terms of material good or bad. Rather, he should be detached in all material circumstances, and taking pleasure in self-realization he should wander about engaged in this liberated life-style, appearing like a retarded person to outsiders.

PURPORT

According to Śrīla Jīva Gosvāmī, this verse describes a type of discipline recommended for the *jñāna-yogīs*, who by intelligence try to understand that they are not their material bodies. One who is engaged in the devotional service of the Lord, however, accepts and rejects material things in terms of their usefulness in the loving service of Lord Kṛṣṇa. One who is trying to preach Kṛṣṇa consciousness should be seen as very intelligent and not *jaḍa-vat,* or stunted, as described here. Although a devotee of the Lord does not act, speak or contemplate for his personal sense gratification, he remains very busy working, speaking and meditating in the devotional service of the Lord. The devotee makes elaborate plans to engage all the fallen souls in Lord Kṛṣṇa's service so they can be purified and go back home, back to Godhead. Merely rejecting material things is not perfect consciousness. One must see everything as the property of the Lord and meant for the Lord's pleasure. One busily engaged in spreading the Kṛṣṇa consciousness movement has no time to make material distinctions and thus automatically comes to the liberated platform.

TEXT 18

शब्दब्रह्मणि निष्णातो न निष्णायात् परे यदि ।
श्रमस्तस्य श्रमफलो ह्यधेनुमिव रक्षतः ॥१८॥

śabda-brahmaṇi niṣṇāto
na niṣṇāyāt pare yadi
śramas tasya śrama-phalo
hy adhenum iva rakṣataḥ

śabda-brahmaṇi—in the Vedic literature; *niṣṇātaḥ*—expert through complete study; *na niṣṇāyāt*—does not absorb the mind; *pare*—in the Supreme; *yadi*—if; *śramaḥ*—labor; *tasya*—his; *śrama*—of great endeavor; *phalaḥ*—the fruit; *hi*—certainly; *adhenum*—a cow that gives no milk; *iva*—like; *rakṣataḥ*—of one who is taking care of.

TRANSLATION

If through meticulous study one becomes expert in reading Vedic literature but makes no endeavor to fix one's mind on the Supreme Personality of Godhead, then one's endeavor is certainly like that of a man who works very hard to take care of a cow that gives no milk. In other words, the fruit of one's laborious study of Vedic knowledge will simply be the labor itself. There will be no other tangible result.

PURPORT

Śrīla Viśvanātha Cakravartī Ṭhākura explains that the word *pare* ("the Supreme") in this verse indicates the Supreme Personality of Godhead rather than the impersonal Brahman, because Lord Kṛṣṇa, the speaker of these instructions, makes references in later verses to His personality as the Supreme. An impersonal interpretation in this case would be *eka-deśānvaya uttara-ślokārtha-tātparya-virodhaḥ*, or a contradictory interpretation that creates illogical conflict with other *ślokas* (verses) spoken in the same context.

It requires great endeavor to take care of a cow. One must either grow food grains to feed the cow or maintain suitable pastures. If the pasture is not properly maintained, poisonous weeds will grow, or snakes will multiply, and there will be danger. Cows are infected by many types of diseases and bugs and must be regularly cleaned and disinfected. Similarly, fences must be maintained around the cow pasture, and there is even more work to be done. If the cow gives no milk, however, then one certainly performs hard labor with no tangible result. Laborious effort is also required to learn the Sanskrit language well enough to discern the subtle and esoteric meaning of the Vedic *mantras*. If after such great labor one does not understand the spiritual body of the Supreme Personality of Godhead, which is the source of all happiness in life, and if one does not surrender to the Lord as the supreme shelter of all things, then one has certainly labored hard with no tangible result other than his own labor. Even a liberated soul who has given up the bodily concept of life will fall down if he does not take shelter of the Supreme Personality of Godhead. The word *niṣṇāta*, or "expert," indicates that one must ultimately achieve the goal of life; otherwise one is not expert. As stated by Caitanya Mahāprabhu, *premā pum-artho mahān:* the actual goal of human life is love of Godhead, and no one can be considered expert without achieving this goal.

TEXT 19

गां दुग्धदोहामसतीं च भार्यां
देहं पराधीनमसत्प्रजां च ।
वित्तं त्वतीर्थीकृतमङ्ग वाचं
हीनां मया रक्षति दुःखदुःखी ॥१९॥

gāṁ dugdha-dohām asatīṁ ca bhāryāṁ
dehaṁ parādhīnam asat-prajāṁ ca
vittaṁ tv atīrthī-kṛtam aṅga vācaṁ
hīnāṁ mayā rakṣati duḥkha-duḥkhī

gām—a cow; *dugdha*—whose milk; *dohām*—already taken; *asatīm*—unchaste; *ca*—also; *bhāryām*—a wife; *deham*—a body; *para*—upon others; *adhīnam*—always dependent; *asat*—useless; *prajām*—children; *ca*—also; *vittam*—wealth; *tu*—but; *atīrthī-kṛtam*—not given to the proper recipient; *aṅga*—O Uddhava; *vācam*—Vedic knowledge; *hīnām*—devoid; *mayā*—of knowledge of Me; *rakṣati*—he takes care of; *duḥkha-duḥkhī*—he who suffers one misery after another.

TRANSLATION

My dear Uddhava, that man is certainly most miserable who takes care of a cow that gives no milk, an unchaste wife, a body totally dependent on others, useless children or wealth not utilized for the right purpose. Similarly, one who studies Vedic knowledge devoid of My glories is also most miserable.

PURPORT

A human being is actually learned or expert when he understands that all material objects perceived through the various senses are expansions of the Supreme Personality of Godhead and that nothing exists without the support of the Supreme Lord. In this verse, through various examples, it is concluded that the power of speech is useless if not engaged in the support of the Supreme Lord. According to Śrīla Viśvanātha Cakravartī Ṭhākura, this verse implies that all of the functions of the various senses are useless if they are not engaged in the glorification of God. Indeed, the *avadhūta brāhmaṇa* previously stated to King Yadu that if the tongue is not controlled, one's entire program of sense control is a failure. One cannot control the tongue unless he vibrates the glories of the Lord.

The example of the milkless cow is significant. A gentleman never kills a cow, and therefore when a cow becomes sterile and no longer gives milk, one must engage in the laborious task of protecting her, since no one will purchase a useless cow. For some time, the greedy owner of a sterile cow may continue thinking, "I have already invested so much money in taking care of this cow, and certainly in the near future she will again become pregnant and give milk." But when this hope is proven futile, he becomes neglectful and indifferent to the health and safety of the animal. Because of such sinful neglect, he must suffer in the next life, after having already suffered because of the sterile cow in the present life.

Similarly, although a man may discover that his wife is neither chaste nor affectionate, he may be so eager to get children that he goes on taking care of such a useless wife, thinking, "I will teach my wife the religious duties of a chaste woman. By hearing historical examples of great women surely her heart will change, and she will become a wonderful wife to me." Unfortunately, the unchaste wife in many cases does not change and also gives a man many useless children who are just as foolish and irreligious as she. Such children never give any happiness to the father, yet the father tediously labors to take care of them.

Also, one who has accumulated wealth by the mercy of God must be vigilant to give in charity to the right person and for the right cause. If such a right person or cause appears and one hesitates and selfishly does not give in charity, one loses his reputation, and in the next life he will be poverty-stricken. One who fails to give properly in charity spends his life anxiously protecting his wealth, which ultimately brings him no fame or happiness.

The previous examples are given to illustrate the uselessness of laboriously studying Vedic knowledge that does not glorify the Supreme Personality of Godhead. Śrīla Jīva Gosvāmī comments that the spiritual vibration of the *Vedas* is meant to bring one to the lotus feet of the Supreme Lord, Kṛṣṇa. Many processes for achieving the Supreme Truth are recommended in the *Upaniṣads* and other Vedic literatures, but because of their innumerable and seemingly contradictory explanations, commentaries and injunctions, one cannot achieve the Absolute Truth, the Personality of Godhead, merely by reading such literature. If, however, one understands Śrī Kṛṣṇa to be the ultimate cause of all causes and reads the *Upaniṣads* and other Vedic literature as glorification of the Supreme Lord, then one can actually become fixed at the Lord's lotus feet. For example, His Divine Grace Śrīla Prabhupāda translated and commented upon *Śrī Īśopaniṣad* in such a way that it brings the reader closer to the Supreme Personality of Godhead. Undoubtedly, the lotus feet of Lord Kṛṣṇa are the only reliable boat by which to cross the turbulent ocean of material existence. Even Lord Brahmā has stated in the Tenth Canto of *Śrīmad-Bhāgavatam* that if one gives up the auspicious path of *bhakti* and takes to the fruitless labor of Vedic speculation, one is just like a fool who beats empty husks in hopes of getting rice. Śrīla Jīva Gosvāmī recommends that one completely ignore dry Vedic speculation because it does not bring one to the point of devotional service to the Absolute Truth, Lord Śrī Kṛṣṇa.

TEXT 20

यस्यां न मे पावनमङ्ग कर्म
स्थित्युद्भवप्राणनिरोधमस्य ।
लीलावतारेप्सितजन्म वा स्याद्
वन्ध्यां गिरं तां बिभृयान्न धीरः ॥२०॥

yasyāṁ na me pāvanam aṅga karma
sthity-udbhava-prāṇa-nirodham asya

līlāvatārepsita-janma vā syād
vandhyāṁ giraṁ tāṁ bibhṛyān na dhīraḥ

yasyām—in which (literature); *na*—not; *me*—My; *pāvanam*—purifying; *aṅga*—O Uddhava; *karma*—activities; *sthiti*—maintenance; *udbhava*—creation; *prāṇa-nirodham*—and annihilation; *asya*—of the material world; *līlā-avatāra*—among the pastime incarnations; *īpsita*—desired; *janma*—appearance; *vā*—or; *syāt*—is; *vandhyām*—barren; *giram*—vibration; *tām*—this; *bibhṛyāt*—should support; *na*—not; *dhīraḥ*—an intelligent person.

TRANSLATION

My dear Uddhava, an intelligent person should never take to literatures that do not contain descriptions of My activities, which purify the whole universe. Indeed, I create, maintain and annihilate the entire material manifestation. Among all My pastime incarnations, the most beloved are Kṛṣṇa and Balarāma. Any so-called knowledge that does not recognize these activities of Mine is simply barren and is not acceptable to those who are actually intelligent.

PURPORT

The words *līlāvatārepsita-janma* are very significant here. The Lord's incarnation for executing wonderful pastimes is called *līlāvatāra*, and such wonderful forms of Viṣṇu are glorified by the names Rāmacandra, Nṛsiṁhadeva, Kūrma, Varāha, and so on. Among all such *līlāvatāras*, however, the most beloved, even to this day, is Lord Kṛṣṇa, the original source of the *viṣṇu-tattva*. The Lord appears in the prison house of Kaṁsa and is immediately transferred to the rural setting of Vṛndāvana, where He exhibits unique childhood pastimes with His cowherd boyfriends, girl friends, parents and well-wishers. After some time, the Lord's pastimes are transferred to Mathurā and Dvārakā, and the extraordinary love of the inhabitants of Vṛndāvana is exhibited in their anguished separation from Lord Kṛṣṇa. Such pastimes of the Lord are *īpsita*, or the reservoir of all loving exchanges with the Absolute Truth. The pure devotees of the Lord are most intelligent and expert and do not pay any attention to useless, fruitless literatures that neglect the highest truth, Lord Kṛṣṇa. Although such literatures are very popular among materialistic persons all over the world, they are completely neglected by the community of pure Vaiṣṇavas. In this verse the Lord explains that the literatures approved for the devotees are those that glorify the Lord's pastimes as the *puruṣa-avatāra* and the *līlāvatāras*, culminating in the personal appearance of Lord Kṛṣṇa Himself, as confirmed in *Brahma-saṁhitā* (5.39):

rāmādi-mūrtiṣu kalā-niyamena tiṣṭhan
nānāvatāram akarod bhuvaneṣu kintu
kṛṣṇaḥ svayaṁ samabhavat paramaḥ pumān yo
govindam ādi-puruṣaṁ tam ahaṁ bhajāmi

"I worship Govinda, the primeval Lord, who manifested Himself personally as Kṛṣṇa and the different *avatāras* in the world in the forms of Rāma, Nṛsiṁha, Vāmana, etc., as His subjective portions."

Even Vedic literatures that neglect the Supreme Personality of Godhead should be ignored. This fact was also explained by Nārada Muni to Śrīla Vyāsadeva, the author of the *Vedas*, when the great Vedavyāsa felt dissatisfied with his work.

TEXT 21

एवं जिज्ञासयापोह्य नानात्वभ्रममात्मनि ।
उपारमेत विरजं मनो मय्यर्प्य सर्वगे ॥२१॥

evaṁ jijñāsayāpohya
nānātva-bhramam ātmani
upārameta virajaṁ
mano mayy arpya sarva-ge

evam—thus (as I have now concluded); *jijñāsayā*—by analytic study; *apohya*—giving up; *nānātva*—of material variety; *bhramam*—the mistake of rotating; *ātmani*—in the self; *upārameta*—one should cease from material life; *virajam*—pure; *manaḥ*—the mind; *mayi*—in Me; *arpya*—fixing; *sarva-ge*—who am all-pervading.

TRANSLATION

Coming to this conclusion of all knowledge, one should give up the false conception of material variety that one imposes upon the soul and thus cease one's material existence. The mind should be fixed in Me since I am all-pervading.

PURPORT

Although in previous verses Lord Kṛṣṇa has described the life-style and approach of the impersonal philosophers who meditate on the distinction between matter and spirit, the Lord here rejects the path of *jñāna*, or speculation, and comes to the final conclusion, *bhakti-yoga.* The path of *jñāna* is interesting only to one who does not know that Lord Kṛṣṇa is the Supreme Personality of Godhead, as stated in *Bhagavad-gītā* (7.19):

bahūnāṁ janmanām ante
jñānavān māṁ prapadyate
vāsudevaḥ sarvam iti
sa mahātmā su-durlabhaḥ

The words *vāsudevaḥ sarvam iti,* or "Vāsudeva is everything," are similar to the words *sarva-ge* found in this verse. One should know why the Personality of Godhead is all-pervading. The first verse of *Śrīmad-Bhāgavatam* states, *janmādy asya yataḥ:* the Supreme Lord is the source of everything. And as stated in the previous verse of this chapter, He creates, maintains and annihilates everything. Thus the Lord is not all-pervading in the manner of air or sunlight; rather, the Lord is all-pervading as the absolute controller who holds in His hands the destiny of every living entity.

Everything is ultimately an expansion of Kṛṣṇa, and therefore there is really no other object of meditation besides Kṛṣṇa. Meditation upon any other object is also meditation on Kṛṣṇa but is imperfectly performed, as confirmed in *Bhagavad-gītā* by the word *avidhi-pūrvakam.* The Lord also states in the *Gītā* that all living entities are on the path back home, back to Godhead. Because of ignorance, however, some of them go backward or stop along the way, foolishly thinking that their journey is finished, when in fact they are suspended in one of the minor potencies of the Supreme Lord. If one wants to intimately understand the nature of the Absolute Truth, one must take to the path of love of Godhead. As stated in *Bhagavad-gītā* (18.55):

bhaktyā mām abhijānāti
yāvān yaś cāsmi tattvataḥ
tato māṁ tattvato jñātvā
viśate tad-anantaram

"One can understand the Supreme Personality as He is only by devotional service. And when one is in full consciousness of the Supreme Lord by such devotion, he can enter into the kingdom of God."

The words *nānātva-bhramam* in this verse indicate false identification with the gross and subtle material bodies. The word *bhramam* indicates a mistake; it can also mean "wandering" or "rotating." The conditioned living entity, because of his mistake of falling into illusion, is wandering through a succession of material bodies, sometimes appearing as a demigod and sometimes as a worm in stool. The word *upārameta* means that one should stop such fruitless wandering and fix one's mind on the Absolute Truth, the Supreme Lord, who is the true object of everyone's love. Such a conclusion is not sentimental but is the result of keen analytic intelligence (*jijñāsayā*). Thus after elaborately explaining to Uddhava many aspects of analytic knowledge, the Lord now comes to the ultimate conclusion, Kṛṣṇa consciousness, pure love of Godhead. Without such love there is no question of eternally fixing one's mind on the Lord.

Quoting from the *Viveka*, Śrīla Madhvācārya states that *nānātva-bhramam* indicates the following illusions: considering the living entity to be the Supreme; considering all living entities to be ultimately one entity without separate individuality; considering that there are many Gods; thinking that Kṛṣṇa is not God; and considering that the material universe is the ultimate reality. All of these illusions are called *bhrama*, or mistakes, but such ignorance can be eliminated at once by the chanting of the holy names of Kṛṣṇa: Hare Kṛṣṇa, Hare Kṛṣṇa, Kṛṣṇa Kṛṣṇa, Hare Hare/ Hare Rāma, Hare Rāma, Rāma Rāma, Hare Hare.

TEXT 22

यद्यनीशो धारयितुं मनो ब्रह्मणि निश्चलम् ।
मयि सर्वाणि कर्माणि निरपेक्षः समाचर ॥२२॥

yady anīśo dhārayituṁ
mano brahmaṇi niścalam
mayi sarvāṇi karmāṇi
nirapekṣaḥ samācara

yadi—if; *anīśaḥ*—incapable; *dhārayitum*—to fix; *manaḥ*—the mind; *brahmaṇi*—on the spiritual platform; *niścalam*—free from sense gratification; *mayi*—in Me; *sarvāṇi*—all; *karmāṇi*—activities; *nirapekṣaḥ*—without trying to enjoy the fruits; *samācara*—execute.

TRANSLATION

My dear Uddhava, if you are not able to free your mind from all material disturbance and thus absorb it completely on the spiritual platform, then perform all your activities as an offering to Me, without trying to enjoy the fruits.

PURPORT

If one offers one's activities to Lord Kṛṣṇa without trying to enjoy the results, one's mind becomes purified. When the mind is purified, transcendental knowledge automatically manifests, since such knowledge is a by-product of pure consciousness. When the mind is absorbed in perfect knowledge, it can be raised to the spiritual platform, as described in *Bhagavad-gītā* (18.54):

brahma-bhūtaḥ prasannātmā
na śocati na kāṅkṣati
samaḥ sarveṣu bhūteṣu
mad-bhaktiṁ labhate parām

"One who is thus transcendentally situated at once realizes the Supreme Brahman. He never laments nor desires to have anything; he is equally disposed to every living entity. In that state he attains pure devotional service unto Me." By absorbing the mind in the transcendental form of Lord Kṛṣṇa, one can surpass the stage of ordinary transcendental knowledge, by which one simply distinguishes oneself from the gross and subtle material bodies. Spiritually enriched by loving devotional service to the Lord, the mind is completely purified of all tinges of illusion. Through intense concentration on one's relationship with the Personality of Godhead one comes to the highest standard of knowledge and becomes an intimate associate of the Personality of Godhead.

By offering one's activities to the Personality of Godhead, one purifies one's mind to some extent and thus comes to the preliminary stage of spiritual awareness. Yet even then one may not be able to fix one's mind completely on the spiritual platform. At that point one should realistically assess one's position, noting the lingering material contamination within the mind. Then, as stated in this verse, one should intensify one's practical devotional work in the service of the Lord. If one artificially considers oneself to be supremely liberated or if one becomes casual on the path of spiritual advancement, there is serious danger of a falldown.

According to Śrīla Jīva Gosvāmī, the Lord previously explained to Uddhava *jñāna-miśrā bhakti*, or devotional service mixed with the impure desire to enjoy transcendental knowledge. In this verse the Lord clearly reveals that transcendental knowledge is an automatic by-product of loving service to the Lord, and in the next verse the Lord begins His explanation of pure devotional service, which is completely sufficient for self-realization. The desire to enjoy spiritual knowledge is certainly a material desire, since the goal is one's personal satisfaction and not the pleasure of the Supreme Lord. Therefore Lord Kṛṣṇa here warns Uddhava that if one is not able to fix one's mind in trance on the spiritual platform, then one should not go on simply theoretically discussing what is Brahman and what is not Brahman. Rather, one should engage in practical devotional service to the Supreme Lord, and then spiritual knowledge will automatically awaken in one's heart. As stated in *Bhagavad-gītā* (10.10):

teṣāṁ satata-yuktānāṁ
bhajatāṁ prīti-pūrvakam
dadāmi buddhi-yogaṁ taṁ
yena mām upayānti te

"To those who are constantly devoted and worship Me with love, I give the understanding by which they can come to Me."

Similarly, in the Tenth Canto of *Śrīmad-Bhāgavatam* Lord Brahmā warns that one should not neglect the auspicious path of *bhakti* and instead take up the useless labor of mental speculation. By mere philosophical speculation one cannot fix one's mind on the spiritual platform. Many great philosophers throughout history had abominable personal habits, which proves that they could not fix themselves on the spiritual platform by mere speculation on philosophical categories. If one is not fortunate enough to have executed devotional service to the Lord in one's past life, and if one is therefore addicted to mere speculation on the differences between matter and spirit, one will not be able to fix one's mind on the spiritual platform. Such a person should give up useless speculation and engage in the practical work of Kṛṣṇa consciousness, absorbing himself twenty-four hours a day in the mission of the Supreme Personality of Godhead. In such missionary work for the Lord's sake, one should never try to enjoy the fruits of one's work. Even though the mind is not completely pure, if one offers the fruits of one's work to the Lord, the mind will quickly come to the standard of pure desirelessness, in which one's only desire is the Lord's satisfaction.

Śrīla Jīva Gosvāmī states that if one does not have faith in the personal form and activities of the Personality of Godhead, one will not have the spiritual strength to remain perpetually on the transcendental platform. In this verse the Lord is definitely bringing Uddhava, and all living entities, to the conclusion of all philosophy—pure devotional service to the Supreme Lord, Kṛṣṇa.

In this regard, Śrīla Bhaktisiddhānta Sarasvatī Ṭhākura points out that one who is bewildered by false ego may not want to offer his activities to the Supreme Personality of Godhead, even though this is the actual way of rising above the influence of the modes of material nature. Because of ignorance one does not know that he is the eternal servant of Kṛṣṇa and instead is attracted by the duality of material illusion. One cannot become free from such illusion by theoretical speculation, but if one offers one's work to the Personality of Godhead, one will clearly understand his eternal, transcendental position as a servant of the Lord.

TEXTS 23–24

श्रद्धालुर्मत्कथाः शृण्वन् सुभद्रा लोकपावनीः ।
गायन्ननुस्मरन् कर्म जन्म चाभिनयन् मुहुः ॥२३॥

मदर्थे धर्मकामार्थानाचरन् मदपाश्रयः ।
लभते निश्चलां भक्तिं मय्युद्धव सनातने ॥२४॥

śraddhālur mat-kathāḥ śṛṇvan
su-bhadrā loka-pāvanīḥ
gāyann anusmaran karma
janma cābhinayan muhuḥ

mad-arthe dharma-kāmārthān
ācaran mad-apāśrayaḥ
labhate niścalāṁ bhaktiṁ
mayy uddhava sanātane

śraddhāluḥ—a faithful person; *mat-kathāḥ*—narrations about Me; *śṛṇvan*—hearing; *su-bhadrāḥ*—which are all-auspicious; *loka*—the entire world; *pāvanīḥ*—purifying; *gāyan*—singing; *anusmaran*—remembering constantly; *karma*—My activities; *janma*—My birth; *ca*—also; *abhinayan*—reliving through dramatical performances, etc.; *muhuḥ*—again and again; *mat-arthe*—for My pleasure; *dharma*—religious activities; *kāma*—sense activities; *arthān*—and commercial activities; *ācaran*—performing; *mat*—in Me; *apāśrayaḥ*—having one's shelter; *labhate*—one obtains; *niścalām*—without deviation; *bhaktim*—devotional service; *mayi*—to Me; *uddhava*—O Uddhava; *sanātane*—dedicated to My eternal form.

TRANSLATION

My dear Uddhava, narrations of My pastimes and qualities are all-auspicious and purify the entire universe. A faithful person who constantly hears, glorifies and remembers such transcendental activities, who through dramatic performances relives My pastimes beginning with My appearance, and who takes full shelter in Me, dedicating his religious, sensual and occupational activities for My satisfaction, certainly obtains unflinching devotional service to Me, the eternal Personality of Godhead.

PURPORT

Those who have faith only in the impersonal effulgent aspect of the Supreme Lord and those who have faith only in the localized Supersoul, the perfect object of mystic meditation located in the heart of every living entity, are considered to be limited and imperfect in their transcendental realization. The process of mystic meditation and impersonal philosophical speculation are both devoid of actual love of God and therefore cannot be considered to be the perfection of human life. Only one who places full faith in the Supreme Personality of Godhead becomes qualified to go back home, back to Godhead.

Lord Kṛṣṇa's pastimes of stealing butter from the elderly *gopīs*, enjoying life with His cowherd boyfriends and the young *gopīs*, playing His flute and engaging in the *rāsa* dance, etc., are all-auspicious spiritual activities, and they are fully described in the Tenth Canto of this work. There are many authorized songs and prayers glorifying these pastimes of the Lord, and by constantly chanting them one will automatically be fixed in *smaraṇam*, or remembrance of the Supreme Personality of Godhead. The Lord exhibited His opulences upon His birth in Kaṁsa's prison and at the birth ceremony subsequently performed by Nanda Mahārāja in Gokula. The Lord further performed many adventurous activities, such as chastising the serpent Kāliya and many other irresponsible demons. One should regularly take part in the ceremonies commemorating Kṛṣṇa's pastimes, such as the Janmāṣṭamī celebration glorifying the Lord's birth. On such days one should worship the Deity of Lord Kṛṣṇa and the spiritual master and thus remember the Lord's pastimes.

The word *dharma* in this verse indicates that one's religious activities should always be in connection with Kṛṣṇa. Therefore, one should give charity in the form of food grains, clothing, etc., to the Vaiṣṇavas and *brāhmaṇas*, and whenever possible one should arrange for the protection of cows, who are very dear to the Lord. The word *kāma* indicates that one should satisfy one's desires with the transcendental paraphernalia of the Lord. One should eat *mahā-prasādam*, food offered to the Deity of Lord Kṛṣṇa, and one should also decorate oneself with the Lord's flower garlands and sandalwood pulp and should place the remnants of the Deity's clothing on one's body. One who lives in a luxurious mansion or apartment should convert his residence into a temple of Lord Kṛṣṇa and invite others to come, chant before the Deity, hear *Bhagavad-gītā* and *Śrīmad-Bhāgavatam* and taste the remnants of the Lord's food, or one may live in a beautiful temple building in the community of Vaiṣṇavas and engage in the same activities. The word *artha* in this verse indicates that one who is inclined toward business should accumulate money to promote the missionary work of the Lord's devotees and not for one's personal sense gratification. Thus one's business activities are also considered to be devotional service to Lord Kṛṣṇa. The word *niścalām* indicates that since Lord Kṛṣṇa is eternally fixed in perfect knowledge and bliss, there is no possibility of disturbance for one who worships the Lord. If we worship anything except the Lord, our worship may be disturbed when our worshipable deity is placed in an awkward position. But because the Lord is supreme, our worship of Him is eternally free of disturbance.

One who engages in hearing, glorifying, remembering and dramatically recreating the pastimes of the Lord will soon be freed from all material desire. Śrīla Jīva Gosvāmī mentions in this connection that one who is advanced in Kṛṣṇa consciousness may specifically be attracted to the pastimes of a devotee in the spiritual world who serves the Lord in a particular way. An advanced devotee in this world may desire to serve the Lord in the same way and thus may take pleasure in dramatically reliving the service of his worshipable devotee-master in the spiritual world. Also, one may take pleasure in spiritual festivals, performances of particular pastimes of Lord Kṛṣṇa, or activities of other devotees of the Lord. In this way, one can continually increase one's faith in the Personality of Godhead. Those who have no desire to hear, glorify or remember the transcendental activities of the Lord are certainly materially polluted and never achieve the highest perfection. Such persons spoil the opportunity of human life by devoting themselves to fleeting mundane topics that produce no eternal benefit. The real meaning of religion is to constantly serve the Supreme Personality of Godhead, whose form is eternal, full of bliss and knowledge. One who has taken full shelter of the Lord is completely uninterested in impersonal speculations about the nature of God and uses his time to advance more and more in the unlimited bliss of pure devotional service.

TEXT 25

सत्सङ्गलब्धया भक्त्या मयि मां स उपासिता ।
स वै मे दर्शितं सद्भिरञ्जसा विन्दते पदम् ॥२५॥

sat-saṅga-labdhayā bhaktyā
mayi māṁ sa upāsitā

sa vai me darśitaṁ sadbhir
añjasā vindate padam

sat—of the devotees of the Lord; *saṅga*—by the association; *labdhayā*—obtained; *bhaktyā*—by devotion; *mayi*—to Me; *mām*—of Me; *saḥ*—he; *upāsitā*—worshiper; *saḥ*—that very person; *vai*—undoubtedly; *me*—My; *darśitam*—revealed; *sadbhiḥ*—by My pure devotees; *añjasā*—very easily; *vindate*—achieves; *padam*—My lotus feet or My eternal abode.

TRANSLATION

One who has obtained pure devotional service by association with My devotees always engages in worshiping Me. Thus he very easily goes to My abode, which is revealed by My pure devotees.

PURPORT

In the previous verses Lord Kṛṣṇa has emphasized the value of surrendering to Him in loving service. One may ask how such surrender or devotion is actually achieved. The Lord gives the answer in this verse. One must live in a society of devotees, and thus automatically one will be engaged twenty-four hours a day in the various processes of devotional service, beginning with *śravaṇam, kīrtanam* and *smaraṇam* (hearing, glorifying and remembering the Lord). The pure devotees of the Lord can reveal the spiritual world by their transcendental sound vibration, making it possible for even a neophyte devotee to experience the Lord's abode. Being thus enlivened, the neophyte makes further progress and gradually becomes qualified to personally serve the Personality of Godhead in the spiritual world. By constantly associating with devotees and learning from them about devotional science, one quickly achieves a deep attachment for the Lord and the Lord's service, and such attachment gradually matures into pure love of Godhead.

Foolish persons say that the various *mantras* composed of names of God, as well as all other *mantras*, are merely material creations with no special value, and therefore any so-called *mantra* or mystical process will ultimately produce the same result. To refute such superficial thinking, the Lord here describes the science of going back home, back to Godhead. One should not accept the bad association of impersonalists, who state that the holy name, form, qualities and pastimes of the Lord are *māyā*, or illusion. *Māyā* is actually an insignificant potency of the almighty Personality of Godhead, and if one ignorantly tries to elevate illusion above the Absolute Truth, one will never experience love of Godhead and will be cast into deep forgetfulness of the Lord. One should not associate with those who are envious of the fortunate devotees who are going back to Godhead. Such envious persons deride the abode of the Lord, which is revealed by the pure devotees to those who have faith in the Lord's message. Envious persons create disturbances among the people in general, who should take shelter of the faithful devotees of the Lord. Unless people hear from pure devotees, it is impossible for them to understand that there is a Supreme Personality of Godhead eternally existing in His own abode, which is self-luminous, full of bliss and knowledge. In this verse, the importance of *saṅga*, association, is clearly explained.

TEXTS 26–27

श्रीउद्धव उवाच

साधुस्तवोत्तमश्लोक मतः कीदृग्विधः प्रभो ।
भक्तिस्त्वय्युपयुज्येत कीदृशी सद्भिरादृता ॥२६॥
एतन्मे पुरुषाध्यक्ष लोकाध्यक्ष जगत्प्रभो ।
प्रणतायानुरक्ताय प्रपन्नाय च कथ्यताम् ॥२७॥

śrī-uddhava uvāca
sādhus tavottama-śloka
mataḥ kīdṛg-vidhaḥ prabho
bhaktis tvayy upayujyeta
kīdṛśī sadbhir ādṛtā

etan me puruṣādhyakṣa
lokādhyakṣa jagat-prabho
praṇatāyānuraktāya
prapannāya ca kathyatām

śrī-uddhavaḥ uvāca—Śrī Uddhava said; *sādhuḥ*—a saintly person; *tava*—in Your; *uttama-śloka*—my dear Lord; *mataḥ*—opinion; *kīdṛk-vidhaḥ*—what kind would he be; *prabho*—my dear Personality of

Godhead; *bhaktiḥ*—devotional service; *tvayi*—unto Your Lordship; *upayujyeta*—deserves to be executed; *kīdṛśī*—what type is it; *sadbhiḥ*—by Your pure devotees such as Nārada; *ādṛtā*—honored; *etat*—this; *me*—to me; *puruṣa-adhyakṣa*—O ruler of the universal controllers; *loka-adhyakṣa*—O Supreme Lord of Vaikuṇṭha; *jagat-prabho*—O God of the universe; *praṇatāya*—unto Your surrendered devotee; *anuraktāya*—who loves You; *prapannāya*—who has no other shelter than You; *ca*—also; *kathyatām*—let this be spoken.

TRANSLATION

Śrī Uddhava said: My dear Lord, O Supreme Personality of Godhead, what type of person do You consider to be a true devotee, and what type of devotional service is approved by great devotees as worthy of being offered to Your Lordship? My dear ruler of the universal controllers, O Lord of Vaikuṇṭha and almighty God of the universe, I am Your devotee, and because I love You I have no other shelter than You. Therefore please explain this to me.

PURPORT

In the previous verse it was stated that one can achieve the Lord's supreme abode by associating with devotees. Therefore, Uddhava naturally inquires about the symptoms of a distinguished devotee whose association can promote one to the kingdom of God. Śrīla Jīva Gosvāmī notes that the Personality of Godhead knows who is actually a sincere devotee because the Lord is always attached to His loving servitors. Similarly, pure devotees can expertly explain the proper methods of devotional service to Lord Kṛṣṇa because they are already absorbed in love of Kṛṣṇa. Uddhava herein requests Lord Kṛṣṇa to describe the qualities of a devotee and asks the Lord to explain the devotional service that the devotees themselves approve as worthy to be offered to the Lord.

Śrīla Viśvanātha Cakravartī Ṭhākura remarks that the word *puruṣādhyakṣa* indicates that Lord Kṛṣṇa is the supreme ruler of the universal controllers headed by Mahā-Viṣṇu, and thus the Lord possesses infinite sovereignty. The term *lokādhyakṣa* indicates that Lord Kṛṣṇa is the ultimate supervising authority of all of the Vaikuṇṭha planets, and therefore the Lord is unlimitedly glorious and perfect. Uddhava further addresses Lord Kṛṣṇa as *jagat-prabhu*, because even in the illusory material world the Lord exhibits His unlimited mercy by personally incarnating to uplift the conditioned souls. The word *praṇatāya* ("Your surrendered devotee") indicates that Uddhava is not proud like ordinary fools who do not enjoy bowing down to the Supreme Personality of Godhead. According to Śrīla Viśvanātha Cakravartī Ṭhākura, Uddhava mentions that he is *anuraktāya*, or completely bound in love to Lord Kṛṣṇa, because unlike other great devotees such as Arjuna, who sometimes worshiped demigods in order to comply with social customs or to show respect for their positions in the scheme of planetary management, Uddhava never worshiped any demigods. Therefore, Uddhava is *prapannāya*, or completely surrendered to Lord Kṛṣṇa, having no other shelter.

TEXT 28

त्वं ब्रह्म परमं व्योम पुरुषः प्रकृतेः परः ।
अवतीर्णोऽसि भगवन् स्वेच्छोपात्तपृथग्वपुः ॥२८॥

tvaṁ brahma paramaṁ vyoma
puruṣaḥ prakṛteḥ paraḥ
avatīrṇo 'si bhagavan
svecchopātta-pṛthag-vapuḥ

tvam—You; *brahma paramam*—the Absolute Truth; *vyoma*—like the sky (You are detached from everything); *puruṣaḥ*—the Personality of Godhead; *prakṛteḥ*—to material nature; *paraḥ*—transcendental; *avatīrṇaḥ*—incarnated; *asi*—You are; *bhagavan*—the Lord; *sva*—of Your own (devotees); *icchā*—according to the desire; *upātta*—accepted; *pṛthak*—different; *vapuḥ*—bodies.

TRANSLATION

My dear Lord, as the Absolute Truth You are transcendental to material nature, and like the sky You are never entangled in any way. Still, being controlled by Your devotees' love, You accept many different forms, incarnating according to Your devotees' desires.

PURPORT

The pure devotees of the Lord propagate devotional service all over the world, and therefore, although separate from the personal form of the Lord, they are considered to be manifestations of God's mercy and potency. As stated in *Caitanya-caritāmṛta* (*Antya* 7.11): *kṛṣṇa-śakti vinā nahe tāra pravartana.*

The Lord is like the sky (*vyoma*) because although expanded everywhere, He is not entangled in anything. He is *prakṛteḥ paraḥ*, or completely transcendental to material nature. The Lord is fully self-satisfied and is therefore indifferent to the affairs of the material world. Still, because of His causeless mercy, the Lord desires to expand pure devotional service, and for this reason He incarnates within the material world to uplift the fallen conditioned souls.

The Lord descends in selected spiritual bodies to please His loving devotees. Sometimes He appears in His original form as Kṛṣṇa. And even Kṛṣṇa Himself appears in different forms to special devotees so that they may fully develop their loving sentiments for Him. Śrīla Jīva Gosvāmī gives several examples of the Lord's special mercy upon His devotees. Lord Kṛṣṇa personally went to the home of Jāmbavān and there displayed a form with slightly angry glances. In that form, the Lord enjoyed a fight with His devotee. The Lord displayed His form as Dattātreya to Atri Muni and similarly bestowed special mercy upon Lord Brahmā, the demigods, Akrūra and innumerable other devotees. And in Vṛndāvana the Lord displayed His most beautiful form as Govinda to the fortunate inhabitants.

Śrīla Madhvācārya has quoted from the *Prakāśa-saṁhitā* as follows. "The Lord accepts different spiritual bodies according to the desire of His devotees. For example, the Lord agreed to become the son of Vasudeva and Devakī. Thus, although Lord Kṛṣṇa has an eternal, blissful spiritual form, He appears to enter within the body of His devotee who becomes His mother. Although we speak of the Lord's 'taking on a body,' the Lord does not change His form, as do the conditioned souls, who must change their material bodies. The Lord appears in His own eternally unchangeable forms. Lord Hari always appears in the forms that are especially desired by His loving devotees, and never in other forms. However, if one thinks that the Lord, in the manner of an ordinary person taking birth, becomes the physical son of Vasudeva or other devotees, then one is victimized by illusion. The Lord merely expands His spiritual potency, causing His pure devotees to think, 'Kṛṣṇa is now my son.' One should understand that the Supreme Personality of Godhead never accepts or rejects a material body, nor does He ever give up His eternal spiritual forms; rather, the Lord eternally manifests His blissful bodies according to the loving sentiments of His eternal pure devotees."

Śrīla Jīva Gosvāmī mentions that the word *vyoma* also indicates the Lord's name of Paravyoma, or the Lord of the spiritual sky. One should not misinterpret this verse to mean that Lord Kṛṣṇa is impersonal, like the material sky, or that the form of Kṛṣṇa is merely another selected incarnation equal to any other. Such casual and whimsical speculations cannot be accepted as actual spiritual knowledge. Śrī Kṛṣṇa is the original Personality of Godhead (*kṛṣṇas tu bhagavān svayam*), and the Lord has explained elaborately in *Bhagavad-gītā* that He is the original source of everything. Therefore, the pure devotees of the Lord are eternally engaged, in full knowledge and bliss, in loving service to the Lord's original form as Kṛṣṇa. The whole purpose of *Śrīmad-Bhāgavatam* is to arouse our love for Lord Kṛṣṇa, and one should not foolishly misunderstand this great purpose.

TEXTS 29–32

श्रीभगवानुवाच

कृपालुरकृतद्रोहस्तितिक्षुः सर्वदेहिनाम् ।
सत्यसारोऽनवद्यात्मा समः सर्वोपकारकः ॥२९॥
कामैरहतधीर्दान्तो मृदुः शुचिरकिञ्चनः ।
अनीहो मितभुक् शान्तः स्थिरो मच्छरणो मुनिः ॥३०॥
अप्रमत्तो गभीरात्मा धृतिमाञ्जितषड्गुणः ।
अमानी मानदः कल्यो मैत्रः कारुणिकः कविः ॥३१॥
आज्ञायैवं गुणान् दोषान् मयादिष्टानपि स्वकान् ।
धर्मान् सन्त्यज्य यः सर्वान् मां भजेत स तु सत्तमः ॥३२॥

śrī-bhagavān uvāca
kṛpālur akṛta-drohas
titikṣuḥ sarva-dehinām

satya-sāro 'navadyātmā
samaḥ sarvopakārakaḥ

kāmair ahata-dhīr dānto
mṛduḥ śucir akiñcanaḥ
anīho mita-bhuk śāntaḥ
sthiro mac-charaṇo muniḥ

apramatto gabhīrātmā
dhṛtimāñ jita-ṣaḍ-guṇaḥ
amānī māna-daḥ kalyo
maitraḥ kāruṇikaḥ kaviḥ

ājñāyaivaṁ guṇān doṣān
mayādiṣṭān api svakān
dharmān santyajya yaḥ sarvān
māṁ bhajeta sa tu sattamaḥ

śrī-bhagavān uvāca—the Supreme Personality of Godhead said; *kṛpāluḥ*—unable to tolerate the suffering of others; *akṛta-drohaḥ*—never injuring others; *titikṣuḥ*—forgiving; *sarva-dehinām*—toward all living entities; *satya-sāraḥ*—one who lives by truth and whose strength and firmness come from truthfulness; *anavadya-ātmā*—a soul free from envy, jealousy, etc.; *samaḥ*—whose consciousness is equal both in happiness and in distresss; *sarva-upakārakaḥ*—always endeavoring as far as possible for the welfare of all others; *kāmaiḥ*—by material desires; *ahata*—undisturbed; *dhīḥ*—whose intelligence; *dāntaḥ*—controlling the external senses; *mṛduḥ*—without a harsh mentality; *śuciḥ*—always well-behaved; *akiñcanaḥ*—without possessiveness; *anīhaḥ*—free from worldly activities; *mita-bhuk*—eating austerely; *śāntaḥ*—controlling the mind; *sthiraḥ*—remaining steady in one's prescribed duty; *mat-śaraṇaḥ*—accepting Me as the only shelter; *muniḥ*—thoughtful; *apramattaḥ*—cautious and sober; *gabhīra-ātmā*—not superficial, and thus unchanging; *dhṛti-mān*—not weak or miserable even in distressing circumstances; *jita*—having conquered; *ṣaṭ-guṇaḥ*—the six material qualities, namely hunger, thirst, lamentation, illusion, old age and death; *amānī*—without desire for prestige; *māna-daḥ*—offering all respects to others; *kalyaḥ*—expert in reviving the Kṛṣṇa consciousness of others; *maitraḥ*—never cheating anyone, and thus a true friend; *kāruṇikaḥ*—acting always due to compassion, not personal ambition; *kaviḥ*—completely learned; *ājñāya*—knowing; *evam*—thus; *guṇān*—good qualities; *doṣān*—bad qualities; *mayā*—by Me; *ādiṣṭān*—taught; *api*—even; *svakān*—one's own; *dharmān*—religious principles; *santyajya*—giving up; *yaḥ*—one who; *sarvān*—all; *mām*—Me; *bhajeta*—worships; *saḥ*—he; *tu*—indeed; *sat-tamaḥ*—the best among saintly persons.

TRANSLATION

The Supreme Personality of Godhead said: O Uddhava, a saintly person is merciful and never injures others. Even if others are aggressive he is tolerant and forgiving toward all living entities. His strength and meaning in life come from the truth itself, he is free from all envy and jealousy, and his mind is equal in material happiness and distress. Thus, he dedicates his time to work for the welfare of all others. His intelligence is never bewildered by material desires, and he has controlled his senses. His behavior is always pleasing, never harsh and always exemplary, and he is free from possessiveness. He never endeavors in ordinary, worldly activities, and he strictly controls his eating. He therefore always remains peaceful and steady. A saintly person is thoughtful and accepts Me as his only shelter. Such a person is very cautious in the execution of his duties and is never subject to superficial transformations, because he is steady and noble, even in a distressing situation. He has conquered over the six material qualities—namely hunger, thirst, lamentation, illusion, old age and death. He is free from all desire for prestige and offers honor to others. He is expert in reviving the Kṛṣṇa consciousness of others and therefore never cheats anyone. Rather, he is a well-wishing friend to all, being most merciful. Such a saintly person must be considered the most learned of men. He perfectly understands that the ordinary religious duties prescribed by Me in various Vedic scriptures possess favorable qualities that purify the performer, and he knows that neglect of such duties constitutes discrepancy in one's life. Having taken complete shelter at My lotus feet, however, a

saintly person ultimately renounces such ordinary religious duties and worships Me alone. He is thus considered to be the best among all living entities.

PURPORT

Verses 29–31 describe twenty-eight qualities of a saintly person, and verse 32 explains the highest perfection of life. According to Śrīla Bhaktisiddhānta Sarasvatī Ṭhākura, the seventeenth quality (*mat-śaraṇa,* or taking complete shelter of Lord Kṛṣṇa) is the most important, and the other twenty-seven qualities automatically appear in one who has become a pure devotee of the Lord. As stated in *Śrīmad-Bhāgavatam* (5.18.12), *yasyāsti bhaktir bhagavaty akiñcanā sarvair guṇais tatra samāsate surāḥ.* The twenty-eight saintly qualities may be described as follows.

(1) *Kṛpālu.* A devotee cannot tolerate seeing the world merged in ignorance and suffering the whiplashes of *māyā.* Therefore he busily engages in distributing Kṛṣṇa consciousness and is called *kṛpālu,* or merciful.

(2) *Akṛta-droha.* Even if someone is offensive toward a devotee, a devotee does not become offensive in return. Indeed, he never acts against the interest of any living entity. One may argue that great Vaiṣṇava kings, such as Mahārāja Yudhiṣṭhira and Parīkṣit Mahārāja, executed many criminals. However, when justice is properly administered by the state, sinful, destructive persons actually benefit from their punishment because they become freed from the severe karmic reactions to their illicit activities. A Vaiṣṇava ruler gives punishment not out of envy or malice, but in faithful obedience to the laws of God. The Māyāvādī philosophers who want to kill God by imagining that He does not exist are certainly *kṛta-droha,* or most injurious to themselves and others. The impersonalist imagines that he himself is supreme and thus creates a most dangerous situation for himself and his followers. Similarly, the *karmīs,* who are dedicated to material sense gratification, are also killers of the self, because by their absorption in material consciousness they lose all chance of experiencing the Absolute Truth and the truth of their own self. Therefore, all living entities who come under the control of materialistic regulations and duties are unnecessarily

harassing themselves and others, and a pure Vaiṣṇava feels great compassion and concern for them. A devotee never uses his mind, body or words to perform any act harmful to the welfare of any living entity.

(3) *Titikṣu.* A devotee forgives and forgets any offense against himself. A Vaiṣṇava is personally detached from his material body, which is made of pus, stool, blood, and so on. Therefore the devotee is able to overlook the obnoxious behavior he sometimes meets with in the course of preaching work and always deals with people as a perfect gentleman. A Vaiṣṇava loudly chants the holy name of the Lord and tolerates and forgives those fallen conditioned souls who are unable to reciprocate properly with a pure devotee.

(4) *Satya-sāra.* A devotee always remembers that he is the eternal servant of the Supreme Personality of Godhead, who is omniscient, the reservoir of all pleasure and the ultimate enjoyer of all activities. By avoiding activities outside devotional service, a devotee remains fixed in the truth, does not uselessly waste time and thus becomes bold, powerful and steady.

(5) *Anavadyātmā.* A devotee knows that the material world is a temporary phantasmagoria and therefore does not envy anyone in any material situation. He never tries to agitate others or criticize them unnecessarily.

(6) *Sama.* A devotee remains steady and equal in material happiness or distress, fame or infamy. His actual wealth is his consciousness of Kṛṣṇa, and he understands that his real self-interest lies outside the scope of material nature. He does not become excited or depressed by external events, but remains fixed in consciousness of the omnipotency of Lord Kṛṣṇa.

(7) *Sarvopakāraka.* Neglecting one's selfish desires and working for the satisfaction of others is called *paropakāra*, whereas causing trouble to others for one's personal gratification is called *parāpakāra*. A devotee always works for the pleasure of Lord Kṛṣṇa, who is the resting place of all living entities, and thus a devotee's activities are ultimately pleasing to everyone. Devotional service to Lord Kṛṣṇa is the perfectional stage of welfare work, since Lord Kṛṣṇa is the supreme controller of everyone's happiness and distress. Foolish persons under the influence of false egotism, considering themselves to be the ultimate well-wishers of others, execute superficial materialistic activities rather than attending to the

eternal happiness of others. Because a devotee remains pure and engages in missionary activities, he is everyone's best friend.

(8) *Kāmair ahata-dhī.* Ordinary persons see all material things as objects for their personal gratification and thus try to acquire or control them. Ultimately a man wants to possess a woman and enjoy sex gratification with her. The Supreme Lord supplies the desired fuel that causes the fire of lust to burn painfully in one's heart, but the Lord does not give self-realization to such a misguided person. Lord Kṛṣṇa is transcendental and neutral, but if one is eager to exploit the Lord's creation, the Lord gives one facility through *māyā,* and one becomes cheated of real happiness by entangling himself in the false role of a great and lusty enjoyer of the world. On the other hand, one who has taken full shelter of Kṛṣṇa is enriched with perfect knowledge and bliss and is not cheated by the seductive appearances of the material world. A pure devotee does not follow the path of the foolish deer, which is seduced by the hunter's horn and killed. A devotee is never attracted by the sensuous entreaties of a beautiful woman, and he avoids hearing from bewildered *karmīs* about the so-called glories of material acquisition. Similarly, a pure devotee is not bewildered by aroma or taste. He does not become attached to sumptuous eating, nor does he spend the whole day making arrangements for bodily comfort. The only actual enjoyer of God's creation is the Lord Himself, and the living entities are secondary enjoyers who experience unlimited pleasure through the Lord's pleasure. This perfect process of experiencing pleasure is called *bhakti-yoga,* or pure devotional service, and a devotee never sacrifices his auspicious position of steady intelligence, even in the face of so-called material opportunity.

(9) *Dānta.* A devotee is naturally repelled by sinful activities and controls his senses by dedicating all his acts to Kṛṣṇa. This requires steady concentration and a cautious mentality.

(10) *Mṛdu.* A materialistic person will always see people as friends or enemies and thus will sometimes justify cruel or small-minded behavior in order to subdue his opponents. Since a devotee has taken shelter of Lord Kṛṣṇa, he does not consider anyone his enemy and is never disturbed by the tendency to desire or enjoy the suffering of others. Thus he is *mṛdu,* or gentle and sublime.

(11) *Śuci.* A devotee never touches that which is impure or improper, and simply by remembering such a pure devotee, one is freed from the

tendency to sin. Because of his perfect behavior, a devotee is called *śuci,* or pure.

(12) *Akiñcana.* A devotee is free from possessiveness and is not eager to enjoy or renounce anything, since he considers everything to be Lord Kṛṣṇa's property.

(13) *Anīha.* A devotee never acts on his own behalf, but rather for the service of Lord Kṛṣṇa. He is therefore aloof from ordinary, worldly affairs.

(14) *Mita-bhuk.* A devotee accepts material sense objects only as far as necessary, to keep himself healthy and fit in Lord Kṛṣṇa's service. He is therefore not entangled by his sense activities and never injures his self-realization. When necessary, a devotee can give up anything for Lord Kṛṣṇa's service, but he does not accept or reject anything for his personal prestige.

(15) *Śānta.* Those trying to exploit the Lord's creation are always disturbed. A devotee, however, is detached from such pointless activities and understands sense gratification to be diametrically opposed to his self-interest. Being always engaged according to the Lord's desire, he remains peaceful.

(16) *Sthira.* Remembering that Lord Kṛṣṇa is the basis of everything, a devotee does not become fearful or impatient.

(17) *Mat-śaraṇa.* A devotee does not take pleasure in anything except serving Lord Kṛṣṇa and is constantly attentive in the execution of his duties. A devotee knows that only Lord Kṛṣṇa can protect him and engage him in useful work.

(18) *Muni.* A devotee is thoughtful and through intelligent contemplation avoids becoming distracted from his spiritual advancement. By intelligence he is freed from doubts about Lord Kṛṣṇa and confronts all problems in life with steady Kṛṣṇa consciousness.

(19) *Apramatta.* One who forgets the Supreme Lord is more or less crazy, but a devotee remains sane by offering his activities to Lord Kṛṣṇa.

(20) *Gabhīrātmā.* As a devotee merges into the ocean of Kṛṣṇa consciousness, his own consciousness becomes deeper and deeper; ordinary, superficial persons hovering on the material platform cannot fathom the extent of a devotee's awareness.

(21) *Dhṛtimān.* By controlling the urges of the tongue and genitals the

devotee remains steady and patient and does not impulsively change his position.

(22) *Jita-ṣaḍ-guṇa.* By spiritual knowledge, a devotee is able to conquer the pushings of hunger, thirst, lamentation, illusion, old age and death.

(23) *Amānī.* A devotee is not puffed up, and even if he is famous, he does not take such fame very seriously.

(24) *Māna-da.* A devotee offers all respects to others, since everyone is part and parcel of Lord Kṛṣṇa.

(25) *Kalya.* A devotee is expert in making people understand the truth of Kṛṣṇa consciousness.

(26) *Maitra.* A devotee does not cheat anyone by encouraging them in the bodily concept of life; rather, by his missionary work a devotee is the true friend of everyone.

(27) *Kāruṇika.* A devotee tries to make people sane and thus is most merciful. He is *para-duḥkha-duḥkhī,* or one who is unhappy to see the unhappiness of others.

(28) *Kavi.* A devotee is expert in studying the transcendental qualities of Lord Kṛṣṇa and is able to show the harmony and compatibility of the Lord's apparently contradictory qualities. This is possible through expert knowledge of the absolute nature of the Lord. Lord Caitanya is softer than a rose and harder than a thunderbolt, but these opposing qualities can easily be understood in terms of the Lord's transcendental nature and purpose. One who is always able to understand the truth of Kṛṣṇa consciousness, without opposition or confusion, is called *kavi,* or most learned.

The position of those on the spiritual path can be understood in terms of their development of the qualities mentioned above. Ultimately, the most important quality is to take shelter of Lord Kṛṣṇa, since the Lord can award all good qualities to His sincere devotee. In the lowest stage of devotional service one acts with a desire to enjoy sense gratification but at the same time tries to offer the fruits to the Lord. This stage is called *karma-miśrā bhakti.* As one gradually purifies himself in devotional service, he becomes detached through knowledge and gains relief from anxiety. In this stage he becomes attached to transcendental knowledge, and therefore this stage is called *jñāna-miśrā bhakti,* or devotional service to

Lord Kṛṣṇa with a desire to enjoy the fruits of transcendental knowledge. But because pure love for Kṛṣṇa is actually the greatest happiness and the natural position of the living entity, a sincere devotee gradually overcomes his desire to enjoy sense gratification and knowledge and comes to the stage of pure devotional service, which is devoid of personal desire. *Na karmāṇi tyajed yogī karmabhis tyajyate hi saḥ:* "The *yogī* should not give up his work, but rather should cultivate detachment by which his material activities will automatically vanish." In other words, one should continue to perform one's prescribed duties, even imperfectly. If one is sincere about advancing in Kṛṣṇa consciousness, then by the strength of *bhakti-yoga* his activities will gradually be transformed into pure loving service.

There are innumerable examples of fruitive workers, mental speculators and materialistic devotees who became perfect by the strength of devotional service. By rendering loving service to Kṛṣṇa, one automatically experiences the greatest pleasure of life and is endowed with perfect knowledge. There is nothing lacking in the process of pure devotional service, and there is no need for any extraneous endeavor to acquire sense pleasure or philosophical satisfaction. One must be completely convinced that simply by serving Kṛṣṇa one will get all perfection in life. Even if one lacks some or all of the above-mentioned qualities, one should sincerely engage in Lord Kṛṣṇa's service, and gradually one's character will become perfect. One who is a sincere devotee of Lord Kṛṣṇa will develop all godly qualities by the mercy of the Lord, and one who is already serving the Lord with the above-mentioned qualities is to be understood as the greatest devotee. As indicated in verse 32, a pure devotee of the Lord is fully aware of the pious advantages of executing duties within the *varṇāśrama* system, and he is similarly aware of the harmful mistake of neglecting such duties. Still, having full faith in the Supreme Personality of Godhead, a devotee gives up all ordinary social and religious activities and engages fully in devotional service. He knows that Lord Kṛṣṇa is the ultimate source of everything and that all perfection comes from Lord Kṛṣṇa alone. Because of his extraordinary faith, the devotee is called *sattama*, or the best among all living beings.

As explained by Śrīla Rūpa Gosvāmī in *Upadeśāmṛta*, a devotee who has not yet developed the good qualities mentioned above but is nevertheless sincerely endeavoring for Kṛṣṇa consciousness should receive the mercy of superior Vaiṣṇavas. One should not necessarily accept intimate association with such an aspirant to pure devotional service, but one should be confident that by chanting the holy names of Kṛṣṇa such a person will eventually attain all perfection. One can imagine the beauty of a society filled with saintly persons, as described in these verses. The wonderful Kṛṣṇa conscious qualities mentioned above are the basis of a peaceful and prosperous society, and if everyone takes to the loving service of Lord Kṛṣṇa, then certainly the present atmosphere of fear, violence, lust, greed and insanity can be replaced by a celestial situation in which all leaders and citizens will be happy. The essential points here are *mat-śaraṇa* ("one should take full shelter of Lord Kṛṣṇa") and *māṁ bhajeta* ("one should worship the Lord through the authorized process"). In this way the entire world can become *sattama*, or most perfect.

TEXT 33

ज्ञात्वाज्ञात्वाथ ये वै मां यावान् यश्चास्मि यादृशः ।
भजन्त्यनन्यभावेन ते मे भक्ततमा मताः ॥३३॥

jñātvājñātvātha ye vai māṁ
yāvān yaś cāsmi yādṛśaḥ
bhajanty ananya-bhāvena
te me bhaktatamā matāḥ

jñātvā—knowing; *ajñātvā*—not knowing; *atha*—thus; *ye*—those who; *vai*—certainly; *mām*—Me; *yāvān*—as; *yaḥ*—who; *ca*—also; *asmi*—I am; *yādṛśaḥ*—how I am; *bhajanti*—worship; *ananya-bhāvena*—with exclusive devotion; *te*—they; *me*—by Me; *bhakta-tamāḥ*—the best devotees; *matāḥ*—are considered.

TRANSLATION

My devotees may or may not know exactly what I am, who I am and how I exist, but if they worship Me with unalloyed love, then I consider them to be the best of devotees.

PURPORT

According to Śrīla Viśvanātha Cakravartī Ṭhākura, although *yāvān* indicates that Lord Kṛṣṇa cannot be limited by time or space, He becomes limited by the love of His pure devotees. For example, Lord Kṛṣṇa never steps one foot out of Vṛndāvana, because of the intense love of its inhabitants for Him. In this way, the Lord comes under the control of His devotees' love. The word *yaḥ* indicates that Kṛṣṇa is the Absolute Truth who appears as the son of Vasudeva, or as Śyāmasundara. *Yādṛśa* indicates that the Lord is *ātmārāma*, or completely self-satisfied, and also *āpta-kāma*, or "one who automatically fulfills all of His desires." Still, being affected by the love of His devotees, the Lord sometimes appears to be *anātmārāma*, or dependent on the love of His devotees, and *anāpta-kāma*, unable to achieve His desire without the cooperation of His devotees. Actually, the Supreme Lord, Kṛṣṇa, is always independent, but He reciprocates the intense love of His devotees and thus appears to be dependent on them, just as He apparently became dependent on Nanda Mahārāja and Yaśodā during His childhood pastimes in Vṛndāvana. The word *ajñātvā* ("inexperienced, lacking knowledge") indicates that sometimes a devotee may not have a proper philosophical understanding of the Personality of Godhead or due to love may temporarily forget the Lord's position. In *Bhagavad-gītā* (11.41) Arjuna says,

sakheti matvā prasabhaṁ yad uktaṁ
he kṛṣṇa he yādava he sakheti
ajānatā mahimānaṁ tavedaṁ
mayā pramādāt praṇayena vāpi

"I have in the past addressed You as 'O Kṛṣṇa,' 'O Yādava,' 'O my friend,' without knowing Your glories. Please forgive whatever I may have done in madness or in love." Arjuna's words *ajānatā mahimānam* have the same meaning as Kṛṣṇa's words *ajñātvā mām* in this verse of the *Bhāgavatam*. Both indicate incomplete understanding of Kṛṣṇa's glories. In *Bhagavad-gītā* Arjuna says, *praṇayena:* his forgetfulness of Kṛṣṇa's supreme position was caused by his love for Him. In this verse, Kṛṣṇa excuses such lapses on the part of His devotees with the words *ajñātvā mām*, which indicate that even though devotees may not fully appreciate His exalted position, Kṛṣṇa accepts their loving service. Thus this verse clearly reveals the supreme position of *bhakti.* Lord Kṛṣṇa also states in *Bhagavad-gītā* (11.54):

bhaktyā tv ananyayā śakya
aham evaṁ-vidho 'rjuna
jñātuṁ draṣṭuṁ ca tattvena
praveṣṭuṁ ca parantapa

"My dear Arjuna, only by undivided devotional service can I be understood as I am, standing before you, and can thus be seen directly. Only in this way can you enter into the mysteries of My understanding."

Although one may develop innumerable saintly qualities, without love of Kṛṣṇa one will not achieve complete success. One must understand the Personality of Godhead as He is and love Him. Even if one is not capable of analytically understanding the position of God, if one simply loves Kṛṣṇa, then one is certainly perfect. Many of the residents of Vṛndāvana had no idea that Kṛṣṇa is the Supreme Personality of Godhead, nor did they know of Kṛṣṇa's potencies or incarnations. They simply loved Kṛṣṇa with their hearts and souls, and therefore they are considered most perfect.

TEXTS 34–41

मल्लिङ्गमद्भक्तजनदर्शनस्पर्शनार्चनम् ।
परिचर्या स्तुतिः प्रह्वगुणकर्मानुकीर्तनम् ॥३४॥
मत्कथाश्रवणे श्रद्धा मदनुध्यानमुद्धव ।
सर्वलाभोपहरणं दास्येनात्मनिवेदनम् ॥३५॥
मज्जन्मकर्मकथनं मम पर्वानुमोदनम् ।
गीतताण्डववादित्रगोष्ठीभिर्मद्गृहोत्सवः ॥३६॥
यात्रा बलिविधानं च सर्ववार्षिकपर्वसु ।
वैदिकी तान्त्रिकी दीक्षा मदीयव्रतधारणम् ॥३७॥
ममार्चास्थापने श्रद्धा स्वतः संहत्य चोद्यमः ।
उद्यानोपवनाक्रीडपुरमन्दिरकर्मणि ॥३८॥

संमार्जनोपलेपाभ्यां सेकमण्डलवर्तनैः ।
गृहशुश्रूषणं मह्यं दासवद् यदमायया ॥३९॥
अमानित्वमदम्भित्वं कृतस्यापरिकीर्तनम् ।
अपि दीपावलोकं मे नोपयुञ्ज्यान्निवेदितम् ॥४०॥
यद् यदिष्टतमं लोके यच्चातिप्रियमात्मनः ।
तत्तन्निवेदयेन्मह्यं तदानन्त्याय कल्पते ॥४१॥

mal-liṅga-mad-bhakta-jana-
darśana-sparśanārcanam
paricaryā stutiḥ prahva-
guṇa-karmānukīrtanam

mat-kathā-śravaṇe śraddhā
mad-anudhyānam uddhava
sarva-lābhopaharaṇaṁ
dāsyenātma-nivedanam

maj-janma-karma-kathanaṁ
mama parvānumodanam
gīta-tāṇḍava-vāditra-
goṣṭhībhir mad-gṛhotsavaḥ

yātrā bali-vidhānaṁ ca
sarva-vārṣika-parvasu
vaidikī tāntrikī dīkṣā
madīya-vrata-dhāraṇam

mamārcā-sthāpane śraddhā
svataḥ saṁhatya codyamaḥ
udyānopavanākrīḍa-
pura-mandira-karmaṇi

sammārjanopalepābhyāṁ
seka-maṇḍala-vartanaiḥ
gṛha-śuśrūṣaṇaṁ mahyaṁ
dāsa-vad yad amāyayā

amānitvam adambhitvaṁ
kṛtasyāparikīrtanam
api dīpāvalokaṁ me
nopayuñjyān niveditam

yad yad iṣṭatamaṁ loke
yac cāti-priyam ātmanaḥ
tat tan nivedayen mahyaṁ
tad ānantyāya kalpate

mat-liṅga—My appearance in this world as the Deity, etc.; *mat-bhakta-jana*—My devotees; *darśana*—seeing; *sparśana*—touching; *arcanam*—and worshiping; *paricaryā*—rendering personal service; *stutiḥ*—offering prayers of glorification; *prahva*—obeisances; *guṇa*—My qualities; *karma*—and activities; *anukīrtanam*—constantly glorifying; *mat-kathā*—topics about Me; *śravaṇe*—in hearing; *śraddhā*—faith due to love; *mat-anudhyānam*—always meditating on Me; *uddhava*—O Uddhava; *sarva-lābha*—all that one acquires; *upaharaṇam*—offering; *dāsyena*—by accepting oneself as My servant; *ātma-nivedanam*—self-surrender; *mat-janma-karma-kathanam*—glorifying My birth and activities; *mama*—My; *parva*—in festivals such as Janmāṣṭamī; *anumodanam*—taking great pleasure; *gīta*—by songs; *tāṇḍava*—dancing; *vāditra*—musical instruments; *goṣṭhībhiḥ*—and discussions among devotees; *mat-gṛha*—in My temple; *utsavaḥ*—festivals; *yātrā*—celebrations; *bali-vidhānam*—making offerings; *ca*—also; *sarva*—in all; *vārṣika*—annual; *parvasu*—in the celebrations; *vaidikī*—mentioned in the *Vedas; tāntrikī*—mentioned in literatures such as the *Pañcarātra; dīkṣā*—initiation; *madīya*—in relation to Me; *vrata*—vows; *dhāraṇam*—observing; *mama*—My; *arcā*—of the Deity form; *sthāpane*—in the installation; *śraddhā*—being faithfully attached; *svataḥ*—by oneself; *saṁhatya*—with others; *ca*—also; *udyamaḥ*—endeavor; *udyāna*—of flower gardens; *upavana*—orchards; *ākrīḍa*—places of pastimes; *pura*—devotional cities; *mandira*—and temples; *karmaṇi*—in the construction; *sammārjana*—by thoroughly sweeping and dusting; *upalepābhyām*—then by smearing water and cow dung; *seka*—by sprinkling scented water; *maṇḍala-vartanaiḥ*—by construction of *maṇḍalas; gṛha*—of the temple, which is My home; *śuśrūṣaṇam*—service; *mahyam*—for My sake; *dāsa-vat*—being like a servant; *yat*—which;

amāyayā—without duplicity; *amānitvam*—being without false prestige; *adambhitvam*—being prideless; *kṛtasya*—one's devotional activities; *aparikīrtanam*—not advertising; *api*—moreover; *dīpa*—of lamps; *avalokam*—the light; *me*—which belong to Me; *na*—not; *upayuñjyāt*—one should engage; *niveditam*—things already offered to others; *yat yat*—anything; *iṣṭa-tamam*—most desired; *loke*—in the material world; *yat ca*—and anything; *ati-priyam*—most dear; *ātmanaḥ*—of oneself; *tat tat*—that very thing; *nivedayet*—one should offer; *mahyam*—unto Me; *tat*—that offering; *ānantyāya*—for immortality; *kalpate*—qualifies one.

TRANSLATION

My dear Uddhava, one can give up false pride and prestige by engaging in the following devotional activities. One may purify oneself by seeing, touching, worshiping, serving, and offering prayers of glorification and obeisances to My form as the Deity and to My pure devotees. One should also glorify My transcendental qualities and activities, hear with love and faith the narrations of My glories and constantly meditate on Me. One should offer to Me whatever one acquires, and accepting oneself as My eternal servant, one should give oneself completely to Me. One should always discuss My birth and activities and enjoy life by participating in festivals, such as Janmāṣṭamī, which glorify My pastimes. In My temple, one should also participate in festivals and ceremonies by singing, dancing, playing musical instruments and discussing Me with other Vaiṣṇavas. One should observe all the regularly celebrated annual festivals by attending ceremonies, pilgrimages and making offerings. One should also observe religious vows such as Ekādaśī and take initiation by the procedures mentioned in the Vedas, Pañcarātra and other similar literatures. One should faithfully and lovingly support the installation of My Deity, and individually or in cooperation with others one should work for the construction of Kṛṣṇa conscious temples and cities as well as flower gardens, fruit gardens and special areas to celebrate My pastimes. One should consider oneself to be My humble servant, without duplicity, and thus should help to clean the temple, which is My home. First one should sweep and dust thoroughly, and then one

should further cleanse with water and cow dung. Having dried the temple, one should sprinkle scented water and decorate the temple with maṇḍalas. One should thus act just like My servant. A devotee should never advertise his devotional activities; therefore his service will not be the cause of false pride. One should never use lamps that are offered to Me for other purposes simply because there is need of illumination, and similarly, one should never offer to Me anything that has been offered to or used by others. Whatever is most desired by one within this material world, and whatever is most dear to oneself—one should offer that very thing to Me. Such an offering qualifies one for eternal life.

PURPORT

In these eight verses Lord Kṛṣṇa ends His discussion of saintly qualities in general and describes the specific characteristics of the devotees of the Lord. Lord Kṛṣṇa has clearly described both here and in *Bhagavad-gītā* that the ultimate goal of life is to surrender fully to Him and become His pure devotee. Herein the Lord elaborately describes the process of devotional service. One should offer everything that one acquires to the Lord, thinking, "Lord Kṛṣṇa has sent these things so that I may serve Him nicely." One ultimately should understand that the minute spirit soul is part and parcel of Lord Kṛṣṇa, and thus one should surrender one's very self to the Lord. Just as an ordinary servant is meek and submissive to his master, similarly, a devotee should always be submissive to his spiritual master, who is a representative of Lord Kṛṣṇa. He should realize how his body and mind are purified simply by his seeing the spiritual master or by accepting on his head the water offered to the spiritual master. It is emphasized in these verses that one should attend Vaiṣṇava festivals. As far as possible, large festivals should be held all over the world so that people can gradually learn how to perfect human life. The words *mamārcā-sthāpane śraddhā* are significant. Here Lord Kṛṣṇa states that one should have faith in His Deity worship, since the Lord is personally present as the Deity. The words *udyānopavanākrīḍa-pura-mandira-karmaṇi* indicate that there should be a serious endeavor to construct beautiful temples and Vaiṣṇava cities with ample parks, orchards and flower gardens. Outstanding examples of such endeavors can be presently seen in India at the Māyāpur Candrodaya Mandira gardens developed by Śrīla Bhavānanda Goswami Viṣṇupāda and in the New Vrindaban community in West Virginia, organized by Śrīla Kīrtanānanda Swami Bhaktipāda.

The words *dīpāvalokaṁ me nopayuñjyān niveditam* indicate that one may never use the Deity's paraphernalia for sense gratification. If there is a shortage of electricity or lights, one may not use the Deity's lamps, nor should one ever offer to Lord Kṛṣṇa paraphernalia previously offered to or used by others. In these verses, the importance of Deity worship and Vaiṣṇava festivals is emphasized in many ways. Lord Kṛṣṇa promises that whoever sincerely performs these activities will certainly go back home, back to Godhead (*tad ānantyāya kalpate*). One should offer his most dear possession to Lord Kṛṣṇa, not that which is superfluous or unwanted. If one is most attached to his family, one should see that his family is engaged in Lord Kṛṣṇa's service. If one is most attached to money, that should be given for propagating Kṛṣṇa consciousness. And if one considers one's intelligence to be most valuable, he should preach Kṛṣṇa consciousness with great logic and reason. If we offer our most valuable possessions to Lord Kṛṣṇa, we will automatically become dear to the Lord and go back to Godhead.

TEXT 42

सूर्योऽग्निर्ब्राह्मणा गावो वैष्णवः खं मरुज्जलम् ।
भूरात्मा सर्वभूतानि भद्र पूजापदानि मे ॥४२॥

sūryo 'gnir brāhmaṇā gāvo
vaiṣṇavaḥ khaṁ maruj jalam
bhūr ātmā sarva-bhūtāni
bhadra pūjā-padāni me

sūryaḥ—the sun; *agniḥ*—fire; *brāhmaṇāḥ*—the *brāhmaṇas; gāvaḥ*—the cows; *vaiṣṇavaḥ*—the devotee of the Lord; *kham*—the sky; *marut*—the wind; *jalam*—water; *bhūḥ*—the earth; *ātmā*—the individual soul; *sarva-bhūtāni*—all living entities; *bhadra*—O saintly Uddhava; *pūjā*—of worship; *padāni*—the places; *me*—of Me.

TRANSLATION

O saintly Uddhava, please know that you may worship Me in the sun, fire, brāhmaṇas, cows, Vaiṣṇavas, sky, wind, water, earth, individual soul and all living entities.

PURPORT

Unless one understands that Lord Kṛṣṇa is all-pervading and that everything is resting within the Lord, one's Kṛṣṇa consciousness is third class and materialistic. It is clearly stated in all Vedic literatures that the Supreme Absolute Truth is the source of everything. Everything is within Him, and He is within everything. To avoid a materialistic conception of Lord Kṛṣṇa, one should not think that the Lord exists only in a particular time and place. Rather, one should understand that He exists at all times and in all places and that one may search for and find Lord Kṛṣṇa within all things. The word *pūjā-padāni* indicates that Lord Kṛṣṇa is all-pervading, but this does not mean that all things are Lord Kṛṣṇa. Lord Kṛṣṇa speaks this verse to clarify His supremacy as the all-pervading Personality of Godhead and to show the path of complete self-realization.

TEXTS 43–45

सूर्ये तु विद्यया त्रय्या हविषाग्नौ यजेत माम् ।
आतिथ्येन तु विप्राग्र्ये गोष्वङ्ग यवसादिना ॥४३॥
वैष्णवे बन्धुसत्कृत्या हृदि खे ध्याननिष्ठया ।
वायौ मुख्यधिया तोये द्रव्यैस्तोयपुरःसरैः ॥४४॥
स्थण्डिले मन्त्रहृदयैर्भोगैरात्मानमात्मनि ।
क्षेत्रज्ञं सर्वभूतेषु समत्वेन यजेत माम् ॥४५॥

sūrye tu vidyayā trayyā
haviṣāgnau yajeta mām
ātithyena tu viprāgrye
goṣv aṅga yavasādinā

vaiṣṇave bandhu-sat-kṛtyā
hṛdi khe dhyāna-niṣṭhayā
vāyau mukhya-dhiyā toye
dravyais toya-puraḥsaraiḥ

sthaṇḍile mantra-hṛdayair
bhogair ātmānam ātmani
kṣetra-jñaṁ sarva-bhūteṣu
samatvena yajeta mām

sūrye—in the sun; *tu*—indeed; *vidyayā trayyā*—by offering selected Vedic hymns of praise, worship and obeisances; *haviṣā*—with offerings of clarified butter; *agnau*—in the fire; *yajeta*—one should worship; *mām*—Me; *ātithyena*—by respectfully receiving them as guests even when uninvited; *tu*—indeed; *vipra*—of *brāhmaṇas; agrye*—in the best; *goṣu*—in the cows; *aṅga*—O Uddhava; *yavasa-ādinā*—by offering grass and other paraphernalia for their maintenance; *vaiṣṇave*—in the Vaiṣṇava; *bandhu*—with loving friendship; *sat-kṛtyā*—by honoring; *hṛdi*—within the heart; *khe*—within the inner space; *dhyāna*—in meditation; *niṣṭhayā*—by being fixed; *vāyau*—in the air; *mukhya*—the most important; *dhiyā*—considering by intelligence; *toye*—in water; *dravyaiḥ*—by material elements; *toya-puraḥ-saraiḥ*—by water, etc.; *sthaṇḍile*—in the earth; *mantra-hṛdayaiḥ*—by application of confidential *mantras; bhogaiḥ*—by offering of materially enjoyable objects; *ātmānam*—the *jīva* soul; *ātmani*—within the body; *kṣetra-jñam*—the Supersoul; *sarva-bhūteṣu*—within all living beings; *samatvena*—seeing Him equally everywhere; *yajeta*—one should worship; *mām*—Me.

TRANSLATION

My dear Uddhava, one should worship Me within the sun by chanting selected Vedic mantras and by performing worship and offering obeisances. One may worship Me within fire by offering oblations of ghee, and one may worship Me among the brāhmaṇas by respectfully receiving them as guests, even when uninvited. I can be worshiped within the cows by offerings of grass and other suitable grains and paraphernalia for the pleasure and health of the cows, and one may worship Me within the Vaiṣṇavas by offer-

ing loving friendship to them and honoring them in all respects. Through steady meditation I am worshiped within the inner space of the heart, and within the air I can be worshiped by knowledge that prāṇa, the life air, is the chief among elements. I am worshiped within water by offerings of water itself along with other elements such as flowers and tulasī leaves, and one may worship Me within the earth by proper application of confidential seed mantras. One may worship Me within the individual living entity by offering food and other enjoyable substances, and one may worship Me within all living entities by seeing the Supersoul within all of them, thus maintaining equal vision.

PURPORT

Significantly, the Lord emphasizes in these three verses that one should worship the Supreme Personality of Godhead who is expanded within all living beings. It is not recommended that one accept any material or spiritual object other than the Lord as supreme. By maintaining steady consciousness of the Lord in His all-pervading feature, one can remain in a worshipful mood twenty-four hours a day. Thus, one will naturally try to engage all material and spiritual elements in the loving service of Lord Kṛṣṇa. If because of ignorance one forgets the Supreme Personality of Godhead, one may become inclined to worship powerful material phenomena independent of the Supreme Lord, or one may foolishly consider oneself to be supreme. One should remain sane and accept the worshipable presence of the Supreme Lord within everything.

TEXT 46

धिष्ण्येष्वित्येषु मद्रूपं शङ्खचक्रगदाम्बुजैः ।
युक्तं चतुर्भुजं शान्तं ध्यायन्नर्चेत् समाहितः ॥४६॥

dhiṣṇyeṣv ity eṣu mad-rūpaṁ
śaṅkha-cakra-gadāmbujaiḥ
yuktaṁ catur-bhujaṁ śāntaṁ
dhyāyann arcet samāhitaḥ

dhiṣṇyeṣu—in the previously mentioned places of worship; *iti*—thus (by the previously mentioned processes); *eṣu*—in them; *mat-rūpam*—

My transcendental form; *śaṅkha*—with the conchshell; *cakra*—Sudarśana disc; *gadā*—club; *ambujaiḥ*—and lotus flower; *yuktam*—equipped; *catuḥ-bhujam*—with four arms; *śāntam*—peaceful; *dhyāyan*—meditating; *arcet*—one should worship; *samāhitaḥ*—with complete attention.

TRANSLATION

Thus, in the previously mentioned places of worship and according to the processes I have described, one should meditate on My peaceful, transcendental form with four arms holding a conchshell, Sudarśana disc, club and lotus flower. In this way, one should worship Me with fixed attention.

PURPORT

The Lord has previously explained that He appears in different transcendental forms to His pure devotees so that they may unlimitedly increase their love of Godhead. Here is given a general description of the four-armed Nārāyaṇa form, which pervades the material world as Supersoul, or Paramātmā. The pure devotees, however, do not meditate upon the Lord within the heart but rather render active service to a specific form of the Lord, such as Rāma or Kṛṣṇa, and thus perfect their realization of Bhagavān, or the Supreme Lord, who engages in transcendental pastimes with His devotees in the spiritual world. Yet even within the material world one can spiritualize one's existence by seeing the Supreme Lord within everything and worshiping Him by constant meditation. As mentioned in the previous verses, one should also go to the temple and specifically worship the Deity and participate in spiritual festivals. One should not be puffed up and claim that because one is meditating on the Lord within nature there is no need to go to the temple. Temple worship has been repeatedly emphasized by the Lord Himself. The word *samāhita* in this verse indicates *samādhi.* If one very carefully worships the Deity or hears and chants about the pastimes of Lord Kṛṣṇa, one is certainly in *samādhi.* By worshiping and glorifying the Lord twenty-four hours a day one becomes a liberated soul and gradually rises completely beyond the influence of the material creation. The living entity is called *ātmā*, or eternal soul, because of his relationship with the Paramātmā, the Supreme Personality of Godhead. By worshiping the Lord, our eternal nature revives, and as we increase our enthusiasm and steadiness in devotional service, material existence fades away.

TEXT 47

इष्टापूर्तेन मामेवं यो यजेत समाहितः ।
लभते मयि सद्भक्तिं मत्स्मृतिः साधुसेवया ॥४७॥

iṣṭā-pūrtena māṁ evaṁ
yo yajeta samāhitaḥ
labhate mayi sad-bhaktiṁ
mat-smṛtiḥ sādhu-sevayā

iṣṭā—by sacrificial performances for one's own benefit; *pūrtena*—and pious works for the benefit of others, such as digging wells; *mām*—Me; *evam*—thus; *yaḥ*—one who; *yajeta*—worships; *samāhitaḥ*—with mind fixed in Me; *labhate*—such a person obtains; *mayi*—in Me; *sat-bhaktim*—unflinching devotional service; *mat-smṛtiḥ*—realized knowledge of Me; *sādhu*—with all superior qualities; *sevayā*—by service.

TRANSLATION

One who has executed sacrificial performances and pious works for My satisfaction, and who thus worships Me with fixed attention, obtains unflinching devotional service unto Me. By the excellent quality of his service such a worshiper obtains realized knowledge of Me.

PURPORT

The word *iṣṭā-pūrtena,* which means "sacrificial performances and pious works," does not indicate deviation from the pure devotional service of the Lord. Lord Kṛṣṇa, or Viṣṇu, is called Yajña, or the Lord of sacrifice, and in *Bhagavad-gītā* (5.29) Lord Kṛṣṇa says, *bhoktāraṁ yajña-tapasām:* "I am the actual enjoyer of all sacrifice." The highest sacrifice is to chant the holy names of the Lord, and by taking shelter of the Lord's names, one will acquire unflinching devotion and realized knowledge of the Absolute Truth. A realized devotee is very attentive in his devotional service, taking it as his life and soul. He keeps himself fit for devotional service by constantly worshiping and glorifying the lotus feet of the spiritual master and the Supreme Personality of Godhead. Such *hari-nāma-kīrtana* and *guru-pūjā* are the only practical methods by which one can achieve pure devotional service. When *hari-kīrtana* is expanded, it is called *kṛṣṇa-saṅkīrtana.* One should not dry up by performing unauthorized austerities or sacrifices; rather, one should engage with all enthusiasm in the great sacrifice of *śrī-kṛṣṇa-saṅkīrtana*, which enables one to easily achieve the highest perfection of human life.

TEXT 48

प्रायेण भक्तियोगेन सत्सङ्गेन विनोद्धव ।
नोपायो विद्यते सम्यक् प्रायणं हि सतामहम् ॥४८॥

prāyeṇa bhakti-yogena
sat-saṅgena vinoddhava
nopāyo vidyate samyak
prāyaṇaṁ hi satām aham

prāyeṇa—for all practical purposes; *bhakti-yogena*—devotional service unto Me; *sat-saṅgena*—which is made possible by association with My devotees; *vinā*—without; *uddhava*—O Uddhava; *na*—not; *upāyaḥ*—any means; *vidyate*—there is; *samyak*—that actually works; *prāyaṇam*—the true path of life or actual shelter; *hi*—because; *satām*—of liberated souls; *aham*—I.

TRANSLATION

My dear Uddhava, I am personally the ultimate shelter and way of life for saintly liberated persons, and thus if one does not engage in My loving devotional service, which is made possible by associating with My devotees, then for all practical purposes, one possesses no effective means for escaping from material existence.

PURPORT

Lord Kṛṣṇa has described to Uddhava the characteristics of *jñāna-yoga* and *bhakti-yoga*, both of which are considered to be spiritual processes. Now, however, Lord Kṛṣṇa clearly indicates that *bhakti-yoga* is the only real means to totally free onself from material existence, and that *bhakti-yoga* is not possible without *sat-saṅga*, or association with other Vaiṣṇavas. On the path of *bhakti-miśra jñāna*, or speculation on the Absolute Truth mixed with devotion, one is still affected by the three modes of material nature. The pure soul, liberated from all material qualities, has no tendency or desire to engage in philosophical speculation, severe austerities or impersonal meditation. The pure soul simply loves Kṛṣṇa and wants to serve Him constantly. *Jīvera 'svarūpa' haya—kṛṣṇera 'nitya-dāsa.'* Pure devotional service to the Lord is called *kevala-bhakti*, whereas devotional service mixed with speculative propensities is called *guṇa-bhūta-bhakti*, or devotional service polluted by the material modes of nature. One who is actually intelligent does not make a show of philosophical wizardry but rather discerns the superiority of pure love of Godhead and takes to the path of *kevala-bhakti*. One who emphasizes so-called intellectual achievements is actually less intelligent, because such a person is more attracted to intelligence than to the pure soul, which is superior. It should be understood, however, that pure devotional service is not nonphilosophical or anti-intellectual. The Absolute Truth is far more extensive than partial truth. Therefore, one who is in full knowledge of Lord Kṛṣṇa has the greatest facility to engage in philosophical analysis, since a pure devotee is working with the entire range of conceptual categories. Those who do not know Lord Kṛṣṇa are attracted to the impersonal Brahman or the localized Paramātmā, but they are not aware of the ultimate category of understanding called Bhagavān, or the Supreme Personality of Godhead. Lacking knowledge of Bhagavān, such imperfect philosophers certainly do not understand the expansion, interaction and withdrawal of the Lord's innumerable potencies and thus cannot fully analyze them. By faithfully accepting everything Lord Kṛṣṇa speaks as the absolute truth, one comes to the mature platform of philosophy and achieves perfect knowledge.

In addition to philosophical or intellectual understanding, pure devotional service also awards all other benefits in life, both material and spiritual; therefore one who for any purpose whatsoever accepts a process other than devotional service has unfortunately misunderstood the nature of pure devotional service to Lord Kṛṣṇa. It is emphasized here that one must cultivate devotional service in the association of other devotees. On the other hand, the *jñāna-yoga* process is cultivated alone, because it is difficult for even two mental speculators to be in the same place without their association degenerating into constant quarrel. Other processes of self-realization are compared to the nipples on a goat's neck. They look just like breast nipples, but they will not give any milk whatsoever. In this regard Śrīla Viśvanātha Cakravartī Ṭhākura has quoted the following verses, spoken by Śrī Uddhava, Śukadeva Gosvāmī and Nārada Muni respectively.

tāpa-trayeṇābhihitasya ghore
santapyamānasya bhavādhvanīha
paśyāmi nānyac charaṇaṁ tavāṅghri-
dvandvātapatrād amṛtābhivarṣāt

"My dear Lord, for one who is being cruelly burned in the blazing fire of material miseries, having fallen into the network of material existence, I do not see any other possible shelter besides Your two lotus feet, which are a shower of nectar extinguishing the fire of suffering." (*Bhāg*. 11.19.9)

saṁsāra-sindhum ati-dustaram uttitīrṣor
nānyaḥ plavo bhagavataḥ puruṣottamasya
līlā-kathā-rasa-niṣevaṇam antareṇa
puṁso bhaved vividha-duḥkha-davārditasya

"Material existence is like an ocean that is extremely difficult to cross. The conditioned souls have fallen into this ocean, which is not cool but rather burns them with the fire of misery. For one who has fallen into this sea and desires to get out, there is no other rescue boat except the constant relishing within oneself of the pastime narrations of the Supreme Personality of Godhead." (*Bhāg*. 12.4.40)

kiṁ vā yogena sāṅkhyena
nyāsa-svādhyāyayor api
kiṁ vā śreyobhir anyaiś ca
na yatrātma-prado hariḥ

"What is the use of the *yoga* system, philosophical speculation, mere renunciation of the world, or Vedic studies? In fact, what is the use of any so-called auspicious process without Lord Kṛṣṇa, who is the source of our very existence?" (*Bhāg.* 4.31.12)

If, as stated in this verse, it is generally (*prāyeṇa*) impossible to escape material bondage without devotional service in the association of devotees, one can simply imagine the probabilities of liberation in Kali-yuga without the Kṛṣṇa consciousness movement. The chances are certainly zero. One may concoct a type of liberation on the mental platform, or one may live in a so-called spiritual society of mutual flattery, but if one actually wants to go back home, back to Godhead, and see with spiritual eyes the beautiful kingdom of God called Kṛṣṇaloka, one must take to Lord Caitanya's movement and worship Lord Kṛṣṇa in the association of the *bhakta-gaṇa*, the devotees of the Lord.

TEXT 49

अथैतत् परमं गुह्यं शृण्वतो यदुनन्दन ।
सुगोप्यमपि वक्ष्यामि त्वं मे भृत्यः सुहृत् सखा ॥४९॥

athaitat paramaṁ guhyaṁ
śṛṇvato yadu-nandana
su-gopyam api vakṣyāmi
tvaṁ me bhṛtyaḥ suhṛt sakhā

atha—thus; *etat*—this; *paramam*—supreme; *guhyam*—secret; *śṛṇvataḥ*—to you who are listening; *yadu-nandana*—O beloved of the Yadu dynasty; *su-gopyam*—most confidential; *api*—even; *vakṣyāmi*—I will speak; *tvam*—you; *me*—of Me; *bhṛtyaḥ*—are the servant; *su-hṛt*—well-wisher; *sakhā*—and friend.

TRANSLATION

My dear Uddhava, O beloved of the Yadu dynasty, because you are My servant, well-wisher and friend, I shall now speak to you the most confidential knowledge. Please hear as I explain these great mysteries to you.

PURPORT

It is stated in the First Chapter of *Śrīmad-Bhāgavatam* (1.1.8), *brūyuḥ snigdhasya śiṣyasya guravo guhyam apy uta:* a bona fide spiritual master naturally reveals all transcendental secrets to a sincere disciple. Śrī Uddhava had completely surrendered to Lord Kṛṣṇa, and then only could the Lord explain such mysteries to him, because without complete faith the transmission of spiritual knowledge is impossible. Other processes of self realization, such as philosophical speculation, are imperfect and unsteady because the performer has personal desires, and there is no definite procedure by which to obtain the full mercy of the Supreme Lord. On the other hand, association with the pure devotees of the Lord is a self-sufficient process that is guaranteed to award the desired result. One must only learn how to associate with the pure devotees and one's life will be perfect. That is the sum and substance of this chapter.

Thus end the purports of the humble servants of His Divine Grace A. C. Bhaktivedanta Swami Prabhupāda to the Eleventh Canto, Eleventh Chapter, of the Śrīmad-Bhāgavatam, *entitled "The Symptoms of Conditioned and Liberated Living Entities."*

CHAPTER TWELVE

Beyond Renunciation and Knowledge

In this chapter the glories of holy association and the superexcellence of the pure love of the residents of Vṛndāvana are described.

The association of saintly devotees destroys the soul's attachment to material life and is capable of bringing even the Supreme Lord, Kṛṣṇa, under one's control. Neither *yoga*, Sāṅkhya philosophy, ordinary religious duties, study of scriptures, austerities, renunciation, works of *iṣṭā* and *pūrtam*, charity, vows of fasting, worship of the Deity, secret *mantras*, visiting of holy places, nor adherence to any major or minor regulative principles can effect the same result. In every age there are demons, monsters, birds and animals who are in the modes of passion and ignorance, and there are also human beings in the categories of businessmen, women, workers, outcastes, and so on, who cannot study the Vedic scriptures. Nevertheless, by the purifying effect of the association of devotees they may all achieve the supreme abode of the Personality of Godhead, whereas without such saintly association, even those very seriously endeavoring in *yoga*, Sāṅkhya study, charity, vows and practice of the renounced order of life may remain incapable of attaining the Supreme Personality of Godhead.

The young damsels of Vraja, ignorant of the true identity of Lord Kṛṣṇacandra, considered Him to be their paramour who would give them pleasure. Yet by the power of their constant association with Śrī Kṛṣṇa, they attained to the supreme Absolute Truth, which even great demigods like Brahmā cannot achieve. The young women of Vṛndāvana displayed such deep attachment to Lord Kṛṣṇa that their minds, which were overflowing with the ecstasy of being with Him, perceived an entire night spent in His company as just a fraction of a second. However, when Akrūra took Śrī Kṛṣṇa along with Baladeva to Mathurā, the *gopīs* then thought each night without Him to be equal in duration to a millennium of the demigods. Being tormented by separation from Lord Kṛṣṇa, they could not imagine anything that could give them satisfaction other than His return. This is the incomparable excellence of the *gopīs'* pure love of God.

The Supreme Lord, Śrī Kṛṣṇa, after imparting these instructions to Uddhava, advised that for the sake of attaining the Absolute Truth, Uddhava should give up all consideration of religion and irreligion as promulgated in the *śrutis* and *smṛtis* and instead take shelter of the example of the women of Vṛndāvana.

TEXTS 1–2

श्रीभगवानुवाच
न रोधयति मां योगो न सांख्यं धर्म एव च ।
न स्वाध्यायस्तपस्त्यागो नेष्टापूर्तं न दक्षिणा ॥ १ ॥
व्रतानि यज्ञश्छन्दांसि तीर्थानि नियमा यमाः ।
यथावरुन्धे सत्सङ्गः सर्वसङ्गापहो हि माम् ॥ २ ॥

śrī-bhagavān uvāca
na rodhayati māṁ yogo
na sāṅkhyaṁ dharma eva ca
na svādhyāyas tapas tyāgo
neṣṭā-pūrtaṁ na dakṣiṇā

vratāni yajñaś chandāṁsi
tīrthāni niyamā yamāḥ
yathāvarundhe sat-saṅgaḥ
sarva-saṅgāpaho hi mām

śrī-bhagavān uvāca—the Supreme Personality of Godhead said; *na rodhayati*—does not control; *mām*—Me; *yogaḥ*—the *aṣṭāṅga-yoga* system; *na*—neither; *sāṅkhyam*—the analytic study of the material elements; *dharmaḥ*—ordinary piety such as nonviolence; *eva*—indeed; *ca*—also; *na*—neither; *svādhyāyaḥ*—chanting the *Vedas; tapaḥ*—penances; *tyāgaḥ*—the renounced order of life; *na*—nor; *iṣṭā-pūrtam*—the performance of sacrifice and public welfare activities such as digging wells or planting trees; *na*—neither; *dakṣiṇā*—charity; *vratāni*—taking vows such as fasting completely on Ekādaśī; *yajñaḥ*—worship of the demigods; *chandāṁsi*—chanting confidential *mantras; tīrthāni*—going to holy places of pilgrimage; *niyamāḥ*—following major instructions for spiritual discipline; *yamāḥ*—and also minor regulations; *yathā*—as;

avarundhe—brings under control; *sat-saṅgaḥ*—association with My devotees; *sarva*—all; *saṅga*—material association; *apahaḥ*—removing; *hi*—certainly; *mām*—Me.

TRANSLATION

The Supreme Personality of Godhead said: My dear Uddhava, by associating with My pure devotees one can destroy one's attachment for all objects of material sense gratification. Such purifying association brings Me under the control of My devotee. One may perform the aṣṭāṅga-yoga system, engage in philosophical analysis of the elements of material nature, practice nonviolence and other ordinary principles of piety, chant the Vedas, perform penances, take to the renounced order of life, execute sacrificial performances and dig wells, plant trees and perform other public welfare activities, give in charity, carry out severe vows, worship the demigods, chant confidential mantras, visit holy places or accept major and minor disciplinary injunctions, but even by performing such activities one does not bring Me under his control.

PURPORT

The commentary of Śrīla Jīva Gosvāmī on these two verses can be summarized as follows. One may serve the devotees of the Lord through ceremonial worship or by actually associating with them. Association with pure devotees is sufficient for self-realization because one can learn everything about spiritual advancement from such devotees. With perfect knowledge one can achieve all that one desires, for the process of devotional service immediately brings the blessings of the Supreme Personality of Godhead. Pure devotional service is transcendental to the modes of nature, and therefore it appears mysterious to the souls conditioned by those modes.

In the previous chapter Lord Kṛṣṇa stated, *haviṣāgnau yajeta mām:* "One may worship Me in fire by offering oblations of ghee." (*Bhāg.* 11.11.43) Also, in verse 38 of the previous chapter it was mentioned that one should construct parks, recreational places, orchards, vegetable gardens, and so on. These serve to attract people to the temples of Kṛṣṇa, where they may directly engage in chanting the holy name of the Lord. Such construction projects may be understood as *pūrtam*, or public welfare activities. Although Lord Kṛṣṇa mentions in these two verses that association with His pure devotees is far more powerful than processes such as *yoga*, philosophical speculation, sacrifices and public welfare activities, these secondary activities also please Lord Kṛṣṇa, but to a lesser extent. Specifically, they please the Lord when performed by devotees rather than by ordinary materialistic persons. Therefore the comparative term *yathā* ("according to proportion") is used. In other words, such practices as sacrifice, austerity and philosophical study may help one become fit for rendering devotional service, and when such activities are performed by devotees aspiring for spiritual advancement, they become somewhat pleasing to the Lord.

One may study the example of *vratāni*, or vows. The injunction that one should fast on Ekādaśī is a permanent vow for all Vaiṣṇavas, and one should not conclude from these verses that one may neglect the Ekādaśī vow. The superiority of *sat-saṅga*, or association with pure devotees, in awarding the fruit of love of Godhead does not mean that one should give up other processes or that these secondary processes are not permanent factors in *bhakti-yoga*. There are many Vedic injunctions instructing one to execute the *agnihotra* sacrifice, and the modern-day followers of Caitanya Mahāprabhu also occasionally execute fire sacrifices. Such sacrifice is recommended by the Lord Himself in the previous chapter, and therefore it should not be given up by the devotees of the Lord. By performing Vedic ritualistic and purificatory processes, one is gradually elevated to the platform of devotional service, whereupon one is able to directly worship the Absolute Truth. One Vedic injunction states, "The result awarded for fasting continuously for one month on six different occasions can easily be achieved simply by accepting a handful of rice offered to Lord Viṣṇu. This facility is especially offered in the Kali-yuga." Nevertheless, regulated fasting on Ekādaśī is not an impediment to spiritual advancement. Rather, it is a perpetual aspect of devotional service and can be considered an auxiliary principle supporting the main principle of worshiping Lord Kṛṣṇa and His devotees. Because such secondary principles help one become fit for executing the primary processes of devotional service, they are also greatly beneficial. Therefore, such secondary principles are widely mentioned throughout Vedic literature. It may be concluded that such secondary principles are essential for advancement in Kṛṣṇa consciousness, and therefore one should never give up the principle of *vrata*, the execution of prescribed vows.

In the previous chapter Śrīla Śrīdhara Svāmī mentioned that the words *ājñāyaivaṁ guṇān doṣān* (*Bhāg.* 11.11.32) indicate that a devotee should select Vedic principles that do not conflict with his service to the Lord. Many of the elaborate Vedic ceremonies and complicated procedures for fasting, demigod worship and *yoga* practice cause great disturbance to the supreme process of *śravaṇaṁ kīrtanaṁ viṣṇoḥ*, hearing and chanting about the Lord; therefore they are rejected by the Vaiṣṇavas. However, the processes helpful to devotional service should be accepted. The example can be given of Mahārāja Yudhiṣṭhira, who was instructed by the dying Bhīṣmadeva. In *Śrīmad-Bhāgavatam* (1.9.27) Bhīṣma instructs King Yudhiṣṭhira in *dāna-dharma*, or public acts of charity, *rāja-dharma*, or the duties of a king, *mokṣa-dharma*, or duties for salvation, *strī-dharma*, or duties for women, and ultimately *bhāgavata-dharma*, or pure devotional service to the Lord. Bhīṣma did not limit his discussion to *bhāgavata-dharma*, because Lord Kṛṣṇa gave Mahārāja Yudhiṣṭhira the devotional service of acting as a king, and to execute his service Yudhiṣṭhira Mahārāja required extensive knowledge of civic affairs. However, one who is not rendering such prescribed devotional service in society should not unnecessarily involve himself in the material world, even by practice of Vedic rituals. Nothing should distract him from the ultimate goal of satisfying Lord Kṛṣṇa.

The principle of not giving up prescribed vows may be further illustrated by the example of Mahārāja Ambarīṣa. In the Ninth Canto of *Śrīmad-Bhāgavatam* we find that although Mahārāja Ambarīṣa performed elaborate Vedic sacrifices, his goal was always the satisfaction of the Lord. The citizens in his kingdom did not desire to go to heaven, because they were always hearing about the glories of Vaikuṇṭha. Ambarīṣa Mahārāja, along with his queen, observed the vow of Ekādaśī and Dvādaśī for one year. Since Ambarīṣa Mahārāja is considered to be a great jewel among Vaiṣṇavas, and since his behavior was always exemplary, it is definitely concluded that such vows as fasting on Ekādaśī are imperative for Vaiṣṇavas. It is further stated in Vedic literature, "If due to negligence a Vaiṣṇava does not fast on Ekādaśī, then his worship of Lord Viṣṇu is useless, and he will go to hell." The members of the International Society for Krishna Consciousness fast from grains and beans on Ekādaśī, and this vow should always be observed by all of its members.

If one falsely thinks that one may obtain the association of Lord Kṛṣṇa merely by great austerities, brilliant studies in Sanskrit literature, magnanimous acts of charity, etc., one's Kṛṣṇa consciousness will be distorted and weakened. One should remember the example of Lord Caitanya, who practiced Kṛṣṇa consciousness by constantly hearing and chanting about Lord Kṛṣṇa. If by fasting, study, austerity or sacrifice one becomes more fit to participate in the *saṅkīrtana* movement of Lord Caitanya, then such activities are also pleasing to Lord Kṛṣṇa. But the Lord clearly explains here that such activities can never become central in the practice of *bhakti-yoga.* They must remain in an auxiliary relationship to the supreme process of *sat-saṅga,* or association with pure devotees who hear and chant the glories of the Lord. Śrīla Madhvācārya has quoted from Vedic literature that if one offends the Lord's devotees and does not learn to associate with them, Lord Viṣṇu personally places barriers in the path of such a person so that he may not enter into the Lord's company.

TEXTS 3–6

सत्सङ्गेन हि दैतेया यातुधाना मृगाः खगाः ।
गन्धर्वाप्सरसो नागाः सिद्धाश्चारणगुह्यकाः ॥ ३ ॥
विद्याधरा मनुष्येषु वैश्याः शूद्राः स्त्रियोऽन्त्यजाः ।
रजस्तमःप्रकृतयस्तस्मिंस्तस्मिन् युगे युगे ॥ ४ ॥
बहवो मत्पदं प्राप्तास्त्वाष्ट्रकायाधवादयः ।
वृषपर्वा बलिर्बाणो मयश्चाथ विभीषणः ॥ ५ ॥
सुग्रीवो हनुमानृक्षो गजो गृध्रो वणिक्पथः ।
व्याधः कुब्जा व्रजे गोप्यो यज्ञपत्न्यस्तथापरे ॥ ६ ॥

sat-saṅgena hi daiteyā
yātudhānā mṛgāḥ khagāḥ
gandharvāpsaraso nāgāḥ
siddhāś cāraṇa-guhyakāḥ

vidyādharā manuṣyeṣu
vaiśyāḥ śūdrāḥ striyo 'ntya-jāḥ
rajas-tamaḥ-prakṛtayas
tasmiṁs tasmin yuge yuge

bahavo mat-padaṁ prāptās
tvāṣṭra-kāyādhavādayaḥ
vṛṣaparvā balir bāṇo
mayaś cātha vibhīṣaṇaḥ

sugrīvo hanumān ṛkṣo
gajo gṛdhro vaṇikpathaḥ
vyādhaḥ kubjā vraje gopyo
yajña-patnyas tathāpare

sat-saṅgena—by association with My devotees; *hi*—certainly; *daiteyāḥ*—the sons of Diti; *yātudhānāḥ*—demons; *mṛgāḥ*—animals; *khagāḥ*—birds; *gandharva*—Gandharvas; *apsarasaḥ*—the society girls of heaven; *nāgāḥ*—snakes; *siddhāḥ*—residents of Siddhaloka; *cāraṇa*—the Cāraṇas; *guhyakāḥ*—the Guhyakas; *vidyādharāḥ*—the residents of Vidyādharaloka; *manuṣyeṣu*—among the human beings; *vaiśyāḥ*—mercantile men; *śūdrāḥ*—laborers; *striyaḥ*—women; *antyajāḥ*—uncivilized men; *rajaḥ-tamaḥ-prakṛtayaḥ*—those bound in the modes of passion and ignorance; *tasmin tasmin*—in each and every; *yuge yuge*—age; *bahavaḥ*—many living entities; *mat*—My; *padam*—abode; *prāptāḥ*—achieved; *tvāṣṭra*—Vṛtrāsura; *kāyādhava*—Prahlāda Mahārāja; *ādayaḥ*—and others like them; *vṛṣaparvā*—named Vṛṣaparvā; *baliḥ*—Bali Mahārāja; *bāṇaḥ*—Bāṇāsura; *mayaḥ*—the demon Maya; *ca*—also; *atha*—thus; *vibhīṣaṇaḥ*—Vibhīṣaṇa, the brother of Rāvaṇa; *sugrīvaḥ*—the monkey king Sugrīva; *hanumān*—the great devotee Hanumān; *ṛkṣaḥ*—Jāmbavān; *gajaḥ*—the devotee-elephant Gajendra; *gṛdhraḥ*—Jaṭāyu the vulture; *vaṇikpathaḥ*—the merchant Tulādhāra; *vyādhaḥ*—Dharma-vyādha; *kubjā*—the former prostitute Kubjā, saved by Lord Kṛṣṇa; *vraje*—in Vṛndāvana; *gopyaḥ*—the *gopīs; yajña-patnyaḥ*—the wives of the *brāhmaṇas* performing sacrifice; *tathā*—similarly; *apare*—others.

TRANSLATION

In every yuga many living entities entangled in the modes of passion and ignorance gained the association of My devotees. Thus, such living entities as the Daityas, Rākṣasas, birds, beasts, Gandharvas, Apsarās, Nāgas, Siddhas, Cāraṇas, Guhyakas and

Vidyādharas, as well as such lower-class human beings as the vaiśyas, śūdras, women and others, were able to achieve My supreme abode. Vṛtrāsura, Prahlāda Mahārāja and others like them also achieved My abode by association with My devotees, as did personalities such as Vṛṣaparvā, Bali Mahārāja, Bāṇāsura, Maya, Vibhīṣaṇa, Sugrīva, Hanumān, Jāmbavān, Gajendra, Jaṭāyu, Tulādhāra, Dharma-vyādha, Kubjā, the gopīs in Vṛndāvana and the wives of the brāhmaṇas who were performing sacrifice.

PURPORT

The Lord has mentioned devotees such as the *gopīs* in Vṛndāvana and also demons like Bāṇāsura to illustrate how He comes under the control of those who surrender to Him. It is understood that devotees like the *gopīs* and others mentioned here obtained pure love of Kṛṣṇa, whereas the demons generally obtained only salvation. Many demons were purified by association with devotees and came to accept devotional service to the Lord as the most important among the various activities in their lives, but the exalted devotees like Prahlāda and Bali Mahārāja know nothing except devotional service, which they accept as their very life. Still, the reformed demons are also mentioned so that readers of *Śrīmad-Bhāgavatam* will understand the enormous benefits one may achieve by associating with devotees of the Lord.

The demon Vṛtrāsura was the pious King Citraketu in his previous life, during which he associated with Śrī Nārada Muni, Śrī Aṅgirā Muni and Lord Saṅkarṣaṇa. Prahlāda Mahārāja, being the son of Hiraṇyakaśipu, is considered a Daitya, or demon. Yet while still in the womb of his mother, Kayādhū, he associated with Nārada Muni by sound vibration. The demon Vṛṣaparvā was abandoned by his mother at birth, but he was raised by a *muni* and became a devotee of Lord Viṣṇu. Bali Mahārāja associated with his grandfather Prahlāda and also with Lord Vāmanadeva. Bali Mahārāja's son, Bāṇāsura, was saved by association with his father and Lord Śiva. He also associated with Lord Kṛṣṇa personally when the Lord cut off all but two of his one thousand arms, which had been awarded as a benediction by Lord Śiva. Understanding the glories of Lord Kṛṣṇa, Bāṇāsura also became a great devotee. The demon Maya Dānava constructed an assembly house for the Pāṇḍavas and also associated with Lord Kṛṣṇa Himself, eventually achieving the shelter of the

Lord. Vibhīṣaṇa was a pious-natured demon, the brother of Rāvaṇa, and he associated with Hanumān and Rāmacandra.

Sugrīva, Hanumān, Jāmbavān and Gajendra are examples of animals who achieved the mercy of the Lord. Jāmbavān, or Ṛkṣarāja, was a member of a race of monkeys. He personally associated with Lord Kṛṣṇa, fighting with Him over the Syamantaka jewel. The elephant Gajendra in a previous life had association with devotees, and at the end of his life as Gajendra he was personally saved by the Lord. Jaṭāyu, the bird who at the cost of his own life assisted Lord Rāmacandra, associated with Śrī Garuḍa and Mahārāja Daśaratha as well as other devotees in *rāma-līlā.* He also personally met with Sītā and Lord Rāma. According to Śrīla Jīva Gosvāmī, the association that the Gandharvas, Apsarās, Nāgas, Siddhas, Cāraṇas, Guhyakas and Vidyādharas had with the devotees is not very prominent and does not need to be mentioned. Vaṇikpatha is a *vaiśya,* and his story is mentioned in the *Mahābhārata* in connection with the pride of Jājali Muni.

The importance of association with devotees is illustrated in the story of Dharma-vyādha, the nonviolent hunter, as described in the *Varāha Purāṇa.* In a previous life he somehow became a *brahma-rākṣasa,* or *brāhmaṇa* ghost, but was eventually saved. In a previous Kali-yuga he had the association of a Vaiṣṇava king named Vāsu. The lady Kubjā associated directly with Lord Kṛṣṇa, and in her previous birth she had associated with Śrī Nārada Muni. The *gopīs* of Vṛndāvana rendered service to saintly persons in their previous births. Having had ample association with devotees, they became *gopīs* in Vṛndāvana in their next lives and associated with the eternally liberated *gopīs* who had descended there. They also had association with Tulasī-devī, or Vṛndā-devī. The wives of the *brāhmaṇas* performing sacrifice had association with women sent by Lord Kṛṣṇa to sell flower garlands and betel nuts and heard about the Lord from them.

TEXT 7

ते नाधीतश्रुतिगणा नोपासितमहत्तमाः ।
अव्रतातप्ततपसः मत्सङ्गान्मामुपागताः ॥ ७ ॥

te nādhīta-śruti-gaṇā
nopāsita-mahattamāḥ

avratātapta-tapasaḥ
mat-saṅgān mām upāgatāḥ

te—they; *na*—not; *adhīta*—having studied; *śruti-gaṇāḥ*—the Vedic literatures; *na*—not; *upāsita*—having worshiped; *mahat-tamaḥ*—great saints; *avrata*—without vows; *atapta*—not having undergone; *tapasaḥ*—austerities; *mat-saṅgāt*—simply by association with Me and My devotees; *mām*—Me; *upāgatāḥ*—they achieved.

TRANSLATION

The persons I have mentioned did not undergo serious studies of the Vedic literature, nor did they worship great saintly persons, nor did they execute severe vows or austerities. Simply by association with Me and My devotees, they achieved Me.

PURPORT

Study of the Vedic literature, worship of those who teach the *śruti-mantras*, acceptance of vows and austerities, etc., as mentioned previously, are helpful processes that please the Supreme Personality of Godhead. In this verse, however, the Lord again explains that all such processes are secondary to the essential process of associating with the Supreme Personality of Godhead and His pure devotees. By other processes one may gain the association of the Lord and His devotees, which will actually give the perfection of life. The word *mat-saṅgāt* can also be read as *sat-saṅgāt*, with the same meaning. In the reading *mat-saṅgāt* ("from association with Me"), *mat* is also understood to indicate "those who are Mine," or the devotees. Śrīla Śrīdhara Svāmī mentions that a pure devotee can advance in Kṛṣṇa consciousness by his own association, since simply by associating with his own activities and consciousness, he associates with the Lord.

TEXT 8

केवलेन हि भावेन गोप्यो गावो नगा मृगाः ।
येऽन्ये मूढधियो नागाः सिद्धा मामीयुरञ्जसा ॥ ८ ॥

kevalena hi bhāvena
gopyo gāvo nagā mṛgāḥ

ye 'nye mūḍha-dhiyo nāgāḥ
siddhā mām īyur añjasā

kevalena—by unalloyed; *hi*—indeed; *bhāvena*—by love; *gopyaḥ*—the *gopīs;* *gāvaḥ*—the Vṛndāvana cows; *nagāḥ*—the unmoving creatures of Vṛndāvana such as the twin *arjuna* trees; *mṛgāḥ*—other animals; *ye*—those; *anye*—others; *mūḍha-dhiyaḥ*—with stunted intelligence; *nāgāḥ*—Vṛndāvana snakes such as Kāliya; *siddhāḥ*—achieving the perfection of life; *mām*—to Me; *īyuḥ*—they went; *añjasā*—quite easily.

TRANSLATION

The inhabitants of Vṛndāvana, including the gopīs, cows, unmoving creatures such as the twin arjuna trees, animals, living entities with stunted consciousness such as bushes and thickets, and snakes such as Kāliya, all achieved the perfection of life by unalloyed love for Me and thus very easily achieved Me.

PURPORT

Although innumerable living entities achieved liberation by association with the Lord and His devotees, many such personalities also executed other processes such as austerity, charity, philosophical speculation, and so on. As we have already explained, such procedures are secondary. But the inhabitants of Vṛndāvana such as the *gopīs* did not know anything except Lord Kṛṣṇa, and their whole purpose in life was simply to love Lord Kṛṣṇa, as indicated here by the words *kevalena hi bhāvena.* Even the trees, bushes and hills such as Govardhana loved Lord Kṛṣṇa. As the Lord explains to His brother, Śrī Baladeva, in the Tenth Canto of *Śrīmad-Bhāgavatam* (10.15.5):

aho amī deva-varāmarārcitaṁ
pādāmbujaṁ te sumanaḥ-phalārhaṇam
namanty upādāya śikhābhir ātmanas
tamo-'pahatyai taru-janma yat-kṛtam

"My dear brother Baladeva, just see how these trees are bowing down with their branches and offering obeisances to Your lotus feet, which are worshipable even by the demigods. Indeed, My dear brother, You are the

Supreme God, and thus these trees have produced fruits and flowers as an offering to You. Although a living entity takes birth as a tree due to the mode of ignorance, certainly by such a birth in Vṛndāvana these trees are destroying all darkness in their lives by serving Your lotus feet."

Although many living entities achieved the mercy of Lord Kṛṣṇa by associating with the Lord and His devotees in various ways, those who take Lord Kṛṣṇa as everything are situated in the highest process of spiritual realization. Therefore the Lord has not bothered to mention in this verse those who achieved perfection through mixed processes, but rather glorifies the unalloyed devotees of Vṛndāvana, headed by the *gopīs*, who knew nothing but Lord Kṛṣṇa. The residents of Vṛndāvana were so satisfied in their relationships with Lord Kṛṣṇa that they did not pollute their loving service with mental speculation or fruitive desires. The *gopīs* served Lord Kṛṣṇa in the conjugal *rasa*, or relationship, whereas according to Śrīla Viśvanātha Cakravartī Ṭhākura the cows loved Lord Kṛṣṇa in *vātsalya-rasa*, or the love of parents for a child, because the cows were always supplying milk to child Kṛṣṇa. Unmoving objects like Govardhana Hill and other hills and mountains loved Lord Kṛṣṇa as a friend, and the ordinary animals, trees and bushes of Vṛndāvana loved Lord Kṛṣṇa in *dāsya-rasa*, or with love of a servant for his master. Snakes like Kāliya also developed this love in servitude, and after relishing their loving service to Lord Kṛṣṇa, all of them went back home, back to Godhead. According to Śrīla Viśvanātha Cakravartī Ṭhākura, all those inhabitants of Vṛndāvana should be considered eternally liberated souls, as expressed by the word *siddhāḥ*, which means "having achieved the perfection of life."

TEXT 9

यं न योगेन सांख्येन दानव्रततपोऽध्वरैः ।
व्याख्यास्वाध्यायसंन्यासैः प्राप्नुयाद् यत्नवानपि ॥ ९ ॥

yaṁ na yogena sāṅkhyena
dāna-vrata-tapo-'dhvaraiḥ
vyākhyā-svādhyāya-sannyāsaiḥ
prāpnuyād yatnavān api

yam—whom; *na*—not; *yogena*—by the mystic *yoga* systems; *sāṅkhyena*—by philosophical speculation; *dāna*—by charity; *vrata*—vows; *tapaḥ*—austerities; *adhvaraiḥ*—or Vedic ritualistic sacrifices; *vyākhyā*—by explaining Vedic knowledge to others; *svādhyāya*—personal study of the *Veda; sannyāsaiḥ*—or by taking the renounced order of life; *prāpnuyāt*—can one obtain; *yatna-vān*—with great endeavor; *api*—even.

TRANSLATION

Even though one engages with great endeavor in the mystic yoga system, philosophical speculation, charity, vows, penances, ritualistic sacrifices, teaching of Vedic mantras to others, personal study of the Vedas, or the renounced order of life, still one cannot achieve Me.

PURPORT

Lord Kṛṣṇa here explains that it is very difficult to achieve His personal association, even for one who seriously endeavors to reach the Absolute Truth. The inhabitants of Vṛndāvana, such as the *gopīs* and cows, were always living with Lord Kṛṣṇa, and thus their association is called *sat-saṅga.* Anyone who is favorably living with the Supreme Personality of Godhead becomes *sat,* or eternal, and thus the association of such a person can immediately award others pure devotional service to the Lord. There is an austerity called *cāndrāyaṇa,* a fast in which one's intake of food is diminished by one mouthful each day as the moon wanes and increased in the same way as the moon waxes. Similarly, there are painstaking ritualistic sacrifices and grueling studies of the Sanskrit Vedic *mantras,* which one may also teach to others. All these tedious activities cannot award the highest perfection of life unless one gets the causeless mercy of the pure devotees of the Lord. As stated in the First Canto of *Śrīmad-Bhāgavatam* (1.2.8):

dharmaḥ sv-anuṣṭhitaḥ puṁsāṁ
viṣvaksena-kathāsu yaḥ
notpādayed yadi ratiṁ
śrama eva hi kevalam

"The occupational activities a man performs according to his own position are only so much useless labor if they do not provoke attraction for the message of the Personality of Godhead."

TEXT 10

रामेण सार्धं मथुरां प्रणीते
श्वाफल्किना मय्यनुरक्तचित्ताः ।
विगाढभावेन न मे वियोग-
तीव्राधयोऽन्यं ददृशुः सुखाय ॥१०॥

rāmeṇa sārdhaṁ mathurāṁ praṇīte
śvāphalkinā mayy anurakta-cittāḥ
vigāḍha-bhāvena na me viyoga-
tīvrādhayo 'nyaṁ dadṛśuḥ sukhāya

rāmeṇa—with Balarāma; *sārdham*—with; *mathurām*—to the city of Mathurā; *praṇīte*—when brought; *śvāphalkinā*—by Akrūra; *mayi*—Myself; *anurakta*—constantly attached; *cittāḥ*—those whose consciousness was; *vigāḍha*—extremely deep; *bhāvena*—by love; *na*—not; *me*—than Me; *viyoga*—of separation; *tīvra*—intense; *ādhayaḥ*—who were experiencing mental distress, anxiety; *anyam*—other; *dadṛśuḥ*—they saw; *sukhāya*—that could make them happy.

TRANSLATION

The residents of Vṛndāvana, headed by the gopīs, were always completely attached to Me with deepest love. Therefore when along with My brother Balarāma I was brought to the city of Mathurā by My uncle Akrūra, the residents of Vṛndāvana suffered extreme mental distress because of separation from Me and could not find any other source of happiness.

PURPORT

This verse especially describes the sentiments of the cowherd girls of Vṛndāvana, the *gopīs*, and Lord Kṛṣṇa here reveals the incomparable love they felt for Him. As explained in the Tenth Canto, Lord Kṛṣṇa's uncle Akrūra, sent by Kaṁsa, came to Vṛndāvana and took Kṛṣṇa and Balarāma back to Mathurā for a wrestling event. The *gopīs* loved Lord Kṛṣṇa so much that in His absence their consciousness was completely absorbed in spiritual love. Thus their Kṛṣṇa consciousness is considered the highest perfectional stage of life. They were always expecting that Lord Kṛṣṇa would finish His business of killing demons and return to them, and therefore their anxiety was an extremely moving, heart-rending display of love. Anyone desiring true happiness must take to the devotional service of the Lord in the spirit of the *gopīs*, giving up everything for the pleasure of the Supreme Lord.

TEXT 11

तास्ताः क्षपाः प्रेष्ठतमेन नीता
मयैव वृन्दावनगोचरेण ।
क्षणार्धवत्ताः पुनरङ्ग तासां
हीना मया कल्पसमा बभूवुः ॥११॥

tās tāḥ kṣapāḥ preṣṭhatamena nītā
mayaiva vṛndāvana-gocareṇa
kṣaṇārdha-vat tāḥ punar aṅga tāsāṁ
hīnā mayā kalpa-samā babhūvuḥ

tāḥ tāḥ—all those; *kṣapāḥ*—nights; *preṣṭha-tamena*—with the most dearly beloved; *nītāḥ*—spent; *mayā*—with Me; *eva*—indeed; *vṛndāvana*—in Vṛndāvana; *go-careṇa*—who can be known; *kṣaṇa*—a moment; *ardha-vat*—like half; *tāḥ*—those very nights; *punaḥ*—again; *aṅga*—dear Uddhava; *tāsām*—for the *gopīs; hīnāḥ*—bereft; *mayā*—of Me; *kalpa*—a day of Brahmā (4,320,000,000 years); *samāḥ*—equal to; *babhūvuḥ*—became.

TRANSLATION

Dear Uddhava, all of those nights that the gopīs spent with Me, their most dearly beloved, in the land of Vṛndāvana seemed to them to pass in less than a moment. Bereft of My association, however, the gopīs felt that those same nights dragged on forever, as if each night were equal to a day of Brahmā.

PURPORT

Śrīla Śrīdhara Svāmī comments as follows. "The *gopīs* suffered extreme anxiety in the absence of Lord Kṛṣṇa, and though outwardly appearing bewildered, they actually achieved the highest perfectional stage of *samādhi.* Their consciousness was intensely and intimately attached to Lord Kṛṣṇa, and by such Kṛṣṇa consciousness their own bodies seemed very far away from them, even though people normally consider their body to be their closest possession. In fact, the *gopīs* did not think about their own existence. Although a young woman normally considers her husband and children to be her dearmost possessions, the *gopīs* did not even consider the existence of their so-called families. Nor could they think of this world or life after death. Indeed, they were not at all aware of these things. Just like great sages who become detached from the names and forms of the material world, the *gopīs* could not think of anything, because they were rapt in loving remembrance of Lord Kṛṣṇa. Just as rivers enter the ocean, similarly, the *gopīs* completely merged into consciousness of Lord Kṛṣṇa through intense love."

Thus a day of Brahmā seemed like a single moment for the *gopīs* when Lord Kṛṣṇa was present with them, and a single moment seemed like a day of Brahmā when Lord Kṛṣṇa was absent. The Kṛṣṇa consciousness of the *gopīs* is the perfection of spiritual life, and the symptoms of such perfection are described here.

TEXT 12

ता नाविदन् मय्यनुषङ्गबद्ध-
धियः स्वमात्मानमदस्तथेदम् ।
यथा समाधौ मुनयोऽब्धितोये
नद्यः प्रविष्टा इव नामरूपे ॥१२॥

tā nāvidan mayy anuṣaṅga-baddha-
dhiyaḥ svam ātmānam adas tathedam
yathā samādhau munayo 'bdhi-toye
nadyaḥ praviṣṭā iva nāma-rūpe

tāḥ—they (the *gopīs*); *na*—not; *avidan*—were aware of; *mayi*—in Me; *anuṣaṅga*—by intimate contact; *baddha*—bound up; *dhiyaḥ*—their consciousness; *svam*—their own; *ātmānam*—body or self; *adaḥ*—something remote; *tathā*—thus considering; *idam*—this which is most near; *yathā*—just as; *samādhau*—in *yoga-samādhi; munayaḥ*—great sages; *abdhi*—of the ocean; *toye*—in the water; *nadyaḥ*—rivers; *praviṣṭāḥ*—having entered; *iva*—like; *nāma*—names; *rūpe*—and forms.

TRANSLATION

My dear Uddhava, just as great sages in yoga trance merge into self-realization, like rivers merging into the ocean, and are thus not aware of material names and forms, similarly, the gopīs of Vṛndāvana were so completely attached to Me within their minds that they could not think of their own bodies, nor of this world, nor of their future lives. Their entire consciousness was simply bound up in Me.

PURPORT

The words *svam ātmānam adas tathedam* indicate that while for ordinary persons one's personal body is the most near and dear thing, the *gopīs* considered their own bodies to be distant and remote, just as a *yogī* in *samādhi* trance considers ordinary things around his physical body or his physical body itself to be most remote. When Kṛṣṇa played on His flute late at night, the *gopīs* immediately forgot everything about their so-called husbands and children and went to dance with Lord Kṛṣṇa in the forest. These controversial points have been clearly explained in the book *Kṛṣṇa*, by His Divine Grace A. C. Bhaktivedanta Swami Prabhupāda. The basic explanation is that Lord Kṛṣṇa is the source of everything, and the *gopīs* are the Lord's own potency. Thus there is no discrepancy or immorality in the almighty Personality of Godhead's loving affairs with His own manifest potency, the *gopīs*, who happen to be the most beautiful young girls in the creation of God.

There is no illusion on the part of the *gopīs*, for they are so attracted to Lord Kṛṣṇa that they do not care to think of anything else. Since all existence is situated within the body of Lord Kṛṣṇa, there is no loss for the *gopīs* when they concentrate on the Lord. It is the nature of very deep love to exclude all objects except the beloved. However, in the material world, where we try to love a limited temporary object such as our nation, family or personal body, our exclusion of other objects constitutes ignorance. But when our love is intensely concentrated on the Supreme

Personality of Godhead, the origin of everything, such concentration cannot be considered ignorance or small-mindedness.

The example of the sages in *samādhi* is given here only to illustrate exclusive concentration on a single object. Otherwise, there is no comparison between the ecstatic love of the *gopīs* and the dry meditation of the *yogīs*, who merely try to understand that they are not their material bodies. Since the *gopīs* had no material bodies to become detached from and were personally dancing with and embracing the Absolute Truth, one can never compare the exalted position of the *gopīs* to that of mere *yogīs*. It is stated that the bliss of impersonal Brahman realization cannot be compared to even an atomic fragment of the blissful ocean of love of Kṛṣṇa. Intimate attachment is like a strong rope that binds the mind and heart. In material life we are bound to that which is temporary and illusory, and therefore such binding of the heart causes great pain. However, if we bind our minds and hearts to the eternal Lord Kṛṣṇa, the reservoir of all pleasure and beauty, then our hearts will expand unlimitedly in the ocean of transcendental bliss.

One should understand that the *gopīs* were not in any way inclined toward impersonal meditation, in which one denies the reality of variegated creation. The *gopīs* did not deny anything; they simply loved Kṛṣṇa and could not think of anything else. They only rejected whatever impeded their concentration on Lord Kṛṣṇa, cursing even their own eyelids, which blinked and thus removed Kṛṣṇa from their sight for a split second. Śrīla Rūpa Gosvāmī has stated that all sincere devotees of the Lord should have the courage to remove from their lives anything that impedes their progressive march back home, back to Godhead.

TEXT 13

मत्कामा रमणं जारमस्वरूपविदोऽबलाः ।
ब्रह्म मां परमं प्रापुः सङ्गाच्छतसहस्रशः ॥१३॥

mat-kāmā ramaṇaṁ jāram
asvarūpa-vido 'balāḥ
brahma māṁ paramaṁ prāpuḥ
saṅgāc chata-sahasraśaḥ

mat—Me; *kāmāḥ*—those who desired; *ramaṇam*—a charming lover; *jāram*—the lover of another's wife; *asvarūpa-vidaḥ*—not knowing My actual situation; *abalāḥ*—women; *brahma*—the Absolute; *mām*—Me; *paramam*—supreme; *prāpuḥ*—they achieved; *saṅgāt*—by association; *śata-sahasraśaḥ*—by hundreds of thousands.

TRANSLATION

All those hundreds of thousands of gopīs, understanding Me to be their most charming lover and ardently desiring Me in that way, were unaware of My actual position. Yet by intimately associating with Me, the gopīs attained Me, the Supreme Absolute Truth.

PURPORT

The words *asvarūpa-vidaḥ* ("not understanding My actual position or form") indicate that the lovely *gopīs* were so completely absorbed in conjugal love for Lord Kṛṣṇa that they were not aware of the Lord's unlimited potencies as the Supreme Personality of Godhead. Śrīla Viśvanātha Cakravartī Ṭhākura explains this and other meanings of the word *asvarūpa-vidaḥ*. In Sanskrit the word *vid* also means "to acquire." Thus, *asvarūpa-vidaḥ* indicates that the *gopīs*, like other pure devotees of the Lord, were not interested in achieving *sārūpya-mukti*, the liberation of acquiring a bodily form similar to the Lord's. Were the *gopīs* to obtain a bodily form like the Lord's, how could the Lord execute His conjugal pastimes of dancing with the *gopīs* and embracing them? Since the *gopīs* had realized their eternal spiritual forms as servitors of the Lord, the word *svarūpa* also may indicate their own spiritual bodies, and thus *asvarūpa-vidaḥ* means that the *gopīs* never thought, as materialists do, of their own bodily beauty. Although the *gopīs* are the most beautiful girls in the Lord's creation, they never thought of their own bodies but rather were always meditating on the transcendental body of Lord Kṛṣṇa. Although we cannot imitate the *gopī's* exalted conjugal feelings, we can follow their superb example of practical Kṛṣṇa consciousness. They naturally took shelter of Lord Kṛṣṇa and achieved the highest perfection of life.

TEXTS 14–15

तस्मात्त्वमुद्धवोत्सृज्य चोदनां प्रतिचोदनाम् ।
प्रवृत्तं च निवृत्तं च श्रोतव्यं श्रुतमेव च ॥१४॥

मामेकमेव शरणमात्मानं सर्वदेहिनाम् ।
याहि सर्वात्मभावेन मया स्या ह्यकुतोभयः ॥१५॥

tasmāt tvam uddhavotsṛjya
codanāṁ praticodanām
pravṛttiṁ ca nivṛttiṁ ca
śrotavyaṁ śrutam eva ca

mām ekam eva śaraṇam
ātmānaṁ sarva-dehinām
yāhi sarvātma-bhāvena
mayā syā hy akuto-bhayaḥ

tasmāt—therefore; *tvam*—you; *uddhava*—O Uddhava; *utsṛjya*—giving up; *codanām*—the regulations of the *Vedas; praticodanām*—the injunctions of supplementary Vedic literatures; *pravṛttim*—injunctions; *ca*—and; *nivṛttim*—prohibitions; *ca*—also; *śrotavyam*—that which is to be heard; *śrutam*—that which has been heard; *eva*—indeed; *ca*—also; *mām*—to Me; *ekam*—alone; *eva*—actually; *śaraṇam*—shelter; *ātmānam*—the Supersoul within the heart; *sarva-dehinām*—of all conditioned souls; *yāhi*—you must go; *sarva-ātma-bhāvena*—with exclusive devotion; *mayā*—by My mercy; *syāḥ*—you should be; *hi*—certainly; *akutaḥ-bhayaḥ*—free from fear in all circumstances.

TRANSLATION

Therefore, My dear Uddhava, abandon the Vedic mantras as well as the procedures of supplementary Vedic literatures and their positive and negative injunctions. Disregard that which has been heard and that which is to be heard. Simply take shelter of Me alone, for I am the Supreme Personality of Godhead, situated within the heart of all conditioned souls. Take shelter of Me wholeheartedly, and by My grace be free from fear in all circumstances.

PURPORT

Śrī Uddhava inquired from Lord Kṛṣṇa about the symptoms of saintly persons and liberated souls, and the Lord has replied in terms of different levels of spiritual advancement, distinguishing between those who are able to understand Lord Kṛṣṇa to be the principal goal of life and those loving devotees who accept Lord Kṛṣṇa and devotional service to Him as the only goal of life. Lord Kṛṣṇa also mentioned that He is captured by His loving devotees and even by those who sincerely associate with His loving devotees. Among all the devotees, the *gopīs* of Vṛndāvana were described by the Lord as having achieved such a rare state of pure devotional service that Lord Kṛṣṇa personally feels constantly indebted to them. According to Śrīla Viśvanātha Cakravartī Ṭhākura, Lord Kṛṣṇa previously kept the *gopīs'* love for Him concealed in His heart because of its confidential nature and the Lord's own gravity. Finally, however, even Lord Kṛṣṇa could not remain silent about the intense love of the *gopīs*, and thus in these verses the Lord reveals to Uddhava how the *gopīs* loved Him in Vṛndāvana and brought Him fully under their control. The Lord would relax in secret places with the loving *gopīs*, and by conjugal spontaneous affection the greatest love was exchanged between them.

As explained by the Lord in *Bhagavad-gītā*, one cannot achieve the perfection of life merely by renouncing the material world or by executing ordinary, sectarian religious principles. One must actually understand the identity of the Supreme Personality of Godhead, and by associating with His pure devotees one must learn to love the Lord in His personal, original form. This love may be expressed in either the conjugal, paternal, fraternal or serving *rasa*, or relationship. The Lord has elaborately explained to Uddhava the system of philosophical analysis of the material world, and now He clearly concludes that it is useless for Uddhava to waste time in fruitive activities or mental speculation. Actually, Lord Kṛṣṇa is hinting that Uddhava should assimilate the example of the *gopīs* and try to advance further in Kṛṣṇa consciousness by following in the footsteps of the cowherd damsels of Vraja. Any conditioned soul who is unsatisfied with the cruel laws of nature, which impose disease, old age and death, should understand that Lord Kṛṣṇa can deliver all living beings from the problems of material existence. There is no need to entangle oneself in unauthorized, sectarian rituals, injunctions or prohibitions. One should simply surrender to Lord Kṛṣṇa, following the example of Śrī Caitanya Mahāprabhu, who is Lord Kṛṣṇa Himself. By the authorized regulated process of *bhakti-yoga*, Kṛṣṇa consciousness, one easily achieves spiritual perfection.

TEXT 16

श्रीउद्धव उवाच
संशयः शृण्वतो वाचं तव योगेश्वरेश्वर ।
न निवर्तत आत्मस्थो येन भ्राम्यति मे मनः ॥१६॥

śrī-uddhava uvāca
saṁśayaḥ śṛṇvato vācaṁ
tava yogeśvareśvara
na nivartata ātma-stho
yena bhrāmyati me manaḥ

śrī-uddhavaḥ uvāca—Śrī Uddhava said; *saṁśayaḥ*—doubt; *śṛṇvataḥ*—of the one who is hearing; *vācam*—the words; *tava*—Your; *yoga-īśvara*—of the lords of mystic power; *īśvara*—You who are the Lord; *na nivartate*—will not go away; *ātma*—in the heart; *sthaḥ*—situated; *yena*—by which; *bhrāmyati*—is bewildered; *me*—my; *manaḥ*—mind.

TRANSLATION

Śrī Uddhava said: O Lord of all masters of mystic power, I have heard Your words, but the doubt in my heart does not go away; thus my mind is bewildered.

PURPORT

In the first verse of the Tenth Chapter of this canto, the Lord stated that one should take shelter of Him and execute one's duties within the *varṇāśrama* system without material desire. Uddhava interpreted this statement as recommending *karma-miśrā bhakti*, or devotional service mixed with a tendency toward fruitive activities. It is a fact that until one understands Lord Kṛṣṇa to be everything, it is not possible to retire from ordinary, worldly duties. Rather, one is encouraged to offer the fruits of such work to the Lord. In verse 4 of the Tenth Chapter, the Lord recommended that one retire from worldly duties and systematically cultivate knowledge, accepting Him as the Supreme. Uddhava understood this instruction to indicate *jñāna-miśrā bhakti,* or devotional service to the Lord mixed with the secondary desire to accumulate knowledge. Beginning with verse 35 of the Tenth Chapter, Uddhava inquired about the process of material conditioning and liberation from material life. The Lord replied elaborately, stating that without devotional service the process of philosophical speculation can never be perfected. In Chapter Eleven, verse 18, the Lord emphasized the importance of faith in the Supreme Personality of Godhead, and in verse 23 Kṛṣṇa extensively widened His discussion of devotional service, emphasizing that one should be faithful and hear and chant the glories of the Lord. The Lord concluded that both the development and perfection of devotional service depend on association with the devotees. In verse 26 of the Eleventh Chapter, Uddhava inquired about the actual ways and means of devotional service and about the symptoms of devotional perfection. And in verse 48 Lord Kṛṣṇa stated that unless one takes to the process of devotional service, one's attempt for liberation will be useless. One must associate with the devotees of the Lord and follow in their footsteps. Finally, in verse 14 of this chapter the Lord categorically rejected the paths of fruitive activities and mental speculation and in verse 15 recommended that one exclusively surrender unto Him with all one's heart.

Having received such elaborate and technical instructions on the perfection of life, Uddhava is bewildered, and his mind is afflicted with doubt about what he should actually do. Lord Kṛṣṇa has described many procedures and the results of such procedures, all of which ultimately lead to the single goal of Lord Kṛṣṇa Himself. Uddhava therefore desires that Lord Kṛṣṇa state in simple terms what should be done. Arjuna makes a similar request of the Lord at the beginning of the Third Chapter of *Bhagavad-gītā.* According to Śrīla Viśvanātha Cakravartī Ṭhākura, Uddhava is stating here, "My dear friend Kṛṣṇa, first You recommended that I perform worldly activities within the *varṇāśrama* system, and then You advised that I reject such activities and take to the path of philosophical research. Now rejecting the path of *jñāna,* You recommend that I simply surrender unto You in *bhakti-yoga.* If I accept Your decision, in the future You may again go back to Your original point and recommend worldly activities." By his boldness in disclosing his mind, Uddhava reveals his intimate friendship with Lord Kṛṣṇa.

TEXT 17

श्रीभगवानुवाच
स एष जीवो विवरप्रसूतिः
प्राणेन घोषेण गुहां प्रविष्टः ।
मनोमयं सूक्ष्ममुपेत्य रूपं
मात्रा स्वरो वर्ण इति स्थविष्ठः ॥१७॥

śrī-bhagavān uvāca
sa eṣa jīvo vivara-prasūtiḥ
prāṇena ghoṣeṇa guhāṁ praviṣṭaḥ
mano-mayaṁ sūkṣmam upetya rūpaṁ
mātrā svaro varṇa iti sthaviṣṭhaḥ

śrī-bhagavān uvāca—the Supreme Personality of Godhead said; *saḥ eṣaḥ*—He Himself; *jīvaḥ*—the Supreme Lord, who gives life to all; *vivara*—within the heart; *prasūtiḥ*—manifest; *prāṇena*—along with the life air; *ghoṣeṇa*—with the subtle manifestation of sound; *guhām*—the heart; *praviṣṭaḥ*—who has entered; *manaḥ-mayam*—perceived by the mind, or controlling the mind even of great demigods like Lord Śiva; *sūkṣmam*—subtle; *upetya*—being situated in; *rūpam*—the form; *mātrā*—the different vocalic lengths; *svaraḥ*—the different intonations; *varṇaḥ*—the different sounds of the alphabet; *iti*—thus; *sthaviṣṭhaḥ*—the gross form.

TRANSLATION

The Supreme Personality of Godhead said: My dear Uddhava, the Supreme Lord gives life to every living being and is situated within the heart along with the life air and primal sound vibration. The Lord can be perceived in His subtle form within the heart by one's mind, since the Lord controls the minds of everyone, even great demigods like Lord Śiva. The Supreme Lord also assumes a gross form as the various sounds of the Vedas, composed of short and long vowels and consonants of different intonations.

PURPORT

Śrīla Viśvanātha Cakravartī Ṭhākura comments as follows on the dialogue between Lord Kṛṣṇa and Uddhava. Uddhava was bewildered and doubtful because Lord Kṛṣṇa explained many different processes such as devotional service, speculative knowledge, renunciation, mystic *yoga*, austerities, pious duties, and so on. However, all of these processes are meant to help the living entities obtain the shelter of Lord Kṛṣṇa, and ultimately no Vedic process should be understood in any other way. Thus Lord Kṛṣṇa explained the entire Vedic system, placing everything in proper order. In fact, Lord Kṛṣṇa was surprised that Uddhava foolishly thought that he was meant to practice every process, as if each method were meant simply for him. Lord Kṛṣṇa therefore wants to inform His devotee, "My dear Uddhava, when I told you that analytic knowledge is to be practiced, pious duties are to be performed, devotional service is obligatory, *yoga* procedures must be observed, austerities are to be executed, etc., I was instructing all living entities, using you as My immediate audience. That which I have spoken, am speaking now and will speak in the future should be understood as guidance for all living entities in different situations. How could you possibly think that you were meant to practice all of the different Vedic processes? I accept you as you are now, My pure devotee. You are not supposed to execute all of these processes." Thus according to Śrīla Viśvanātha Cakravartī Ṭhākura, the Lord, with lighthearted and encouraging words, reveals to Uddhava the deep purpose behind the variety of Vedic procedures.

Lord Kṛṣṇa became manifest from the mouth of Lord Brahmā in the form of the *Vedas.* The word *vivara-prasūti* in this verse also indicates that the Lord is manifest within the *ādhārādi-cakras* situated within the body of Lord Brahmā. The word *ghoṣeṇa* means "subtle sound," and *guhāṁ praviṣṭaḥ* also indicates that Lord Kṛṣṇa enters within the *ādhāra-cakra.* The Lord can further be perceived within other *cakras* such as the *maṇipūraka-cakra,* located around the navel, and the *viśuddhi-cakra.* The Sanskrit alphabet is composed of short and long vowels, and consonants pronounced with high and low tones, and utilizing these vibrations the different branches of Vedic literatures are manifested as a gross form of the Supreme Personality of Godhead. According to *Bhagavad-gītā,* such literatures deal mostly with the three modes of material nature: *traiguṇya-viṣayā vedā nistrai-guṇyo bhavārjuna.* Śrīla Śrīdhara Svāmī explains that due to the control of the illusory energy, *māyā,* the Personality of Godhead appears to the conditioned souls as part of the material universe. The imagined imposition of gross and subtle material qualities on the Personality of Godhead is called *avidyā*, or ignorance, and through such ignorance the living entity considers himself to be the doer of his own activities and becomes bound up in the network of *karma*. The *Vedas* therefore order an entangled soul to observe positive and negative injunctions to purify his existence. These procedures are called *pravṛtti-mārga*, or the path of regulated fruitive activities. When one has purified one's existence, one gives up this gross stage of fruitive activities because it is detrimental to the practice of pure devotional service. By firm faith one may then worship the Personality of Godhead. One who has developed perfect Kṛṣṇa consciousness no longer has to perform ritualistic duties. As stated in *Bhagavad-gītā*, *tasya kāryaṁ na vidyate*.

According to Śrīla Jīva Gosvāmī, this verse may be understood in another way. The word *jīva* indicates Lord Kṛṣṇa, who gives life to the residents of Vṛndāvana, and *vivara-prasūti* indicates that although Lord Kṛṣṇa eternally performs His pastimes in the spiritual world, beyond the vision of the conditioned souls, He also enters within the material universe to display these same pastimes. The words *guhāṁ praviṣṭaḥ* indicates that after displaying such pastimes, the Lord withdraws them and enters into His unmanifest pastimes, or those pastimes not manifest to the conditioned souls. In this case, *mātrā* indicates the transcendental senses of the Lord, *svara* indicates the Lord's transcendental sound vibration and singing, and the word *varṇa* indicates the transcendental form of the Lord. The word *sthaviṣṭha*, or "gross manifestation," means that the Lord becomes manifest in the material world even to those devotees who are not completely advanced in Kṛṣṇa consciousness and whose vision is not completely purified. *Mano-maya* indicates that somehow or other Lord Kṛṣṇa is to be kept within one's mind; and for the nondevotees Lord Kṛṣṇa is *sūkṣma*, or most subtle, because He cannot be known. Thus different *ācāryas* have glorified Lord Kṛṣṇa in different ways through the transcendental sound vibration of this verse.

TEXT 18

यथानलः खेऽनिलबन्धुरुष्मा
बलेन दारुण्यधिमथ्यमानः ।
अणुः प्रजातो हविषा समेधते
तथैव मे व्यक्तिरियं हि वाणी ॥१८॥

yathānalaḥ khe 'nila-bandhur uṣmā
balena dāruṇy adhimathyamānaḥ
aṇuḥ prajāto haviṣā samedhate
tathaiva me vyaktir iyaṁ hi vāṇī

yathā—just as; *analaḥ*—fire; *khe*—in the space within wood; *anila*—air; *bandhuḥ*—whose help; *uṣmā*—heat; *balena*—strongly; *dāruṇi*—within the wood; *adhimathyamānaḥ*—being kindled by friction; *aṇuḥ*—very tiny; *prajātaḥ*—is born; *haviṣā*—with ghee (clarified butter); *samedhate*—it increases; *tathā*—similarly; *eva*—indeed; *me*—My; *vyaktiḥ*—manifestation; *iyam*—this; *hi*—certainly; *vāṇī*—the Vedic sounds.

TRANSLATION

When kindling wood is rubbed together, heat is produced by contact with air, and by vigorously rubbing the sticks, a spark of fire appears. Once the fire is kindled, ghee is added and the fire blazes. Similarly, I become manifest in the sound vibration of the Vedas.

PURPORT

Lord Kṛṣṇa here explains the most confidential meaning of Vedic knowledge. The *Vedas* first regulate ordinary material work and channel the fruits into ritualistic sacrifices, which ostensibly reward the performer with future benefits. The real purpose of these sacrifices, however, is to accustom a materialistic worker to offering the fruits of his work to a superior Vedic authority. An expert fruitive worker gradually exhausts the possibilities of material enjoyment and naturally gravitates toward the superior stage of philosophical speculation on his existential situation. By increased knowledge, one becomes aware of the unlimited glories of the Supreme and gradually takes to the process of loving devotional service to the transcendental Absolute Truth. Lord Kṛṣṇa is the goal of Vedic knowledge, as the Lord states in *Bhagavad-gītā: vedaiś ca sarvair aham eva vedyaḥ.* The Lord gradually becomes manifest in the progression of Vedic rituals, just as fire is gradually manifest by the rubbing of firewood. The words *haviṣā samedhate* ("the fire increases by addition of ghee") indicate that by the progressive advancement of Vedic sacrifice, the fire of spiritual knowledge gradually blazes, illuminating everything and destroying the chain of fruitive work.

Lord Kṛṣṇa considered Uddhava to be the most qualified person to hear this elaborate transcendental knowledge; therefore the Lord mercifully instructs Uddhava so that he may enlighten the sages at Badarikāśrama, thus fulfilling the purpose of the sages' lives.

TEXT 19

एवं गदिः कर्म गतिर्विसर्गो
घ्राणो रसो दृक् स्पर्शः श्रुतिश्च ।
सङ्कल्पविज्ञानमथाभिमानः
सूत्रं रजःसत्त्वतमोविकारः ॥१९॥

evaṁ gadiḥ karma gatir visargo
ghrāṇo raso dṛk sparśaḥ śrutiś ca
saṅkalpa-vijñānam athābhimānaḥ
sūtraṁ rajaḥ-sattva-tamo-vikāraḥ

evam—thus; *gadiḥ*—speech; *karma*—the function of the hands; *gatiḥ*—the function of the legs; *visargaḥ*—the functions of the genital and anus; *ghrāṇaḥ*—smell; *rasaḥ*—taste; *dṛk*—sight; *sparśaḥ*—touch; *śrutiḥ*—hearing; *ca*—also; *saṅkalpa*—the mind's function; *vijñānam*—the function of intelligence and consciousness; *atha*—moreover; *abhimānaḥ*—the function of false ego; *sūtram*—the function of *pradhāna*, or the subtle cause of material nature; *rajaḥ*—of the mode of passion; *sattva*—goodness; *tamaḥ*—and of ignorance; *vikāraḥ*—the transformation.

TRANSLATION

The functions of the working senses—the organ of speech, the hands, the legs, the genital and the anus—and the functions of the knowledge-acquiring senses—the nose, tongue, eyes, skin and ears—along with the functions of the subtle senses of mind, intelligence, consciousness and false ego, and the function of the subtle pradhāna and the interaction of the three modes of material nature, should be understood as My materially manifest form.

PURPORT

By the word *gadi*, or "speech," the Lord concludes His discussion about His manifestation as Vedic vibrations and describes the functions of the other working senses, along with the knowledge-acquiring senses, the subtle functions of consciousness, *pradhāna* and the interaction of the three modes of material nature. A Kṛṣṇa conscious person sees the entire material world as a manifestation of the Lord's potencies. There is therefore no legitimate scope for material sense gratification, because everything is an expansion from the Supreme Personality of Godhead and belongs to Him. One who can understand the expansion of the Lord within subtle and gross material manifestations gives up his desire to live in this world. In the spiritual world everything is eternal, full of bliss and knowledge. The exclusive feature of the material world is that here the living entity dreams that he is lord. A sane person, giving up this hallucination, finds no attractive features in the kingdom of *māyā* and therefore returns home, back to Godhead.

TEXT 20

अयं हि जीवस्त्रिवृदब्जयोनि-
रव्यक्त एको वयसा स आद्यः ।
विश्लिष्टशक्तिर्बहुधेव भाति
बीजानि योनिं प्रतिपद्य यद्वत् ॥२०॥

ayaṁ hi jīvas tri-vṛd abja-yonir
avyakta eko vayasā sa ādyaḥ
viśliṣṭa-śaktir bahudheva bhāti
bījāni yoniṁ pratipadya yadvat

ayam—this; *hi*—certainly; *jīvaḥ*—the supreme living entity who gives life to others; *tri-vṛt*—containing the three modes of material nature; *abja*—of the universal lotus flower; *yoniḥ*—the source; *avyaktaḥ*—unmanifest (materially); *ekaḥ*—alone; *vayasā*—in course of time; *saḥ*—He; *ādyaḥ*—eternal; *viśliṣṭa*—divided; *śaktiḥ*—potencies;

bahudhā—in many divisions; *iva*—like; *bhāti*—He appears; *bījāni*—seeds; *yonim*—in an agricultural field; *pratipadya*—falling; *yat-vat*—just like.

TRANSLATION

When many seeds are placed in an agricultural field, innumerable manifestations of trees, bushes, vegetables, and so on, will arise from a single source, the soil. Similarly, the Supreme Personality of Godhead, who gives life to all and is eternal, originally exists beyond the scope of the cosmic manifestation. In the course of time, however, the Lord, who is the resting place of the three modes of nature and the source of the universal lotus flower in which the cosmic manifestation takes place, divides His material potencies and thus appears to be manifest in innumerable forms, although He is one.

PURPORT

Śrīla Vīrarāghavācārya comments that one may question as to whom the cosmic manifestation, consisting of demigods, men, animals, plants, planets, space, etc., actually belongs. Lord Kṛṣṇa now eradicates any doubt about the source of the cosmic manifestation. The word *tri-vṛt* indicates that the three modes of nature are not independent but are under superior control. The suffix *vṛt* means the *vartanam*, or "existence," of the three modes of material nature within the Supreme Personality of Godhead. Analyzing the term *abja-yoni*, *ap* indicates "water," and *ja* indicates "birth." Thus *abja* means the complex material universe, which sprouts from Garbhodakaśāyī Viṣṇu, who lies in the Garbhodaka Ocean. *Yoni*, or "source," indicates the Personality of Godhead, and thus *abja-yoni* means that the Lord is the source of all cosmic manifestations; indeed, all creation takes place within the Lord. Since the three modes of material nature are under the superior control of the Lord, material objects helplessly undergo creation and annihilation within the universal shell by the will of the Lord. The term *avyakta* indicates the Lord's subtle spiritual form, which exists alone before the material creation. The Lord's original form, being spiritual, does not undergo birth, transformation or death. It is eternal. In the course of time, the Lord's material potencies are divided and manifest as bodies, bodily paraphernalia, sense objects, bodily expansions, false ego and false proprietorship. Thus the Lord expands His conscious living potency called *jīva-śakti*, which is manifest in innumerable material forms such as those of men, demigods, animals, and so on. From the example of the seeds sown in an agricultural field, we can understand that innumerable manifestations may arise from a single source. Similarly, although the Lord is one, He becomes manifest in innumerable forms through the expansion of His different potencies.

TEXT 21

यस्मिन्निदं प्रोतमशेषमोतं
पटो यथा तन्तुवितानसंस्थः ।
य एष संसारतरुः पुराणः
कर्मात्मकः पुष्पफले प्रसूते ॥२१॥

yasminn idaṁ protam aśeṣam otaṁ
paṭo yathā tantu-vitāna-saṁsthaḥ
ya eṣa saṁsāra-taruḥ purāṇaḥ
karmātmakaḥ puṣpa-phale prasūte

yasmin—in whom; *idam*—this universe; *protam*—woven crosswise; *aśeṣam*—the whole; *otam*—and lengthwise; *paṭaḥ*—a cloth; *yathā*—just like; *tantu*—of the threads; *vitāna*—in the expansion; *saṁsthaḥ*—situated; *yaḥ*—that which; *eṣaḥ*—this; *saṁsāra*—of material existence; *taruḥ*—the tree; *purāṇaḥ*—existing since time immemorial; *karma*—toward fruitive activities; *ātmakaḥ*—naturally inclined; *puṣpa*—the first result, blossoming; *phale*—and the fruit; *prasūte*—being produced.

TRANSLATION

Just as woven cloth rests on the expansion of lengthwise and crosswise threads, similarly the entire universe is expanded on the lengthwise and crosswise potency of the Supreme Personality of Godhead and is situated within Him. The conditioned soul has been accepting material bodies since time immemorial, and these bodies are like great trees sustaining one's material existence. Just

as a tree first blossoms and then produces fruit, similarly the tree of material existence, one's material body, produces the various results of material existence.

PURPORT

Before a tree produces fruit, blossoms appear. Similarly, the word *puṣpa-phale*, according to Śrīla Viśvanātha Cakravartī Ṭhākura, indicates the happiness and distress of material existence. One's material life may appear to be blossoming, but ultimately there will appear the bitter fruits of old age, death and other catastrophes. Attachment to the material body, which is always inclined toward sense gratification, is the root cause of material existence, and it is therefore called *saṁsāra-taru.* The tendency to exploit the external energy of the Supreme Lord has existed since time immemorial, as expressed by the words *purāṇaḥ karmātmakaḥ.* The material universe is an expansion of the illusory potency of the Supreme Lord and is always dependent on Him and nondifferent from Him. This simple understanding can relieve the conditioned souls from endless wandering in the unhappy kingdom of *māyā.*

The word *puṣpa-phale* may also be understood as meaning sense gratification and liberation. The tree of material existence will be further explained in the following verses.

TEXTS 22–23

द्वे अस्य बीजे शतमूलस्त्रिनालः
पञ्चस्कन्धः पञ्चरसप्रसूतिः ।
दशैकशाखो द्विसुपर्णनीड-
स्त्रिवल्कलो द्विफलोऽर्कं प्रविष्टः ॥२२॥
अदन्ति चैकं फलमस्य गृध्रा
ग्रामेचरा एकमरण्यवासाः ।
हंसा य एकं बहुरूपमिज्यै-
र्मायामयं वेद स वेद वेदम् ॥२३॥

dve asya bīje śata-mūlas tri-nālaḥ
pañca-skandhaḥ pañca-rasa-prasūtiḥ

daśaika-śākho dvi-suparṇa-nīḍas
tri-valkalo dvi-phalo 'rkaṁ praviṣṭaḥ

adanti caikaṁ phalam asya gṛdhrā
grāme-carā ekam araṇya-vāsāḥ
haṁsā ya ekaṁ bahu-rūpam ijyair
māyā-mayaṁ veda sa veda vedam

dve—two; *asya*—of this tree; *bīje*—seeds; *śata*—hundreds; *mūlaḥ*—of roots; *tri*—three; *nālaḥ*—lower trunks; *pañca*—five; *skandhaḥ*—upper trunks; *pañca*—five; *rasa*—saps; *prasūtiḥ*—producing; *daśa*—ten; *eka*—plus one; *śākhaḥ*—branches; *dvi*—two; *suparṇa*—of birds; *nīḍaḥ*—a nest; *tri*—three; *valkalaḥ*—types of bark; *dvi*—two; *phalaḥ*—fruits; *arkam*—the sun; *praviṣṭaḥ*—extending into; *adanti*—they eat or enjoy; *ca*—also; *ekam*—one; *phalam*—fruit; *asya*—of this tree; *gṛdhrāḥ*—those who are lusty for material enjoyment; *grāme*—in householder life; *carāḥ*—living; *ekam*—another; *araṇya*—in the forest; *vāsāḥ*—those who live; *haṁsāḥ*—swanlike men, saintly persons; *yaḥ*—one who; *ekam*—one only, the Supersoul; *bahu-rūpam*—appearing in many forms; *ijyaiḥ*—by the help of those who are worshipable, the spiritual masters; *māyā-mayam*—produced by the potency of the Supreme Lord; *veda*—knows; *saḥ*—such a person; *veda*—knows; *vedam*—the actual meaning of the Vedic literature.

TRANSLATION

This tree of material existence has two seeds, hundreds of roots, three lower trunks and five upper trunks. It produces five flavors and has eleven branches and a nest made by two birds. The tree is covered by three types of bark, gives two fruits and extends up to the sun. Those lusty after material enjoyment and dedicated to family life enjoy one of the tree's fruits, and swanlike men in the renounced order of life enjoy the other fruit. One who with the help of the bona fide spiritual masters can understand this tree to be a manifestation of the potency of the one Supreme Truth appearing in many forms actually knows the meaning of the Vedic literature.

PURPORT

The two seeds of this tree are sinful and pious activities, and the hundreds of roots are the living entities' innumerable material desires, which chain them to material existence. The three lower trunks represent the three modes of material nature, and the five upper trunks represent the five gross material elements. The tree produces five flavors—sound, form, touch, taste and aroma—and has eleven branches—the five working senses, the five knowledge-acquiring senses and the mind. Two birds, namely the individual soul and the Supersoul, have made their nest in this tree, and the three types of bark are air, bile and mucus, the constituent elements of the body. The two fruits of this tree are happiness and distress.

Those who are busy trying to enjoy the company of beautiful women, money and other luxurious aspects of illusion enjoy the fruit of unhappiness. One should remember that even in the heavenly planets there is anxiety and death. Those who have renounced material goals and taken to the path of spiritual enlightenment enjoy the fruit of happiness. One who takes the assistance of bona fide spiritual masters can understand that this elaborate tree is simply the manifestation of the external potency of the Supreme Personality of Godhead, who is ultimately one without a second. If one can see the Supreme Lord as the ultimate cause of everything, then his knowledge is perfect. Otherwise, if one is entangled in Vedic rituals or Vedic speculation without knowledge of the Supreme Lord, he has not achieved the perfection of life.

TEXT 24

एवं गुरूपासनयैकभक्त्या
विद्याकुठारेण शितेन धीरः ।
विवृश्च्य जीवाशयमप्रमत्तः
सम्पद्य चात्मानमथ त्यजास्त्रम् ॥२४॥

evaṁ gurūpāsanayaika-bhaktyā
vidyā-kuṭhāreṇa śitena dhīraḥ
vivṛścya jīvāśayam apramattaḥ
sampadya cātmānam atha tyajāstram

evam—thus (with the knowledge I have given you); *guru*—of the spiritual master; *upāsanayā*—developed by worship; *eka*—unalloyed; *bhaktyā*—by loving devotional service; *vidyā*—of knowledge; *kuṭhāreṇa*—by the ax; *śitena*—sharp; *dhīraḥ*—one who is steady by knowledge; *vivṛścya*—cutting down; *jīva*—of the living entity; *āśayam*—the subtle body (filled with designations created by the three modes of material nature); *apramattaḥ*—being very careful in spiritual life; *sampadya*—achieving; *ca*—and; *ātmānam*—the Supreme Personality of Godhead; *atha*—then; *tyaja*—you should give up; *astram*—the means by which you achieved perfection.

TRANSLATION

With steady intelligence you should develop unalloyed devotional service by careful worship of the spiritual master, and with the sharpened ax of transcendental knowledge you should cut off the subtle material covering of the soul. Upon realizing the Supreme Personality of Godhead, you should then give up that ax of analytic knowledge.

PURPORT

Because Uddhava had achieved the perfection of personal association with Lord Kṛṣṇa, there was no need for him to maintain the mentality of a conditioned soul, and thus, as described here by the words *sampadya cātmānam*, Uddhava could personally serve the lotus feet of the Lord in the spiritual world. Indeed, Uddhava requested this opportunity at the beginning of this great conversation. As stated here, *gurūpāsanayaika-bhaktyā:* one can achieve pure devotional service by worshiping a bona fide spiritual master. It is not recommended here that one give up pure devotional service or one's spiritual master. Rather, it is clearly stated by the words *vidyā-kuṭhāreṇa* that one should cultivate knowledge of the material world as described by Lord Kṛṣṇa in this chapter. One should fully understand that each and every aspect of the material creation is the expansion of the illusory potency of the Lord. Such knowledge works as a sharpened ax to cut down the roots of material existence. In this way, even the stubborn subtle body, created by the three modes of nature, is cut to pieces, and one becomes *apramatta*, or sane and cautious in Kṛṣṇa consciousness.

Lord Kṛṣṇa has clearly explained in this chapter that the cowherd damsels of Vṛndāvana were not interested in an analytical approach to life. They simply loved Lord Kṛṣṇa and could not think of anything else. Lord Caitanya Mahāprabhu taught that all His devotees should follow in the footsteps of the cowherd damsels of Vraja in order to develop the highest intensity of selfless love of Godhead. Lord Kṛṣṇa has elaborately analyzed the nature of the material world so that the conditioned souls, who are trying to enjoy it, can cut down the tree of material existence with this knowledge. The words *sampadya cātmānam* indicate that a person with such knowledge has no further material existence, because he has already achieved the Personality of Godhead. Such a person should not loiter in the kingdom of *māyā*, perpetually refining his understanding of the illusory creation. One who has accepted Lord Kṛṣṇa as everything may enjoy eternal bliss in the Lord's service. Yet even though he remains in this world, he has no more business with it and gives up the analytical procedures for negating it. Lord Kṛṣṇa therefore tells Uddhava, *tyajāstram:* "Give up the ax of analytic knowledge by which you have cut down your sense of proprietorship and residence in the material world."

Thus end the purports of the humble servants of His Divine Grace A. C. Bhaktivedanta Swami Prabhupāda, to the Eleventh Canto, Twelfth Chapter, of the Śrīmad-Bhāgavatam, *entitled "Beyond Renunciation and Knowledge."*

CHAPTER THIRTEEN

The Haṁsa-avatāra Answers the Questions of the Sons of Brahmā

In this chapter, Lord Śrī Kṛṣṇa explains to Uddhava how human beings, overwhelmed by sense gratification, become bound by the three modes of nature, and how to renounce these modes. The Lord then describes how He appeared in His form of Haṁsa before Brahmā and the four sages headed by Sanaka and revealed to them various confidential truths.

The three modes—goodness, passion and ignorance—are related to material intelligence, not to the soul. One should conquer the lower modes of passion and ignorance by the mode of goodness, and then one must surpass the mode of goodness by acting in the transcendental mode of pure goodness. By associating with things in the mode of goodness, one becomes more fully situated in that mode. The three modes increase their different influences through various types of scripture, water, place, time, beneficiaries of activity, natures of activity, birth, meditation, *mantras*, purificatory rituals, and so on.

Lacking discrimination, one identifies with the material body, and consequently the mode of passion, which produces misery, takes over the mind, which is normally in the mode of goodness. As the mind evolves its function of decision and doubt, it creates intolerable hankerings for sense gratification. Unfortunate persons who are bewildered by the urges of the mode of passion become the slaves of their senses. Even though they know that the eventual result of their work will be suffering, they cannot avoid engaging in such fruitive work. A discriminating person, on the other hand, keeps himself detached from the objects of the senses and, by utilizing appropriate renunciation, takes shelter of unalloyed devotional service.

Lord Brahmā himself has no material cause. He is the cause of the creation of all living beings and is the greatest among all the demigods. Yet even Brahmā is always suffering agitation of the mind on account of the duties he has to perform; therefore, when he was questioned by his sons headed by Sanaka, who were born from his mind, about the means for driving away desires for sense gratification, he was incapable of giving them an answer. In order to receive some insight into this matter, he took shelter of the Supreme Personality of Godhead, whereupon the Supreme Lord appeared before him in the form of the swan incarnation, Lord Haṁsa. Lord Haṁsa proceeded to give instructions about the categorical identity of the self, the different states of consciousness (wakeful awareness, sleep and deep sleep) and the means for conquering over material existence. The sages headed by Sanaka became freed from all their doubts by hearing the words of the Lord and worshiped Him with pure devotion in mature love of God.

TEXT 1

श्रीभगवानुवाच
सत्त्वं रजस्तम इति गुणा बुद्धेर्न चात्मनः ।
सत्त्वेनान्यतमौ हन्यात् सत्त्वं सत्त्वेन चैव हि ॥ १ ॥

śrī-bhagavān uvāca
sattvaṁ rajas tama iti
guṇā buddher na cātmanaḥ
sattvenānyatamau hanyāt
sattvaṁ sattvena caiva hi

śrī-bhagavān uvāca—the Supreme Personality of Godhead said; *sattvam*—goodness; *rajaḥ*—passion; *tamaḥ*—ignorance; *iti*—thus known; *guṇāḥ*—the modes of material nature; *buddheḥ*—pertain to material intelligence; *na*—not; *ca*—also; *ātmanaḥ*—to the soul; *sattvena*—by the material mode of goodness; *anyatamau*—the other two (passion and ignorance); *hanyāt*—may be destroyed; *sattvam*—the material mode of goodness; *sattvena*—by purified goodness; *ca*—also (may be destroyed); *eva*—certainly; *hi*—indeed.

TRANSLATION

The Supreme Personality of Godhead said: The three modes of material nature, namely goodness, passion and ignorance, pertain to material intelligence and not to the spirit soul. By development

of material goodness one can conquer the modes of passion and ignorance, and by cultivation of transcendental goodness one may free oneself even from material goodness.

PURPORT

Goodness in the material world never exists in a pure form. Therefore, it is common knowledge that on the material platform no one is working without personal motivation. In the material world goodness is always mixed with some amount of passion and ignorance, whereas spiritual, or purified, goodness (*viśuddha-sattva*) represents the liberated platform of perfection. Materially, one is proud to be an honest, compassionate man, but unless one is fully Kṛṣṇa conscious one will speak truths that are not ultimately significant, and one will give mercy that is ultimately useless. Because the onward march of material time removes all situations and persons from the material stage, our so-called mercy and truth apply to situations that shortly will not exist. Real truth is eternal, and real mercy means to situate people in eternal truth. Still, for an ordinary person, cultivation of material goodness may be a preliminary stage on the road to Kṛṣṇa consciousness. For example, it is stated in the Tenth Canto of *Śrīmad-Bhāgavatam* that one who is addicted to meat-eating cannot understand the pastimes of Lord Kṛṣṇa. By cultivation of the material mode of goodness, however, one may become a vegetarian and perhaps come to appreciate the sublime process of Kṛṣṇa consciousness. Since it is clearly stated in *Bhagavad-gītā* that the material modes of nature constantly rotate, one must take advantage of an elevated position in material goodness to step onto the transcendental platform. Otherwise, as the wheel of time turns one will again go into the darkness of material ignorance.

TEXT 2

सत्त्वाद् धर्मो भवेद् वृद्धात् पुंसो मद्भक्तिलक्षणः ।
सात्त्विकोपासया सत्त्वं ततो धर्मः प्रवर्तते ॥ २ ॥

sattvād dharmo bhaved vṛddhāt
puṁso mad-bhakti-lakṣaṇaḥ
sāttvikopāsayā sattvaṁ
tato dharmaḥ pravartate

sattvāt—from the mode of goodness; *dharmaḥ*—religious principles; *bhavet*—arise; *vṛddhāt*—which are strengthened; *puṁsaḥ*—of a person; *mat-bhakti*—by devotional service to Me; *lakṣaṇaḥ*—characterized; *sāttvika*—of things in the mode of goodness; *upāsayā*—by serious cultivation; *sattvam*—the mode of goodness; *tataḥ*—from that mode; *dharmaḥ*—religious principles; *pravartate*—arise.

TRANSLATION

When the living entity becomes strongly situated in the mode of goodness, then religious principles, characterized by devotional service to Me, become prominent. One can strengthen the mode of goodness by cultivation of those things that are already situated in goodness, and thus religious principles arise.

PURPORT

Since the three modes of material nature are constantly in conflict, vying for supremacy, how is it possible that the mode of goodness can subdue the modes of passion and ignorance? Lord Kṛṣṇa here explains how one can be strongly fixed in the mode of goodness, which automatically gives rise to religious principles. In the Fourteenth Chapter of *Bhagavad-gītā*, Lord Kṛṣṇa elaborately explains the things that are in goodness, passion and ignorance. Thus, by choosing food, attitudes, work, recreation, etc., strictly in the mode of goodness, one will become situated in that mode. The usefulness of *sattva-guṇa*, or the mode of goodness, is that it produces religious principles aimed at and characterized by devotional service to Lord Kṛṣṇa. Without such devotional service to the Lord, the mode of goodness is considered useless and merely another aspect of material illusion. The word *vṛddhāt*, or "strengthened, increased," indicates clearly that one should come to the platform of *viśuddha-sattva*, or purified goodness. The word *vṛddhāt* indicates growth, and growth should not be stopped until full maturity is reached. The full maturity of goodness is called *viśuddha-sattva*, or the transcendental platform on which there is no trace of any other quality. In pure goodness all knowledge automatically manifests, and one can easily understand one's eternal loving relationship with Lord Kṛṣṇa. That is the actual meaning and purpose of *dharma*, or religious principles.

Śrīla Madhvācārya points out in this regard that an increase in the mode of goodness strengthens religious principles and the invigorated execution of religious principles strengthens the mode of goodness. In that way, one can advance higher and higher in the mode of spiritual happiness.

TEXT 3

धर्मो रजस्तमो हन्यात् सत्त्ववृद्धिरनुत्तमः ।
आशु नश्यति तन्मूलो ह्यधर्म उभये हते ॥ ३ ॥

dharmo rajas tamo hanyāt
sattva-vṛddhir anuttamaḥ
āśu naśyati tan-mūlo
hy adharma ubhaye hate

dharmaḥ—religious principles based on devotional service; *rajaḥ*—the mode of passion; *tamaḥ*—the mode of ignorance; *hanyāt*—destroy; *sattva*—of goodness; *vṛddhiḥ*—by the increase; *anuttamaḥ*—the greatest; *āśu*—quickly; *naśyati*—is destroyed; *tat*—of passion and ignorance; *mūlaḥ*—the root; *hi*—certainly; *adharmaḥ*—irreligion; *ubhaye hate*—when both are destroyed.

TRANSLATION

Religious principles, strengthened by the mode of goodness, destroy the influence of passion and ignorance. When passion and ignorance are overcome, their original cause, irreligion, is quickly vanquished.

TEXT 4

आगमोऽपः प्रजा देशः कालः कर्म च जन्म च ।
ध्यानं मन्त्रोऽथ संस्कारो दशैते गुणहेतवः ॥ ४ ॥

āgamo 'paḥ prajā deśaḥ
kālaḥ karma ca janma ca
dhyānaṁ mantro 'tha saṁskāro
daśaite guṇa-hetavaḥ

āgamaḥ—religious scriptures; *apaḥ*—water; *prajāḥ*—association with people in general or one's children; *deśaḥ*—place; *kālaḥ*—time; *karma*—activities; *ca*—also; *janma*—birth; *ca*—also; *dhyānam*—meditation; *mantraḥ*—chanting of *mantras;* *atha*—and; *saṁskāraḥ*—rituals for purification; *daśa*—ten; *ete*—these; *guṇa*—of the modes of nature; *hetavaḥ*—causes.

TRANSLATION

According to the quality of religious scriptures, water, one's association with one's children or with people in general, the particular place, the time, activities, birth, meditation, chanting of mantras, and purificatory rituals, the modes of nature become differently prominent.

PURPORT

The ten items mentioned above possess superior and inferior qualities and are thus identified as being in goodness, passion or ignorance. One can increase the mode of goodness by selecting religious scriptures in goodness, pure water, friendship with other persons in goodness, and so on. One should scrupulously avoid any of these ten items that may be polluted by an inferior mode of nature.

TEXT 5

तत्तत् सात्त्विकमेवैषां यद् यद् वृद्धाः प्रचक्षते ।
निन्दन्ति तामसं तत्तद् राजसं तदुपेक्षितम् ॥ ५ ॥

tat tat sāttvikam evaiṣāṁ
yad yad vṛddhāḥ pracakṣate
nindanti tāmasaṁ tat tad
rājasaṁ tad-upekṣitam

tat tat—those things; *sāttvikam*—in the mode of goodness; *eva*—indeed; *eṣām*—among the ten items; *yat yat*—whatever; *vṛddhāḥ*—the sages of the past, such as Vyāsadeva, who are expert in Vedic knowledge; *pracakṣate*—they praise; *nindanti*—they scorn; *tāmasam*—in the mode of ignorance; *tat tat*—those things; *rājasam*—in the mode of passion; *tat*—by the sages; *upekṣitam*—left alone, neither praised nor criticized.

TRANSLATION

Among the ten items I have just mentioned, the great sages who understand Vedic knowledge have praised and recommended those that are in the mode of goodness, criticized and rejected those in the mode of ignorance, and shown indifference to those in the mode of passion.

TEXT 6

सात्त्विकान्येव सेवेत पुमान् सत्त्वविवृद्धये ।
ततो धर्मस्ततो ज्ञानं यावत् स्मृतिरपोहनम् ॥ ६ ॥

sāttvikāny eva seveta
pumān sattva-vivṛddhaye
tato dharmas tato jñānaṁ
yāvat smṛtir apohanam

sāttvikāni—things in the mode of goodness; *eva*—indeed; *seveta*—he should cultivate; *pumān*—a person; *sattva*—the mode of goodness; *vivṛddhaye*—in order to increase; *tataḥ*—from that (increase in goodness); *dharmaḥ*—one is fixed in religious principles; *tataḥ*—from that (religion); *jñānam*—knowledge is manifest; *yāvat*—until; *smṛtiḥ*—self-realization, remembering one's eternal identity; *apohanam*—driving away (the illusory identification with the material body and mind).

TRANSLATION

Until one revives one's direct knowledge of the spirit soul and drives away the illusory identification with the material body and mind caused by the three modes of nature, one must cultivate those things in the mode of goodness. By increasing the mode of goodness one automatically can understand and practice religious principles, and by such practice transcendental knowledge is awakened.

PURPORT

One who desires to cultivate the mode of goodness must consider the following points. One should study religious scriptures that teach detachment from mental speculation and material sense gratification, not scriptures that provide rituals and *mantras* to increase material ignorance.

Such materialistic scriptures do not give attention to the Supreme Personality of Godhead and thus are basically atheistic. One should accept pure water for quenching thirst and cleaning the body. There is no need for a devotee to use colognes, perfume, whiskey, beer, etc., which are all polluted manifestations of water. One should associate with persons who are cultivating detachment from the material world and not with those who are materially attached or sinful in their behavior. One should live in a solitary place where devotional service is practiced and discussed among Vaiṣṇavas. One should not be spontaneously attracted to busy highways, shopping centers, sports stadiums, and so on. Concerning time, one should rise by four o'clock in the morning and utilize the auspicious *brāhma-muhūrta* to advance in Kṛṣṇa consciousness. Similarly, one should avoid the sinful influence of hours such as midnight, when ghosts and demons are encouraged to become active. Concerning work, one should execute one's prescribed duties, follow the regulative principles of spiritual life and utilize all of one's energy for pious purposes. Time should not be wasted in frivolous or materialistic activities, of which there are now literally millions in modern society. One can cultivate birth in the mode of goodness by accepting the second birth of initiation from a bona fide spiritual master and learning to chant the Hare Kṛṣṇa *mantra.* One should not accept initiation or so-called spiritual birth in unauthorized mystical or religious cults in the modes of passion and ignorance. One should meditate upon the Supreme Personality of Godhead as the enjoyer of all sacrifices, and similarly, one should meditate on the lives of great devotees and saintly persons. One should not meditate on lusty women and envious men. Concerning *mantras,* one should follow the example of Śrī Caitanya Mahāprabhu by chanting the Hare Kṛṣṇa *mantra* and not other songs, verses, poetry or *mantras* that glorify the kingdom of illusion. Purificatory rituals should be performed to purify the spirit soul and not to bring down material blessings on one's material household.

One who increases the mode of goodness will certainly become fixed in religious principles, and automatically knowledge will arise. As knowledge increases one is able to understand the eternal spirit soul and the Supreme Soul, Lord Kṛṣṇa. Thus the soul becomes free from the artificial imposition of the gross and subtle material bodies caused by the modes of material nature. Spiritual knowledge burns to ashes the material designations that cover the living entity, and one's real, eternal life begins.

TEXT 7

वेणुसङ्घर्षजो वह्निर्दग्ध्वा शाम्यति तद्वनम् ।
एवं गुणव्यत्ययजो देहः शाम्यति तत्क्रियः ॥ ७ ॥

veṇu-saṅgharṣa-jo vahnir
dagdhvā śāmyati tad-vanam
evaṁ guṇa-vyatyaya-jo
dehaḥ śāmyati tat-kriyaḥ

veṇu—of bamboo; *saṅgharṣa-jaḥ*—generated by the friction; *vahniḥ*—fire; *dagdhvā*—having burned; *śāmyati*—is pacified; *tat*—of bamboo; *vanam*—the forest; *evam*—thus; *guṇa*—of the modes of nature; *vyatyaya-jaḥ*—generated by interaction; *dehaḥ*—the material body; *śāmyati*—is pacified; *tat*—as the fire; *kriyaḥ*—performing the same action.

TRANSLATION

In a bamboo forest the wind sometimes rubs the bamboo stalks together, and such friction generates a blazing fire that consumes the very source of its birth, the bamboo forest. Thus, the fire is automatically calmed by its own action. Similarly, by the competition and interaction of the material modes of nature, the subtle and gross material bodies are generated. If one uses his mind and body to cultivate knowledge, then such enlightenment destroys the influence of the modes of nature that generated one's body. Thus, like the fire, the body and mind are pacified by their own actions in destroying the source of their birth.

PURPORT

The word *guṇa-vyatyaya-jaḥ* is significant in this verse. *Vyatyaya* indicates change or inversion in the normal order of things. Śrīla Bhaktisiddhānta Sarasvatī Ṭhākura has described the concept of *vyatyaya* by giving the Sanskrit synonym *vaiṣamya*, which indicates inequality or disproportionate diversity. Thus, it is understood by the term *guṇa-vyatyaya-jaḥ* that the body is generated by the unstable relationships of the three modes of material nature, which exist everywhere in constantly changing proportions. There is constant strife among the modes of nature. A good person is sometimes torn by passion, and a passionate person sometimes wants to give up everything and rest. An ignorant person may sometimes become disgusted with his depraved life, and a passionate person may sometimes indulge in bad habits in the mode of ignorance. Due to the interactive conflict of the modes of nature, one wanders throughout material nature creating one body after another by one's own work, *karma.* As it is said, variety is the mother of enjoyment, and the variety of material modes gives hope to the conditioned souls that by changing their material situation their unhappiness and frustration can be turned into happiness and satisfaction. But even if one acquires relative material happiness, that will soon be disturbed by the inevitable flux of the material modes.

TEXT 8

श्रीउद्धव उवाच
विदन्ति मर्त्याः प्रायेण विषयान् पदमापदाम् ।
तथापि भुञ्जते कृष्ण तत् कथं श्वखराजवत् ॥ ८ ॥

śrī-uddhava uvāca
vidanti martyāḥ prāyeṇa
viṣayān padam āpadām
tathāpi bhuñjate kṛṣṇa
tat kathaṁ śva-kharāja-vat

śrī-uddhavaḥ uvāca—Śrī Uddhava said; *vidanti*—they know; *martyāḥ*—human beings; *prāyeṇa*—generally; *viṣayān*—sense gratification; *padam*—a situation; *āpadām*—of many miserable conditions; *tathā api*—even so; *bhuñjate*—they enjoy; *kṛṣṇa*—O Kṛṣṇa; *tat*—such sense gratification; *katham*—how is it possible; *śva*—dogs; *khara*—asses; *aja*—and goats; *vat*—just like.

TRANSLATION

Śrī Uddhava said: My dear Kṛṣṇa, generally human beings know that material life brings great future unhappiness, and still they try to enjoy material life. My dear Lord, how can one in knowledge act just like a dog, an ass or a goat?

PURPORT

The standard methods of enjoyment in the material world are sex, money and false prestige, all of which are obtained with great suffering and eventually lost. One engaged in material life suffers in the present and has only a very bleak future to look forward to in the continuing cycle of birth and death. Thus, how can human beings who have seen these things and know them very well continue to enjoy life like dogs, asses and goats? Often a dog will approach a bitch for sex, but the lady dog may not be attracted and will show her teeth, snarl and threaten the poor dog with serious injury. Still he goes about his business trying to get a little sex pleasure. Similarly, many times a dog risks being beaten or shot while stealing some food in a place where he knows he should not go. The ass is very attracted to the she-ass, but the lady ass often kicks him in the legs. Similarly, the ass's master gives the ass a handful of grass, which the poor ass could get anywhere, and then burdens him with great loads. The goat is generally raised for slaughter, and even when the goat is brought into the slaughterhouse he shamelessly goes after the lady goat to get sex pleasure. In this way, even at the risk of being shot, bitten, beaten and slaughtered, animals persist in their foolish sense gratification. How can an educated human being commit himself to such a condemned way of life, wherein the result is practically the same as that of the animals? If by cultivating the mode of goodness one's life is filled with happiness, enlightenment and future rewards, why would anyone cultivate the modes of passion and ignorance? This is Uddhava's question.

TEXTS 9–10

श्रीभगवानुवाच
अहमित्यन्यथाबुद्धिः प्रमत्तस्य यथा हृदि ।
उत्सर्पति रजो घोरं ततो वैकारिकं मनः ॥९॥
रजोयुक्तस्य मनसः सङ्कल्पः सविकल्पकः ।
ततः कामो गुणध्यानाद् दुःसहः स्याद्धि दुर्मतेः॥१०॥

śrī-bhagavān uvāca
aham ity anyathā-buddhiḥ
pramattasya yathā hṛdi

utsarpati rajo ghoraṁ
tato vaikārikaṁ manaḥ

rajo-yuktasya manasaḥ
saṅkalpaḥ sa-vikalpakaḥ
tataḥ kāmo guṇa-dhyānād
duḥsahaḥ syād dhi durmateḥ

śrī-bhagavān uvāca—the Supreme Personality of Godhead said; *aham*—false identification with the material body and mind; *iti*—thus; *anyathā-buddhiḥ*—illusory knowledge; *pramattasya*—of one who is bereft of actual intelligence; *yathā*—accordingly; *hṛdi*—within the mind; *utsarpati*—arises; *rajaḥ*—passion; *ghoram*—which brings terrible suffering; *tataḥ*—then; *vaikārikam*—(originally) in the mode of goodness; *manaḥ*—the mind; *rajaḥ*—in passion; *yuktasya*—of that which is engaged; *manasaḥ*—of the mind; *saṅkalpaḥ*—material determination; *sa-vikalpakaḥ*—along with variation and alternation; *tataḥ*—from that; *kāmaḥ*—full-fledged material desire; *guṇa*—in the modes of nature; *dhyānāt*—from concentration; *duḥsahaḥ*—unbearable; *syāt*—it must so be; *hi*—certainly; *durmateḥ*—of a foolish person.

TRANSLATION

The Supreme Personality of Godhead said: My dear Uddhava, a person bereft of intelligence first falsely identifies himself with the material body and mind, and when such false knowledge arises within one's consciousness, material passion, the cause of great suffering, pervades the mind, which by nature is situated in goodness. Then the mind, contaminated by passion, becomes absorbed in making and changing many plans for material advancement. Thus, by constantly thinking of the modes of material nature, a foolish person is afflicted with unbearable material desires.

PURPORT

Those who are trying to enjoy material sense gratification are not actually intelligent, although they consider themselves most intelligent. Although such foolish persons themselves criticize the miseries of material life in innumerable books, songs, newspapers, television programs, civic committees, etc., they cannot desist from material life for a single moment. The process by which one is helplessly bound in illusion is clearly described here.

A materialistic person is always thinking, "Oh, what a beautiful house. I wish we could buy it" or "What a beautiful woman. I wish I could touch her" or "What a powerful position. I wish I could occupy it," and so on. The words *saṅkalpaḥ sa-vikalpakaḥ* indicate that a materialist is always making new plans or modifying his old plans to increase his material enjoyment, although in his saner moments he admits that material life is full of suffering. The mind is created from the mode of goodness, as described in Sāṅkhya philosophy, and the natural, peaceful situation of the mind is pure love of Kṛṣṇa, in which there is no mental disturbance, disappointment or confusion. Artificially, the mind is dragged down to a lower platform in passion or ignorance, and thus one is never satisfied.

TEXT 11

करोति कामवशगः कर्माण्यविजितेन्द्रियः ।
दुःखोदर्काणि सम्पश्यन् रजोवेगविमोहितः ॥११॥

karoti kāma-vaśa-gaḥ
karmāṇy avijitendriyaḥ
duḥkhodarkāṇi sampaśyan
rajo-vega-vimohitaḥ

karoti—performs; *kāma*—of material desires; *vaśa*—under the control; *gaḥ*—having gone; *karmāṇi*—fruitive activities; *avijita*—uncontrolled; *indriyaḥ*—whose senses; *duḥkha*—unhappiness; *udarkāṇi*—bringing as a future result; *sampaśyan*—seeing clearly; *rajaḥ*—of the mode of passion; *vega*—by the force; *vimohitaḥ*—bewildered.

TRANSLATION

One who does not control the material senses comes under the control of material desires and is thus bewildered by the strong waves of the mode of passion. Such a person executes material activities, although clearly seeing that the result will be future unhappiness.

TEXT 12

रजस्तमोभ्यां यदपि विद्वान् विक्षिप्तधीः पुनः ।
अतन्द्रितो मनो युञ्जन् दोषदृष्टिर्न सज्जते ॥१२॥

rajas-tamobhyāṁ yad api
vidvān vikṣipta-dhīḥ punaḥ
atandrito mano yuñjan
doṣa-dṛṣṭir na sajjate

rajaḥ-tamobhyām—by the modes of passion and ignorance; *yat api*—even though; *vidvān*—a learned person; *vikṣipta*—bewildered; *dhīḥ*—the intelligence; *punaḥ*—again; *atandritaḥ*—carefully; *manaḥ*—the mind; *yuñjan*—engaging; *doṣa*—the contamination of material attachment; *dṛṣṭiḥ*—seeing clearly; *na*—not; *sajjate*—becomes attached.

TRANSLATION

Although the intelligence of a learned person may be bewildered by the modes of passion and ignorance, he should again carefully bring the mind under control. By clearly seeing the contamination of the modes of nature, he does not become attached.

TEXT 13

अप्रमत्तोऽनुयुञ्जीत मनो मय्यर्पयञ्छनैः ।
अनिर्विण्णो यथाकालं जितश्वासो जितासनः ॥१३॥

apramatto 'nuyuñjīta
mano mayy arpayañ chanaiḥ
anirviṇṇo yathā-kālaṁ
jita-śvāso jitāsanaḥ

apramattaḥ—attentive and grave; *anuyuñjīta*—one should fix; *manaḥ*—the mind; *mayi*—in Me; *arpayan*—placing; *śanaiḥ*—gradually, step by step; *anirviṇṇaḥ*—without being lazy or morose; *yathā-kālam*—at least three times a day (dawn, noon and sunset); *jita*—having conquered; *śvāsaḥ*—the breathing process; *jita*—having conquered; *āsanaḥ*—the sitting postures.

TRANSLATION

A person should be attentive and grave and never lazy or morose. Mastering the yoga procedures of breathing and sitting properly, one should practice placing the mind in Me at dawn, noon and sunset, and thus gradually the mind should be completely absorbed in Me.

TEXT 14

एतावान् योग आदिष्टो मच्छिष्यैः सनकादिभिः।
सर्वतो मन आकृष्य मय्यद्धावेश्यते यथा ॥१४॥

etāvān yoga ādiṣṭo
mac-chiṣyaiḥ sanakādibhiḥ
sarvato mana ākṛṣya
mayy addhāveśyate yathā

etāvān—actually this; *yogaḥ*—yoga system; *ādiṣṭaḥ*—instructed; *mat-śiṣyaiḥ*—by My devotees; *sanaka-ādibhiḥ*—headed by Sanaka-kumāra; *sarvataḥ*—from all sides; *manaḥ*—the mind; *ākṛṣya*—withdrawing; *mayi*—in Me; *addhā*—directly; *āveśyate*—is absorbed; *yathā*—accordingly.

TRANSLATION

The actual yoga system as taught by My devotees, headed by Sanaka-kumāra, is simply this: Having withdrawn the mind from all other objects, one should directly and appropriately absorb it in Me.

PURPORT

The word *yathā* ("accordingly" or "properly") indicates that like Uddhava one should hear directly from Lord Kṛṣṇa or His bona fide representative and directly (*addhā*) fix the mind in Lord Kṛṣṇa.

TEXT 15

श्रीउद्धव उवाच

यदा त्वं सनकादिभ्यो येन रूपेण केशव ।
योगमादिष्टवानेतद् रूपमिच्छामि वेदितुम् ॥१५॥

śrī-uddhava uvāca
yadā tvaṁ sanakādibhyo
yena rūpeṇa keśava
yogam ādiṣṭavān etad
rūpam icchāmi veditum

śrī-uddhavaḥ uvāca—Śrī Uddhava said; *yadā*—when; *tvam*—You; *sanaka-ādibhyaḥ*—to Sanaka, etc.; *yena*—by which; *rūpeṇa*—form; *keśava*—my dear Keśava; *yogam*—the process of fixing the mind in the Absolute Truth; *ādiṣṭavān*—You have instructed; *etat*—that; *rūpam*—form; *icchāmi*—I desire; *veditum*—to know.

TRANSLATION

Śrī Uddhava said: My dear Keśava, at what time and in what form did You instruct the science of yoga to Sanaka and others? I now desire to know about these things.

TEXT 16

श्रीभगवानुवाच
पुत्रा हिरण्यगर्भस्य मानसाः सनकादयः ।
पप्रच्छुः पितरं सूक्ष्मां योगस्यैकान्तिकीं गतिम् ॥ १६ ॥

śrī-bhagavān uvāca
putrā hiraṇyagarbhasya
mānasāḥ sanakādayaḥ
papracchuḥ pitaraṁ sūkṣmāṁ
yogasyaikāntikīṁ gatim

śrī-bhagavān uvāca—the Supreme Personality of Godhead; *putrāḥ*—the sons; *hiraṇya-garbhasya*—of Lord Brahmā; *mānasāḥ*—born of the mind; *sanaka-ādayaḥ*—headed by Sanaka Ṛṣi; *papracchuḥ*—inquired; *pitaram*—from their father (Brahmā); *sūkṣmām*—subtle and therefore difficult to understand; *yogasya*—of the science of *yoga;* *ekāntikīm*—the supreme; *gatim*—destination.

TRANSLATION

The Supreme Personality of Godhead said: Once, the mental sons of Lord Brahmā, namely, the sages headed by Sanaka, inquired from their father about the difficult subject matter of the supreme goal of yoga.

TEXT 17

सनकादय ऊचुः

गुणेष्वाविशते चेतो गुणाश्चेतसि च प्रभो ।
कथमन्योन्यसंत्यागो मुमुक्षोरतितितीर्षोः ॥१७॥

sanakādaya ūcuḥ
guṇeṣv āviśate ceto
guṇāś cetasi ca prabho
katham anyonya-santyāgo
mumukṣor atititīrṣoḥ

sanaka-ādayaḥ ūcuḥ—the sages headed by Sanaka said; *guṇeṣu*—in the sense objects; *āviśate*—directly enters; *cetaḥ*—the mind; *guṇāḥ*—the sense objects; *cetasi*—within the mind; *ca*—also (enter); *prabho*—O Lord; *katham*—what is the process; *anyonya*—of the mutual relationship between the sense objects and the mind; *santyāgaḥ*—renunciation; *mumukṣoḥ*—of one desiring liberation; *atititīrṣoḥ*—of one desiring to cross over sense gratification.

TRANSLATION

The sages headed by Sanaka said: O Lord, people's minds are naturally attracted to material sense objects, and similarly the sense objects in the form of desire enter within the mind. Therefore, how can a person who desires liberation, who desires to cross over activities of sense gratification, destroy this mutual relationship between the sense objects and the mind? Please explain this to us.

PURPORT

As described above, as long as one is a conditioned soul the modes of material nature, manifested in the form of sense objects, constantly disturb the mind, and by their harassment one is deprived of the actual perfection of life.

TEXT 18

श्रीभगवानुवाच
एवं पृष्टो महादेवः स्वयंभूर्भूतभावनः ।
ध्यायमानः प्रश्नबीजं नाभ्यपद्यत कर्मधीः ॥१८॥

śrī-bhagavān uvāca
evaṁ pṛṣṭo mahā-devaḥ
svayambhūr bhūta-bhāvanaḥ
dhyāyamānaḥ praśna-bījaṁ
nābhyapadyata karma-dhīḥ

śrī-bhagavān uvāca—the Supreme Personality of Godhead said; *evam*—thus; *pṛṣṭaḥ*—questioned; *mahā-devaḥ*—the great god Brahmā; *svayam-bhūḥ*—without material birth (born directly from the body of Garbhodakaśāyī Viṣṇu); *bhūta*—of all conditioned souls; *bhāvanaḥ*—the creator (of their conditioned life); *dhyāyamānaḥ*—seriously considering; *praśna*—of the question; *bījam*—the essential truth; *na abhyapadyata*—did not reach; *karma-dhīḥ*—intelligence bewildered by his own activities of creation.

TRANSLATION

The Supreme Personality of Godhead said: My dear Uddhava, Brahmā himself, who is born directly from the body of the Lord and who is the creator of all living entities within the material world, being the best of the demigods, seriously contemplated the question of his sons headed by Sanaka. The intelligence of Brahmā, however, was affected by his own activities of creation, and thus he could not discover the essential answer to this question.

PURPORT

Śrīla Jīva Gosvāmī has quoted three verses from the Second Canto of *Śrīmad-Bhāgavatam* as follows. In the Ninth Chapter, verse 32, Lord Kṛṣṇa blessed Brahmā with realized knowledge of the Lord's actual form, qualities and activities. In the Ninth Chapter, verse 37, the Lord ordered Brahmā to rigidly carry out the Lord's injunctions and affirmed that Brahmā would thus never be bewildered in his cosmic decision-making. In the Sixth Chapter, verse 34, Lord Brahmā assured his son Nārada, "O Nārada, because I have caught hold of the lotus feet of the Supreme Personality of Godhead, Hari, with great zeal, whatever I say has never proved to have been false, nor is the progress of my mind ever deterred, nor are my senses ever degraded by temporary attachment to matter."

In the present verse in this Thirteenth Chapter of the Eleventh Canto, Lord Kṛṣṇa states that Brahmā unfortunately did become bewildered by his creative functions, thus providing a grave lesson to all of the Lord's empowered representatives. Although one may be elevated to an exalted position in the Lord's transcendental service, at any moment there is danger of false pride polluting one's devotional mentality.

TEXT 19

स मामचिन्तयद् देवः प्रश्नपारतितीर्षया ।
तस्याहं हंसरूपेण सकाशमगमं तदा ॥१९॥

sa mām acintayad devaḥ
praśna-pāra-titīrṣayā
tasyāhaṁ haṁsa-rūpeṇa
sakāśam agamaṁ tadā

saḥ—he (Lord Brahmā); *mām*—Me; *acintayat*—remembered; *devaḥ*—the original demigod; *praśna*—of the question; *pāra*—the end, conclusion (the answer); *titīrṣayā*—with a desire to attain, understand; *tasya*—unto him; *aham*—I; *haṁsa-rūpeṇa*—in My form of Haṁsa; *sakāśam*—visible; *agamam*—became; *tadā*—at that time.

TRANSLATION

Lord Brahmā desired to attain the answer to the question that was puzzling him, and thus he fixed his mind in Me, the Supreme Lord. At that time, in My form of Haṁsa, I became visible to Lord Brahmā.

PURPORT

Haṁsa means "swan," and the specific ability of the swan is to separate a mixture of milk and water, extracting the rich, milky portion. Similarly, Lord Kṛṣṇa appeared as Haṁsa, or the swan, in order to separate the pure consciousness of Lord Brahmā from the modes of material nature.

TEXT 20

दृष्ट्वा मां त उपव्रज्य कृत्वा पादाभिवन्दनम् ।
ब्रह्माणमग्रतः कृत्वा पप्रच्छुः को भवानिति ॥२०॥

dṛṣṭvā māṁ ta upavrajya
kṛtvā pādābhivandanam
brahmāṇam agrataḥ kṛtvā
papracchuḥ ko bhavān iti

dṛṣṭvā—thus seeing; *māṃ*—Me; *te*—they (the sages); *upavrajya*—approaching; *kṛtvā*—offering; *pāda*—at the lotus feet; *abhivandanam*—obeisances; *brahmāṇam*—Lord Brahmā; *agrataḥ*—in front; *kṛtvā*—keeping; *papracchuḥ*—they asked; *kaḥ bhavān*—"who are You, sir?"; *iti*—thus.

TRANSLATION

Thus seeing Me, the sages, placing Brahmā in the lead, came forward and worshiped My lotus feet. Then they frankly asked Me, "Who are You?"

PURPORT

Śrīla Bhaktisiddhānta Sarasvatī Ṭhākura comments, "When Brahmā was unable to answer the question placed by the sages, he fixed his mind in thought of the Supreme Lord. The Lord then assumed the form of Haṁsa and appeared before Lord Brahmā and the sages, who proceeded to inquire about the specific identity of the Lord."

TEXT 21

इत्यहं मुनिभिः पृष्टस्तत्त्वजिज्ञासुभिस्तदा ।
यदवोचमहं तेभ्यस्तदुद्धव निबोध मे ॥२१॥

ity ahaṁ munibhiḥ pṛṣṭas
tattva-jijñāsubhis tadā
yad avocam ahaṁ tebhyas
tad uddhava nibodha me

iti—thus; *aham*—I; *munibhiḥ*—by the sages; *pṛṣṭaḥ*—questioned; *tattva*—the truth about the goal of *yoga; jijñāsubhiḥ*—by those desiring to know; *tadā*—at that time; *yat*—that which; *avocam*—spoke; *aham*—I; *tebhyaḥ*—unto them; *tat*—that; *uddhava*—My dear Uddhava; *nibodha*—please learn; *me*—from Me.

TRANSLATION

My dear Uddhava, the sages, being eager to understand the ultimate truth of the yoga system, thus inquired from Me. Now please hear as I explain that which I spoke unto the sages.

TEXT 22

वस्तुनो यद्यनानात्व आत्मनः प्रश्न ईदृशः ।
कथं घटेत वो विप्रा वक्तुर्वा मे क आश्रयः ॥२२॥

vastuno yady anānātva
ātmanaḥ praśna īdṛśaḥ
kathaṁ ghaṭeta vo viprā
vaktur vā me ka āśrayaḥ

vastunaḥ—of the essential reality; *yadi*—if; *anānātve*—in the concept of nonindividuality; *ātmanaḥ*—of the *jīva* soul; *praśnaḥ*—question; *īdṛśaḥ*—such; *katham*—how; *ghaṭeta*—is it possible or appropriate; *vaḥ*—of you who are asking; *viprāḥ*—O *brāhmaṇas; vaktuḥ*—of the speaker; *vā*—or; *me*—of Me; *kaḥ*—what is; *āśrayaḥ*—the real situation or resting place.

TRANSLATION

My dear brāhmaṇas, if, when asking Me who I am, you believe that I am also a jīva soul and that there is no ultimate difference between us since all souls are ultimately one without individuality, then how is your question possible or appropriate? Ultimately, what is the real situation or resting place both of yourselves and of Me?

PURPORT

Āśraya means "the resting place" or "shelter." Lord Kṛṣṇa's question "What is our actual resting place or shelter?" means "What is our ultimate nature or constitutional position?" This is because no one can come to rest or be satisfied unless one is in one's natural position. The example is given that one may travel all over the world, but ultimately one becomes satisfied by returning to one's own home. Similarly, a crying child is satisfied when embraced by its own mother. By inquiring about the shelter or resting place of Himself and the *brāhmaṇas,* the Lord is indicating the eternal, constitutional position of every living entity.

If Lord Kṛṣṇa were also in the *jīva* category, and if all living entities including Him were thus equal, there would be no deep purpose in one living entity inquiring and another answering. Only one who is in a superior position can meaningfully answer important questions. It may be argued that the bona fide spiritual master answers all the questions of the disciple, and yet the *guru* is in the *jīva* category. The answer is that the bona fide spiritual master speaks not on his own behalf but as a representative of the Supreme Personality of Godhead, who is in the Viṣṇu category. A so-called *guru* speaking on his own behalf as a *jīva* soul is useless and is unable to meaningfully answer serious questions. Thus, the sages' question *ko bhavān* ("Who are You?") indicates that the Supreme Personality of Godhead is eternally an individual person. And because the sages headed by Lord Brahmā offered obeisances and worshiped the Lord, it is understood that He is the Supreme Personality of Godhead. Lord Brahmā, as the first created being in this universe, could not accept any other living entity except the Lord as worshipable.

Lord Kṛṣṇa's actual purpose is to explain the ultimate perfection of *yoga*, which the sages were desiring to know. If one becomes fixed in transcendental knowledge, the mutual attraction between the material mind and the material sense objects automatically ceases. The spiritual mind is not attracted to material objects of gratification, and thus by spiritualizing the mind, material existence automatically slackens. By questioning the propriety of the sages' question, the Lord is assuming the position of the spiritual master and preparing to give valuable instructions. One should never be envious of a bona fide spiritual master, especially if, as in the case of Lord Haṁsa speaking to the sages headed by Brahmā and Sanaka-kumāra, the *guru* is the Supreme Personality of Godhead Himself.

TEXT 23

पञ्चात्मकेषु भूतेषु समानेषु च वस्तुतः ।
को भवानिति वः प्रश्नो वाचारम्भो ह्यनर्थकः ॥२३॥

pañcātmakeṣu bhūteṣu
samāneṣu ca vastutaḥ
ko bhavān iti vaḥ praśno
vācārambho hy anarthakaḥ

pañca—of five elements; *ātmakeṣu*—made of; *bhūteṣu*—thus existing; *samāneṣu*—being the same; *ca*—also; *vastutaḥ*—in essence; *kaḥ*—who; *bhavān*—are You; *iti*—thus; *vaḥ*—your; *praśnaḥ*—question; *vācā*—merely with words; *ārambhaḥ*—such an endeavor; *hi*—certainly; *anarthakaḥ*—without real meaning or purpose.

TRANSLATION

If by asking Me "Who are You?" you were referring to the material body, then I must point out that all material bodies are constituted of five elements, namely earth, water, fire, air and ether. Thus, you should have asked, "Who are you five?" If you consider

that all material bodies are ultimately one, being constituted essentially of the same elements, then your question is still meaningless, since there would be no deep purpose in distinguishing one body from another. Thus, it appears that in asking My identity, you are merely speaking words, without any real meaning or purpose.

PURPORT

Śrīla Viśvanātha Cakravartī Ṭhākura explains this verse as follows. "In the previous verse Lord Kṛṣṇa demonstrated that if the sages accepted the impersonal philosophy that all living beings are ultimately one in all respects, their question 'Who are You?' was meaningless, since there would be no philosophical basis to distinguish one manifestation of spirit soul from another. In this verse the Lord refutes the false identification with the material body composed of five elements. If the sages accepted the body as the self, then their question was meaningless, since they would have to ask, 'Who are you five?' If the sages replied that although the body is composed basically of five elements and these elements combine and thus form one unique substance, then the Lord has already replied by the words *samāneṣu ca vastutaḥ.* The bodies of human beings, demigods, animals, etc., are all composed of the same five elements and are essentially the same. Therefore the question 'Who are You?' is ultimately meaningless. Thus, if one accepts either the theory that all living entities are ultimately the same or the theory that all living entities are ultimately nondifferent from their material bodies, in both cases the question of the sages is meaningless.

"The sages might argue that even among learned persons it is common practice to ask questions and give answers on many subjects as a part of normal life. The sages could point out that Lord Kṛṣṇa also distinguished among them, by His saying *viprāḥ*, 'O *brāhmaṇas*,' and *vaḥ*, or 'your [question],' as expressed in this verse. In this way it is seen that the Lord also accepts the ordinary customs of questions and answers. To answer this argument, Lord Kṛṣṇa states, *vācārambho hy anarthakaḥ.* The Lord states, 'My addressing you as *brāhmaṇas* is merely an exhibition of words if we are ultimately not different. I merely reciprocated with your approach to Me. Therefore, if we are ultimately one, neither My statement nor your question has any real meaning. I can conclude therefore by your question to Me that you are all not actually very intelligent. Therefore, why are you inquiring after ultimate knowledge? Aren't you all embarrassed?' "

Śrīla Madhvācārya points out in this regard that the question of the sages was not appropriate, since they had already seen their father, Lord Brahmā, worshiping the lotus feet of Lord Haṁsa. Since their spiritual master and father was worshiping Lord Haṁsa, they should have immediately understood the Lord's position, and their question is thus meaningless.

TEXT 24

मनसा वचसा दृष्ट्या गृह्यतेऽन्यैरपीन्द्रियैः ।
अहमेव न मत्तोऽन्यदिति बुध्यध्वमञ्जसा ॥२४॥

manasā vacasā dṛṣṭyā
gṛhyate 'nyair apīndriyaiḥ
aham eva na matto 'nyad
iti budhyadhvam añjasā

manasā—by the mind; *vacasā*—by speech; *dṛṣṭyā*—by sight; *gṛhyate*—is perceived and thus accepted; *anyaiḥ*—by others; *api*—even; *indriyaiḥ*—senses; *aham*—I; *eva*—indeed; *na*—not; *mattaḥ*—besides Me; *anyat*—anything else; *iti*—thus; *budhyadhvam*—you should all understand; *añjasā*—by straightforward analysis of the facts.

TRANSLATION

Within this world, whatever is perceived by the mind, speech, eyes or other senses is Me alone and nothing besides Me. All of you please understand this by a straightforward analysis of the facts.

PURPORT

Lord Kṛṣṇa has already explained that if the sages consider all living entities to be the same, or if they consider the living entity to be the same as his body, then their question "Who are You?" is inappropriate. Now the Lord refutes the conception that He is a Supreme God far beyond and different from everything within this world. Modern agnostic philosophers preach that God created the world and then retired or went away. According to them, God has no tangible connection with this world, nor does He interfere in human affairs. Ultimately, they claim, God is so great that He cannot be known; therefore no one should waste time trying to understand God. To refute such foolish ideas, the Lord here explains that since everything is the expansion of His potency, He is not different from anything. Nothing can exist separately from the Supreme Personality of Godhead, and thus everything shares in the Lord's nature, although some manifestations are superior and others inferior. The Lord is testing the intelligence of the sages by pointing out various contradictions in their questions. Even if the Lord is supreme, He is not different from His creation; therefore, what is the meaning of the question "Who are You?" We can clearly see that the Lord is paving the way for a deep discussion of spiritual knowledge.

TEXT 25

गुणेष्वाविशते चेतो गुणाश्चेतसि च प्रजाः ।
जीवस्य देह उभयं गुणाश्चेतो मदात्मनः ॥२५॥

guṇeṣv āviśate ceto
guṇāś cetasi ca prajāḥ
jīvasya deha ubhayaṁ
guṇāś ceto mad-ātmanaḥ

guṇeṣu—in the sense objects; *āviśate*—enters; *cetaḥ*—the mind; *guṇāḥ*—the sense objects; *cetasi*—in the mind; *ca*—also (enter); *prajāḥ*—My dear sons; *jīvasya*—of the living entity; *dehaḥ*—the outward body, existing as designation; *ubhayam*—both of these; *guṇāḥ*—the sense objects; *cetaḥ*—the mind; *mat-ātmanaḥ*—having Me as the Supreme Soul.

TRANSLATION

My dear sons, the mind has a natural proclivity to enter into the material sense objects, and similarly the sense objects enter into

the mind; but both this material mind and the sense objects are merely designations that cover the spirit soul, who is part and parcel of Me.

PURPORT

Lord Kṛṣṇa in the form of Haṁsa-avatāra, on the pretext of finding contradictions in the simple inquiry of the sons of Brahmā ("Who are You?"), is actually preparing to teach the sages perfect spiritual knowledge, but only after first rejecting two false concepts of life, namely that all living entities are the same in all respects and that the living entity is identical with his outward or subtle body. Lord Kṛṣṇa now answers the difficult question that puzzled even Lord Brahmā. According to Śrīla Viśvanātha Cakravartī Ṭhākura, the sons of Lord Brahmā were thinking as follows. "Our dear Lord, if it is indeed true that we are unintelligent, still Your Lordship has stated that You are actually everything because everything is the expansion of Your potency. Therefore, You are also the mind and the sense objects, which are the subject matter of our question. The material sense objects always enter into the functions of the mind, and similarly, the mind always enters into the material sense objects. Thus, it is proper that we inquire from Your Lordship about the process by which the sense objects will no longer enter the mind and the mind will no longer enter the sense objects. Please be merciful and give us the answer." The Lord answers as follows. "My dear sons, it is a fact that the mind enters into the material sense objects and the sense objects into the mind. Thus, although the living entity is actually part and parcel of Me, being, as I am also, eternally conscious, and although the eternal form of the living entity is spiritual, in conditioned life the living entity artificially imposes upon himself the mind and sense objects, which act as covering designations of the eternal soul. Since it is the natural function of the material mind and sense objects to mutually interact, how can you possibly endeavor to prevent such a mutual attraction? Since both the material mind and sense objects are useless, they both should be completely given up, and thus automatically you will be free from all material duality."

Śrīla Śrīdhara Svāmī points out that the symptom of the material mind is the tendency to consider oneself to be the ultimate doer and enjoyer. Naturally, one with such a puffed-up mentality is helplessly attracted by the sense objects. One who considers himself to be the doer and enjoyer will be irresistibly attracted to the means for attaining sense gratification and false prestige, namely, exploitation of material objects. Above the material mind, however, is intelligence, which can perceive the existence of the eternal spirit soul. It is not possible to separate the material mind from the sense objects, because they naturally exist together. Therefore, by intelligence, one must realize one's eternal form as spirit soul, part and parcel of the Lord, and completely reject the bogus material mentality. One who revives his original spiritual mentality becomes automatically detached from material attraction. Therefore, one should cultivate knowledge of the falsity of sense gratification. When the mind or senses are attracted to material enjoyment, the superior intelligence must immediately detect such illusion. In this way, one should purify one's mentality. By devotional service to the Lord, such detachment and intelligence automatically awaken, and by full understanding of one's original spiritual form, one is properly situated in eternal consciousness.

TEXT 26

गुणेषु चाविशच्चित्तमभीक्ष्णं गुणसेवया ।
गुणाश्च चित्तप्रभवा मद्रूप उभयं त्यजेत् ॥२६॥

guṇeṣu cāviśac cittam
abhīkṣṇaṁ guṇa-sevayā
guṇāś ca citta-prabhavā
mad-rūpa ubhayaṁ tyajet

guṇeṣu—in the sense objects; *ca*—and; *āviśat*—entered; *cittam*—the mind; *abhīkṣṇam*—again and again; *guṇa-sevayā*—by sense gratification; *guṇāḥ*—and the material sense objects; *ca*—also; *citta*—within the mind; *prabhavāḥ*—existing prominently; *mat-rūpaḥ*—one who has realized that he is not different from Me, and who is thus absorbed in My form, pastimes, etc.; *ubhayam*—both (the mind and sense objects); *tyajet*—should give up.

TRANSLATION

A person who has thus achieved Me by understanding that he is not different from Me realizes that the material mind is lodged

within the sense objects, because of constant sense gratification, and that the material objects are existing prominently within the material mind. Having understood My transcendental nature, he gives up both the material mind and its objects.

PURPORT

The Lord again states here that it is most difficult to separate the material mind from its objects because the material mind by definition considers itself to be the doer and enjoyer of everything. It must be understood that giving up the material mind does not mean giving up all mental activities, but instead means purifying the mind and engaging one's enlightened mentality in the devotional service of the Lord. Since time immemorial the material mind and senses have been in contact with the sense objects; therefore, how is it possible for the material mind to give up its objects, which are the basis of its existence? And not only does the mind reach out to material objects, but also, because of the mind's desires, the material objects cannot remain out of the mind, helplessly entering at every moment. Thus, separation between the mind and sense objects is not actually feasible, nor does it serve any purpose. If one retains a material mentality, considering oneself to be supreme, one may renounce sense gratification, considering it to be ultimately the cause of unhappiness, but one will not be able to remain on such an artificial platform, nor will such renunciation serve any real purpose. Without surrender to the lotus feet of the Lord, mere renunciation cannot take one out of this material world.

Just as the sun's rays are part of the sun, the living entities are part of the Supreme Personality of Godhead. When the living entity is completely absorbed in his identity as the part and parcel of the Personality of Godhead, he becomes actually wise and easily gives up the material mind and sense objects. The word *mad-rūpaḥ* in this verse indicates absorption of the mind in the form, qualities, pastimes and associates of the Supreme Personality of Godhead. Immersed in such ecstatic meditation, one should render devotional service to the Lord, and this will automatically drive away the influence of sense gratification. By himself, the living entity does not have the potency to give up his false identification with the material mind and sense objects, but by worshiping the Lord in the mood of being His eternal part-and-parcel servant, one is infused with the Lord's potency, which easily drives away the darkness of ignorance.

TEXT 27

जाग्रत् स्वप्नः सुषुप्तं च गुणतो बुद्धिवृत्तयः ।
तासां विलक्षणो जीवः साक्षित्वेन विनिश्चितः ॥२७॥

jāgrat svapnaḥ suṣuptaṁ ca
guṇato buddhi-vṛttayaḥ
tāsāṁ vilakṣaṇo jīvaḥ
sākṣitvena viniścitaḥ

jāgrat—being awake; *svapnaḥ*—dreaming; *su-suptam*—deep sleep; *ca*—also; *guṇataḥ*—caused by the modes of nature; *buddhi*—of intelligence; *vṛttayaḥ*—the functions; *tāsām*—from such functions; *vilakṣaṇaḥ*—possessing different characteristics; *jīvaḥ*—the living entity; *sākṣitvena*—with the characteristic of being a witness; *viniścitaḥ*—is ascertained.

TRANSLATION

Waking, sleeping and deep sleep are the three functions of the intelligence and are caused by the modes of material nature. The living entity within the body is ascertained to possess characteristics different from these three states and thus remains as a witness to them.

PURPORT

The spirit soul actually has nothing to do with the material world, having no permanent or natural relationship with it. Real renunciation means to give up the illusory identification with matter in its subtle and gross forms. *Suṣuptam*, or deep sleep, indicates sleeping without any dreams or conscious activity. These three states are described by Lord Kṛṣṇa as follows:

sattvāj jāgaraṇaṁ vidyād
rajasā svapnam ādiśet

prasvāpaṁ tamasā jantos
turīyaṁ triṣu santatam

"One should know that wakefulness is born of the mode of goodness, dreams from the mode of passion, and deep dreamless sleep from the mode of ignorance. The fourth element, pure consciousness, is different from these three and pervades them." (*Bhāg.* 11.25.20) Real freedom means *sākṣitvena*, or to exist as a witness to the functions of illusion. Such an advantageous position is achieved by development of Kṛṣṇa consciousness.

TEXT 28

यर्हि संसृतिबन्धोऽयमात्मनो गुणवृत्तिदः ।
मयि तुर्ये स्थितो जह्यात् त्यागस्तद् गुणचेतसाम् ॥२८॥

yarhi saṁsṛti-bandho 'yam
ātmano guṇa-vṛtti-daḥ
mayi turye sthito jahyāt
tyāgas tad guṇa-cetasām

yarhi—whereas; *saṁsṛti*—of material intelligence or material existence; *bandhaḥ*—bondage; *ayam*—this is; *ātmanaḥ*—of the soul; *guṇa*—in the modes of nature; *vṛtti-daḥ*—that which gives occupations; *mayi*—in Me; *turye*—in the fourth element (beyond wakefulness, dreaming and deep sleep); *sthitaḥ*—being situated; *jahyāt*—one should give up; *tyāgaḥ*—renunciation; *tat*—at that time; *guṇa*—of the material sense objects; *cetasām*—and of the material mind.

TRANSLATION

The spirit soul is trapped in the bondage of material intelligence, which awards him constant engagement in the illusory modes of nature. But I am the fourth stage of consciousness, beyond wakefulness, dreaming and deep sleep. Becoming situated in Me, the soul should give up the bondage of material consciousness. At that time, the living entity will automatically renounce the material sense objects and the material mind.

PURPORT

Lord Kṛṣṇa now specifically answers the questions that the sages originally placed before Lord Brahmā. Ultimately, the spirit soul has nothing to do with the material sense objects and modes of nature. But because of one's false identification with the material body, the modes of nature are empowered to engage one in illusory occupations. By destroying this false identification with matter, the soul gives up the illusory occupations awarded by the modes of nature. It is clearly stated in this verse that the living entity is not empowered to independently free himself from illusion, but must situate himself in Kṛṣṇa consciousness, in full awareness of the Supreme Lord.

TEXT 29

अहङ्कारकृतं बन्धमात्मनोऽर्थविपर्ययम् ।
विद्वान् निर्विद्य संसारचिन्तां तुर्ये स्थितस्त्यजेत् ॥२९॥

ahaṅkāra-kṛtaṁ bandham
ātmano 'rtha-viparyayam
vidvān nirvidya saṁsāra-
cintāṁ turye sthitas tyajet

ahaṅkāra—by false ego; *kṛtam*—produced; *bandham*—bondage; *ātmanaḥ*—of the soul; *artha*—of that which is really valuable; *viparyayam*—being the opposite; *vidvān*—one who knows; *nirvidya*—being detached; *saṁsāra*—in material existence; *cintām*—constant thoughts; *turye*—in the fourth element, the Lord; *sthitaḥ*—being situated; *tyajet*—should give up.

TRANSLATION

The false ego of the living entity places him in bondage and awards him exactly the opposite of what he really desires. Therefore, an intelligent person should give up his constant anxiety to enjoy material life and remain situated in the Lord, who is beyond the functions of material consciousness.

PURPORT

Śrīla Śrīdhara Svāmī comments as follows. "How does material existence cause the bondage of the living entity, and how can such bondage be given up? The Lord explains this here by the word *ahaṅkāra-kṛtam.* Because of false ego, one is bound up in the network of illusion. *Artha-viparyayam* indicates that although the living entity desires blissful life, eternity and knowledge, he adopts procedures that actually cover over his eternal, blissful nature and give him exactly the opposite result. The living entity does not want death and suffering, but these are actually the results of material existence, which is therefore useless for all practical purposes. An intelligent person should contemplate the unhappiness of material life and thus become situated in the transcendental Lord. The word *saṁsāra-cintām* can be understood as follows. *Saṁsāra*, or material existence, indicates material intelligence, because material existence only occurs because of the living entity's false intellectual identification with the material world. Because of this misidentification, one becomes overwhelmed with *saṁsāra-cintām*, anxiety to enjoy the material world. One should become situated in the Lord and give up such useless anxiety."

TEXT 30

यावन्नानार्थधीः पुंसो न निवर्तेत युक्तिभिः ।
जागर्त्यपि स्वपन्नज्ञः स्वप्ने जागरणं यथा ॥३०॥

yāvan nānārtha-dhīḥ puṁso
na nivarteta yuktibhiḥ
jāgarty api svapann ajñaḥ
svapne jāgaraṇaṁ yathā

yāvat—as long as; *nānā*—of many; *artha*—values; *dhīḥ*—the conception; *puṁsaḥ*—of a person; *na*—does not; *nivarteta*—subside; *yuktibhiḥ*—by the appropriate methods (described by Me); *jāgarti*—being awake; *api*—although; *svapan*—sleeping, dreaming; *ajñaḥ*—one who does not see things as they are; *svapne*—in a dream; *jāgaraṇam*—being awake; *yathā*—just as.

TRANSLATION

According to My instructions, one should fix the mind in Me alone. If, however, one continues to see many different values and goals in life rather than seeing everything within Me, then although apparently awake, one is actually dreaming due to incomplete knowledge, just as one may dream that one has awakened from a dream.

PURPORT

One who is not Kṛṣṇa conscious cannot understand that everything is resting within Lord Kṛṣṇa, and thus it is impossible for him to retire from material sense gratification. One may adopt a particular process of salvation and consider oneself to be "saved"; nevertheless, his material conditioning will remain and thus he will maintain his attachment to the material world. While one is dreaming he sometimes imagines that he has awakened from a dream and is experiencing normal consciousness. Similarly, one may consider oneself to be saved, but if he remains absorbed in making material value judgments between good and bad, without reference to devotional service to the Supreme Lord, he is understood to be a conditioned soul covered by the illusory identification with matter.

TEXT 31

असत्त्वादात्मनोऽन्येषां भावानां तत्कृता भिदा ।
गतयो हेतवश्चास्य मृषा स्वप्नदृशो यथा ॥३१॥

asattvād ātmano 'nyeṣāṁ
bhāvānāṁ tat-kṛtā bhidā
gatayo hetavaś cāsya
mṛṣā svapna-dṛśo yathā

asattvāt—because of lacking factual existence; *ātmanaḥ*—from the Supreme Personality of Godhead; *anyeṣām*—of others; *bhāvānām*—states of existence; *tat*—by them; *kṛtā*—created; *bhidā*—difference or separation; *gatayaḥ*—destinations such as going to heaven; *hetavaḥ*—

fruitive activities, which are the cause of future rewards; *ca*—also; *asya*—of the living entity; *mṛṣā*—false; *svapna*—of a dream; *dṛśaḥ*—of the seer; *yathā*—just as.

TRANSLATION

Those states of existence that are conceived of as separate from the Supreme Personality of Godhead have no actual existence, although they create a sense of separation from the Absolute Truth. Just as the seer of a dream imagines many different activities and rewards, similarly, because of the sense of an existence separate from the Lord's existence, the living entity falsely performs fruitive activities, thinking them to be the cause of future rewards and destinations.

PURPORT

Śrīla Viśvanātha Cakravartī Ṭhākura comments as follows: "Although Lord Kṛṣṇa in His form of Haṁsa-avatāra has condemned the intelligence that sees duality and separate values within the material world, the *Vedas* themselves institute the system of *varṇāśrama-dharma*, by which the entire human society is divided into different castes, occupations and spiritual statuses. Therefore, how can the Lord recommend that one give up one's faith in this Vedic system? The answer is given in this verse as follows. The words *anyeṣāṁ bhāvānām*, or 'of other states of existence,' refer to the innumerable divisions of false identification with the material body, mind, occupation, and so on. Such identification is illusion, and the material divisions of the *varṇāśrama* system are certainly based on this illusion. The Vedic literatures promise heavenly rewards such as residence in upper planetary systems and prescribe the means to acquire such rewards. However, both the rewards and the means for achieving them are ultimately illusion. Since this world is the Lord's creation, one cannot deny that its existence is also real; yet the living entity who identifies the creations of this world as belonging to himself is certainly in illusion. The example may be given that horns are real and rabbits are real, but if one imagines a rabbit's horns, that is certainly illusion, though a rabbit's horns may occur in a dream. Similarly, the living entity dreams of a permanent relationship within the material world. One may dream that one is feasting on sumptuous sweet rice prepared with milk and sugar, but there is no actual nutritional value in the dream of royal feasting."

Śrīla Bhaktisiddhānta Sarasvatī Ṭhākura remarks in this regard that just as one soon forgets the experience of a dream after awakening, similarly, a liberated soul in Kṛṣṇa consciousness does not see anything substantial in even the most exalted rewards offered by the *Vedas*, such as promotion to the heavenly planets. Therefore Lord Kṛṣṇa advised Arjuna in *Bhagavad-gītā* to remain fixed in self-realization, without being deviated by fruitive rituals performed in the name of religion.

TEXT 32

यो जागरे बहिरनुक्षणधर्मिणोऽर्थान्
भुङ्क्ते समस्तकरणैर्हृदि तत्सदृक्षान् ।
स्वप्ने सुषुप्त उपसंहरते स एकः
स्मृत्यन्वयात्त्रिगुणवृत्तिदृगिन्द्रियेशः ॥३२॥

yo jāgare bahir anukṣaṇa-dharmiṇo 'rthān
bhuṅkte samasta-karaṇair hṛdi tat-sadṛkṣān
svapne suṣupta upasaṁharate sa ekaḥ
smṛty-anvayāt tri-guṇa-vṛtti-dṛg indriyeśaḥ

yaḥ—the living entity who; *jāgare*—while awake; *bahiḥ*—external; *anukṣaṇa*—momentary; *dharmiṇaḥ*—qualities; *arthān*—the body and mind and their experiences; *bhuṅkte*—enjoys; *samasta*—with all; *karaṇaiḥ*—the senses; *hṛdi*—within the mind; *tat-sadṛkṣān*—experiences similar to those in wakefulness; *svapne*—in dreams; *suṣupte*—in deep dreamless sleep; *upasaṁharate*—merges into ignorance; *saḥ*—he; *ekaḥ*—one; *smṛti*—of memory; *anvayāt*—by the succession; *tri-guṇa*—of the three stages wakefulness, dream and dreamless sleep; *vṛtti*—functions; *dṛk*—seeing; *indriya*—of the senses; *īśaḥ*—becomes the lord.

TRANSLATION

While awake the living entity enjoys with all of his senses the fleeting characteristics of the material body and mind; while dreaming he enjoys similar experiences within the mind; and in

deep dreamless sleep all such experiences merge into ignorance. By remembering and contemplating the succession of wakefulness, dreaming and deep sleep, the living entity can understand that he is one throughout the three stages of consciousness and is transcendental. Thus, he becomes the lord of the senses.

PURPORT

In verse 30 of this chapter Lord Kṛṣṇa stated that one must retire from material duality by the proper means, which the Lord now explains. One may first consider the three phases of consciousness mentioned above and then understand one's own transcendental position as spirit soul. One experiences childhood, boyhood, adolescence, adulthood, middle age and old age, and throughout these phases one is experiencing things while awake and while dreaming. Similarly, one may, by careful intelligence, understand one's lack of consciousness during deep sleep, and thus through intelligence one may have experience of lack of consciousness.

One may argue that it is actually the senses that experience during wakefulness and that it is the mind that experiences during dreams. However, the Lord here states, *indriyeśaḥ:* the living entity is actually the lord of the senses and mind, although temporarily he has become a victim of their influence. By Kṛṣṇa consciousness one may resume one's rightful position as master of the mental and sensory faculties. Also, since the living entity can remember his experiences in these three stages of consciousness, he is ultimately the experiencing agent or the seer of all phases of consciousness. He remembers, "I saw so many things in my dream, and then my dream ended and I didn't see anything. Now I'm waking up." This universal experience can be understood by everyone, and thus everyone can understand that one's actual identity is separate from the material body and mind.

TEXT 33

एवं विमृश्य गुणतो मनसस्त्र्यवस्था
मन्मायया मयि कृता इति निश्चितार्थाः।
संछिद्य हार्दमनुमानसदुक्तितीक्ष्ण-
ज्ञानासिना भजत माखिलसंशयाधिम्॥३३॥

evaṁ vimṛśya guṇato manasas try-avasthā
man-māyayā mayi kṛtā iti niścitārthāḥ
sañchidya hārdam anumāna-sad-ukti-tīkṣṇa-
jñānāsinā bhajata mākhila-saṁśayādhim

evam—thus; *vimṛśya*—considering; *guṇataḥ*—by the modes of nature; *manasaḥ*—of the mind; *tri-avasthāḥ*—the three states of consciousness; *mat-māyayā*—by the influence of My illusory potency; *mayi*—in Me; *kṛtāḥ*—imposed; *iti*—thus; *niścita-arthāḥ*—those who have ascertained the actual meaning of the soul; *sañchidya*—cutting off; *hārdam*—situated in the heart; *anumāna*—by logic; *sat-ukti*—and by the instructions of sages and the Vedic literatures; *tīkṣṇa*—sharpened; *jñāna*—of knowledge; *asinā*—by the sword; *bhajata*—all of you worship; *mā*—Me; *akhila*—of all; *saṁśaya*—doubts; *ādhim*—the cause (false ego).

TRANSLATION

You should consider how, by the influence of My illusory energy, these three states of the mind, caused by the modes of nature, have been artificially imagined to exist in Me. Having definitely ascertained the truth of the soul, you should utilize the sharpened sword of knowledge, acquired by logical reflection and from the instructions of sages and Vedic literatures, to completely cut off the false ego, which is the breeding ground of all doubts. All of you should then worship Me, who am situated within the heart.

PURPORT

One who has obtained transcendental knowledge is no longer dependent on the three stages of ordinary consciousness, namely waking, dreaming and dreamless sleep. One thus rids one's material mind of the tendency to become the enjoyer of the inferior energy of the Lord, and one sees everything as part and parcel of the Lord's potency, meant only for the enjoyment of the Lord Himself. In such a state of consciousness, one naturally surrenders fully to the Lord's devotional service, which Lord Haṁsa here advises the sons of Lord Brahmā to take up.

TEXT 34

ईक्षेत विभ्रममिदं मनसो विलासं
दृष्टं विनष्टमतिलोलमलातचक्रम् ।
विज्ञानमेकमुरुधेव विभाति माया
स्वप्नस्त्रिधा गुणविसर्गकृतो विकल्पः ॥३४॥

īkṣeta vibhramam idaṁ manaso vilāsaṁ
dṛṣṭaṁ vinaṣṭam ati-lolam alāta-cakram
vijñānam ekam urudheva vibhāti māyā
svapnas tridhā guṇa-visarga-kṛto vikalpaḥ

īkṣeta—one should see; *vibhramam*—as illusion or mistake; *idam*—this (material world); *manasaḥ*—of the mind; *vilāsam*—appearance or jumping; *dṛṣṭam*—here today; *vinaṣṭam*—gone tomorrow; *ati-lolam*—extremely flickering; *alāta-cakram*—just like the moving red line created by whirling a fiery stick; *vijñānam*—the spirit soul, by nature fully conscious; *ekam*—is one; *urudhā*—in many divisions; *iva*—as if; *vibhāti*—appears; *māyā*—this is illusion; *svapnaḥ*—merely a dream; *tridhā*—in three divisions; *guṇa*—of the modes of nature; *visarga*—by the transformation; *kṛtaḥ*—created; *vikalpaḥ*—variety of perception or imagination.

TRANSLATION

One should see that the material world is a distinct illusion appearing in the mind, because material objects have an extremely flickering existence and are here today and gone tomorrow. They can be compared to the streaking red line created by whirling a fiery stick. The spirit soul by nature exists in the single state of pure consciousness. However, in this world he appears in many different forms and stages of existence. The modes of nature divide the soul's consciousness into normal wakefulness, dreaming and dreamless sleep. All such varieties of perception, however, are actually māyā and exist only like a dream.

PURPORT

The Lord now describes an additional process for transcending the illusory interaction of the material mind and material sense objects. *Lāsa* means "jumping" or "dancing," and thus *manaso vilāsam* here indicates that the material mind is jumping superficially from one conception of life to another. Our original consciousness, however, is one (*vijñānam ekam*). Therefore, one should carefully study the flickering "here today, gone tomorrow" nature of the material world and detach oneself from the illusory variety of *māyā.*

TEXT 35

दृष्टिं ततः प्रतिनिवर्त्य निवृत्ततृष्ण-
स्तूष्णीं भवेन्निजसुखानुभवो निरीहः ।
संदृश्यते क्व च यदीदमवस्तुबुद्ध्या
त्यक्तं भ्रमाय न भवेत् स्मृतिरानिपातात्॥३५॥

dṛṣṭiṁ tataḥ pratinivartya nivṛtta-tṛṣṇas
tūṣṇīṁ bhaven nija-sukhānubhavo nirīhaḥ
sandṛśyate kva ca yadīdam avastu-buddhyā
tyaktaṁ bhramāya na bhavet smṛtir ā-nipātāt

dṛṣṭim—sight; *tataḥ*—from that illusion; *pratinivartya*—pulling away; *nivṛtta*—ceased; *tṛṣṇaḥ*—material hankering; *tūṣṇīm*—silent; *bhavet*—one should become; *nija*—one's own (of the soul); *sukha*—happiness; *anubhavaḥ*—perceiving; *nirīhaḥ*—without material activities; *sandṛśyate*—is observed; *kva ca*—sometimes; *yadi*—if; *idam*—this material world; *avastu*—of not being reality; *buddhyā*—by the consciousness; *tyaktam*—given up; *bhramāya*—further illusion; *na*—not; *bhavet*—may become; *smṛtiḥ*—remembrance; *ā-nipātāt*—until giving up the material body.

TRANSLATION

Having understood the temporary illusory nature of material things, and thus having pulled one's vision away from illusion, one should remain without material desires. By experiencing the happiness of the soul, one should give up material speaking and activities. If sometimes one must observe the material world, one should remember that it is not ultimate reality and therefore one

has given it up. By such constant remembrance up till the time of death, one will not again fall into illusion.

PURPORT

To maintain the material body one cannot avoid eating and sleeping. In these and other ways, one will sometimes be forced to deal with the material world and the physical aspects of one's own body. At such times one should remember that the material world is not actual reality and that therefore one has given it up to become Kṛṣṇa conscious. By such constant remembrance, by enjoying spiritual bliss within oneself and by retiring from any material activities of the mind, speech or body, one will not fall into material illusion.

Śrīla Bhaktisiddhānta Sarasvatī Ṭhākura comments as follows. "The living entity, while living in the external energy of the Lord, should give up any anxiety for sense gratification and should not act for his personal enjoyment. Rather, one should search out spiritual bliss through devotional service to the Supreme Lord. By reviving one's relationship with Lord Kṛṣṇa, one will understand that if one accepts any material object for one's personal enjoyment, attachment will inevitably develop, and thus one will be bewildered by illusion. By gradually developing one's spiritual body, one will no longer desire to enjoy anything within the material world."

TEXT 36

देहं च नश्वरमवस्थितमुत्थितं वा
सिद्धो न पश्यति यतोऽध्यगमत् स्वरूपम् ।
दैवादपेतमथ दैववशादुपेतं
वासो यथा परिकृतं मदिरामदान्धः ॥३६॥

deham ca naśvaram avasthitam utthitaṁ vā
siddho na paśyati yato 'dhyagamat svarūpam
daivād apetam atha daiva-vaśād upetaṁ
vāso yathā parikṛtaṁ madirā-madāndhaḥ

deham—the material body; *ca*—also; *naśvaram*—to be destroyed; *avasthitam*—seated; *utthitam*—risen; *vā*—or; *siddhaḥ*—one who is perfect; *na paśyati*—does not see; *yataḥ*—because; *adhyagamat*—he has achieved; *sva-rūpam*—his actual spiritual identity; *daivāt*—by destiny; *apetam*—departed; *atha*—or thus; *daiva*—of destiny; *vaśāt*—by the control; *upetam*—achieved; *vāsaḥ*—clothes; *yathā*—just as; *parikṛtam*—placed on the body; *madirā*—of liquor; *mada*—by the intoxication; *andhaḥ*—blinded.

TRANSLATION

Just as a drunken man does not notice if he is wearing his coat or shirt, similarly, one who is perfect in self-realization and who has thus achieved his eternal identity does not notice whether the temporary body is sitting or standing. Indeed, if by God's will the body is finished or if by God's will he obtains a new body, a self-realized soul does not notice, just as a drunken man does not notice the situation of his outward dress.

PURPORT

A Kṛṣṇa conscious person who has achieved his spiritual identity does not accept sense gratification in the material world as the goal of his life. He is constantly engaged in the service of the Lord and knows that the temporary body and flickering mind are material. By superior intelligence in Kṛṣṇa consciousness he remains engaged in the Lord's service. The example of a drunken man in this verse is very nice. It is common knowledge that at mundane social gatherings men become drunk and lose all awareness of their external situation. Similarly, a liberated soul has already achieved his spiritual body and therefore knows that his continued existence does not depend on the material body. A liberated soul does not, however, inflict punishment on the body but rather remains neutral, naturally accepting his destiny as the will of the Supreme.

TEXT 37

देहोऽपि दैववशगः खलु कर्म यावत्
स्वारम्भकं प्रतिसमीक्षत एव सासुः ।
तं सप्रपञ्चमधिरूढसमाधियोगः
स्वाप्नं पुनर्न भजते प्रतिबुद्धवस्तुः ॥३७॥

deho 'pi daiva-vaśa-gaḥ khalu karma yāvat
svārambhakaṁ pratisamīkṣata eva sāsuḥ
taṁ sa-prapañcam adhirūḍha-samādhi-yogaḥ
svāpnaṁ punar na bhajate pratibuddha-vastuḥ

dehaḥ—the body; *api*—even; *daiva*—of the Supreme; *vaśa-gaḥ*—under the control; *khalu*—indeed; *karma*—the chain of fruitive activities; *yāvat*—as long as; *sva-ārambhakam*—that which initiates or perpetuates itself; *pratisamīkṣate*—goes on living and waiting; *eva*—certainly; *sa-asuḥ*—along with the vital air and senses; *tam*—that (body); *sa-prapañcam*—with its variety of manifestations; *adhirūḍha*—highly situated; *samādhi*—the stage of perfection; *yogaḥ*—in the *yoga* system; *svāpnam*—just like a dream; *punaḥ*—again; *na bhajate*—does not worship or cultivate; *pratibuddha*—one who is enlightened; *vastuḥ*—in the supreme reality.

TRANSLATION

The material body certainly moves under the control of supreme destiny and therefore must continue to live along with the senses and vital air as long as one's karma is in effect. A self-realized soul, however, who is awakened to the absolute reality and who is thus highly situated in the perfect stage of yoga, will never again surrender to the material body and its manifold manifestations, knowing it to be just like a body visualized in a dream.

PURPORT

Although Lord Kṛṣṇa recommended in the previous verse that a self-realized soul not give attention to the body, it is clear from the Lord's statement here that one should not foolishly starve or injure the body, but should patiently wait until the chain of one's previous fruitive work has completely exhausted itself. At that time the body will automatically die according to destiny. The following doubt may then arise: If a Kṛṣṇa conscious person pays proper attention to the maintenance of the body, is there danger of again becoming attached to it? Lord Kṛṣṇa here states that one who is highly elevated in Kṛṣṇa consciousness, having understood Lord Kṛṣṇa to be the actual *vastu*, or reality, never again surrenders to the illusory identification with the material body, which is just like the body seen in a dream.

TEXT 38

मयैतदुक्तं वो विप्रा गुह्यं यत् सांख्ययोगयोः ।
जानीत मागतं यज्ञं युष्मद्धर्मविवक्षया ॥३८॥

mayaitad uktaṁ vo viprā
guhyaṁ yat sāṅkhya-yogayoḥ
jānīta māgataṁ yajñaṁ
yuṣmad-dharma-vivakṣayā

mayā—by Me; *etat*—this (knowledge); *uktam*—has been spoken; *vaḥ*—unto you; *viprāḥ*—O *brāhmaṇas; guhyam*—confidential; *yat*—which; *sāṅkhya*—of the philosophical method of distinguishing matter from spirit; *yogayoḥ*—and the *aṣṭāṅga-yoga* system; *jānīta*—please understand; *mā*—Me; *āgatam*—who has arrived; *yajñam*—as Viṣṇu, the Supreme Lord of sacrifice; *yuṣmat*—your; *dharma*—religious duties; *vivakṣayā*—with the desire to explain.

TRANSLATION

My dear brāhmaṇas, I have now explained to you the confidential knowledge of Sāṅkhya, by which one philosophically distinguishes matter from spirit, and of aṣṭāṅga-yoga, by which one links up with the Supreme. Please understand that I am the Supreme Personality of Godhead, Viṣṇu, and that I have appeared before you desiring to explain your actual religious duties.

PURPORT

To increase the faith of Lord Brahmā's sons and establish the prestige of His teachings, Lord Kṛṣṇa now formally identifies Himself as the Supreme Personality of Godhead, Viṣṇu. As stated in Vedic literature, *yajño vai viṣṇuḥ.* After explaining the *sāṅkhya-* and *aṣṭāṅga-yoga* systems, the Lord clearly answers the original question of the sages, "Who are You, sir?" Thus, Lord Brahmā and his sons were enlightened by Lord Haṁsa.

TEXT 39

अहं योगस्य सांख्यस्य सत्यस्यर्तस्य तेजसः ।
परायणं द्विजश्रेष्ठाः श्रियः कीर्तेर्दमस्य च ॥३९॥

ahaṁ yogasya sāṅkhyasya
satyasyartasya tejasaḥ
parāyaṇaṁ dvija-śreṣṭhāḥ
śriyaḥ kīrter damasya ca

aham—I; *yogasya*—of the *yoga* system; *sāṅkhyasya*—of the system of analytic philosophy; *satyasya*—of virtuous action; *ṛtasya*—of truthful religious principles; *tejasaḥ*—of power; *para-ayaṇam*—the ultimate shelter; *dvija-śreṣṭhāḥ*—O best of the *brāhmaṇas; śriyaḥ*—of beauty; *kīrteḥ*—of fame; *damasya*—of self-control; *ca*—also.

TRANSLATION

O best of the brāhmaṇas, please know that I am the supreme shelter of the yoga system, analytic philosophy, virtuous action, truthful religious principles, power, beauty, fame and self-control.

PURPORT

According to Śrīla Śrīdhara Svāmī, the synonymous words *satyasya* and *ṛtasya* refer to, respectively, the proper or virtuous execution of religious principles and a convincing presentation of religion. Śrīla Viśvanātha Cakravartī Ṭhākura points out that the sons of Brahmā were struck with wonder at the presentation of the Supreme Personality of Godhead and were thinking, "What wonderful knowledge we have just heard." The Lord, recognizing their astonishment, spoke this verse to confirm their understanding of Him.

TEXT 40

मां भजन्ति गुणाः सर्वे निर्गुणं निरपेक्षकम् ।
सुहृदं प्रियमात्मानं साम्यासङ्गादयोऽगुणाः ॥४०॥

māṁ bhajanti guṇāḥ sarve
nirguṇaṁ nirapekṣakam
suhṛdaṁ priyam ātmānaṁ
sāmyāsaṅgādayo 'guṇāḥ

mām—Me; *bhajanti*—serve and take shelter of; *guṇāḥ*—qualities; *sarve*—all; *nirguṇam*—free from the modes of nature; *nirapekṣakam*—detached; *su-hṛdam*—the well-wisher; *priyam*—the most dear; *ātmānam*—the Supersoul; *sāmya*—being equally situated everywhere; *asaṅga*—detachment; *ādayaḥ*—and so on; *aguṇāḥ*—free from the transformation of the material modes.

TRANSLATION

All superior transcendental qualities, such as being beyond the modes of nature, detached, the well-wisher, the most dear, the Supersoul, equally situated everywhere, and free from material entanglement—all such qualities, free from the transformations of material qualities, find their shelter and worshipable object in Me.

PURPORT

Because in the previous verse Lord Kṛṣṇa explained His exalted nature, the sons of Brahmā might have slightly doubted the Lord's position, thinking that they had detected some pride within the Lord's mind. Therefore, they may have doubted the instructions they had just received from Lord Haṁsa. Anticipating any such reluctance, the Lord immediately clarifies the situation in the present verse. The Lord explains that, unlike ordinary living entities even up to the standard of Brahmā, the Lord's transcendental body is not different from His eternal Self and has no material qualities such as false egotism. The Lord's transcendental form is eternal, full of knowledge and bliss, and is thus *nirguṇam*, beyond the modes of nature. Because the Lord completely ignores the so-called enjoyment offered by the illusory energy, He is called *nirapekṣakam*, and being the best well-wisher of His devotees, He is called *suhṛdam. Priyam* indicates that the Lord is the supreme lovable object and that He establishes wonderful affectionate relationships with His devotees. *Sāmya* indicates that the Lord is neutral and detached in all material situations. These and other exalted qualities find their shelter and worshipable object in the Lord, who does not take material designations into consideration but awards His mercy to anyone who takes shelter of Him. In *Śrīmad-Bhāgavatam* (1.16.26–30) mother Bhūmi, the predominating deity of the earth, gives a list of some of the Lord's transcendental qualities, and even more are found in *The Nectar of Devotion.* Actually, the Lord's qualities are unlimited, but a small sample is given here simply to establish the Lord's transcendental position.

Śrīla Madhvācārya has quoted from the *Kāla-saṁhitā* as follows. "The demigods are not actually perfectly endowed with transcendental qualities. Indeed, their opulences are limited, and therefore they worship the Supreme Personality of Godhead, the Absolute Truth, who is simultaneously free of all material qualities and completely endowed with all transcendental qualities, which exist in His personal body."

TEXT 41

इति मे छिन्नसन्देहा मुनयः सनकादयः ।
सभाजयित्वा परया भक्त्यागृणत संस्तवैः ॥४१॥

iti me chinna-sandehā
munayaḥ sanakādayaḥ
sabhājayitvā parayā
bhaktyāgṛṇata saṁstavaiḥ

iti—thus; *me*—by Me; *chinna*—destroyed; *sandehāḥ*—all their doubts; *munayaḥ*—the sages; *sanaka-ādayaḥ*—headed by Sanaka-kumāra; *sabhājayitvā*—fully worshiping Me; *parayā*—characterized by transcendental love; *bhaktyā*—with devotion; *agṛṇata*—they chanted My glories; *saṁstavaiḥ*—with beautiful hymns.

TRANSLATION

My dear Uddhava, thus all of the doubts of the sages headed by Sanaka were destroyed by My words. Fully worshiping Me with transcendental love and devotion, they chanted My glories with excellent hymns.

TEXT 42

तैरहं पूजितः सम्यक् संस्तुतः परमर्षिभिः ।
प्रत्येयाय स्वकं धाम पश्यतः परमेष्ठिनः ॥४२॥

tair ahaṁ pūjitaḥ samyak
saṁstutaḥ paramarṣibhiḥ
pratyeyāya svakaṁ dhāma
paśyataḥ parameṣṭhinaḥ

taiḥ—by them; *aham*—I; *pūjitaḥ*—worshiped; *samyak*—perfectly; *saṁstutaḥ*—perfectly glorified; *parama-ṛṣibhiḥ*—by the greatest of sages; *pratyeyāya*—I returned; *svakam*—to My own; *dhāma*—abode; *paśyataḥ parameṣṭhinaḥ*—as Lord Brahmā looked on.

TRANSLATION

The greatest of sages, headed by Sanaka Ṛṣi, thus perfectly worshiped and glorified Me, and as Lord Brahmā looked on, I returned to My own abode.

Thus end the purports of the humble servants of His Divine Grace A. C. Bhaktivedanta Swami Prabhupāda to the Eleventh Canto, Thirteenth Chapter, of the Śrīmad-Bhāgavatam, *entitled "The Haṁsa-avatāra Answers the Questions of the Sons of Brahmā."*

CHAPTER FOURTEEN

Lord Kṛṣṇa Explains the Yoga System to Śrī Uddhava

In this chapter, Kṛṣṇa explains that devotional service to the Supreme Lord is the most excellent method of spiritual practice. He also speaks about the process of meditation.

Śrī Uddhava wanted to know which process of spiritual advancement is the best. He also desired to hear about the superexcellence of devotional service free from ulterior motives. The Supreme Personality of Godhead replied to him that the original process of religion revealed in the *Vedas* had become lost during the time of annihilation. At the beginning of the new creation, therefore, the Supreme Lord spoke it again to Brahmā. Brahmā repeated it to Manu, Manu spoke it to the sages headed by Bhṛgu Muni, and these sages in turn instructed this eternal religion to the demigods and demons. Because of the living entities' multitude of diverse desires, this system of religion was elaborately explained in different ways. Thus different philosophies arose, including various atheistic doctrines. Because the living entity, bewildered by illusion, is incapable of ascertaining his eternal benefit, he mistakenly identifies ordinary vows of penance, austerity, etc., to be the topmost spiritual practice. But the only true means of achieving happiness is to meditate on offering everything to the Supreme Lord. In this way one becomes free from all desires for selfish gratification through enjoyment of mundane sense objects, and he becomes released from all hankering for either enjoyment or liberation.

The Lord then proceeded to describe the superior process of devotional service, which destroys countless sinful reactions and produces many symptoms of spiritual happiness, such as the standing of the hairs on end. Pure devotion, having the power to purify the heart, enables one to achieve the association of the Supreme Personality of Godhead, and because the devotee is very dear to the Lord and is always close to Him, he is able in turn to purify the entire universe. By virtue of his unflinching devotion to the Lord, the devotee can never be completely diverted by the objects of sense enjoyment, even if he is not able to gain control over his senses in the beginning. One desiring to attain the perfection of life is advised to give up all material processes of elevation as well as the association of women. He should then merge his mind constantly in thought of Lord Kṛṣṇa. Finally, the Lord instructed Śrī Uddhava about the true object of meditation.

TEXT 1

श्रीउद्धव उवाच
वदन्ति कृष्ण श्रेयांसि बहूनि ब्रह्मवादिनः ।
तेषां विकल्पप्राधान्यमुताहो एकमुख्यता ॥ १ ॥

śrī-uddhava uvāca
vadanti kṛṣṇa śreyāṁsi
bahūni brahma-vādinaḥ
teṣāṁ vikalpa-prādhānyam
utāho eka-mukhyatā

śrī-uddhavaḥ uvāca—Śrī Uddhava said; *vadanti*—they speak; *kṛṣṇa*—my dear Kṛṣṇa; *śreyāṁsi*—processes for advancement in life; *bahūni*—many; *brahma-vādinaḥ*—the learned sages who have explained the Vedic literature; *teṣām*—of all such processes; *vikalpa*—of varieties of perception; *prādhānyam*—supremacy; *uta*—or; *aho*—indeed; *eka*—of one; *mukhyatā*—being most important.

TRANSLATION

Śrī Uddhava said: My dear Kṛṣṇa, the learned sages who explain Vedic literature recommend various processes for perfecting one's life. Considering these varieties of viewpoint, my Lord, please tell me whether all these processes are equally important, or whether one of them is supreme.

PURPORT

In order to clearly establish the exalted position of *bhakti-yoga*, or pure devotional service to the Supreme Lord, Śrī Uddhava requests Lord

Kṛṣṇa to identify the supreme among all processes of self-realization. Not all Vedic processes lead directly to the ultimate goal, pure love of God; some only gradually elevate the consciousness of the living entity. For the purpose of giving a general outline of the process of self-realization, sages may discuss the various methods of elevation. But when the time comes to ascertain the most perfect process, the secondary methods must be cleared from the path.

TEXT 2

भवतोदाहृतः स्वामिन् भक्तियोगोऽनपेक्षितः ।
निरस्य सर्वतः सङ्गं येन त्वय्याविशेन्मनः ॥ २ ॥

bhavatodāhṛtaḥ svāmin
bhakti-yogo 'napekṣitaḥ
nirasya sarvataḥ saṅgaṁ
yena tvayy āviśen manaḥ

bhavatā—by You; *udāhṛtaḥ*—clearly stated; *svāmin*—O my Lord; *bhakti-yogaḥ*—devotional service; *anapekṣitaḥ*—without material desires; *nirasya*—removing; *sarvataḥ*—in all respects; *saṅgam*—material association; *yena*—by which (devotional service); *tvayi*—in Your Lordship; *āviśet*—may enter; *manaḥ*—the mind.

TRANSLATION

My dear Lord, You have clearly explained the process of unalloyed devotional service, by which a devotee removes all material association from his life, enabling him to fix his mind in You.

PURPORT

It is now clearly established that pure devotional service is the supreme process for fixing the mind in the Supreme Truth, Lord Kṛṣṇa. The next point to be clarified is this: Can everyone practice this process, or is it limited to an elite class of transcendentalists? In discussing the relative advantages of different spiritual processes, one must immediately ascertain the goal of spiritual life and then isolate the process that actually awards this goal. Processes must be defined in terms of primary and secondary functions. A method that gives one the highest perfection is primary, whereas processes that merely assist or enhance the primary function are considered secondary. The mind is most flickering and unsteady; therefore by clear intelligence one must fix oneself in a progressive mode of life, and thus one can achieve the Absolute Truth in this lifetime. This is the sober purpose of Lord Kṛṣṇa's conversation with Śrī Uddhava.

TEXT 3

श्रीभगवानुवाच
कालेन नष्टा प्रलये वाणीयं वेदसंज्ञिता ।
मयादौ ब्रह्मणे प्रोक्ता धर्मो यस्यां मदात्मकः ॥ ३ ॥

śrī-bhagavān uvāca
kālena naṣṭā pralaye
vāṇīyaṁ veda-saṁjñitā
mayādau brahmaṇe proktā
dharmo yasyāṁ mad-ātmakaḥ

śrī-bhagavān uvāca—the Supreme Personality of Godhead said; *kālena*—by the influence of time; *naṣṭā*—lost; *pralaye*—at the time of annihilation; *vāṇī*—message; *iyam*—this; *veda-saṁjñitā*—consisting of the *Vedas; mayā*—by Me; *ādau*—at the time of creation; *brahmaṇe*—unto Lord Brahmā; *proktā*—spoken; *dharmaḥ*—religious principles; *yasyām*—in which; *mat-ātmakaḥ*—identical with Me.

TRANSLATION

The Supreme Personality of Godhead said: By the influence of time, the transcendental sound of Vedic knowledge was lost at the time of annihilation. Therefore, when the subsequent creation took place, I spoke the Vedic knowledge to Brahmā because I Myself am the religious principles enunciated in the Vedas.

PURPORT

Lord Kṛṣṇa explains to Uddhava that although many processes and concepts of spiritual realization are described in the *Vedas*, the *Vedas* ultimately recommend devotional service to the Supreme Lord. Lord Kṛṣṇa is the reservoir of all pleasure, and His devotees directly enter into the Lord's *hlādinī,* or pleasure-giving, potency. Somehow or other one must fix one's mind in Lord Kṛṣṇa, and that is not possible without devotional service. One who has not developed his attraction to Lord Kṛṣṇa cannot restrain the senses from inferior engagements. Since other Vedic processes do not actually award Lord Kṛṣṇa to the practitioner, they cannot offer the highest benefit in life. The transcendental sound of the *Vedas* is itself the highest evidence, but one whose senses and mind are entangled in sense gratification and mental speculation, and whose heart is therefore covered by material dust, cannot directly receive the transcendental Vedic message. Thus one cannot appreciate the exalted position of devotional service to the Lord.

TEXT 4

तेन प्रोक्ता स्वपुत्राय मनवे पूर्वजाय सा ।
ततो भृग्वादयोऽगृह्णन् सप्त ब्रह्ममहर्षयः ॥ ४ ॥

tena proktā sva-putrāya
manave pūrva-jāya sā
tato bhṛgv-ādayo 'gṛhṇan
sapta brahma-maharṣayaḥ

tena—by Brahmā; *proktā*—spoken; *sva-putrāya*—to his son; *manave*—to Manu; *pūrva-jāya*—the oldest; *sā*—that Vedic knowledge; *tataḥ*—from Manu; *bhṛgu-ādayaḥ*—those headed by Bhṛgu Muni; *agṛhṇan*—accepted; *sapta*—seven; *brahma*—in Vedic literature; *mahārṣayaḥ*—most learned sages.

TRANSLATION

Lord Brahmā spoke this Vedic knowledge to his eldest son Manu, and the seven great sages headed by Bhṛgu Muni then accepted the same knowledge from Manu.

PURPORT

Everyone engages in a certain way of life based on one's own nature and propensities. *Bhakti-yoga* is the natural activity of one whose nature is completely purified by association with the Supreme Lord. Other processes are meant for those whose nature is still affected by the material modes, and thus such processes, along with their results, are themselves also materially contaminated. Devotional service to the Lord, however, is a pure spiritual process, and by executing it with a pure consciousness one comes directly in touch with the Personality of Godhead, who describes Himself in *Bhagavad-gītā* (9.2) as *pavitram idam uttamam*, the supreme pure. The system of *paramparā*, or disciplic succession, is illustrated in this and the previous verse. The spiritual masters in Caitanya Mahāprabhu's movement are part of such a disciplic succession, and through them the same Vedic knowledge spoken by Brahmā to Manu is still available.

TEXTS 5–7

तेभ्यः पितृभ्यस्तत्पुत्रा देवदानवगुह्यकाः ।
मनुष्याः सिद्धगन्धर्वाः सविद्याधरचारणाः ॥ ५ ॥
किन्देवाः किन्नरा नागा रक्षःकिम्पुरुषादयः ।
बह्व्यस्तेषां प्रकृतयो रजःसत्त्वतमोभुवः ॥ ६ ॥
याभिर्भूतानि भिद्यन्ते भूतानां पतयस्तथा ।
यथाप्रकृति सर्वेषां चित्रा वाचः स्रवन्ति हि ॥ ७ ॥

tebhyaḥ pitṛbhyas tat-putrā
deva-dānava-guhyakāḥ
manuṣyāḥ siddha-gandharvāḥ
sa-vidyādhara-cāraṇāḥ

kindevāḥ kinnarā nāgā
rakṣaḥ-kimpuruṣādayaḥ
bahvyas teṣāṁ prakṛtayo
rajaḥ-sattva-tamo-bhuvaḥ

yābhir bhūtāni bhidyante
bhūtānāṁ patayas tathā
yathā-prakṛti sarveṣāṁ
citrā vācaḥ sravanti hi

tebhyaḥ—from them (Bhṛgu Muni, etc.); *pitṛbhyaḥ*—from the forefathers; *tat*—their; *putrāḥ*—sons, descendants; *deva*—the demigods; *dānava*—demons; *guhyakāḥ*—the Guhyakas; *manuṣyāḥ*—human beings; *siddha-gandharvāḥ*—Siddhas and Gandharvas; *sa-vidyādhara-cāraṇāḥ*—along with Vidyādharas and Cāraṇas; *kindevāḥ*—a different human species; *kinnarāḥ*—half-humans; *nāgāḥ*—snakes; *rakṣaḥ*—demons; *kimpuruṣa*—an advanced race of monkeys; *ādayaḥ*—and so on; *bahvyaḥ*—many different; *teṣām*—of such living entities; *prakṛtayaḥ*—desires or natures; *rajaḥ-sattva-tamaḥ-bhuvaḥ*—being generated from the three modes of material nature; *yābhiḥ*—by such material desires or tendencies; *bhūtāni*—all such living entities; *bhidyante*—appear divided in many material forms; *bhūtānām*—and their; *patayaḥ*—leaders; *tathā*—divided in the same way; *yathā-prakṛti*—according to propensity or desire; *sarveṣām*—of all of them; *citrāḥ*—variegated; *vācaḥ*—Vedic rituals and *mantras; sravanti*—flow down; *hi*—certainly.

TRANSLATION

From the forefathers headed by Bhṛgu Muni and other sons of Brahmā appeared many children and descendants, who assumed different forms as demigods, demons, human beings, Guhyakas, Siddhas, Gandharvas, Vidyādharas, Cāraṇas, Kindevas, Kinnaras, Nāgas, Kimpuruṣas, and so on. All of the many universal species, along with their respective leaders, appeared with different natures and desires generated from the three modes of material nature. Therefore, because of the different characteristics of the living entities within the universe, there are a great many Vedic rituals, mantras and rewards.

PURPORT

If one is curious why Vedic literatures recommend so many different methods of worship and advancement, the answer is given here. Bhṛgu, Marīci, Atri, Aṅgirā, Pulastya, Pulaha and Kratu are the seven great *brāhmaṇa* sages and forefathers of this universe. The Kindevas are a race of human beings who are, like the demigods, completely free from fatigue, sweat and body odor. Seeing them, one may thus ask, *kiṁ devāḥ:* "Are they demigods?" Actually, they are human beings living on another planet within the universe. The Kinnaras are so called because they are *kiñcin narāḥ*, or "a little like human beings." The Kinnaras have either a human head or human body (but not both) combined with a nonhuman form. The Kimpuruṣas are so called because they resemble human beings and thus prompt the question *kiṁ puruṣāḥ:* "Are these human beings?" Actually, they are a race of monkeys who are almost like human beings.

Śrīla Bhaktisiddhānta Sarasvatī Ṭhākura explains that this verse describes the varieties of forgetfulness of the Supreme Personality of Godhead. The different Vedic *mantras* and rituals are especially meant for the different species of intelligent beings throughout the universe; but this proliferation of Vedic formulas indicates only the variety of material illusion and not a variety of ultimate purpose. The ultimate purpose of the many Vedic injunctions is one—to know and love the Supreme Personality of Godhead. The Lord Himself is emphatically explaining this to Śrī Uddhava.

TEXT 8

एवं प्रकृतिवैचित्र्याद् भिद्यन्ते मतयो नृणाम् ।
पारम्पर्येण केषाञ्चित् पाषण्डमतयोऽपरे ॥ ८ ॥

evaṁ prakṛti-vaicitryād
bhidyante matayo nṛṇām
pāramparyeṇa keṣāñcit
pāṣaṇḍa-matayo 'pare

evam—thus; *prakṛti*—of nature or desires; *vaicitryāt*—due to the great variety; *bhidyante*—are divided; *matayaḥ*—philosophies of life; *nṛṇām*—among human beings; *pāramparyeṇa*—by tradition or disciplic succession; *keṣāñcit*—among some people; *pāṣaṇḍa*—atheistic; *matayaḥ*—philosophies; *apare*—others.

TRANSLATION

Thus, due to the great variety of desires and natures among human beings, there are many different theistic philosophies of

life, which are handed down through tradition, custom and disciplic succession. There are other teachers who directly support atheistic viewpoints.

PURPORT

The word *keṣāñcit* refers to those persons in various parts of the world who are ignorant of the Vedic conclusion and thus concoct many unauthorized and ultimately fruitless philosophies of life. *Pāṣaṇḍa-matayaḥ* refers to those who directly oppose the Vedic conclusion. Śrīla Viśvanātha Cakravartī Ṭhākura has given a most interesting example, as follows. The water of the Ganges is always pure and very sweet. On the banks of that great river, however, there are several types of poisonous trees whose roots drink up the Ganges water from the soil and use it to produce poisonous fruits. Similarly, those who are atheistic or demoniac utilize their association with Vedic knowledge to produce the poisonous fruits of atheistic or materialistic philosophy.

TEXT 9

मन्मायामोहितधियः पुरुषाः पुरुषर्षभ ।
श्रेयो वदन्त्यनेकान्तं यथाकर्म यथारुचि ॥ ९ ॥

man-māyā-mohita-dhiyaḥ
puruṣāḥ puruṣarṣabha
śreyo vadanty anekāntaṁ
yathā-karma yathā-ruci

mat-māyā—by My illusory potency; *mohita*—bewildered; *dhiyaḥ*—those whose intelligence; *puruṣāḥ*—people; *puruṣa-ṛṣabha*—O best among men; *śreyaḥ*—what is good for people; *vadanti*—they speak; *aneka-antam*—in innumerable ways; *yathā-karma*—according to their own activities; *yathā-ruci*—according to what pleases them.

TRANSLATION

O best among men, the intelligence of human beings is bewildered by My illusory potency, and thus, according to their

own activities and whims, they speak in innumerable ways about what is actually good for people.

PURPORT

Unlike the Supreme Personality of Godhead, the individual living entity is not omniscient, therefore his activities and pleasures do not represent the whole truth. According to one's individual way of doing things (*yathā-karma*) and one's personal preference (*yathā-ruci*), one speaks to others about what is good for them. Everyone thinks, "What is good for me is good for everyone." Actually, the best thing for everyone is to surrender to the Supreme Personality of Godhead, Lord Kṛṣṇa, and thus realize one's eternal nature of bliss and knowledge. Without knowledge of the Absolute Truth, many so-called learned people are whimsically advising other whimsical people who also lack perfect knowledge of the actual goal of life.

TEXT 10

धर्ममेके यशश्चान्ये कामं सत्यं दमं शमम् ।
अन्ये वदन्ति स्वार्थं वा ऐश्वर्यं त्यागभोजनम् ।
केचिद् यज्ञं तपो दानं व्रतानि नियमान् यमान् ॥१०॥

dharmam eke yaśaś cānye
kāmaṁ satyaṁ damaṁ śamam
anye vadanti svārthaṁ vā
aiśvaryaṁ tyāga-bhojanam
kecid yajñaṁ tapo dānaṁ
vratāni niyamān yamān

dharmam—pious activities; *eke*—some people; *yaśaḥ*—fame; *ca*—also; *anye*—others; *kāmam*—sense gratification; *satyam*—truthfulness; *damam*—self-control; *śamam*—peacefulness; *anye*—others; *vadanti*—propound; *sva-artham*—pursuing one's self-interest; *vai*—certainly; *aiśvaryam*—opulence or political influence; *tyāga*—renunciation; *bhojanam*—consumption; *kecit*—some people; *yajñam*—sacrifice; *tapaḥ*—austerity; *dānam*—charity; *vratāni*—taking vows; *niyamān*—regular religious duties; *yamān*—strict regulative discipline.

TRANSLATION

Some say that people will be happy by performing pious religious activities. Others say that happiness is attained through fame, sense gratification, truthfulness, self-control, peace, self-interest, political influence, opulence, renunciation, consumption, sacrifice, penance, charity, vows, regulated duties or strict disciplinary regulation. Each process has its proponents.

PURPORT

Dharmam eke refers to those atheistic philosophers called *karma-mīmāṁsakas,* who state that one should not waste time worrying about a kingdom of God that no one has ever seen and from which no one has ever returned; rather, one should expertly utilize the laws of *karma,* performing fruitive activities in such a way that one will always be well situated. Concerning fame, it is said that as long as the fame of a human being is sung in the pious planets, he may live for thousands of years in material heaven. *Kāmam* refers to Vedic texts like the *Kāma-sūtra* as well as millions of modern books that advise one about sex pleasure. Some people state that the highest virtue in life is honesty; others say it is self-control, peace of mind and so on. Each viewpoint has proponents and "scriptures." Others say that law, order and morality are the highest good, whereas still others propose political influence as the real self-interest of human beings. Some state that one should give away one's material possessions to the needy; others state that one should try to enjoy this life as far as possible; and others recommend daily rituals, disciplinary vows, penances, and so on.

TEXT 11

आद्यन्तवन्त एवैषां लोकाः कर्मविनिर्मिताः ।
दुःखोदर्कास्तमोनिष्ठाः क्षुद्रा मन्दाः शुचार्पिताः ॥११॥

ādy-anta-vanta evaiṣāṁ
lokāḥ karma-vinirmitāḥ
duḥkhodarkās tamo-niṣṭhāḥ
kṣudrā mandāḥ śucārpitāḥ

ādi-anta-vantaḥ—possessing a beginning and end; *eva*—undoubtedly; *eṣām*—of them (the materialistic); *lokāḥ*—achieved destinations; *karma*—by one's material work; *vinirmitāḥ*—produced; *duḥkha*—misery; *udarkāḥ*—bringing as the future result; *tamaḥ*—ignorance; *niṣṭhāḥ*—situated in; *kṣudrāḥ*—meager; *mandāḥ*—wretched; *śucā*—with lamentation; *arpitāḥ*—filled.

TRANSLATION

All the persons I have just mentioned obtain temporary fruits from their material work. Indeed, the meager and miserable situations they achieve bring future unhappiness and are based on ignorance. Even while enjoying the fruits of their work, such persons are filled with lamentation.

PURPORT

Those who have grasped temporary material things, mistaking them to be ultimate reality, are not considered very intelligent by anyone except themselves. Such foolish persons are always in anxiety because by the laws of nature the very fruits of their work are constantly being transformed in ways neither desired nor expected. The performer of Vedic rituals can elevate himself to heavenly planets, whereas one who is atheistic has the privilege of transferring himself to hell. The entire panorama of material existence is actually uninteresting and dull (*mandāḥ*). One can make no real progress within the material world; therefore one should take to Kṛṣṇa consciousness and prepare oneself to go back home, back to Godhead.

TEXT 12

मय्यर्पितात्मनः सभ्य निरपेक्षस्य सर्वतः ।
मयात्मना सुखं यत्तत् कुतः स्याद् विषयात्मनाम् ॥१२॥

mayy arpitātmanaḥ sabhya
nirapekṣasya sarvataḥ
mayātmanā sukhaṁ yat tat
kutaḥ syād viṣayātmanām

mayi—in Me; *arpita*—fixed; *ātmanaḥ*—of one whose consciousness; *sabhya*—O learned Uddhava; *nirapekṣasya*—of one bereft of material desires; *sarvataḥ*—in all respects; *mayā*—with Me; *ātmanā*—with the Supreme Personality of Godhead or with one's own spiritual body; *sukham*—happiness; *yat tat*—such; *kutaḥ*—how; *syāt*—could it be; *viṣaya*—in material sense gratification; *ātmanām*—of those who are attached.

TRANSLATION

O learned Uddhava, those who fix their consciousness in Me, giving up all material desires, share with Me a happiness that cannot possibly be experienced by those engaged in sense gratification.

PURPORT

The actual purport of Vedic knowledge is explained in this verse. The word *viṣayātmanām* includes those who are cultivating material peace of mind, self-control and speculative philosophy. But even if such persons rise to the platform of *sattva-guṇa*, the mode of goodness, they do not attain perfection, because *sattva-guṇa*, being material, is also part and parcel of *māyā*, or illusion. As stated by Śrī Nārada Muni,

kiṁ vā yogena sāṅkhyena
nyāsa-svādhyāyayor api
kiṁ vā śreyobhir anyaiś ca
na yatrātma-prado hariḥ

"The Supreme Personality of Godhead is not inclined to award Himself even to one who executes the *yoga* system, speculative philosophy, the renounced order of life or Vedic studies. Indeed, no so-called materially auspicious process can induce the Lord to reveal Himself." (*Bhāg*. 4.31.12) According to Śrīla Śrīdhara Svāmī, one enjoys the happiness spoken of in this verse while associating, in one's own spiritual body, with the supreme transcendental form of the Lord. The Lord's transcendental form is filled with infinite, wonderful qualities, and the happiness of being with the Lord is unlimited. Unfortunately, materialistic people cannot possibly imagine such happiness, since they are not at all inclined to love the Supreme Personality of Godhead.

TEXT 13

अकिञ्चनस्य दान्तस्य शान्तस्य समचेतसः ।
मया सन्तुष्टमनसः सर्वाः सुखमया दिशः ॥१३॥

akiñcanasya dāntasya
śāntasya sama-cetasaḥ
mayā santuṣṭa-manasaḥ
sarvāḥ sukha-mayā diśaḥ

akiñcanasya—of one who does not desire anything; *dāntasya*—whose senses are controlled; *śāntasya*—peaceful; *sama-cetasaḥ*—whose consciousness is equal everywhere; *mayā*—with Me; *santuṣṭa*—completely satisfied; *manasaḥ*—whose mind; *sarvāḥ*—all; *sukha-mayāḥ*—full of happiness; *diśaḥ*—directions.

TRANSLATION

One who does not desire anything within this world, who has achieved peace by controlling his senses, whose consciousness is equal in all conditions and whose mind is completely satisfied in Me finds only happiness wherever he goes.

PURPORT

A devotee who is always meditating upon Lord Kṛṣṇa experiences transcendental sound, touch, form, flavor and aroma in the pastimes of the Lord. These sublime perceptions are certainly due to the causeless mercy of Lord Kṛṣṇa upon one whose mind and senses are completely satisfied in Him. Such a person finds only happiness wherever he goes. Śrīla Viśvanātha Cakravartī Ṭhākura gives the example that when a very wealthy man travels all over the world, at every place he stays he always enjoys the same luxurious standard of comfort. Similarly, one who has developed Kṛṣṇa consciousness is never separated from happiness, because Lord Kṛṣṇa is all-pervading. The word *kiñcana* indicates the so-called enjoyable things of this world. One who is *akiñcana* has correctly understood that material sense gratification is simply the glare of illusion, and therefore such a person is *dāntasya*, or self-controlled, *śāntasya*, or peaceful, and *mayā santuṣṭa-manasaḥ*, or completely satisfied with his transcendental experience of the Supreme Personality of Godhead.

TEXT 14

न पारमेष्ठ्यं न महेन्द्रधिष्ण्यं
न सार्वभौमं न रसाधिपत्यम् ।
न योगसिद्धीरपुनर्भवं वा
मय्यर्पितात्मेच्छति मद् विनान्यत् ॥१४॥

na pārameṣṭhyaṁ na mahendra-dhiṣṇyaṁ
na sārvabhaumaṁ na rasādhipatyam
na yoga-siddhīr apunar-bhavaṁ vā
mayy arpitātmecchati mad vinānyat

na—not; *pārameṣṭhyam*—the position or abode of Lord Brahmā; *na*—never; *mahā-indra-dhiṣṇyam*—the position of Lord Indra; *na*—neither; *sārvabhaumam*—empire on the earth; *na*—nor; *rasa-ādhipatyam*—sovereignty in the lower planetary systems; *na*—never; *yoga-siddhīḥ*—the eightfold *yoga* perfections; *apunaḥ-bhavam*—liberation; *vā*—nor; *mayi*—in Me; *arpita*—fixed; *ātmā*—consciousness; *icchati*—he desires; *mat*—Me; *vinā*—without; *anyat*—anything else.

TRANSLATION

One who has fixed his consciousness in Me does not desire the position or abode of Lord Brahmā or Lord Indra, nor an empire on the earth, nor sovereignty in the lower planetary systems, nor the eightfold perfection of yoga, nor liberation from birth and death. Such a person desires Me alone.

PURPORT

The position of the *akiñcana* pure devotee is described in this verse. Śrī Priyavrata Mahārāja is an example of a great devotee who was not interested in universal sovereignty because his love was completely absorbed in the lotus feet of the Lord. Even the greatest material enjoyment appears most insignificant and useless to a pure devotee of the Lord.

TEXT 15

न तथा मे प्रियतम आत्मयोनिर्न शङ्करः ।
न च सङ्कर्षणो न श्रीर्नैवात्मा च यथा भवान् ॥१५॥

na tathā me priyatama
ātma-yonir na śaṅkaraḥ
na ca saṅkarṣaṇo na śrīr
naivātmā ca yathā bhavān

na—not; *tathā*—in the same way; *me*—to Me; *priya-tamaḥ*—most dear; *ātma-yoniḥ*—Lord Brahmā, who is born from My body; *na*—nor; *śaṅkaraḥ*—Lord Śiva; *na*—nor; *ca*—also; *saṅkarṣaṇaḥ*—My direct expansion Lord Saṅkarṣaṇa; *na*—nor; *śrīḥ*—the goddess of fortune; *na*—nor; *eva*—certainly; *ātmā*—My own self as the Deity; *ca*—also; *yathā*—as much as; *bhavān*—you.

TRANSLATION

My dear Uddhava, even Lord Brahmā, Lord Śiva, Lord Saṅkarṣaṇa, the goddess of fortune Lakṣmī and indeed My own self are not as dear to Me as you are.

PURPORT

The Lord has described in the previous verses the unalloyed love of His pure devotees for Him, and now the Lord describes His love for His devotees. *Ātma-yoni* means Lord Brahmā, who is born directly from the Lord's body. Lord Śiva always gives great pleasure to Lord Kṛṣṇa by his constant meditation upon Him, and Saṅkarṣaṇa, or Balarāma, is the Lord's brother in *kṛṣṇa-līlā.* The goddess of fortune is the Lord's wife, and the word *ātmā* here indicates the Lord's own self as the Deity. None of these personalities—even the Lord's own self—are as dear to Him as His pure devotee Uddhava, an *akiñcana* devotee of the Lord. Śrīla Madhvācārya cites from Vedic literature the example that a gentleman sometimes neglects his own interest and that of his children to give charity to a poor beggar. Similarly, the Lord gives preference to a helpless devotee who depends completely on His mercy. The only way to obtain the Lord's mercy is through His causeless love, and the Lord is most lovingly inclined toward those devotees who are most dependent on Him, just as ordinary mothers and fathers worry more about their helpless children than about those who are self-sufficient. Thus even if one lacks any material qualification, one should simply depend upon the Supreme Personality of Godhead, without any other interest, and surely one will achieve the highest perfection of life.

TEXT 16

निरपेक्षं मुनिं शान्तं निर्वैरं समदर्शनम् ।
अनुव्रजाम्यहं नित्यं पूयेयेत्यङ्घ्रिरेणुभिः ॥१६॥

nirapekṣaṁ muniṁ śāntaṁ
nirvairaṁ sama-darśanam
anuvrajāmy ahaṁ nityaṁ
pūyeyety aṅghri-reṇubhiḥ

nirapekṣam—without personal desire; *munim*—always thinking of assisting Me in My pastimes; *śāntam*—peaceful; *nirvairam*—not inimical to anyone; *sama-darśanam*—equal consciousness everywhere; *anuvrajāmi*—follow; *aham*—I; *nityam*—always; *pūyeya*—I may be purified (I will purify the universe within Me); *iti*—thus; *aṅghri*—of the lotus feet; *reṇubhiḥ*—by the dust.

TRANSLATION

I desire to purify with the dust of the lotus feet of My devotees the material worlds, which are situated within Me. Thus, I always follow the footsteps of My pure devotees, who are free from all personal desire, rapt in thought of My pastimes, peaceful, without any feelings of enmity, and of equal disposition everywhere.

PURPORT

Just as the devotees always follow the footsteps of Lord Kṛṣṇa, similarly Lord Kṛṣṇa, being a devotee of His devotees, follows the footsteps of His devotees. A pure servitor of the Lord is always meditating on the pastimes of the Lord and considering how to assist the Lord in His mission. All the material universes are situated in Śrī Kṛṣṇa's body, as demonstrated to Arjuna, mother Yaśodā and others. Lord Kṛṣṇa is the Supreme Personality of Godhead, and therefore there is no question of impurity in the Lord. Still, the Lord desires to purify the universes situated within Him by taking the dust of the lotus feet of His pure devotees. Without the dust of the lotus feet of the devotees, it is not possible to engage in pure devotional service, without which one cannot directly experience transcendental bliss. Lord Kṛṣṇa thought, "I have established this strict rule that one can enjoy My transcendental bliss only through devotional service obtained from the dust of the lotus feet of My devotees. Since I also desire to experience My own bliss, I will observe the standard procedure and accept the dust of My devotees' feet." Śrīla Madhvācārya points out that Lord Kṛṣṇa follows the footsteps of His devotees in order to purify them. As the Lord walks along behind His pure devotees, the wind blows the dust of the Lord's feet in the front of His devotees, who then become purified by contact with such transcendental dust. One should not foolishly look for material logic in these transcendental pastimes of the Lord. It is simply a question of love between the Lord and His devotees.

TEXT 17

निष्किञ्चना मय्यनुरक्तचेतसः
शान्ता महान्तोऽखिलजीववत्सलाः ।
कामैरनालब्धधियो जुषन्ति ते
यन्नैरपेक्ष्यं न विदुः सुखं मम ॥१७॥

niṣkiñcanā mayy anurakta-cetasaḥ
śāntā mahānto 'khila-jīva-vatsalāḥ
kāmair anālabdha-dhiyo juṣanti te
yan nairapekṣyaṁ na viduḥ sukhaṁ mama

niṣkiñcanāḥ—without any desire for sense gratification; *mayi*—in Me, the Supreme Lord; *anurakta-cetasaḥ*—mind constantly attached; *śāntāḥ*—peaceful; *mahāntaḥ*—great souls without false ego; *akhila*—to all; *jīva*—living entities; *vatsalāḥ*—affectionate well-wishers; *kāmaiḥ*—

by opportunities for sense gratification; *anālabdha*—untouched and unaffected; *dhiyaḥ*—whose consciousness; *juṣanti*—experience; *te*—they; *yat*—which; *nairapekṣyam*—achieved only by complete detachment; *na viduḥ*—they do not know; *sukham*—happiness; *mama*—My.

TRANSLATION

Those who are without any desire for personal gratification, whose minds are always attached to Me, who are peaceful, without false ego and merciful to all living entities, and whose consciousness is never affected by opportunities for sense gratification—such persons enjoy in Me a happiness that cannot be known or achieved by those lacking such detachment from the material world.

PURPORT

The pure devotees always experience transcendental bliss in their service to Śrī Kṛṣṇa, the reservoir of pleasure; thus they are completely detached from material pleasure and do not desire even liberation. Since all others have some personal desire, they cannot experience such happiness. Pure devotees always desire to give Kṛṣṇa conscious happiness to all others, and therefore they are called *mahāntaḥ*, or great souls. In the course of a devotee's service, many opportunities for sense gratification arise, but a pure devotee is not tempted or attracted and does not fall down from his exalted transcendental position.

TEXT 18

बाध्यमानोऽपि मद्भक्तो विषयैरजितेन्द्रियः ।
प्रायः प्रगल्भया भक्त्या विषयैर्नाभिभूयते ॥१८॥

bādhyamāno 'pi mad-bhakto
viṣayair ajitendriyaḥ
prāyaḥ pragalbhayā bhaktyā
viṣayair nābhibhūyate

bādhyamānaḥ—being harassed; *api*—even though; *mat-bhaktaḥ*—My devotee; *viṣayaiḥ*—by the sense objects; *ajita*—without having conquered; *indriyaḥ*—the senses; *prāyaḥ*—generally; *pragalbhayā*—effective and strong; *bhaktyā*—by devotion; *viṣayaiḥ*—by sense gratification; *na*—not; *abhibhūyate*—is defeated.

TRANSLATION

My dear Uddhava, not having fully conquered his senses, My devotee may be harassed by material desires, but because of his unflinching devotion for Me, he will not be defeated by sense gratification.

PURPORT

Abhibhūyate indicates falling down into the material world and being defeated by *māyā.* But even though one's senses are not fully conquered, one who has unflinching devotion for Lord Kṛṣṇa does not run the risk of being separated from Him. The words *pragalbhayā bhaktyā* indicate a person who has great devotion for Lord Kṛṣṇa, and not one who desires to commit sinful activities and chant Hare Kṛṣṇa to avoid the reaction. Because of previous bad habits and immaturity, even a sincere devotee may be harassed by lingering attraction to the bodily concept of life; but his unflinching devotion for Lord Kṛṣṇa will act. Śrīla Viśvanātha Cakravartī Ṭhākura gives the following two examples. A great warrior may be struck by the weapon of his enemy, but because of his courage and strength he is not killed or defeated. He accepts the blow and goes on to victory. Similarly, one may contract a serious disease, but if he takes the proper medicine he is quickly cured.

If those who follow the impersonal system of speculation and austerity deviate even slightly from their path, they fall down. A devotee, however, even though immature, never falls from the path of devotional service. Even if he displays occasional weakness, he is still considered a devotee if his devotion to Lord Kṛṣṇa is very strong. As the Lord states in *Bhagavad-gītā* (9.30):

api cet su-durācāro
bhajate mām ananya-bhāk
sādhur eva sa mantavyaḥ
samyag vyavasito hi saḥ

"Even if one commits the most abominable actions, if he is engaged in devotional service he is to be considered saintly because he is properly situated."

TEXT 19

यथाग्निः सुसमृद्धार्चिः करोत्येधांसि भस्मसात् ।
तथा मद्विषया भक्तिरुद्धवैनांसि कृत्स्नशः ॥१९॥

yathāgniḥ su-samṛddhārciḥ
karoty edhāṁsi bhasmasāt
tathā mad-viṣayā bhaktir
uddhavaināṁsi kṛtsnaśaḥ

yathā—just as; *agniḥ*—fire; *su-samṛddha*—blazing; *arciḥ*—whose flames; *karoti*—turns; *edhāṁsi*—firewood; *bhasma-sāt*—into ashes; *tathā*—similarly; *mat-viṣayā*—with Me as the object; *bhaktiḥ*—devotion; *uddhava*—O Uddhava; *enāṁsi*—sins; *kṛtsnaśaḥ*—completely.

TRANSLATION

My dear Uddhava, just as a blazing fire turns firewood into ashes, similarly, devotion unto Me completely burns to ashes sins committed by My devotees.

PURPORT

One should carefully note that the Lord refers to devotion that is like a blazing fire. To commit sinful activity on the strength of chanting the holy name is the greatest offense, and the devotion of one who commits this offense cannot be compared to a blazing fire of love for Kṛṣṇa. As stated in the previous verse, a sincere loving devotee, because of immaturity or previous bad habits, may be disturbed by his senses even though he has accepted Lord Kṛṣṇa as the only goal in his life. But if even by chance the devotee accidentally falls down without premeditation or indifference, the Lord immediately burns to ashes his sinful reactions, just as a blazing fire immediately consumes an insignificant piece of wood. Lord Kṛṣṇa is glorious, and one who takes exclusive shelter of the Lord receives the unique benefits of devotional service to the Supreme Personality of Godhead.

TEXT 20

न साधयति मां योगो न सांख्यं धर्म उद्धव ।
न स्वाध्यायस्तपस्त्यागो यथा भक्तिर्ममोर्जिता॥२०॥

na sādhayati māṁ yogo
na sāṅkhyaṁ dharma uddhava
na svādhyāyas tapas tyāgo
yathā bhaktir mamorjitā

na—not; *sādhayati*—brings under control; *mām*—Me; *yogaḥ*—the *yoga* system; *na*—nor; *sāṅkhyam*—the system of Sāṅkhya philosophy; *dharmaḥ*—pious activities within the *varṇāśrama* system; *uddhava*—My dear Uddhava; *na*—not; *svādhyāyaḥ*—Vedic study; *tapaḥ*—austerity; *tyāgaḥ*—renunciation; *yathā*—as; *bhaktiḥ*—devotional service; *mama*—unto Me; *ūrjitā*—strongly developed.

TRANSLATION

My dear Uddhava, the unalloyed devotional service rendered to Me by My devotees brings Me under their control. I cannot be thus controlled by those engaged in mystic yoga, Sāṅkhya philosophy, pious work, Vedic study, austerity or renunciation.

PURPORT

One may make Kṛṣṇa the goal of mystic *yoga*, Sāṅkhya philosophy, etc.; yet such activities do not please the Lord as much as direct loving service, which one practices by hearing and chanting about the Lord and executing His mission. Śrīla Rūpa Gosvāmī states, *jñāna-karmādy-anāvṛtam:* a devotee should simply depend on Kṛṣṇa and should not unnecessarily complicate his loving service with tendencies toward fruitive work or mental speculation. The residents of Vṛndāvana simply depend on Lord Kṛṣṇa. When the great serpent Aghāsura appeared in the precincts of Vraja, the cowherd boys, completely confident in their friendship with Lord Kṛṣṇa, fearlessly marched into the serpent's gigantic mouth. Such pure love for Kṛṣṇa brings the Lord under the control of the devotee.

TEXT 21

भक्त्याहमेकया ग्राह्यः श्रद्धयात्मा प्रियः सताम् ।
भक्तिः पुनाति मन्निष्ठा श्वपाकानपि सम्भवात् ॥२१॥

bhaktyāham ekayā grāhyaḥ
śraddhayātmā priyaḥ satām
bhaktiḥ punāti man-niṣṭhā
śva-pākān api sambhavāt

bhaktyā—by devotional service; *aham*—I; *ekayā*—unalloyed; *grāhyaḥ*—am to be obtained; *śraddhayā*—by faith; *ātmā*—the Supreme Personality of Godhead; *priyaḥ*—the object of love; *satām*—of the devotees; *bhaktiḥ*—pure devotional service; *punāti*—purifies; *mat-niṣṭhā*—fixing Me as the only goal; *śva-pākān*—dog-eaters; *api*—even; *sambhavāt*—from the contamination of low birth.

TRANSLATION

Only by practicing unalloyed devotional service with full faith in Me can one obtain Me, the Supreme Personality of Godhead. I am naturally dear to My devotees, who take Me as the only goal of their loving service. By engaging in such pure devotional service, even the dog-eaters can purify themselves from the contamination of their low birth.

PURPORT

Sambhavāt indicates *jāti-doṣāt*, or the pollution of low birth. *Jāti-doṣa* does not refer to mundane social, economic or professional status, but rather to one's degree of spiritual enlightenment. All around the world, many people are born into rich and powerful families, but they often acquire abominable habits that are part of their so-called family tradition. However, even unfortunate persons who are taught from birth to engage in sinful activities can at once be purified by the potency of pure devotional service. Such service must have Lord Kṛṣṇa as the only goal (*man-niṣṭhā*), must be rendered with full faith (*śraddhayā*), and must be unalloyed, or without any selfish motivation (*ekayā*).

TEXT 22

धर्मः सत्यदयोपेतो विद्या वा तपसान्विता ।
मद्भक्त्यापेतमात्मानं न सम्यक् प्रपुनाति हि ॥२२॥

dharmaḥ satya-dayopeto
vidyā vā tapasānvitā
mad-bhaktyāpetam ātmānaṁ
na samyak prapunāti hi

dharmaḥ—religious principles; *satya*—with truthfulness; *dayā*—and mercy; *upetaḥ*—endowed; *vidyā*—knowledge; *vā*—or; *tapasā*—with austerity; *anvitā*—endowed; *mat-bhaktyā*—devotional service to Me; *apetam*—bereft of; *ātmānam*—consciousness; *na*—not; *samyak*—completely; *prapunāti*—purifies; *hi*—certainly.

TRANSLATION

Religious activities endowed with honesty and mercy or knowledge obtained with great penance cannot completely purify one's consciousness if they are bereft of loving service to Me.

PURPORT

Although pious religious work, truthfulness, mercy, penances and knowledge partially purify one's existence, they do not take out the root of material desires. Thus the same desires will reappear at a later time. After an extensive program of material gratification, one becomes eager to perform austerities, acquire knowledge, perform selfless work and in general purify one's existence. After sufficient piety and purification, however, one again becomes eager for material enjoyment. When clearing an agricultural field one must uproot the unwanted plants, otherwise with the coming of rain everything will grow back as it was. Pure devotional service to the Lord uproots one's material desires, so that there is no danger of relapsing into a degraded life of material gratification. In the eternal kingdom of God, loving reciprocation between the Lord and His devotees is manifest. One who has not come to this stage of enlightenment must remain on the material platform, which is always full of discrepancies and contradictions. Thus everything is incomplete and imperfect without loving service to the Lord.

TEXT 23

कथं विना रोमहर्षं द्रवता चेतसा विना ।
विनानन्दाश्रुकलया शुध्येद् भक्त्या विनाशयः ॥२३॥

kathaṁ vinā roma-harṣaṁ
dravatā cetasā vinā
vinānandāśru-kalayā
śudhyed bhaktyā vināśayaḥ

katham—how; *vinā*—without; *roma-harṣam*—standing of the hairs on end; *dravatā*—melted; *cetasā*—heart; *vinā*—without; *vinā*—without; *ānanda*—of bliss; *aśru-kalayā*—the flowing of tears; *śudhyet*—can be purified; *bhaktyā*—loving service; *vinā*—without; *āśayaḥ*—the consciousness.

TRANSLATION

If one's hairs do not stand on end, how can the heart melt? And if the heart does not melt, how can tears of love flow from the eyes? If one does not cry in spiritual happiness, how can one render loving service to the Lord? And without such service, how can the consciousness be purified?

PURPORT

Loving service to the Lord is the only process that can completely purify one's consciousness; such service produces waves of ecstatic love that completely cleanse the soul. As mentioned earlier by Lord Kṛṣṇa to Śrī Uddhava, other processes such as self-control, pious activities, mystic *yoga*, penances, etc., certainly purify the mind, as stated in many authorized literatures. Such processes, however, do not completely remove the desire to perform forbidden activities. But pure devotional service rendered in love of Godhead is so powerful that it burns to ashes any obstacle encountered on the path of progress. The Lord has stated in this chapter that loving service to Him is a blazing fire that burns to ashes all impediments. In contrast, the small fires of mental speculation or mystic *yoga* can be extinguished by sinful desires at any moment. Thus, by hearing *Śrīmad-Bhāgavatam* one should ignite the blazing fire of loving service to the Lord and burn to ashes the network of material illusion.

TEXT 24

वाग् गद्गदा द्रवते यस्य चित्तं
रुदत्यभीक्ष्णं हसति क्वचिच्च ।
विलज्ज उद्गायति नृत्यते च
मद्भक्तियुक्तो भुवनं पुनाति ॥२४॥

vāg gadgadā dravate yasya cittaṁ
rudaty abhīkṣṇaṁ hasati kvacic ca
vilajja udgāyati nṛtyate ca
mad-bhakti-yukto bhuvanaṁ punāti

vāk—speech; *gadgadā*—choked up; *dravate*—melts; *yasya*—of whom; *cittam*—the heart; *rudati*—cries; *abhīkṣṇam*—again and again; *hasati*—laughs; *kvacit*—sometimes; *ca*—also; *vilajjaḥ*—ashamed; *udgāyati*—sings out loudly; *nṛtyate*—dances; *ca*—also; *mat-bhakti-yuktaḥ*—one fixed in devotional service to Me; *bhuvanam*—the universe; *punāti*—purifies.

TRANSLATION

A devotee whose speech is sometimes choked up, whose heart melts, who cries continually and sometimes laughs, who feels ashamed and cries out loudly and then dances—a devotee thus fixed in loving service to Me purifies the entire universe.

PURPORT

Vāg gadgadā refers to a highly emotional state in which the throat is choked up and one cannot express oneself. *Vilajjaḥ* indicates that a devotee sometimes feels embarrassment due to bodily functions and memories of past sinful activities. In this condition, a devotee loudly cries out the holy name of Kṛṣṇa and sometimes dances in ecstasy. As stated here, such a devotee purifies the three worlds.

By melting of the heart, one becomes very steady in spiritual life. Normally, one whose heart easily melts is thought to be unsteady; but because Lord Kṛṣṇa is the stable foundation of all existence, one whose heart melts in love of Kṛṣṇa becomes most stable and cannot be disturbed by opposing arguments, bodily suffering, mental problems, supernatural disasters or the interference of envious persons. Because such a devotee is fixed in loving service to the Lord, he becomes the very heart of the Personality of Godhead.

TEXT 25

यथाग्निना हेम मलं जहाति
ध्मातं पुनः स्वं भजते च रूपम् ।
आत्मा च कर्मानुशयं विधूय
मद्भक्तियोगेन भजत्यथो माम् ॥२५॥

yathāgninā hema malaṁ jahāti
dhmātaṁ punaḥ svaṁ bhajate ca rūpam
ātmā ca karmānuśayaṁ vidhūya
mad-bhakti-yogena bhajaty atho mām

yathā—just as; *agninā*—by fire; *hema*—gold; *malam*—impurities; *jahāti*—gives up; *dhmātam*—smelted; *punaḥ*—again; *svam*—its own; *bhajate*—enters; *ca*—also; *rūpam*—form; *ātmā*—the spirit soul or consciousness; *ca*—also; *karma*—of fruitive activities; *anuśayam*—the resultant contamination; *vidhūya*—removing; *mat-bhakti-yogena*—by loving service to Me; *bhajati*—worships; *atho*—thus; *mām*—Me.

TRANSLATION

Just as gold, when smelted in fire, gives up its impurities and returns to its pure brilliant state, similarly, the spirit soul, absorbed in the fire of bhakti-yoga, is purified of all contamination caused by previous fruitive activities and returns to its original position of serving Me in the spiritual world.

PURPORT

According to Śrīla Viśvanātha Cakravartī Ṭhākura, this verse indicates that the devotee goes back home, back to Godhead, and there worships Lord Kṛṣṇa in his original spiritual body, which is compared to the original pure form of smelted gold. Gold alloyed with inferior metals cannot be purified by water and soap; similarly, the heart's impurities cannot be removed by superficial processes. Only the fire of love of Godhead can cleanse one's soul and send one back home, back to Godhead, to engage in eternal loving service to the Lord.

TEXT 26

यथा यथात्मा परिमृज्यतेऽसौ
मत्पुण्यगाथाश्रवणाभिधानैः ।
तथा तथा पश्यति वस्तु सूक्ष्मं
चक्षुर्यथैवाञ्जनसम्प्रयुक्तम् ॥२६॥

yathā yathātmā parimṛjyate 'sau
mat-puṇya-gāthā-śravaṇābhidhānaiḥ
tathā tathā paśyati vastu sūkṣmaṁ
cakṣur yathaivāñjana-samprayuktam

yathā yathā—as much as; *ātmā*—the spirit soul, the conscious entity; *parimṛjyate*—is cleansed of material contamination; *asau*—he; *mat-puṇya-gāthā*—the pious narrations of My glories; *śravaṇa*—by hearing; *abhidhānaiḥ*—and by chanting; *tathā tathā*—exactly in that proportion; *paśyati*—he sees; *vastu*—the Absolute Truth; *sūkṣmam*—subtle, being nonmaterial; *cakṣuḥ*—the eye; *yathā*—just as; *eva*—certainly; *añjana*—with medicinal ointment; *samprayuktam*—treated.

TRANSLATION

When a diseased eye is treated with medicinal ointment it gradually recovers its power to see. Similarly, as a conscious living entity cleanses himself of material contamination by hearing and chanting the pious narrations of My glories, he regains his ability to see Me, the Absolute Truth, in My subtle spiritual form.

PURPORT

The Lord is called *sūkṣmam* because He is pure spiritual consciousness, without any tinge of material energy. If one chants and hears the holy name and glories of Kṛṣṇa with great sincerity, there is immediately a transcendental effect. We can immediately see the spiritual world and pastimes of the Lord if we fully surrender to the process mentioned here. A blind person feels perpetual gratitude to a doctor who restores his sight. Similarly, we sing *cakṣu-dāna dila ye, janme janme prabhu sei:* the bona fide spiritual master, the representative of Lord Kṛṣṇa, restores our spiritual sight, and thus he is our eternal lord and master.

TEXT 27

विषयान् ध्यायतश्चित्तं विषयेषु विषज्जते ।
मामनुस्मरतश्चित्तं मय्येव प्रविलीयते ॥२७॥

viṣayān dhyāyataś cittaṁ
viṣayeṣu viṣajjate
mām anusmarataś cittaṁ
mayy eva pravilīyate

viṣayān—objects of sense gratification; *dhyāyataḥ*—of one who is meditating on; *cittam*—the consciousness; *viṣayeṣu*—in the objects of gratification; *viṣajjate*—becomes attached; *mām*—Me; *anusmarataḥ*—of one remembering constantly; *cittam*—the consciousness; *mayi*—in Me; *eva*—certainly; *pravilīyate*—is absorbed.

TRANSLATION

The mind of one meditating upon the objects of sense gratification is certainly entangled in such objects, but if one constantly remembers Me, then the mind is absorbed in Me.

PURPORT

One should not think that one can attain complete transcendental knowledge of Kṛṣṇa by mechanically engaging in worship of the Lord. Lord Kṛṣṇa states here that one must endeavor constantly to keep the Lord within one's mind. *Anusmarataḥ*, or constant remembrance, is possible for one who always chants and hears the glories of Lord Kṛṣṇa. It is therefore stated, *śravaṇam, kīrtanam, smaraṇam:* the process of devotional service begins with hearing (*śravaṇam*) and chanting (*kīrtanam*), from which remembrance (*smaraṇam*) develops. One who constantly thinks of the objects of material gratification becomes attached to them; similarly, one who constantly keeps Lord Kṛṣṇa within his mind becomes absorbed in the Lord's transcendental nature and thus becomes qualified to render personal service to the Lord in His own abode.

TEXT 28

तस्मादसदभिध्यानं यथा स्वप्नमनोरथम् ।
हित्वा मयि समाधत्स्व मनो मद्भावभावितम् ॥२८॥

tasmād asad-abhidhyānaṁ
yathā svapna-manoratham
hitvā mayi samādhatsva
mano mad-bhāva-bhāvitam

tasmāt—therefore; *asat*—material; *abhidhyānam*—processes of elevation which absorb one's attention; *yathā*—just as; *svapna*—in a dream; *manaḥ-ratham*—mental concoction; *hitvā*—giving up; *mayi*—in Me; *samādhatsva*—completely absorb; *manaḥ*—the mind; *mat-bhāva*—by consciousness of Me; *bhāvitam*—purified.

TRANSLATION

Therefore, one should reject all material processes of elevation, which are like the mental creations of a dream, and should completely absorb one's mind in Me. By constantly thinking of Me, one becomes purified.

PURPORT

The word *bhāvitam* means "caused to be." As explained in *Bhagavad-gītā,* material existence is an unstable platform subject to the constant disturbances of creation and annihilation. One who absorbs his consciousness in Kṛṣṇa, however, attains to Kṛṣṇa's nature and is therefore described as *mad-bhāva-bhāvitam,* or one situated in real existence because of Kṛṣṇa consciousness. The Lord here concludes His analysis of different processes of human perfection.

TEXT 29

स्त्रीणां स्त्रीसङ्गिनां सङ्गं त्यक्त्वा दूरत आत्मवान् ।
क्षेमे विविक्त आसीनश्चिन्तयेन्मामतन्द्रितः ॥२९॥

strīṇāṁ strī-saṅgināṁ saṅgaṁ
tyaktvā dūrata ātmavān
kṣeme vivikta āsīnaś
cintayen mām atandritaḥ

strīṇām—of women; *strī*—to women; *saṅginām*—of those who are attached or intimately associated; *saṅgam*—association; *tyaktvā*—giving up; *dūrataḥ*—far away; *ātma-vān*—being conscious of the self; *kṣeme*—fearless; *vivikte*—in a separated or isolated place; *āsīnaḥ*—sitting; *cintayet*—one should concentrate; *mām*—on Me; *atandritaḥ*—with great care.

TRANSLATION

Being conscious of the eternal self, one should give up association with women and those intimately associated with women. Sitting fearlessly in a solitary place, one should concentrate the mind on Me with great attention.

PURPORT

One who has intimate contact with women and becomes attached to them will gradually lose his determination to go back home, back to Godhead. Association with lusty men gives exactly the same result. Therefore, one is advised to be fearless and to sit down in a solitary place, or a place where there are no lusty men and women committing spiritual suicide. Without fear of failure or of unhappiness in life, one should remain with sincere devotees of the Lord. *Atandrita* means that one should not compromise this principle but should be rigid and cautious. All this is possible only for one who is *ātmavān*, or fixed in practical understanding of the eternal soul.

TEXT 30

न तथास्य भवेत् क्लेशो बन्धश्चान्यप्रसङ्गतः ।
योषित्सङ्गाद् यथा पुंसो यथा तत्सङ्गिसङ्गतः ॥३०॥

na tathāsya bhavet kleśo
bandhaś cānya-prasaṅgataḥ
yoṣit-saṅgād yathā puṁso
yathā tat-saṅgi-saṅgataḥ

na—not; *tathā*—like that; *asya*—of him; *bhavet*—could be; *kleśaḥ*—suffering; *bandhaḥ*—bondage; *ca*—and; *anya-prasaṅgataḥ*—from any other attachment; *yoṣit*—of women; *saṅgāt*—from attachment; *yathā*—just as; *puṁsaḥ*—of a man; *yathā*—similarly; *tat*—to women; *saṅgi*—of those attached; *saṅgataḥ*—from the association.

TRANSLATION

Of all kinds of suffering and bondage arising from various attachments, none is greater than the suffering and bondage arising from attachment to women and intimate contact with those attached to women.

PURPORT

One should make a great endeavor to give up intimate contact with women and those fond of women. A learned gentleman will automatically be on guard if placed in intimate contact with lusty women. In the company of lusty men, however, the same man may engage in all kinds of social dealings and thus be contaminated by their polluted mentality. Association with lusty men is often more dangerous than association with women and should be avoided by all means. There are innumerable verses in the *Bhāgavatam* describing the intoxication of material lust. Suffice it to say that a lusty man becomes exactly like a dancing dog and, by the influence of Cupid, loses all gravity, intelligence and direction in life. The Lord warns here that one who surrenders to the illusory form of a woman suffers unbearably in this life and the next.

TEXT 31

श्रीउद्धव उवाच

यथा त्वामरविन्दाक्ष यादृशं वा यदात्मकम् ।
ध्यायेन्मुमुक्षुरेतन्मे ध्यानं त्वं वक्तुमर्हसि ॥३१॥

śrī-uddhava uvāca
yathā tvām aravindākṣa
yādṛśaṁ vā yad-ātmakam
dhyāyen mumukṣur etan me
dhyānaṁ tvaṁ vaktum arhasi

śrī-uddhavaḥ uvāca—Śrī Uddhava said; *yathā*—in what way; *tvām*—You; *aravinda-akṣa*—O my dear lotus-eyed Kṛṣṇa; *yādṛśam*—of what specific nature; *vā*—or; *yat-ātmakam*—in what specific form; *dhyāyet*—should meditate; *mumukṣuḥ*—one who desires liberation; *etat*—this; *me*—to me; *dhyānam*—meditation; *tvam*—You; *vaktum*—to speak or explain; *arhasi*—ought.

TRANSLATION

Śrī Uddhava said: My dear lotus-eyed Kṛṣṇa, by what process should one who desires liberation meditate upon You, of what specific nature should his meditation be, and upon which form should he meditate? Kindly explain to me this topic of meditation.

PURPORT

It has already been elaborately explained by the Supreme Lord that without loving devotional service rendered to Him in the association of devotees, no other process of self-realization will work. Therefore it may be asked why Uddhava is again referring to the system of meditation, *dhyāna.* The *ācāryas* explain that one cannot fully appreciate the beauty and perfection of *bhakti-yoga* unless one sees its superiority to all other processes. Through comparative analysis, the devotees become fully ecstatic in their appreciation of *bhakti-yoga.* It should also be understood that although Uddhava asks about those who aspire for liberation, he is not actually a *mumukṣu,* or salvationist; rather, he is asking questions for the benefit of those who are not on the platform of love of Godhead. Uddhava wants to hear this knowledge for his personal appreciation and so that those who pursue salvation, or liberation, can be protected and redirected to the path of pure devotional service to the Supreme Lord.

TEXTS 32–33

श्रीभगवानुवाच
सम आसन आसीनः समकायो यथासुखम् ।
हस्तावुत्सङ्ग आधाय स्वनासाग्रकृतेक्षणः ॥३२॥
प्राणस्य शोधयेन्मार्गं पूरकुम्भकरेचकैः ।
विपर्ययेणापि शनैरभ्यसेन्निर्जितेन्द्रियः ॥३३॥

śrī-bhagavān uvāca
sama āsana āsīnaḥ
sama-kāyo yathā-sukham
hastāv utsaṅga ādhāya
sva-nāsāgra-kṛtekṣaṇaḥ

prāṇasya śodhayen mārgaṁ
pūra-kumbhaka-recakaiḥ
viparyayeṇāpi śanair
abhyasen nirjitendriyaḥ

śrī-bhagavān uvāca—the Supreme Personality of Godhead said; *same*—having a level surface; *āsane*—on the seat; *āsīnaḥ*—sitting; *sama-kāyaḥ*—sitting with the body straight and erect; *yathā-sukham*—sitting comfortably; *hastau*—the two hands; *utsaṅge*—in the lap; *ādhāya*—placing; *sva-nāsa-agra*—on the tip of one's own nose; *kṛta*—focusing; *īkṣaṇaḥ*—the glance; *prāṇasya*—of the breath; *śodhayet*—should purify; *mārgam*—the pathway; *pūra-kumbhaka-recakaiḥ*—by the mechanical breathing exercises, or *prāṇāyāma; viparyayeṇa*—by reversing the processes, namely *recaka, kumbhaka* and *pūraka; api*—also; *śanaiḥ*—following the process step by step; *abhyaset*—one should practice *prāṇāyāma; nirjita*—having controlled; *indriyaḥ*—the senses.

TRANSLATION

The Supreme Personality of Godhead said: Sitting on a level seat that is not too high or too low, keeping the body straight and erect yet comfortable, placing the two hands on one's lap and focusing the eyes on the tip of one's nose, one should purify the pathways

of breathing by practicing the mechanical exercises of pūraka, kumbhaka and recaka, and then one should reverse the procedure (recaka, kumbhaka, pūraka). Having fully controlled the senses, one may thus practice prāṇāyāma step by step.

PURPORT

According to this procedure, the hands are to be placed palms upward, one on top of the other. Thus, one may practice *prāṇāyāma* through mechanical breath control in order to achieve steadiness of the mind. As stated in the *yoga-śāstra, antar-lakṣyo bahir-dṛṣṭiḥ sthira-cittaḥ susaṅgataḥ:* "The eyes, which generally see externally, must be turned inward, and thus the mind is steadied and fully controlled."

TEXT 34

हृद्यविच्छिन्नमोङ्कारं घण्टानादं बिसोर्णवत् ।
प्राणेनोदीर्य तत्राथ पुनः संवेशयेत् स्वरम् ॥३४॥

hṛdy avicchinnam oṁkāraṁ
ghaṇṭā-nādaṁ bisorṇa-vat
prāṇenodīrya tatrātha
punaḥ saṁveśayet svaram

hṛdi—in the heart; *avicchinnam*—uninterrupted, continuous; *oṁkāram*—the sacred vibration *oṁ; ghaṇṭā*—like a bell; *nādam*—sound; *bisa-ūrṇa-vat*—like the fiber running up the lotus stalk; *prāṇena*—by the wind of *prāṇa; udīrya*—pushing upward; *tatra*—therein (at a distance of twelve thumb-breadths); *atha*—thus; *punaḥ*—again; *saṁveśayet*—one should join together; *svaram*—the fifteen vibrations produced with *anusvāra.*

TRANSLATION

Beginning from the mūlādhāra-cakra, one should move the life air continuously upward like the fibers in the lotus stalk until one reaches the heart, where the sacred syllable oṁ is situated like the sound of a bell. One should thus continue raising the sacred

syllable upward the distance of twelve aṅgulas, and there the oṁkāra should be joined together with the fifteeen vibrations produced with anusvāra.

PURPORT

It appears that the *yoga* system is somewhat technical and difficult to perform. *Anusvāra* refers to a nasal vibration pronounced after the fifteen Sanskrit vowels. The complete explanation of this process is extremely complicated and obviously unsuitable for this age. From this description we can appreciate the sophisticated achievements of those who in former ages practiced mystic meditation. Despite such appreciation, however, we should stick firmly to the simple, foolproof method of meditation prescribed for the present age, the chanting of Hare Kṛṣṇa, Hare Kṛṣṇa, Kṛṣṇa Kṛṣṇa, Hare Hare/ Hare Rāma, Hare Rāma, Rāma Rāma, Hare Hare.

TEXT 35

एवं प्रणवसंयुक्तं प्राणमेव समभ्यसेत् ।
दशकृत्वस्त्रिषवणं मासादर्वाग् जितानिलः ॥३५॥

evaṁ praṇava-saṁyuktaṁ
prāṇam eva samabhyaset
daśa-kṛtvas tri-ṣavaṇaṁ
māsād arvāg jitānilaḥ

evam—thus; *praṇava*—with the syllable *oṁ; saṁyuktam*—joined; *prāṇam*—the *prāṇāyāma* system of controlling the bodily airs; *eva*—indeed; *samabhyaset*—one should carefully practice; *daśa-kṛtvaḥ*—ten times; *tri-savanam*—at sunrise, noon and sunset; *māsāt*—one month; *arvāk*—after; *jita*—one will conquer; *anilaḥ*—the life air.

TRANSLATION

Being fixed in the oṁkāra, one should carefully practice the prāṇāyāma system ten times at each sunrise, noon and sunset. Thus, after one month one will have conquered the life air.

TEXTS 36–42

हृत्पुण्डरीकमन्तःस्थमूर्ध्वनालमधोमुखम् ।
ध्यात्वोर्ध्वमुखमुन्निद्रमष्टपत्रं सकर्णिकम् ।
कर्णिकायां न्यसेत् सूर्यसोमाग्नीनुत्तरोत्तरम् ॥३६॥
वह्निमध्ये स्मरेद् रूपं ममैतद् ध्यानमङ्गलम् ।
समं प्रशान्तं सुमुखं दीर्घचारुचतुर्भुजम् ॥३७॥
सुचारुसुन्दरग्रीवं सुकपोलं शुचिस्मितम् ।
समानकर्णविन्यस्तस्फुरन्मकरकुण्डलम् ॥३८॥
हेमाम्बरं घनश्यामं श्रीवत्सश्रीनिकेतनम् ।
शङ्खचक्रगदापद्मवनमालाविभूषितम् ॥३९॥
नूपुरैर्विलसत्पादं कौस्तुभप्रभया युतम् ।
द्युमत्किरीटकटककटिसूत्राङ्गदायुतम् ॥४०॥
सर्वाङ्गसुन्दरं हृद्यं प्रसादसुमुखेक्षणम् ।
सुकुमारमभिध्यायेत् सर्वाङ्गेषु मनो दधत् ॥४१॥
इन्द्रियाणीन्द्रियार्थेभ्यो मनसाकृष्य तन्मनः ।
बुद्ध्या सारथिना धीरः प्रणयेन्मयि सर्वतः ॥४२॥

hṛt-puṇḍarīkam antaḥ-stham
ūrdhva-nālam adho-mukham
dhyātvordhva-mukham unnidram
aṣṭa-patraṁ sa-karṇikam
karṇikāyāṁ nyaset sūrya-
somāgnīn uttarottaram

vahni-madhye smared rūpaṁ
mamaitad dhyāna-maṅgalam
samaṁ praśāntaṁ su-mukhaṁ
dīrgha-cāru-catur-bhujam

su-cāru-sundara-grīvaṁ
su-kapolaṁ śuci-smitam

samāna-karṇa-vinyasta-
sphuran-makara-kuṇḍalam

hemāmbaraṁ ghana-śyāmaṁ
śrīvatsa-śrī-niketanam
śaṅkha-cakra-gadā-padma-
vanamālā-vibhūṣitam

nūpurair vilasat-pādaṁ
kaustubha-prabhayā yutam
dyumat-kirīṭa-kaṭaka-
kaṭi-sūtrāṅgadāyutam

sarvāṅga-sundaraṁ hṛdyaṁ
prasāda-sumukhekṣaṇam
su-kumāram abhidhyāyet
sarvāṅgeṣu mano dadhat

indriyāṇīndriyārthebhyo
manasākṛṣya tan manaḥ
buddhyā sārathinā dhīraḥ
praṇayen mayi sarvataḥ

hṛt—in the heart; *puṇḍarīkam*—lotus flower; *antaḥ-stham*—situated within the body; *ūrdhva-nālam*—having erected the lotus stalk; *adhaḥ-mukham*—with eyes half closed, staring at the tip of the nose; *dhyātvā*—having fixed the mind in meditation; *ūrdhva-mukham*—enlivened; *un-nidram*—alert without dozing off; *aṣṭa-patram*—with eight petals; *sa-karṇikam*—with the whorl of the lotus; *karṇikāyām*—within the whorl; *nyaset*—one should place by concentration; *sūrya*—the sun; *soma*—moon; *agnīn*—and fire; *uttara-uttaram*—in order, one after the other; *vahni-madhye*—within the fire; *smaret*—one should meditate; *rūpam*—upon the form; *mama*—My; *etat*—this; *dhyāna-maṅgalam*—the auspicious object of meditation; *samam*—balanced, all the parts of the body proportionate; *praśāntam*—gentle; *su-mukham*—cheerful; *dīrgha-cāru-catuḥ-bhujam*—having four beautiful long arms; *su-cāru*—

charming; *sundara*—beautiful; *grīvam*—neck; *su-kapolam*—beautiful forehead; *śuci-smitam*—having a pure smile; *samāna*—alike; *karṇa*—in the two ears; *vinyasta*—situated; *sphurat*—glowing; *makara*—shaped like sharks; *kuṇḍalam*—earrings; *hema*—golden colored; *ambaram*—dress; *ghana-śyāmam*—the color of a dark rain cloud; *śrī-vatsa*—the unique curl of hair on the Lord's chest; *śrī-niketanam*—the abode of the goddess of fortune; *śaṅkha*—with the conchshell; *cakra*—Sudarśana disc; *gadā*—club; *padma*—lotus; *vana-mālā*—and a garland of forest flowers; *vibhūṣitam*—decorated; *nūpuraiḥ*—with ankle bells and bracelets; *vilasat*—shining; *pādam*—the lotus feet; *kaustubha*—of the Kaustubha gem; *prabhayā*—with the effulgence; *yutam*—enriched; *dyumat*—shining; *kirīṭa*—crown or helmet; *kaṭaka*—gold bracelets; *kaṭi-sūtra*—a band for the waist or upper hip; *aṅgada*—bracelets; *āyutam*—equipped with; *sarva-aṅga*—all the parts of the body; *sundaram*—beautiful; *hṛdyam*—charming; *prasāda*—with mercy; *sumukha*—smiling; *īkṣaṇam*—His glance; *su-kumāram*—most delicate; *abhidhyāyet*—one should meditate; *sarva-aṅgeṣu*—in all the parts of the body; *manaḥ*—the mind; *dadhat*—placing; *indriyāṇi*—the material senses; *indriya-arthebhyaḥ*—from the object of the senses; *manasā*—by the mind; *ākṛṣya*—pulling back; *tat*—that; *manaḥ*—mind; *buddhyā*—by intelligence; *sārathinā*—which is like the driver of a chariot; *dhīraḥ*—being grave and self-controlled; *praṇayet*—one should strongly lead; *mayi*—unto Me; *sarvataḥ*—in all limbs of the body.

TRANSLATION

Keeping the eyes half closed and fixed on the tip of one's nose, being enlivened and alert, one should meditate on the lotus flower situated within the heart. This lotus has eight petals and is situated on an erect lotus stalk. One should meditate on the sun, moon and fire, placing them one after the other within the whorl of that lotus flower. Placing My transcendental form within the fire, one should meditate upon it as the auspicious goal of all meditation. That form is perfectly proportioned, gentle and cheerful. It possesses four beautiful long arms, a charming, beautiful neck, a handsome forehead, a pure smile and glowing, shark-shaped earrings suspended from two identical ears. That spiritual form is the color of

a dark rain cloud and is garbed in golden-yellowish silk. The chest of that form is the abode of Śrīvatsa and the goddess of fortune, and that form is also decorated with a conchshell, disc, club, lotus flower and garland of forest flowers. The two brilliant lotus feet are decorated with ankle bells and bracelets, and that form exhibits the Kaustubha gem along with an effulgent crown. The upper hips are beautified by a golden belt, and the arms are decorated with valuable bracelets. All of the limbs of that beautiful form capture the heart, and the face is beautified by merciful glancing. Pulling the senses back from the sense objects, one should be grave and self-controlled and should use the intelligence to strongly fix the mind upon all of the limbs of My transcendental body. Thus one should meditate upon that most delicate transcendental form of Mine.

PURPORT

Lord Kṛṣṇa here answers Uddhava's question concerning the correct procedure, nature and object of meditation for those desiring liberation.

TEXT 43

तत् सर्वव्यापकं चित्तमाकृष्यैकत्र धारयेत् ।
नान्यानि चिन्तयेद् भूयः सुस्मितं भावयेन्मुखम् ॥४३॥

tat sarva-vyāpakaṁ cittam
ākṛṣyaikatra dhārayet
nānyāni cintayed bhūyaḥ
su-smitaṁ bhāvayen mukham

tat—therefore; *sarva*—in all the parts of the body; *vyāpakam*—spread; *cittam*—consciousness; *ākṛṣya*—pulling back; *ekatra*—in one place; *dhārayet*—one should concentrate; *na*—not; *anyāni*—other limbs of the body; *cintayet*—one should meditate on; *bhūyaḥ*—again; *su-smitam*—wonderfully smiling or laughing; *bhāvayet*—one should concentrate on; *mukham*—the face.

TRANSLATION

One should then pull the consciousness back from all the limbs of that transcendental body. At that time, one should meditate only on the wonderfully smiling face of the Lord.

TEXT 44

तत्र लब्धपदं चित्तमाकृष्य व्योम्नि धारयेत् ।
तच्च त्यक्त्वा मदारोहो न किञ्चिदपि चिन्तयेत् ॥४४॥

tatra labdha-padaṁ cittam
ākṛṣya vyomni dhārayet
tac ca tyaktvā mad-āroho
na kiñcid api cintayet

tatra—in such meditation on the Lord's face; *labdha-padam*—being established; *cittam*—consciousness; *ākṛṣya*—withdrawing; *vyomni*—in the sky; *dhārayet*—one should meditate; *tat*—such meditation in the sky as the cause of material manifestation; *ca*—also; *tyaktvā*—giving up; *mat*—to Me; *ārohaḥ*—having ascended; *na*—not; *kiñcit*—anything; *api*—at all; *cintayet*—one should think of.

TRANSLATION

Being established in meditation on the Lord's face, one should then withdraw the consciousness and fix it in the sky. Then giving up such meditation, one should become established in Me and give up the process of meditation altogether.

PURPORT

As one becomes established in pure consciousness, the duality of "I am meditating and this is the object of my meditation" vanishes, and one comes to the stage of spontaneous relationship with the Personality of Godhead. Every living entity is originally part and parcel of the Supreme Lord, and when that forgotten eternal relationship is revived one experiences remembrance of the Absolute Truth. In that stage, described here as *mad-ārohaḥ*, one no longer sees oneself as a meditator nor the Lord as a mere object of meditation, but rather one enters the spiritual sky for an eternal life of bliss and knowledge in direct loving relationship with the Lord.

Uddhava originally inquired about the procedure of meditation for those desiring liberation. The word *labdha-padam* indicates that when one fixes the mind upon the Lord's face, one achieves full liberation. In the postliberation phase one then proceeds to render service to the original Personality of Godhead. By giving up the concept of being a meditator, one casts off the last small remnant of illusory energy and sees the Lord as He actually is.

TEXT 45

एवं समाहितमतिर्मामेवात्मानमात्मनि ।
विचष्टे मयि सर्वात्मन् ज्योतिर्ज्योतिषि संयुतम् ॥४५॥

evaṁ samāhita-matir
mām evātmānam ātmani
vicaṣṭe mayi sarvātman
jyotir jyotiṣi saṁyutam

evam—thus; *samāhita*—completely fixed; *matiḥ*—consciousness; *mām*—Me; *eva*—indeed; *ātmānam*—the individual soul; *ātmani*—within the individual soul; *vicaṣṭe*—sees; *mayi*—in Me; *sarva-ātman*—in the Supreme Personality of Godhead; *jyotiḥ*—the sunrays; *jyotiṣi*—within the sun; *saṁyutam*—united.

TRANSLATION

One who has completely fixed his mind in Me should see Me within his own soul and should see the individual soul within Me, the Supreme Personality of Godhead. Thus, he sees the individual souls united with the Supreme Soul, just as one sees the sun's rays completely united with the sun.

PURPORT

In the spiritual world everything is naturally effulgent because that is the nature of spirit. Thus when one sees the individual soul as part and parcel of the Supreme Lord, the experience can be compared to seeing the sun's rays emanating from the sun. The Supreme Lord is within the living entity, and simultaneously the living entity is within the Lord. But in both cases the Supreme Lord, and not the living entity, is the maintainer and controller. How happy everyone could be by taking to Kṛṣṇa consciousness and finding the Supreme Lord, Kṛṣṇa, within everything and everything within Kṛṣṇa. Liberated life in Kṛṣṇa consciousness is so pleasurable that the greatest misfortune is to be without such consciousness. Śrī Kṛṣṇa is kindly explaining in many different ways the supremacy of Kṛṣṇa consciousness, and fortunate persons will understand the sincere message of the Lord.

TEXT 46

ध्यानेनेत्थं सुतीव्रेण युञ्जतो योगिनो मनः ।
संयास्यत्याशु निर्वाणं द्रव्यज्ञानक्रियाभ्रमः ॥४६॥

dhyānenetthaṁ su-tīvreṇa
yuñjato yogino manaḥ
saṁyāsyaty āśu nirvāṇaṁ
dravya-jñāna-kriyā-bhramaḥ

dhyānena—by meditation; *ittham*—as thus mentioned; *su-tīvreṇa*—extremely concentrated; *yuñjataḥ*—of one practicing; *yoginaḥ*—of the *yogī; manaḥ*—the mind; *saṁyāsyati*—will go together; *āśu*—quickly; *nirvāṇam*—to extinction; *dravya-jñāna-kriyā*—based on perception of material objects, knowledge and activities; *bhramaḥ*—the illusory identification.

TRANSLATION

When the yogī thus controls his mind by intensely concentrated meditation, his illusory identification with material objects, knowledge and activities is very quickly extinguished.

PURPORT

Because of false material identification, we accept our own body and mind, the bodies and minds of others, and supernatural material control to be ultimate realities. Supernatural control refers to the bodies and minds of the demigods, who ultimately are humble servitors of the Supreme Personality of Godhead. Even the mighty sun, which displays immense potencies, obediently treads its universal path by the order of Lord Kṛṣṇa.

It is clearly seen in this chapter that *haṭha-yoga, karma-yoga, rāja-yoga,* etc., are part and parcel of *bhakti-yoga* and do not actually exist separately. The goal of life is Lord Kṛṣṇa, and one must eventually come to the stage of pure devotion if one desires to perfect one's meditation or *yoga* practice. In the mature stage of devotion, as described in this chapter, one becomes free from the artificial duality of meditator and object of meditation, and one spontaneously engages in hearing about and glorifying the Supreme Absolute Truth. Such activities of *bhakti-yoga* are natural because they spring from spontaneous love. When one revives one's original nature as the loving servitor of Lord Kṛṣṇa, other *yoga* processes cease to be interesting. Uddhava was a pure devotee even before the Lord began His instruction; therefore it was not expected that Uddhava would give up the supreme platform of being a personal associate of the Lord to take up the mechanical exercises of the *yoga* system. *Bhakti-yoga,* or devotional service, is so elevated that even in the beginning stages of practice one is considered liberated, because all of one's activities are executed under proper guidance for the pleasure of the Lord. In the *haṭha-yoga* system one is concerned with bodily control, and in *jñāna-yoga* one is concerned with speculative knowledge. In both systems one endeavors selfishly, desiring to become a great *yogī* or a philosopher. Such egoistic activity is described in this verse as *kriyā.* One must give up the illusory designations of *dravya, jñāna* and *kriyā* and come to the prideless stage of loving service to the Lord.

Thus end the purports of the humble servants of His Divine Grace A. C. Bhaktivedanta Swami Prabhupāda to the Eleventh Canto, Fourteenth Chapter, of the Śrīmad-Bhāgavatam, *entitled "Lord Kṛṣṇa Explains the Yoga System to Śrī Uddhava."*

CHAPTER FIFTEEN

Lord Kṛṣṇa's Description of Mystic Yoga Perfections

This chapter describes the eight primary and ten minor mystic perfections. They are developed by fixing one's mind in *yoga*, but they are ultimately obstructions to achieving the spiritual abode of Lord Viṣṇu.

Being questioned by Uddhava, Lord Śrī Kṛṣṇa describes the characteristics of the eighteen mystic perfections and the particular kind of meditation by which each is achieved. In conclusion, Kṛṣṇa states that for one who desires to perform pure devotional service to the Personality of Godhead, the achievement of these mystic perfections is a waste of time, because they distract one from proper worship. All these perfections are automatically offered to a pure devotee, but he does not accept them. Unless used in the *yoga* of devotional service, these perfections are valueless. A devotee simply sees that the Personality of Godhead is always present everywhere, both externally and internally, and depends completely upon Him.

TEXT 1

श्रीभगवानुवाच
जितेन्द्रियस्य युक्तस्य जितश्वासस्य योगिनः ।
मयि धारयतश्चेत उपतिष्ठन्ति सिद्धयः ॥ १ ॥

śrī-bhagavān uvāca
jitendriyasya yuktasya
jita-śvāsasya yoginaḥ
mayi dhārayataś ceta
upatiṣṭhanti siddhayaḥ

śrī-bhagavān uvāca—the Supreme Personality of Godhead said; *jita-indriyasya*—of one who has conquered his senses; *yuktasya*—who has steadied the mind; *jita-śvāsasya*—and conquered his breathing system; *yoginaḥ*—of such a *yogī; mayi*—in Me; *dhārayataḥ*—fixing; *cetaḥ*—his consciousness; *upatiṣṭhanti*—appear; *siddhayaḥ*—the mystic perfections of *yoga.*

TRANSLATION

The Supreme Personality of Godhead said: My dear Uddhava, the mystic perfections of yoga are acquired by a yogī who has conquered his senses, steadied his mind, conquered the breathing process and fixed his mind in Me.

PURPORT

There are eight primary mystic perfections, such as *aṇimā-siddhi,* and ten secondary perfections. In this Fifteenth Chapter Lord Kṛṣṇa will explain that such mystic perfections are actually impediments to the development of Kṛṣṇa consciousness, and that therefore one should not desire them.

TEXT 2

श्रीउद्धव उवाच
कया धारणया कास्वित् कथं वा सिद्धिरच्युत ।
कति वा सिद्धयो ब्रूहि योगिनां सिद्धिदो भवान् ॥ २ ॥

śrī-uddhava uvāca
kayā dhāraṇayā kā svit
kathaṁ vā siddhir acyuta
kati vā siddhayo brūhi
yogināṁ siddhi-do bhavān

śrī-uddhavaḥ uvāca—Śrī Uddhava said; *kayā*—by what; *dhāraṇayā*—process of meditation; *kā svit*—which indeed; *katham*—in what manner; *vā*—or; *siddhiḥ*—mystic perfection; *acyuta*—My dear Lord; *kati*—how many; *vā*—or; *siddhayaḥ*—perfections; *brūhi*—please speak; *yoginām*—of all *yogīs; siddhi-daḥ*—the giver of mystic perfections; *bhavān*—You.

TRANSLATION

Śrī Uddhava said: My dear Lord Acyuta, by what process can mystic perfection be achieved, and what is the nature of such perfection? How many mystic perfections are there? Please explain these things to me. Indeed, You are the bestower of all mystic perfections.

TEXT 3

श्रीभगवानुवाच
सिद्धयोऽष्टादश प्रोक्ता धारणा योगपारगैः ।
तासामष्टौ मत्प्रधाना दशैव गुणहेतवः ॥ ३ ॥

śrī-bhagavān uvāca
siddhayo 'ṣṭādaśa proktā
dhāraṇā yoga-pāra-gaiḥ
tāsām aṣṭau mat-pradhānā
daśaiva guṇa-hetavaḥ

śrī-bhagavān uvāca—the Supreme Personality of Godhead said; *siddhayaḥ*—mystic perfections; *aṣṭādaśa*—eighteen; *proktāḥ*—are declared; *dhāraṇāḥ*—meditations; *yoga*—of *yoga; pāra-gaiḥ*—by the masters; *tāsām*—of the eighteen; *aṣṭau*—eight; *mat-pradhānāḥ*—have their shelter in Me; *daśa*—ten; *eva*—indeed; *guṇa-hetavaḥ*—are manifested from the material mode of goodness.

TRANSLATION

The Supreme Personality of Godhead said: The masters of the yoga system have declared that there are eighteen types of mystic perfection and meditation, of which eight are primary, having their shelter in Me, and ten are secondary, appearing from the material mode of goodness.

PURPORT

Śrīla Viśvanātha Cakravartī Ṭhākura explains the word *mat-pradhānāḥ* as follows. Lord Kṛṣṇa is naturally the shelter of the eight primary mystic potencies and meditations because such perfections emanate from the Lord's personal potency, and thus they are fully developed only within the Lord Himself and the Lord's personal associates. When materialistic persons mechanically acquire such potencies, the perfections awarded are of an inferior degree and are considered to be manifestations of *māyā*, illusion. A pure devotee of the Lord automatically receives from the Lord wonderful potencies to execute his devotional service. If for sense gratification one mechanically endeavors to acquire mystic perfections, then these perfections are certainly considered to be inferior expansions of the Lord's external potency.

TEXTS 4–5

अणिमा महिमा मूर्तेर्लघिमा प्राप्तिरिन्द्रियैः ।
प्राकाम्यं श्रुतदृष्टेषु शक्तिप्रेरणमीशिता ॥ ४ ॥
गुणेष्वसङ्गो वशिता यत्कामस्तदवस्यति ।
एता मे सिद्धयः सौम्य अष्टावौत्पत्तिका मताः ॥ ५ ॥

aṇimā mahimā mūrter
laghimā prāptir indriyaiḥ
prākāmyaṁ śruta-dṛṣṭeṣu
śakti-preraṇam īśitā

guṇeṣv asaṅgo vaśitā
yat-kāmas tad avasyati
etā me siddhayaḥ saumya
aṣṭāv autpattikā matāḥ

aṇimā—the perfection of becoming smaller than the smallest; *mahimā*—becoming greater than the greatest; *mūrteḥ*—of the body; *laghimā*—becoming lighter than the lightest; *prāptiḥ*—acquisition; *indriyaiḥ*—by the senses; *prākāmyam*—obtaining or performing whatever one desires; *śruta*—things invisible, about which one only hears; *dṛṣṭeṣu*—and things visible; *śakti-preraṇam*—manipulating the subpotencies of *māyā; īśitā*—the perfection of controlling; *guṇeṣu*—in the modes of material nature; *asaṅgaḥ*—being unobstructed; *vaśitā*—the power to bring others under control; *yat*—whatever; *kāmaḥ*—desire (there may be); *tat*—that; *avasyati*—one can obtain; *etāḥ*—these; *me*—My (potencies); *siddhayaḥ*—mystic perfections; *saumya*—O gentle Uddhava; *aṣṭau*—eight; *autpattikāḥ*—natural and unexcelled; *matāḥ*—understood to be.

TRANSLATION

Among the eight primary mystic perfections those three by which one adjusts one's own body are aṇimā, becoming smaller than the smallest; mahimā, becoming greater than the greatest; and laghimā, becoming lighter than the lightest. Through the perfection of prāpti one acquires whatever one desires, and through prākāmya-siddhi one experiences any enjoyable object, either in this world or the next. Through īśitā-siddhi one can manipulate the subpotencies of māyā, and through the controlling potency called vaśitā-siddhi one is unimpeded by the three modes of nature. One who has acquired kāmāvasāyitā-siddhi can obtain anything from anywhere, to the highest possible limit. My dear gentle Uddhava, these eight mystic perfections are considered to be naturally existing and unexcelled within this world.

PURPORT

Through *aṇimā-siddhi* one can become so small that one can enter a stone or pass through any obstacle. Through *mahimā-siddhi* one becomes so great that one covers everything, and through *laghimā* one becomes so light that one can ride on the sun's rays into the sun planet. Through *prāpti-siddhi* one can acquire anything from anywhere and can even touch the moon with one's finger. By this mystic perfection one can also enter into the senses of any other living entity through the predominating deities of the particular senses; and by thus utilizing the senses of others, one can acquire anything. Through *prākāmya* one can experience any enjoyable object, either in this world or the next, and through *īśitā*, or the controlling potency, one can manipulate the subpotencies of *māyā*, which are material. In other words, even by acquiring mystic powers one cannot pass beyond the control of illusion; however, one may manipulate the subpotencies of illusion. Through *vaśitā*, or the power to control, one can bring others under one's dominion or keep oneself beyond the control of the three modes of nature. Ultimately, one acquires through *kāmāvasāyitā* the maximum powers of control, acquisition and enjoyment. The word *autpattikāḥ* in this verse indicates being original, natural and unexcelled. These eight mystic potencies originally exist in the Supreme Personality of Godhead, Kṛṣṇa, in the superlative degree. Lord Kṛṣṇa becomes so small that He enters within the atomic particles, and He becomes so large that as Mahā-Viṣṇu He breathes out millions of universes. The Lord can become so light or subtle that even great mystic *yogīs* cannot perceive Him, and the Lord's acquisitive power is perfect, because He keeps the total existence eternally within His body. The Lord certainly can enjoy whatever He likes, control all energies, dominate all other persons and exhibit complete omnipotency. Therefore it is to be understood that these eight mystic perfections are insignificant expansions of the mystic potency of the Lord, who in *Bhagavad-gītā* is called Yogeśvara, the Supreme Lord of all mystic potencies. These eight perfections are not artificial, but are natural and unexcelled because they originally exist in the Supreme Personality of Godhead.

TEXTS 6–7

अनूर्मिमत्त्वं देहेऽस्मिन् दूरश्रवणदर्शनम् ।
मनोजवः कामरूपं परकायप्रवेशनम् ॥ ६ ॥
स्वच्छन्दमृत्युर्देवानां सहक्रीडानुदर्शनम् ।
यथासङ्कल्पसंसिद्धिराज्ञाप्रतिहतागतिः ॥ ७ ॥

anūrmimattvaṁ dehe 'smin
dūra-śravaṇa-darśanam
mano-javaḥ kāma-rūpaṁ
para-kāya-praveśanam

svacchanda-mṛtyur devānāṁ
saha-krīḍānudarśanam
yathā-saṅkalpa-saṁsiddhir
ājñāpratihatā gatiḥ

anūrmi-mattvam—being undisturbed by hunger, thirst, etc.; *dehe asmin*—in this body; *dūra*—things very far away; *śravaṇa*—hearing; *darśanam*—and seeing; *manaḥ-javaḥ*—moving the body at the speed of the mind; *kāma-rūpam*—assuming any body that one desires; *para-*

kāya—the bodies of others; *praveśanam*—entering; *sva-chanda*—according to one's own desire; *mṛtyuḥ*—dying; *devānām*—of the demigods; *saha*—together with (the celestial girls); *krīḍā*—the sporting pastimes; *anudarśanam*—witnessing; *yathā*—according to; *saṅkalpa*—one's determination; *saṁsiddhiḥ*—perfect accomplishment; *ājñā*—order; *apratihatā*—unimpeded; *gatiḥ*—whose progress.

TRANSLATION

The ten secondary mystic perfections arising from the modes of nature are the powers of freeing oneself from hunger and thirst and other bodily disturbances, hearing and seeing things far away, moving the body at the speed of the mind, assuming any form one desires, entering the bodies of others, dying when one desires, witnessing the pastimes between the demigods and the celestial girls called Apsarās, completely executing one's determination and giving orders whose fulfillment is unimpeded.

TEXTS 8–9

त्रिकालज्ञत्वमद्वन्द्वं परचित्ताद्यभिज्ञता ।
अग्न्यर्काम्बुविषादीनां प्रतिष्टम्भोऽपराजयः ॥८ ॥
एताश्चोद्देशतः प्रोक्ता योगधारणसिद्धयः ।
यया धारणया या स्याद् यथा वा स्यान्निबोध मे॥ ९ ॥

tri-kāla-jñatvam advandvaṁ
para-cittādy-abhijñatā
agny-arkāmbu-viṣādīnāṁ
pratiṣṭambho 'parājayaḥ

etāś coddeśataḥ proktā
yoga-dhāraṇa-siddhayaḥ
yayā dhāraṇayā yā syād
yathā vā syān nibodha me

tri-kāla-jñatvam—the perfection of knowing past, present and future; *advandvam*—being unaffected by dualities such as heat and cold; *para*—of others; *citta*—the mind; *ādi*—and so on; *abhijñatā*—

knowing; *agni*—of fire; *arka*—the sun; *ambu*—water; *viṣa*—of poison; *ādīnām*—and so on; *pratiṣṭambhaḥ*—checking the potency; *aparājayaḥ*—not being conquered by others; *etāḥ*—these; *ca*—also; *uddeśataḥ*—merely by mentioning their names and characteristics; *proktāḥ*—are described; *yoga*—of the *yoga* system; *dhāraṇa*—of meditation; *siddhayaḥ*—perfections; *yayā*—by which; *dhāraṇayā*—meditation; *yā*—which (perfection); *syāt*—may occur; *yathā*—by which means; *vā*—or; *syāt*—may occur; *nibodha*—please learn; *me*—from Me.

TRANSLATION

The power to know past, present and future; tolerance of heat, cold and other dualities; knowing the minds of others; checking the influence of fire, sun, water, poison, and so on; and remaining unconquered by others—these constitute five perfections of the mystic process of yoga and meditation. I am simply listing these here according to their names and characteristics. Now please learn from Me how specific mystic perfections arise from specific meditations and also of the particular processes involved.

PURPORT

According to the *ācāryas* these five perfections are considered to be quite inferior to the others already mentioned, since they involve more or less ordinary physical and mental manipulations. According to Śrīla Madhvācārya, in the perfection called *agny-arkāmbu-viṣādīnāṁ pratiṣṭambhaḥ*, or checking the influence of fire, sun, water, poison, and so on, the term "and so on" refers to one's remaining invulnerable to all types of weapons as well as attacks by nails, teeth, beating, curses and other such sources.

TEXT 10

भूतसूक्ष्मात्मनि मयि तन्मात्रं धारयेन्मनः ।
अणिमानमवाप्नोति तन्मात्रोपासको मम ॥१०॥

bhūta-sūkṣmātmani mayi
tan-mātraṁ dhārayen manaḥ

aṇimānam avāpnoti
tan-mātropāsako mama

bhūta-sūkṣma—of the subtle elements; *ātmani*—in the soul; *mayi*—in Me; *tat-mātram*—on the subtle, elemental forms of perception; *dhārayet*—one should concentrate; *manaḥ*—the mind; *aṇimānam*—the mystic perfection called *aṇimā; avāpnoti*—obtains; *tat-mātra*—in the subtle elements; *upāsakaḥ*—the worshiper; *mama*—My.

TRANSLATION

One who worships Me in My atomic form pervading all subtle elements, fixing his mind on that alone, obtains the mystic perfection called aṇimā.

PURPORT

Aṇimā refers to the mystic ability to make oneself smaller than the smallest and thus able to enter within anything. The Supreme Personality of Godhead is within the atoms and atomic particles, and one who perfectly fixes his mind in that subtle atomic form of the Lord acquires the mystic potency called *aṇimā*, by which one can enter within even the most dense matter such as stone.

TEXT 11

महत्तत्त्वात्मनि मयि यथासंस्थं मनो दधत् ।
महिमानमवाप्नोति भूतानां च पृथक् पृथक् ॥११॥

mahat-tattvātmani mayi
yathā-saṁsthaṁ mano dadhat
mahimānam avāpnoti
bhūtānāṁ ca pṛthak pṛthak

mahat-tattva—of the total material energy; *ātmani*—in the Soul; *mayi*—in Me; *yathā*—according to; *saṁstham*—the particular situation; *manaḥ*—the mind; *dadhat*—fixing; *mahimānam*—the mystic perfection called *mahimā; avāpnoti*—one achieves; *bhūtānām*—of the material elements; *ca*—also; *pṛthak pṛthak*—each one individually.

TRANSLATION

One who absorbs his mind in the particular form of the mahat-tattva and thus meditates upon Me as the Supreme Soul of the total material existence achieves the mystic perfection called mahimā. By further absorbing the mind in the situation of each individual element such as the sky, air, fire, and so on, one progressively acquires the greatness of each material element.

PURPORT

There are innumerable verses in Vedic literatures explaining that the Supreme Personality of Godhead is qualitatively not different from His creation and thus a *yogī* may meditate upon the total material existence as a manifestation of the external potency of the Lord. Once the *yogī* has established his realization that the material creation is not different from the Lord, he obtains the perfection called *mahimā-siddhi.* By realizing the Lord's presence in each individual element the *yogī* also acquires the greatness of each element. However, the pure devotees are not very interested in such perfections because they are surrendered to the Personality of Godhead, who exhibits such perfections to the infinite degree. Being always protected by the Lord, the pure devotees save their precious time to chant Hare Kṛṣṇa, Hare Kṛṣṇa, Kṛṣṇa Kṛṣṇa, Hare Hare/ Hare Rāma, Hare Rāma, Rāma Rāma, Hare Hare. Thus they achieve for themselves and others *saṁsiddhi,* or the supreme perfection, pure love of Godhead, Kṛṣṇa consciousness, by which one expands one's existence beyond the total material creation to the spiritual planets called Vaikuṇṭha.

TEXT 12

परमाणुमये चित्तं भूतानां मयि रञ्जयन् ।
कालसूक्ष्मार्थतां योगी लघिमानमवाप्नुयात् ॥१२॥

paramāṇu-maye cittaṁ
bhūtānāṁ mayi rañjayan
kāla-sūkṣmārthatāṁ yogī
laghimānam avāpnuyāt

parama-aṇu-maye—in the form of atoms; *cittam*—his consciousness; *bhūtānām*—of the material elements; *mayi*—in Me; *rañjayan*—attaching; *kāla*—of time; *sūkṣma*—subtle; *arthatām*—being the substance; *yogī*—the *yogī; laghimānam*—the mystic perfection *laghimā; avāpnuyāt*—may obtain.

TRANSLATION

I exist within everything, and I am therefore the essence of the atomic constituents of material elements. By attaching his mind to Me in this form, the yogī may achieve the perfection called laghimā, by which he realizes the subtle atomic substance of time.

PURPORT

Śrīmad-Bhāgavatam elaborately explains that *kāla*, or time, is the transcendental form of the Lord that moves the material world. Since the five gross elements are composed of atoms, the atomic particles are the subtle substance or manifestation of the movements of time. More subtle than time is the Personality of Godhead Himself, who expands His potency as the time factor. By understanding all these things clearly the *yogī* obtains *laghimā-siddhi*, or the power to make himself lighter than the lightest.

TEXT 13

धारयन् मय्यहंतत्त्वे मनो वैकारिकेऽखिलम् ।
सर्वेन्द्रियाणामात्मत्वं प्राप्तिं प्राप्नोति मन्मनाः ॥१३॥

dhārayan mayy ahaṁ-tattve
mano vaikārike 'khilam
sarvendriyāṇām ātmatvaṁ
prāptiṁ prāpnoti man-manāḥ

dhārayan—concentrating; *mayi*—in Me; *aham-tattve*—within the element of false ego; *manaḥ*—the mind; *vaikārike*—in that which is produced from the mode of goodness; *akhilam*—completely; *sarva*—of all living entities; *indriyāṇām*—of the senses; *ātmatvam*—proprietorship;

prāptim—the mystic perfection of acquisition; *prāpnoti*—obtains; *mat-manāḥ*—the *yogī* whose mind is fixed in Me.

TRANSLATION

Fixing his mind completely in Me within the element of false ego generated from the mode of goodness, the yogī obtains the power of mystic acquisition, by which he becomes the proprietor of the senses of all living entities. He obtains such perfection because his mind is absorbed in Me.

PURPORT

It is significant that in order to acquire each mystic perfection one must fix one's mind on the Supreme Personality of Godhead. Śrīla Bhaktisiddhānta Sarasvatī Ṭhākura states that those who pursue such perfections without fixing the mind in the Supreme Lord acquire a gross and inferior reflection of each mystic potency. Those who are not conscious of the Lord cannot actually synchronize their minds perfectly with the universal functions and therefore cannot elevate their mystic opulences to the universal platform.

TEXT 14

महत्यात्मनि यः सूत्रे धारयेन्मयि मानसम् ।
प्राकाम्यं पारमेष्ठ्यं मे विन्दतेऽव्यक्तजन्मनः॥१४॥

mahaty ātmani yaḥ sūtre
dhārayen mayi mānasam
prākāmyaṁ pārameṣṭhyaṁ me
vindate 'vyakta-janmanaḥ

mahati—in the *mahat-tattva; ātmani*—in the Supersoul; *yaḥ*—one who; *sūtre*—characterized by the chain of fruitive activities; *dhārayet*—should concentrate; *mayi*—in Me; *mānasam*—the mental activities; *prākāmyam*—the mystic perfection called *prākāmya; pārameṣṭhyam*—most excellent; *me*—from Me; *vindate*—obtains or enjoys; *avyakta-janmanaḥ*—from Him whose appearance in this world cannot be materially perceived.

TRANSLATION

One who concentrates all mental activities in Me as the Supersoul of that phase of the mahat-tattva which manifests the chain of fruitive activities obtains from Me, whose appearance is beyond material perception, the most excellent mystic perfection called prākāmya.

PURPORT

Śrīla Vīrarāghava Ācārya explains that the word *sūtra*, or "thread," is used to indicate that the *mahat-tattva* sustains one's fruitive activities just as a thread sustains a row of jewels. Thus by fixed meditation on the Supreme Personality of Godhead, who is the soul of the *mahat-tattva*, one can achieve the most excellent perfection called *prākāmya*. *Avyakta-janmanaḥ* indicates that the Supreme Personality of Godhead appears from the *avyakta*, or the spiritual sky, or that His birth is *avyakta*, beyond the perception of material senses. Unless one accepts the transcendental form of the Supreme Personality of Godhead, there is no possibility of obtaining *prākāmya* or any other genuine mystic perfection.

TEXT 15

विष्णौ त्र्यधीश्वरे चित्तं धारयेत् कालविग्रहे ।
स ईशित्वमवाप्नोति क्षेत्रज्ञक्षेत्रचोदनाम् ॥१५॥

viṣṇau try-adhīśvare cittaṁ
dhārayet kāla-vigrahe
sa īśitvam avāpnoti
kṣetrajña-kṣetra-codanām

viṣṇau—in Lord Viṣṇu, the Supersoul; *tri-adhīśvare*—the supreme controller of *māyā*, which consists of three modes of nature; *cittam*—the consciousness; *dhārayet*—one concentrates; *kāla*—of time, the prime mover; *vigrahe*—in the form; *saḥ*—he, the *yogī*; *īśitvam*—the mystic perfection of controlling; *avāpnoti*—obtains; *kṣetra-jña*—the conscious living entity; *kṣetra*—and the body with its designations; *codanām*—impelling.

TRANSLATION

One who concentrates his consciousness in Viṣṇu, the Supersoul, the prime mover and Supreme Lord of the external energy consisting of three modes, obtains the mystic perfection of controlling other conditioned souls, their material bodies and bodily designations.

PURPORT

We should remember that mystic perfection never enables a living entity to challenge the supremacy of the Personality of Godhead. In fact, one cannot obtain such perfections without the mercy of the Supreme Lord; thus one's controlling power can never disturb the plan of Lord Kṛṣṇa. One is allowed to exhibit mystic control only within the confines of the law of God, and even a great *yogī* who transgresses the law of God by his so-called mystic opulences will be severely punished, as revealed in the story of Durvāsā Muni cursing Ambarīṣa Mahārāja.

TEXT 16

नारायणे तुरीयाख्ये भगवच्छब्दशब्दिते ।
मनो मय्यादधद् योगी मद्धर्मा वशितामियात् ॥१६॥

nārāyaṇe turīyākhye
bhagavac-chabda-śabdite
mano mayy ādadhad yogī
mad-dharmā vaśitām iyāt

nārāyaṇe—in the Supreme Lord, Nārāyaṇa; *turīya-ākhye*—known as the fourth, beyond the three modes of material nature; *bhagavat*—full of all opulences; *śabda-śabdite*—known by the word; *manaḥ*—the mind; *mayi*—in Me; *ādadhat*—placing; *yogī*—the *yogī; mat-dharmā*—being endowed with My nature; *vaśitām*—the mystic opulence called *vaśitā; iyāt*—may obtain.

TRANSLATION

The yogī who places his mind in My form of Nārāyaṇa, known as the fourth factor, full of all opulences, becomes endowed with My nature and thus obtains the mystic perfection called vaśitā.

PURPORT

In *Bhagavad-gītā* (7.13) Lord Kṛṣṇa states,

tribhir guṇa-mayair bhāvair
ebhiḥ sarvam idaṁ jagat
mohitaṁ nābhijānāti
mām ebhyaḥ param avyayam

"Deluded by the three modes [goodness, passion and ignorance], the whole world does not know Me, who am above the modes and inexhaustible." Thus the Lord is called *turīya*, or the fourth factor beyond the three modes of nature. According to Śrīla Vīrarāghava Ācārya, *turīya* also indicates that the Lord is beyond the three ordinary phases of consciousness, namely wakefulness, dreaming and dreamless sleep. *Bhagavac-chabda-śabdite* indicates that the Lord is known as Bhagavān, or the possessor of unlimited opulences, principally beauty, fame, wealth, knowledge, renunciation and intelligence.

In conclusion, one can obtain the mystic opulence *vaśitā*, or freedom from the modes of nature, by meditating upon the Lord as *turīya*, the fourth factor beyond those modes. Everything depends upon the favor of the Supreme Personality of Godhead.

TEXT 17

निर्गुणे ब्रह्मणि मयि धारयन् विशदं मनः ।
परमानन्दमाप्नोति यत्र कामोऽवसीयते ॥१७॥

nirguṇe brahmaṇi mayi
dhārayan viśadaṁ manaḥ
paramānandam āpnoti
yatra kāmo 'vasīyate

nirguṇe—without qualities; *brahmaṇi*—in Brahman; *mayi*—in Me; *dhārayan*—concentrating; *viśadam*—pure; *manaḥ*—the mind; *parama-ānandam*—the greatest happiness; *āpnoti*—obtains; *yatra*—wherein; *kāmaḥ*—desire; *avasīyate*—is completely fulfilled.

TRANSLATION

One who fixes the pure mind in Me in My manifestation as the impersonal Brahman obtains the greatest happinesss, wherein all of his desires are completely fulfilled.

PURPORT

Paramānanda, or "the greatest happiness," here indicates the greatest material happiness, since it is clearly stated in *Śrīmad-Bhāgavatam* that a devotee has no personal desire, or *kāma*. One who has personal desire is certainly within the material world, and on the material platform the greatest happiness is *kāmāvasāyitā-siddhi*, or the perfection of completely obtaining anything that one desires.

TEXT 18

श्वेतद्वीपपतौ चित्तं शुद्धे धर्ममये मयि ।
धारयञ्छ्वेततां याति षडूर्मिरहितो नरः ॥१८॥

śvetadvīpa-patau cittaṁ
śuddhe dharma-maye mayi
dhārayañ chvetatāṁ yāti
ṣaḍ-ūrmi-rahito naraḥ

śveta-dvīpa—of the white island, the abode of Kṣīrodakaśāyī Viṣṇu; *patau*—in the Lord; *cittam*—consciousness; *śuddhe*—in the personification of goodness; *dharma-maye*—in He who is always situated in piety; *mayi*—in Me; *dhārayan*—concentrating; *śvetatām*—pure existence; *yāti*—obtains; *ṣaṭ-ūrmi*—the six waves of material disturbance; *rahitaḥ*—freed from; *naraḥ*—a person.

TRANSLATION

A human being who concentrates on Me as the upholder of religious principles, the personification of purity and the Lord of Śvetadvīpa obtains the pure existence in which he is freed from the six waves of material disturbance, namely hunger, thirst, decay, death, grief and illusion.

PURPORT

The Lord now begins to explain the processes for obtaining the ten secondary mystic perfections derived from the modes of nature. Within the material world Lord Viṣṇu, addressed here as *śvetadvīpa-pati*, the Lord of Śvetadvīpa, governs the material mode of goodness and is thus called *śuddha* and *dharma-maya*, or the personification of purity and piety. By worshiping Lord Viṣṇu as the personification of material goodness one obtains the material benediction of freedom from bodily disturbance.

TEXT 19

मय्याकाशात्मनि प्राणे मनसा घोषमुद्वहन् ।
तत्रोपलब्धा भूतानां हंसो वाचः शृणोत्यसौ ॥१९॥

mayy ākāśātmani prāṇe
manasā ghoṣam udvahan
tatropalabdhā bhūtānāṁ
haṁso vācaḥ śṛṇoty asau

mayi—in Me; *ākāśa-ātmani*—in the personification of the sky; *prāṇe*—in the life air; *manasā*—with the mind; *ghoṣam*—the transcendental sound; *udvahan*—concentrating on; *tatra*—there in the sky; *upalabdhāḥ*—perceived; *bhūtānām*—of all living entities; *haṁsaḥ*—the purified living entity; *vācaḥ*—words or speaking; *śṛṇoti*—hears; *asau*—he.

TRANSLATION

That purified living entity who fixes his mind on the extraordinary sound vibrations occurring within Me as the personified sky and total life air is then able to perceive within the sky the speaking of all living entities.

PURPORT

Speech occurs by vibrating air within the sky. One who meditates on the Supreme Lord as the personified sky and air thereby acquires the ability to hear that which is vibrated at great distance. The word *prāṇa* indicates that the Lord is the personified life air of the individual living entities and for the total aggregate of life forms. Ultimately, the pure devotees meditate on the supreme vibration—Hare Kṛṣṇa, Hare Kṛṣṇa, Kṛṣṇa Kṛṣṇa, Hare Hare/ Hare Rāma, Hare Rāma, Rāma Rāma, Hare Hare—and are thus able to hear the speech originating from liberated living entities far beyond the material universe. Any living entity can hear such discussions by reading *Śrīmad-Bhāgavatam, Bhagavad-gītā* and other such literatures. One who has properly understood the opulences of the Supreme Personality of Godhead finds all perfection, mystic and otherwise, in Kṛṣṇa consciousness.

TEXT 20

चक्षुस्त्वष्टरि संयोज्य त्वष्टारमपि चक्षुषि ।
मां तत्र मनसा ध्यायन् विश्वं पश्यति दूरतः ॥२०॥

cakṣus tvaṣṭari saṁyojya
tvaṣṭāram api cakṣuṣi
māṁ tatra manasā dhyāyan
viśvaṁ paśyati dūrataḥ

cakṣuḥ—the eyes; *tvaṣṭari*—in the sun; *saṁyojya*—merging; *tvaṣṭāram*—the sun; *api*—also; *cakṣuṣi*—in one's eyes; *mām*—Me; *tatra*—there, in the mutual merging of sun and eye; *manasā*—with the mind; *dhyāyan*—meditating; *viśvam*—everything; *paśyati*—he sees; *dūrataḥ*—far away.

TRANSLATION

Merging one's sight into the sun planet and then the sun planet into one's eyes, one should meditate with the mind on Me existing within the combination of sun and vision; thus one acquires the power to see any distant thing.

TEXT 21

मनो मयि सुसंयोज्य देहं तदनुवायुना ।
मद्धारणानुभावेन तत्रात्मा यत्र वै मनः ॥२१॥

mano mayi su-saṁyojya
dehaṁ tad-anuvāyunā
mad-dhāraṇānubhāvena
tatrātmā yatra vai manaḥ

manaḥ—the mind; *mayi*—in Me; *su-saṁyojya*—completely absorbing; *deham*—the material body; *tat*—the mind; *anu-vāyunā*—by the wind that follows; *mat-dhāraṇā*—of meditation in Me; *anubhāvena*—by the potency; *tatra*—there; *ātmā*—the material body (goes); *yatra*—wherever; *vai*—certainly; *manaḥ*—the mind (goes).

TRANSLATION

The yogī who completely absorbs his mind in Me, and who then makes use of the wind that follows the mind to absorb the material body in Me, obtains through the potency of meditation on Me the mystic perfection by which his body immediately follows his mind wherever it goes.

PURPORT

Tad-anuvāyunā indicates the particular subtle air that follows the mind. When the *yogī* merges this air together with the body and mind in Kṛṣṇa by the potency of meditation on the Lord, his gross material body, like the subtle air, can follow the mind anywhere. This perfection is called *mano-javaḥ*.

TEXT 22

यदा मन उपादाय यद् यद् रूपं बुभूषति ।
तत्तद् भवेन्मनोरूपं मद्योगबलमाश्रयः ॥२२॥

yadā mana upādāya
yad yad rūpaṁ bubhūṣati
tat tad bhaven mano-rūpaṁ
mad-yoga-balam āśrayaḥ

yadā—when; *manaḥ*—the mind; *upādāya*—applying; *yat yat*—whatever; *rūpam*—form; *bubhūṣati*—one desires to assume; *tat tat*—that very form; *bhavet*—may appear; *manaḥ-rūpam*—the form desired by the mind; *mat-yoga-balam*—My inconceivable mystic potency, by which I manifest innumerable forms; *āśrayaḥ*—being the shelter.

TRANSLATION

When the yogī, applying his mind in a certain way, desires to assume a particular form, that very form immediately appears. Such perfection is possible by absorbing the mind in the shelter of My inconceivable mystic potency, by which I assume innumerable forms.

PURPORT

This perfection is called *kāma-rūpa*, or the ability to assume any form that one desires, even the form of a demigod. The pure devotees absorb their minds in a particular type of service to Lord Kṛṣṇa and thus gradually assume a spiritual body for an eternal life of bliss and knowledge. Thus anyone who takes to the process of chanting the holy names of Kṛṣṇa and follows the regulative principles of human life can acquire the ultimate perfection of *kāma-rūpa*, assuming an eternal, spiritual body in the kingdom of God.

TEXT 23

परकायं विशन् सिद्ध आत्मानं तत्र भावयेत् ।
पिण्डं हित्वा विशेत् प्राणो वायुभूतः षडङ्घ्रिवत्॥२३॥

para-kāyaṁ viśan siddha
ātmānaṁ tatra bhāvayet
piṇḍaṁ hitvā viśet prāṇo
vāyu-bhūtaḥ ṣaḍaṅghri-vat

para—of another; *kāyam*—the body; *viśan*—desiring to enter; *siddhaḥ*—one perfected in *yoga* practice; *ātmānam*—oneself; *tatra*—in that body; *bhāvayet*—imagines; *piṇḍam*—one's own gross body; *hitvā*—giving up; *viśet*—one should enter; *prāṇaḥ*—in the subtle body; *vāyu-bhūtaḥ*—becoming just like the wind; *ṣaṭ-aṅghri-vat*—like the bee, who easily moves from one flower to another.

TRANSLATION

When a perfect yogī desires to enter another's body, he should meditate upon himself within the other body, and then giving up his own gross body he should enter the other's body through the pathways of air, as easily as a bee leaves a flower and flies into another.

PURPORT

As air is inhaled into the body through the nostrils and mouth, similarly, the life air of the *yogī's* subtle body travels through the pathways of external air and easily enters into the body of another person, just as the bee easily flies from flower to flower. One may admire a heroic man or beautiful woman and desire to experience life within their extraordinary material body. Such opportunities are available through the mystic perfection called *para-kāya-praveśanam.* Pure devotees, being absorbed in meditation upon the spiritual form of the Supreme Personality of Godhead, are not actually attracted to any material body. Thus the devotees remain transcendental and satisfied on the platform of eternal life.

TEXT 24

पार्ष्ण्यापीड्य गुदं प्राणं हृदुरःकण्ठमूर्धसु ।
आरोप्य ब्रह्मरन्ध्रेण ब्रह्म नीत्वोत्सृजेत्तनुम् ॥२४॥

pārṣṇyāpīḍya gudaṁ prāṇaṁ
hṛd-uraḥ-kaṇṭha-mūrdhasu
āropya brahma-randhreṇa
brahma nītvotsṛjet tanum

pārṣṇyā—with the heel of the foot; *āpīḍya*—blocking; *gudam*—the anus; *prāṇam*—the vital air carrying the living entity; *hṛt*—from the heart; *uraḥ*—to the chest; *kaṇṭha*—to the neck; *mūrdhasu*—and to the head; *āropya*—placing; *brahma-randhreṇa*—by the spiritual seat at the top of the head; *brahma*—to the spiritual world or impersonal Brahman (or any other destination one has selected); *nītvā*—leading (the soul); *utsṛjet*—one should give up; *tanum*—the material body.

TRANSLATION

The yogī who has achieved the mystic perfection called svacchanda-mṛtyu blocks the anus with the heel of the foot and then lifts the soul from the heart to the chest, to the neck and finally to the head. Situated within the brahma-randhra, the yogī then gives up his material body and guides the spirit soul to the selected destination.

PURPORT

This mystic opulence of *svacchanda-mṛtyu*, or dying at will, was wonderfully exhibited by Bhīṣmadeva at the end of the Battle of Kurukṣetra. According to Śrīla Śrīdhara Svāmī, the term *brahma*, as used in this verse, is an example of *upalakṣaṇa*, or the use of a general term to indicate various concepts. *Brahma* here indicates the particular destination selected by the *yogī*, namely the spiritual sky, the impersonal *brahmajyoti* or any other destination that has attracted the *yogī's* mind.

TEXT 25

विहरिष्यन् सुराक्रीडे मत्स्थं सत्त्वं विभावयेत् ।
विमानेनोपतिष्ठन्ति सत्त्ववृत्तीः सुरस्त्रियः ॥२५॥

vihariṣyan surākrīḍe
mat-sthaṁ sattvaṁ vibhāvayet
vimānenopatiṣṭhanti
sattva-vṛttīḥ sura-striyaḥ

vihariṣyan—desiring to enjoy; *sura*—of the demigods; *ākrīḍe*—in the pleasure gardens; *mat*—in Me; *stham*—situated; *sattvam*—the mode of goodness; *vibhāvayet*—one should meditate on; *vimānena*—by airplane; *upatiṣṭhanti*—they arrive; *sattva*—in the mode of goodness; *vṛttīḥ*—appearing; *sura*—of the demigods; *striyaḥ*—the women.

TRANSLATION

The yogī who desires to enjoy in the pleasure gardens of the demigods should meditate on the purified mode of goodness, which is situated within Me, and then the heavenly women, generated from the mode of goodness, will approach him in airplanes.

TEXT 26

यथा सङ्कल्पयेद् बुद्ध्या यदा वा मत्परः पुमान् ।
मयि सत्ये मनो युञ्जंस्तथा तत् समुपाश्नुते ॥२६॥

yathā saṅkalpayed buddhyā
yadā vā mat-paraḥ pumān
mayi satye mano yuñjaṁs
tathā tat samupāśnute

yathā—by which means; *saṅkalpayet*—one may determine or resolve; *buddhyā*—by the mind; *yadā*—when; *vā*—or; *mat-paraḥ*—having faith in Me; *pumān*—the *yogī; mayi*—in Me; *satye*—whose desire always becomes truth; *manaḥ*—the mind; *yuñjan*—absorbing; *tathā*—by that means; *tat*—that very purpose; *samupāśnute*—he obtains.

TRANSLATION

A yogī who has faith in Me, absorbing his mind in Me and knowing that My purpose is always fulfilled, will always achieve his purpose by the very means he has determined to follow.

PURPORT

In this verse the word *yadā* ("whenever") indicates that by the mystic power called *yathā-saṅkalpa-saṁsiddhi* one will achieve one's objective even if one pursues it at an inauspicious time. Lord Kṛṣṇa is called *satya-saṅkalpa*, or He whose desire, intention, purpose or resolve always comes to pass.

Śrīla Bhaktisiddhānta Sarasvatī Ṭhākura mentions that one should determine to revive one's lost relationship with the Supreme Lord Kṛṣṇa through the infallible means of devotional service, which can be executed at any time or in any place. There are many books giving proper guidance for achieving Lord Kṛṣṇa, and the following are mentioned: Śrīla Jīva Gosvāmī's *Saṅkalpa-kalpavṛkṣa*, Śrīla Kṛṣṇadāsa Kavirāja's *Śrī Govinda-līlāmṛta*, Śrīla Viśvanātha Cakravartī's *Śrī Kṛṣṇa-bhāvanāmṛta* and *Saṅkalpa-kalpadruma*, and Śrīla Bhaktivinoda Ṭhākura's *Śrī Gaurāṅga-smaraṇa-maṅgala.* In the modern age, His Divine Grace A. C. Bhaktivedanta Swami Prabhupāda has given us over sixty large volumes of transcendental literature, which can fix us firmly on the path back home, back to Godhead. Our *saṅkalpa*, or determination, should be practical and not useless. We should resolve to make a permanent solution to the problems of life by going back home, back to Godhead.

TEXT 27

यो वै मद्भावमापन्न ईशितुर्वशितुः पुमान् ।
कुतश्चिन्न विहन्येत तस्य चाज्ञा यथा मम ॥२७॥

yo vai mad-bhāvam āpanna
īśitur vaśituḥ pumān
kutaścin na vihanyeta
tasya cājñā yathā mama

yaḥ—one who (a *yogī*); *vai*—indeed; *mat*—from Me; *bhāvam*—nature; *āpannaḥ*—achieved; *īśituḥ*—from the supreme ruler; *vaśituḥ*—the supreme controller; *pumān*—a person (*yogī*); *kutaścit*—in any way; *na vihanyeta*—cannot be frustrated; *tasya*—his; *ca*—also; *ājñā*—order, command; *yathā*—just as; *mama*—Mine.

TRANSLATION

A person who perfectly meditates on Me acquires My nature of being the supreme ruler and controller. His order, like Mine, can never be frustrated by any means.

PURPORT

By the command of the Supreme Personality of Godhead the entire creation is moving. As stated in *Bhagavad-gītā* (9.10),

mayādhyakṣeṇa prakṛtiḥ
sūyate sa-carācaram
hetunānena kaunteya
jagad viparivartate

"This material nature is working under My direction, O son of Kuntī, and it is producing all moving and unmoving beings. By its rule this manifestation is created and annihilated again and again." Similarly, Caitanya Mahāprabhu has given His command that people all over the world should take to Kṛṣṇa consciousness. The sincere devotees of the Lord should go all over the world repeating the Lord's command. In this way, they can share in His mystic opulence of giving orders that cannot be counteracted.

TEXT 28

मद्भक्त्या शुद्धसत्त्वस्य योगिनो धारणाविदः ।
तस्य त्रैकालिकी बुद्धिर्जन्ममृत्यूपबृंहिता ॥२८॥

mad-bhaktyā śuddha-sattvasya
yogino dhāraṇā-vidaḥ
tasya trai-kālikī buddhir
janma-mṛtyūpabṛṁhitā

mat-bhaktyā—by devotion to Me; *śuddha-sattvasya*—of one whose existence is purified; *yoginaḥ*—of a *yogī;* *dhāraṇā-vidaḥ*—who knows the process of meditation; *tasya*—of him; *trai-kālikī*—functioning in three phases of time, namely past, present and future; *buddhiḥ*—intelligence; *janma-mṛtyu*—birth and death; *upabṛṁhitā*—including.

TRANSLATION

A yogī who has purified his existence by devotion to Me and who thus expertly knows the process of meditation obtains knowledge of past, present and future. He can therefore see the birth and death of himself and others.

PURPORT

After having explained the eight primary and ten secondary mystic perfections of *yoga*, the Lord now explains the five inferior potencies.

TEXT 29

अग्न्यादिभिर्न हन्येत मुनेर्योगमयं वपुः ।
मद्योग शान्तचित्तस्य यादसामुदकं यथा ॥२९॥

agny-ādibhir na hanyeta
muner yoga-mayaṁ vapuḥ
mad-yoga-śānta-cittasya
yādasām udakaṁ yathā

agni—by fire; *ādibhiḥ*—and so on (sun, water, poison, etc.); *na*—not; *hanyeta*—can be injured; *muneḥ*—of a wise *yogī; yoga-mayam*—fully cultivated in *yoga* science; *vapuḥ*—the body; *mat-yoga*—by devotional connection with Me; *śānta*—pacified; *cittasya*—whose consciousness; *yādasām*—of the aquatics; *udakam*—water; *yathā*—just as.

TRANSLATION

Just as the bodies of aquatics cannot be injured by water, similarly, the body of a yogī whose consciousness is pacified by devotion to Me and who is fully developed in yoga science cannot be injured by fire, sun, water, poison, and so forth.

PURPORT

The creatures dwelling in the ocean are never injured by water; rather, they enjoy life within the watery medium. Similarly, for one skilled in the techniques of *yoga*, fending off attacks by weapons, fire, poison, and so on, is a recreational activity. Prahlāda Mahārāja was attacked by his father in all these ways, but because of his perfect Kṛṣṇa consciousness he was not injured. The pure devotees of the Lord depend fully on the mercy of Lord Kṛṣṇa, who possesses mystic opulences to an infinite degree and is therefore known as Yogeśvara, the master of all mystic power. Because devotees are always connected to Lord Kṛṣṇa, they do not feel any need to separately develop powers already possessed unlimitedly by their Lord, master and protector.

If a human being falls into the middle of the ocean he quickly drowns, whereas the fish enjoy happiness sporting in the same waves. Similarly, the conditioned souls have fallen into the ocean of material existence and are drowning in the reactions to their sinful activities, whereas the devotees recognize this world to be the potency of the Lord and enjoy pleasurable pastimes within it by fully engaging in the loving service of Lord Kṛṣṇa.

TEXT 30

मद्विभूतीरभिध्यायन् श्रीवत्सास्त्रविभूषिताः ।
ध्वजातपत्रव्यजनैः स भवेदपराजितः ॥३०॥

mad-vibhūtīr abhidhyāyan
śrīvatsāstra-vibhūṣitāḥ
dhvajātapatra-vyajanaiḥ
sa bhaved aparājitaḥ

mat—My; *vibhūtīḥ*—opulent incarnations; *abhidhyāyan*—meditating upon; *śrīvatsa*—with the Lord's Śrīvatsa opulence; *astra*—and weapons; *vibhūṣitāḥ*—decorated; *dhvaja*—with flags; *ātapatra*—with ceremonial umbrellas; *vyajanaiḥ*—and different types of fans; *saḥ*—he, the devotee-*yogī; bhavet*—becomes; *aparājitaḥ*—unconquerable by others.

TRANSLATION

My devotee becomes unconquerable by meditating on My opulent incarnations, which are decorated with Śrīvatsa and various weapons and are endowed with imperial paraphernalia such as flags, ornamental umbrellas and fans.

PURPORT

The imperial paraphernalia of the Lord's opulent incarnations indicates His omnipotency, and the devotees become unconquerable by meditating on the Lord's powerful, royally equipped incarnations. As stated by Bilvamaṅgala Ṭhākura in *Kṛṣṇa-karṇāmṛta*, verse 107,

bhaktis tvayi sthiratarā bhagavan yadi syād
daivena naḥ phalati divya-kiśora-mūrtiḥ
muktiḥ svayaṁ mukulitāñjaliḥ sevate 'smān
dharmārtha-kāma-gatayaḥ samaya-pratīkṣāḥ

"My dear Lord, if we develop unflinching devotional service unto You, then automatically Your transcendental, youthful form is revealed to us.

Thus liberation herself waits with folded hands to serve us, and the ultimate goals of religiosity, economic development and sense gratification patiently wait to render service to us."

TEXT 31

उपासकस्य मामेवं योगधारणया मुनेः ।
सिद्धयः पूर्वकथिता उपतिष्ठन्त्यशेषतः ॥३१॥

upāsakasya mām evaṁ
yoga-dhāraṇayā muneḥ
siddhayaḥ pūrva-kathitā
upatiṣṭhanty aśeṣataḥ

upāsakasya—of one who is worshiping; *mām*—Me; *evam*—thus; *yoga-dhāraṇayā*—by the process of mystic meditation; *muneḥ*—of a learned person; *siddhayaḥ*—the mystic perfections; *pūrva*—previously; *kathitāḥ*—described; *upatiṣṭhanti*—approach; *aśeṣataḥ*—in all respects.

TRANSLATION

A learned devotee who worships Me through yoga meditation certainly obtains in all respects the mystic perfections that I have described.

PURPORT

The word *yoga-dhāraṇayā* indicates that each devotee obtains the particular perfection for which he has qualified himself. The Lord thus concludes His discussion of *yoga-siddhis.*

TEXT 32

जितेन्द्रियस्य दान्तस्य जितश्वासात्मनो मुनेः ।
मद्धारणां धारयतः का सा सिद्धिः सुदुर्लभा ॥३२॥

jitendriyasya dāntasya
jita-śvāsātmano muneḥ
mad-dhāraṇāṁ dhārayataḥ
kā sā siddhiḥ su-durlabhā

jita-indriyasya—of one who has conquered his senses; *dāntasya*—who is disciplined and self-controlled; *jita-śvāsa*—who has conquered his breathing; *ātmanaḥ*—and conquered the mind; *muneḥ*—of such a sage; *mat*—in Me; *dhāraṇām*—meditation; *dhārayataḥ*—who is conducting; *kā*—what is; *sā*—that; *siddhiḥ*—perfection; *su-durlabhā*—which is very difficult to achieve.

TRANSLATION

For a sage who has conquered his senses, breathing and mind, who is self-controlled and always absorbed in meditation on Me, what mystic perfection could possibly be difficult to achieve?

PURPORT

Śrīla Śrīdhara Svāmī comments as follows. "Lord Kṛṣṇa here expresses that there is no need to practice many different processes, for by completely carrying out even one of the above-mentioned procedures one controls one's senses, becomes absorbed in Him and thus achieves all mystic perfections."

Śrīla Jīva Gosvāmī notes that one must meditate on the transcendental form of the Lord, which is free from any material designation. This is the essence of advancing in the *yoga* system; thus one acquires all mystic perfections very easily from the personal body of the Personality of Godhead.

TEXT 33

अन्तरायान् वदन्त्येता युञ्जतो योगमुत्तमम् ।
मया सम्पद्यमानस्य कालक्षपणहेतवः ॥३३॥

antarāyān vadanty etā
yuñjato yogam uttamam
mayā sampadyamānasya
kāla-kṣapaṇa-hetavaḥ

antarāyān—impediments; *vadanti*—they say; *etāḥ*—these mystic perfections; *yuñjataḥ*—of one engaging in; *yogam*—connection with the

Absolute; *uttamam*—the supreme stage; *mayā*—with Me; *sampadya-mānasya*—of one who is becoming completely opulent; *kāla*—of time; *kṣapaṇa*—of the interruption, waste; *hetavaḥ*—causes.

TRANSLATION

Learned experts in devotional service state that the mystic perfections of yoga that I have mentioned are actually impediments and are a waste of time for one who is practicing the supreme yoga, by which one achieves all perfection in life directly from Me.

PURPORT

It is common sense that whatever is a useless waste of time should be given up; therefore one should not pray to God for mystic *yoga* perfections. For a pure devotee, who has no material desire, even impersonal liberation is a useless disturbance in his life, and what to speak of the material perfections of *yoga*, which cannot even be compared to impersonal liberation. Such mystic perfections may be wonderful for an immature and inexperienced person, but they are not impressive for a learned man who has understood the Supreme Personality of Godhead. Simply by obtaining Lord Kṛṣṇa one dwells within an infinite ocean of mystic opulences; therefore he should not waste precious time pursuing separate mystic perfections.

TEXT 34

जन्मौषधितपोमन्त्रैर्यावतीरिह सिद्धयः ।
योगेनाप्नोति ताः सर्वा नान्यैर्योगगतिं व्रजेत् ॥३४॥

janmauṣadhi-tapo-mantrair
yāvatīr iha siddhayaḥ
yogenāpnoti tāḥ sarvā
nānyair yoga-gatiṁ vrajet

janma—by birth; *auṣadhi*—herbs; *tapaḥ*—austerities; *mantraiḥ*—and by *mantras; yāvatīḥ*—as many as there are; *iha*—in this world; *siddhayaḥ*—perfections; *yogena*—by devotional service to Me; *āpnoti*—one obtains; *tāḥ*—those; *sarvāḥ*—all of them; *na*—not; *anyaiḥ*—by other methods; *yoga-gatim*—the actual perfection of *yoga; vrajet*—one can achieve.

TRANSLATION

Whatever mystic perfections can be achieved by good birth, herbs, austerities and mantras can all be achieved by devotional service to Me; indeed, one cannot achieve the actual perfection of yoga by any other means.

PURPORT

By taking birth as a demigod one is automatically endowed with many mystic perfections. Simply by birth on Siddhaloka one automatically acquires all of the eight principal perfections of *yoga.* Similarly, by birth as a fish one becomes invulnerable to water, by birth as a bird one gets the mystic perfection of flying, and by birth as a ghost one gets the mystic perfection of disappearing and entering into the bodies of others. Patañjali Muni states that the mystic perfections of *yoga* can be achieved by birth, herbs, austerities and *mantras.* The Lord states, however, that such perfections are ultimately a waste of time and an impediment to achieving the actual perfection of *yoga,* Kṛṣṇa consciousness.

Those who give up the process of *bhakti-yoga* and shop around for other objects of meditation besides Kṛṣṇa are certainly not very intelligent. Those who claim to be *yogīs* but pursue the satisfaction of their own senses are certainly *kuyogīs,* or *bhogi-yogīs.* Such *kuyogīs* cannot understand that just as they have tiny senses, the Absolute Truth has absolute senses, nor can they understand that *yoga* is actually meant to satisfy the absolute senses of the Lord. Therefore, persons who give up the lotus feet of Lord Kṛṣṇa in order to pursue so-called happiness in mystic perfection will undoubtedly be frustrated in their attempt. By meditating exclusively on the Supreme Personality of Godhead one can achieve *yoga-gati,* the ultimate goal of *yoga,* which means living on Lord Kṛṣṇa's planet and there enjoying spiritual opulences.

TEXT 35

सर्वासामपि सिद्धीनां हेतुः पतिरहं प्रभुः ।
अहं योगस्य सांख्यस्य धर्मस्य ब्रह्मवादिनाम् ॥३५॥

sarvāsām api siddhīnāṁ
hetuḥ patir ahaṁ prabhuḥ

ahaṁ yogasya sāṅkhyasya
dharmasya brahma-vādinām

sarvāsām—of all of them; *api*—indeed; *siddhīnām*—of the mystic perfections; *hetuḥ*—the cause; *patiḥ*—the protector; *aham*—I am; *prabhuḥ*—the Lord; *aham*—I; *yogasya*—of unalloyed meditation on Me; *sāṅkhyasya*—of analytic knowledge; *dharmasya*—of work executed without personal desire; *brahma-vādinām*—of the learned community of Vedic teachers.

TRANSLATION

My dear Uddhava, I am the cause, the protector and the Lord of all mystic perfections, of the yoga system, of analytic knowledge, of pure activity and of the community of learned Vedic teachers.

PURPORT

According to Śrīla Śrīdhara Svāmī, the word *yoga* here indicates liberation from material life, and *sāṅkhya* indicates the means of obtaining liberation. Thus Lord Kṛṣṇa is not merely the Lord of material *yoga* perfections, but of the highest liberated perfections as well. One can obtain *sāṅkhya*, or knowledge leading to liberation, by performing pious activities, and Lord Kṛṣṇa is also the cause, protector and Lord of such activities as well as of the learned teachers who instruct ordinary people in the means of piety. In many different ways Lord Kṛṣṇa is the real object of meditation and worship for every living entity. Lord Kṛṣṇa through the expansion of His potencies is everything, and this simple understanding, called Kṛṣṇa consciousness, is the supreme perfection of the *yoga* system.

TEXT 36

अहमात्मान्तरो बाह्योऽनावृतः सर्वदेहिनाम् ।
यथा भूतानि भूतेषु बहिरन्तः स्वयं तथा ॥३६॥

aham ātmāntaro bāhyo
'nāvṛtaḥ sarva-dehinām
yathā bhūtāni bhūteṣu
bahir antaḥ svayaṁ tathā

aham—I; *ātmā*—the Supreme Lord; *āntaraḥ*—existing within as the Supersoul; *bāhyaḥ*—existing externally in My all-pervading feature; *anāvṛtaḥ*—uncovered; *sarva-dehinām*—of all living entities; *yathā*—just as; *bhūtāni*—the material elements; *bhūteṣu*—among living entities; *bahiḥ*—externally; *antaḥ*—internally; *svayam*—Myself; *tathā*—in the same way.

TRANSLATION

Just as the same material elements exist within and outside of all material bodies, similarly, I cannot be covered by anything else. I exist within everything as the Supersoul and outside of everything in My all-pervading feature.

PURPORT

Lord Kṛṣṇa is the entire basis of meditation for all *yogīs* and philosophers, and here the Lord clarifies His absolute position. Since the Lord is within everything, one might think that the Lord is divided into pieces. However, the word *anāvṛta*, or "completely uncovered," indicates that nothing can interrupt, disturb or in any way infringe upon the supreme existence of the Absolute Truth, the Personality of Godhead. There is no actual separation between the internal and external existence of the material elements, which continuously exist everywhere. Similarly, the Supreme Personality of Godhead is all-pervading and is the ultimate perfection of everything.

Thus end the purports of the humble servants of His Divine Grace A. C. Bhaktivedanta Swami Prabhupāda to the Eleventh Canto, Fifteenth Chapter, of the Śrīmad-Bhāgavatam, *entitled "Lord Kṛṣṇa's Description of Mystic Yoga Perfections."*

CHAPTER SIXTEEN

The Lord's Opulence

In this chapter the Personality of Godhead, Lord Śrī Kṛṣṇa, describes His manifest opulences in terms of His specific potencies of knowledge, strength, influence, and so on.

Śrī Uddhava offered glorification to Lord Śrī Kṛṣṇa, the Supreme Personality of Godhead and ultimate shelter of all holy places, saying, "The Supreme Lord has no beginning and no end. He is the cause of the birth, maintenance and destruction of all living entities. He is the soul of all beings, and by secretly taking up residence within all living bodies He sees everything. The conditioned souls, on the other hand, are bewildered by His external energy and thus are unable to see Him." After offering such prayers at the lotus feet of Lord Kṛṣṇa, Śrī Uddhava revealed his desire to know about the Lord's various opulences in heaven, on earth, in hell and in all directions. Lord Śrī Kṛṣṇa then described all these opulences, after which He commented that all power, beauty, fame, opulence, humility, charity, charm, good fortune, valor, tolerance and wisdom—wherever they are manifest—are simply expansions from Himself. It therefore cannot be truthfully said that a material object actually possesses these opulences. Such conceptions are the results of mentally combining two ideas to produce an object that exists only in the imagination, such as a sky flower. Material opulences are not substantially true, and therefore one should not become too involved in meditating upon them. The pure devotees of the Supreme Lord utilize their intelligence to properly regulate the activities of their speech, mind and vital force and thus perfect their existence in Kṛṣṇa consciousness.

TEXT 1

श्रीउद्धव उवाच

त्वं ब्रह्म परमं साक्षादनाद्यन्तमपावृतम् ।
सर्वेषामपि भावानां त्राणस्थित्यप्ययोद्भवः ॥ १ ॥

śrī-uddhava uvāca
tvaṁ brahma paramaṁ sākṣād
anādy-antam apāvṛtam
sarveṣām api bhāvānāṁ
trāṇa-sthity-apyayodbhavaḥ

śrī-uddhavaḥ uvāca—Śrī Uddhava said; *tvam*—You are; *brahma*—the greatest; *paramam*—the supreme; *sākṣāt*—Himself; *anādi*—without beginning; *antam*—without end; *apāvṛtam*—unlimited by anything else; *sarveṣām*—of all; *api*—indeed; *bhāvānām*—things which exist; *trāṇa*—the protector; *sthiti*—the life-giver; *apyaya*—the destruction; *udbhavaḥ*—and the creation.

TRANSLATION

Śrī Uddhava said: My dear Lord, You are beginningless and endless, the Absolute Truth Himself, unlimited by anything else. You are the protector and life-giver, the destruction and creation of all things that exist.

PURPORT

Brahma means the greatest of all and the cause of everything. Uddhava here addresses the Lord as the *paramam*, or supreme *brahma*, because in His feature as Bhagavān the Lord is the highest feature of the Absolute Truth and the shelter of unlimited spiritual opulences. Unlike those of ordinary living entities, the Lord's opulences cannot be restricted by time, and thus the Lord is *anādy-antam*, without beginning or end, and *apāvṛtam*, unhindered by any superior or equal potency. The opulence of the material world is also resting within the Lord, who alone can protect, maintain, create and destroy the material world. In this chapter, Śrī Uddhava inquires from the Lord about His spiritual and material opulences in order to refine his appreciation of the Lord's position as the Absolute Truth. Even Lord Viṣṇu, the ultimate creator of the material world, is an expansion of Lord Kṛṣṇa, and thus Śrī Uddhava wishes to fully appreciate the unique status of his personal friend.

TEXT 2

उच्चावचेषु भूतेषु दुर्ज्ञेयमकृतात्मभिः ।
उपासते त्वां भगवन् याथातथ्येन ब्राह्मणाः ॥ २ ॥

uccāvaceṣu bhūteṣu
durjñeyam akṛtātmabhiḥ
upāsate tvāṁ bhagavan
yāthā-tathyena brāhmaṇāḥ

ucca—in the superior; *avaceṣu*—and the inferior; *bhūteṣu*—created objects and entities; *durjñeyam*—hard to understand; *akṛta-ātmabhiḥ*—by the impious; *upāsate*—they worship; *tvām*—You; *bhagavan*—my dear Lord; *yāthā-tathyena*—in truth; *brāhmaṇāḥ*—those dedicated to the Vedic conclusion.

TRANSLATION

My dear Lord, although it is difficult for the impious to understand that You are situated in all superior and inferior creations, those brāhmaṇas who are actual knowers of the Vedic conclusion worship You in truth.

PURPORT

The behavior of saintly persons is also to be taken as evidence, and therefore it is here stated that although ignorant, impious persons are bewildered before the Lord's all-pervading feature, those with purified, clear consciousness worship the Lord as He is. In this chapter Śrī Uddhava inquires about the Lord's opulences, and here the words *uccāvaceṣu bhūteṣu* ("within superior and inferior creations") clearly refer to the Lord's external opulences, those manifested in the material world. The saintly *brāhmaṇas*, or Vaiṣṇavas, worship Lord Kṛṣṇa within all things and yet recognize the variety in the Lord's creation. For example, in worshiping the Deity, the devotees will select the nicest flowers, fruits and ornaments for decorating the transcendental form of the Lord. Similarly, although the Lord is present in the heart of every conditioned soul, the devotee will give more attention to a conditioned soul interested in the message of Lord Kṛṣṇa. Although the Lord is everywhere, the devotees make distinctions, for the sake of the Lord's service, between His presence in superior (*ucca*) and inferior (*avaceṣu*) creations.

TEXT 3

येषु येषु च भूतेषु भक्त्या त्वां परमर्षयः ।
उपासीनाः प्रपद्यन्ते संसिद्धिं तद् वदस्व मे ॥ ३ ॥

yeṣu yeṣu ca bhūteṣu
bhaktyā tvāṁ paramarṣayaḥ
upāsīnāḥ prapadyante
saṁsiddhiṁ tad vadasva me

yeṣu yeṣu—in which various; *ca*—also; *bhūteṣu*—forms; *bhaktyā*—with devotion; *tvām*—You; *parama-ṛṣayaḥ*—the great sages; *upāsīnāḥ*—worshiping; *prapadyante*—achieve; *saṁsiddhim*—perfection; *tat*—that; *vadasva*—please speak; *me*—to me.

TRANSLATION

Please tell me of the perfections that great sages achieve by worshiping You with devotion. Also, kindly explain which of Your different forms they worship.

PURPORT

Śrī Uddhava here inquires about the spiritual opulences of the Lord, which consist primarily of His *viṣṇu-tattva* expansions such as Vāsudeva, Saṅkarṣaṇa, Pradyumna and Aniruddha. By worshiping different plenary expansions of the Lord one achieves particular perfections, and Śrī Uddhava wants to know about this.

TEXT 4

गूढश्चरसि भूतात्मा भूतानां भूतभावन ।
न त्वां पश्यन्ति भूतानि पश्यन्तं मोहितानि ते ॥ ४ ॥

gūḍhaś carasi bhūtātmā
bhūtānāṁ bhūta-bhāvana
na tvāṁ paśyanti bhūtāni
paśyantaṁ mohitāni te

gūḍhaḥ—hidden; *carasi*—You are engaged; *bhūta-ātmā*—the Supersoul; *bhūtānām*—of the living entities; *bhūta-bhāvana*—O maintainer of all living beings; *na*—not; *tvām*—You; *paśyanti*—they see; *bhūtāni*—living entities; *paśyantam*—who are seeing; *mohitāni*—bewildered; *te*—by You.

TRANSLATION

O my Lord, maintainer of all, although You are the Supersoul of the living entities, You remain hidden. Thus being bewildered by You, the living entities cannot see You, although You are seeing them.

PURPORT

The Lord exists as the Supersoul within everything. He also appears in various incarnations or sometimes empowers a devotee to act as an incarnation. All such forms of the Lord are unknown to the nondevotees. The bewildered conditioned souls think that the supreme enjoyer, Śrī Kṛṣṇa, is actually meant to be enjoyed by them for their sense gratification. Praying to God for specific material benedictions and assuming God's creation to be their personal property, the nondevotees cannot understand the actual form of the Lord. They therefore remain foolish and bewildered. Within the universe everything is subject to creation, maintenance and destruction, and thus the Supersoul is the only actual controller in the material world. Unfortunately, when the Supersoul appears in various incarnations to clarify His position, ignorant persons think that the Supersoul is merely another creation of the modes of material nature. As stated in this verse, they cannot see that person who is actually seeing them, and simply remain bewildered.

TEXT 5

याः काश्च भूमौ दिवि वै रसायां
विभूतयो दिक्षु महाविभूते ।
ता मह्यमाख्याह्यनुभावितास्ते
नमामि ते तीर्थपदाङ्घ्रिपद्मम् ॥ ५ ॥

yāḥ kāś ca bhūmau divi vai rasāyāṁ
vibhūtayo dikṣu mahā-vibhūte
tā mahyam ākhyāhy anubhāvitās te
namāmi te tīrtha-padāṅghri-padmam

yāḥ kāḥ—whatever; *ca*—also; *bhūmau*—on the earth; *divi*—in heaven; *vai*—indeed; *rasāyām*—in hell; *vibhūtayaḥ*—potencies; *dik-*

ṣu—in all directions; *mahā-vibhūte*—O supremely potent; *tāḥ*—those; *mahyam*—unto me; *ākhyāhi*—please explain; *anubhāvitāḥ*—manifested; *te*—by You; *namāmi*—I offer my humble obeisances; *te*—Your; *tīrtha-pada*—the abode of all holy places; *aṅghri-padmam*—at the lotus feet.

TRANSLATION

O supremely potent Lord, please explain to me Your innumerable potencies, which You manifest on the earth, in heaven, in hell and indeed in all directions. I offer my humble obeisances at Your lotus feet, which are the shelter of all holy places.

PURPORT

Uddhava here inquires about the Lord's material and spiritual potencies, as manifested within our universe. Just as ordinary animals or insects living in human cities cannot appreciate the scientific, cultural or military achievements of man, similarly, foolish materialists cannot appreciate the mighty opulences of the Personality of Godhead, even those manifested within our universe. For the appreciation of ordinary human beings Uddhava requests the Lord to reveal exactly how and in what forms He expands His potencies. As already explained, the Lord is the essential ingredient of all that exists, and thus any mighty or opulent manifestation must ultimately rest on the Lord Himself.

TEXT 6

श्रीभगवानुवाच

एवमेतदहं पृष्टः प्रश्नं प्रश्नविदां वर ।
युयुत्सुना विनशने सपत्नैरर्जुनेन वै ॥ ६ ॥

śrī-bhagavān uvāca
evam etad ahaṁ pṛṣṭaḥ
praśnaṁ praśna-vidāṁ vara
yuyutsunā vinaśane
sapatnair arjunena vai

śrī-bhagavān uvāca—the Supreme Personality of Godhead said; *evam*—thus; *etat*—this; *aham*—I; *pṛṣṭaḥ*—was asked; *praśnam*—the question or topic; *praśna-vidām*—of those who know how to inquire; *vara*—you who are the best; *yuyutsunā*—by him who desired to fight; *vinaśane*—in the Battle of Kurukṣetra; *sapatnaiḥ*—with his rivals or enemies; *arjunena*—by Arjuna; *vai*—indeed.

TRANSLATION

The Supreme Personality of Godhead said: O best of those who know how to inquire, on the Battlefield of Kurukṣetra, Arjuna, desiring to fight with his rivals, asked Me the same question that you are now posing.

PURPORT

Lord Kṛṣṇa was pleased that His two friends, Arjuna and Uddhava, had posed the same question regarding the opulences of the Personality of Godhead. Lord Kṛṣṇa considered it wonderful that His two dear friends had asked exactly the same question.

TEXT 7

ज्ञात्वा ज्ञातिवधं गर्ह्यमधर्मं राज्यहेतुकम् ।
ततो निवृत्तो हन्ताहं हतोऽयमिति लौकिकः ॥ ७ ॥

jñātvā jñāti-vadhaṁ garhyam
adharmaṁ rājya-hetukam
tato nivṛtto hantāhaṁ
hato 'yam iti laukikaḥ

jñātvā—being aware; *jñāti*—of his relatives; *vadham*—the killing; *garhyam*—abominable; *adharmam*—irreligion; *rājya*—to acquire a kingdom; *hetukam*—having as the motive; *tataḥ*—from such activity; *nivṛttaḥ*—retired; *hantā*—the killer; *aham*—I am; *hataḥ*—killed; *ayam*—this group of relatives; *iti*—thus; *laukikaḥ*—mundane.

TRANSLATION

On the Battlefield of Kurukṣetra Arjuna thought that killing his relatives would be an abominable, irreligious activity, motivated only by his desire to acquire a kingdom. He therefore desisted

from the battle, thinking, "I would be the killer of my relatives. They would be destroyed." Thus Arjuna was afflicted with mundane consciousness.

PURPORT

Lord Kṛṣṇa here explains to Uddhava the circumstances in which Śrī Arjuna posed his questions.

TEXT 8

स तदा पुरुषव्याघ्रो युक्त्या मे प्रतिबोधितः ।
अभ्यभाषत मामेवं यथा त्वं रणमूर्धनि ॥ ८ ॥

sa tadā puruṣa-vyāghro
yuktyā me pratibodhitaḥ
abhyabhāṣata mām evaṁ
yathā tvaṁ raṇa-mūrdhani

saḥ—he; *tadā*—at that time; *puruṣa-vyāghraḥ*—the tiger among men; *yuktyā*—by logical argument; *me*—by Me; *pratibodhitaḥ*—enlightened in real knowledge; *abhyabhāṣata*—addressed questions; *mām*—to Me; *evam*—thus; *yathā*—just as; *tvam*—you; *raṇa*—of the battle; *mūrdhani*—in the front.

TRANSLATION

At that time I enlightened Arjuna, the tiger among men, with logical arguments, and thus in the front of the battle Arjuna addressed Me with questions in the same way that you are now inquiring.

TEXT 9

अहमात्मोद्धवामीषां भूतानां सुहृदीश्वरः ।
अहं सर्वाणि भूतानि तेषां स्थित्युद्भवाप्ययः ॥ ९ ॥

aham ātmoddhavāmīṣāṁ
bhūtānāṁ suhṛd īśvaraḥ

ahaṁ sarvāṇi bhūtāni
teṣāṁ sthity-udbhavāpyayaḥ

aham—I am; *ātmā*—the Supersoul; *uddhava*—O Uddhava; *amīṣām*—of these; *bhūtānām*—living entities; *su-hṛt*—the well-wisher; *īśvaraḥ*—the supreme controller; *aham*—I am; *sarvāṇi bhūtāni*—all entities; *teṣām*—of them; *sthiti*—the maintenance; *udbhava*—creation; *apyayaḥ*—and annihilation.

TRANSLATION

My dear Uddhava, I am the Supersoul of all living entities, and therefore I am naturally their well-wisher and supreme controller. Being the creator, maintainer and annihilator of all entities, I am not different from them.

PURPORT

Śrīla Śrīdhara Svāmī points out that the Personality of Godhead maintains an ablative and genitive relationship with His opulences. In other words, the Lord is not different from all living entities, because they are coming from Him and they belong to Him. The Lord gave a similar explanation to Arjuna in the Tenth Chapter of *Bhagavad-gītā* (10.20), beginning with the same words, *aham ātmā.* Although the Lord describes His external, or material, opulences, the Lord's position is always transcendental and nonmaterial. Just as the living soul within the body gives life to the body, similarly, the Lord, by His supreme potency, gives life to all universal opulences.

TEXT 10

अहं गतिर्गतिमतां कालः कलयतामहम् ।
गुणानां चाप्यहं साम्यं गुणिन्यौत्पत्तिको गुणः॥१०॥

ahaṁ gatir gatimatāṁ
kālaḥ kalayatām aham
guṇānāṁ cāpy ahaṁ sāmyaṁ
guṇiny autpattiko guṇaḥ

aham—I am; *gatiḥ*—the ultimate goal; *gati-matām*—of those who seek progress; *kālaḥ*—time; *kalayatām*—of those who exert control; *aham*—I am; *guṇānām*—of the modes of material nature; *ca*—also; *api*—even; *aham*—I am; *sāmyam*—material equilibrium; *guṇini*—in the pious; *autpattikaḥ*—natural; *guṇaḥ*—virtue.

TRANSLATION

I am the ultimate goal of all those seeking progress, and I am time among those who exert control. I am the equilibrium of the modes of material nature, and I am natural virtue among the pious.

TEXT 11

गुणिनामप्यहं सूत्रं महतां च महानहम् ।
सूक्ष्माणामप्यहं जीवो दुर्जयानामहं मनः ॥११॥

guṇinām apy ahaṁ sūtraṁ
mahatāṁ ca mahān aham
sūkṣmāṇām apy ahaṁ jīvo
durjayānām ahaṁ manaḥ

guṇinām—among things possessing qualities; *api*—indeed; *aham*—I am; *sūtram*—the primary *sūtra-tattva; mahatām*—among great things; *ca*—also; *mahān*—the total material manifestation; *aham*—I am; *sūkṣmāṇām*—among subtle things; *api*—indeed; *aham*—I am; *jīvaḥ*—the spirit soul; *durjayānām*—among things difficult to conquer; *aham*—I am; *manaḥ*—the mind.

TRANSLATION

Among things possessing qualities I am the primary manifestation of nature, and among great things I am the total material creation. Among subtle things I am the spirit soul, and of things that are difficult to conquer I am the mind.

TEXT 12

हिरण्यगर्भो वेदानां मन्त्राणां प्रणवस्त्रिवृत् ।
अक्षराणामकारोऽस्मि पदानि च्छन्दसामहम् ॥१२॥

hiraṇyagarbho vedānāṁ
mantrāṇāṁ praṇavas tri-vṛt
akṣarāṇām a-kāro 'smi
padāni cchandasām aham

hiraṇya-garbhaḥ—Lord Brahmā; *vedānām*—of the *Vedas; mantrāṇām*—of *mantras; praṇavaḥ*—the *oṁkāra; tri-vṛt*—consisting of three letters; *akṣarāṇām*—of letters; *a-kāraḥ*—the first letter, *a; asmi*—I am; *padāni*—the three-line Gāyatrī *mantra; chandasām*—among sacred meters; *aham*—I am.

TRANSLATION

Among the Vedas I am their original teacher, Lord Brahmā, and of all mantras I am the three-lettered oṁkāra. Among letters I am the first letter, "a," and among sacred meters I am the Gāyatrī mantra.

TEXT 13

इन्द्रोऽहं सर्वदेवानां वसूनामस्मि हव्यवाट् ।
आदित्यानामहं विष्णू रुद्राणां नीललोहितः ॥१३॥

indro 'haṁ sarva-devānāṁ
vasūnām asmi havya-vāṭ
ādityānām ahaṁ viṣṇū
rudrāṇāṁ nīla-lohitaḥ

indraḥ—Lord Indra; *aham*—I am; *sarva-devānām*—among the demigods; *vasūnām*—among the Vasus; *asmi*—I am; *havya-vāṭ*—the carrier of oblations, the fire-god Agni; *ādityānām*—among the sons of Aditi; *aham*—I am; *viṣṇuḥ*—Viṣṇu; *rudrāṇām*—among the Rudras; *nīla-lohitaḥ*—Lord Śiva.

TRANSLATION

Among the demigods I am Indra, and among the Vasus I am Agni, the god of fire. I am Viṣṇu among the sons of Aditi, and among the Rudras I am Lord Śiva.

PURPORT

Lord Viṣṇu appeared among the sons of Aditi as Vāmanadeva.

TEXT 14

ब्रह्मर्षीणां भृगुरहं राजर्षीणामहं मनुः ।
देवर्षीणां नारदोऽहं हविर्धान्यस्मि धेनुषु ॥१४॥

brahmarṣīṇāṁ bhṛgur ahaṁ
rājarṣīṇām ahaṁ manuḥ
devarṣīṇāṁ nārado 'haṁ
havirdhāny asmi dhenuṣu

brahma-ṛṣīṇām—among the saintly *brāhmaṇas; bhṛguḥ*—Bhṛgu Muni; *aham*—I am; *rāja-ṛṣīṇām*—among the saintly kings; *aham*—I am; *manuḥ*—Manu; *deva-ṛṣīṇām*—among the saintly demigods; *nāradaḥ*—Nārada Muni; *aham*—I am; *havirdhānī*—Kāmadhenu; *asmi*—I am; *dhenuṣu*—among cows.

TRANSLATION

Among saintly brāhmaṇas I am Bhṛgu Muni, and I am Manu among saintly kings. I am Nārada Muni among saintly demigods, and I am Kāmadhenu among cows.

TEXT 15

सिद्धेश्वराणां कपिलः सुपर्णोऽहं पतत्रिणाम् ।
प्रजापतीनां दक्षोऽहं पितॄणामहमर्यमा ॥१५॥

siddheśvarāṇāṁ kapilaḥ
suparṇo 'haṁ patatriṇām
prajāpatīnāṁ dakṣo 'haṁ
pitṝṇām aham aryamā

siddha-īśvarāṇām—among perfected beings; *kapilaḥ*—I am Lord Kapila; *suparṇaḥ*—Garuḍa; *aham*—I am; *patatriṇām*—among birds; *prajāpatīnām*—among the progenitors of mankind; *dakṣaḥ*—Dakṣa; *aham*—I am; *pitṝṇām*—among the forefathers; *aham*—I am; *aryamā*—Aryamā.

TRANSLATION

I am Lord Kapila among perfected beings and Garuḍa among birds. I am Dakṣa among the progenitors of mankind, and I am Aryamā among the forefathers.

TEXT 16

मां विद्ध्युद्धव दैत्यानां प्रह्लादमसुरेश्वरम् ।
सोमं नक्षत्रौषधीनां धनेशं यक्षरक्षसाम् ॥१६॥

māṁ viddhy uddhava daityānāṁ
prahlādam asureśvaram
somaṁ nakṣatrauṣadhīnāṁ
dhaneśaṁ yakṣa-rakṣasām

mām—Me; *viddhi*—you should know; *uddhava*—My dear Uddhava; *daityānām*—among the sons of Diti, the demons; *prahlādam*—Prahlāda Mahārāja; *asura-īśvaram*—the lord of the *asuras; somam*—the moon; *nakṣatra-oṣadhīnām*—among the stars and herbs; *dhana-īśam*—the lord of wealth, Kuvera; *yakṣa-rakṣasām*—among the Yakṣas and Rākṣasas.

TRANSLATION

My dear Uddhava, among the demoniac sons of Diti know Me to be Prahlāda Mahārāja, the saintly lord of the asuras. Among the stars and herbs I am their lord, Candra (the moon), and among Yakṣas and Rākṣasas I am the lord of wealth, Kuvera.

TEXT 17

ऐरावतं गजेन्द्राणां यादसां वरुणं प्रभुम् ।
तपतां द्युमतां सूर्यं मनुष्याणां च भूपतिम् ॥१७॥

airāvataṁ gajendrāṇāṁ
yādasāṁ varuṇaṁ prabhum
tapatāṁ dyumatāṁ sūryaṁ
manuṣyāṇāṁ ca bhū-patim

airāvatam—the elephant Airāvata; *gaja-indrāṇām*—among lordly elephants; *yādasām*—among aquatics; *varuṇam*—Varuṇa; *prabhum*—

the lord of seas; *tapatām*—among things that heat; *dyu-matām*—among things that illuminate; *sūryam*—I am the sun; *manuṣyāṇām*—among human beings; *ca*—also; *bhū-patim*—the king.

TRANSLATION

I am Airāvata among lordly elephants, and among aquatics I am Varuṇa, the lord of the seas. Among all things that heat and illuminate I am the sun, and among human beings I am the king.

PURPORT

It is significant to know that Lord Kṛṣṇa is represented within this universe by the lord or supreme in all categories. No one can be as aristocratic and perfect as Śrī Kṛṣṇa, nor can anyone estimate the glories of Śrī Kṛṣṇa. Lord Kṛṣṇa is without doubt the Supreme Personality of Godhead.

TEXT 18

उच्चैःश्रवास्तुरङ्गाणां धातूनामस्मि काञ्चनम् ।
यमः संयमतां चाहं सर्पाणामस्मि वासुकिः ॥१८॥

uccaiḥśravās turaṅgāṇāṁ
dhātūnām asmi kāñcanam
yamaḥ saṁyamatāṁ cāham
sarpāṇām asmi vāsukiḥ

uccaiḥśravāḥ—the horse Uccaiḥśravā; *turaṅgāṇām*—among horses; *dhātūnām*—among metals; *asmi*—I am; *kāñcanam*—gold; *yamaḥ*—Yamarāja; *saṁyamatām*—among those who punish and suppress; *ca*—also; *aham*—I; *sarpāṇām*—among serpents; *asmi*—am; *vāsukiḥ*—Vāsuki.

TRANSLATION

Among horses I am Uccaiḥśravā, and I am gold among metals. I am Yamarāja among those who suppress and punish, and among serpents I am Vāsuki.

TEXT 19

नागेन्द्राणामनन्तोऽहं मृगेन्द्रः शृङ्गिदंष्ट्रिणाम् ।
आश्रमाणामहं तुर्यो वर्णानां प्रथमोऽनघ ॥१९॥

nāgendrāṇām ananto 'haṁ
mṛgendraḥ śṛṅgi-daṁṣṭriṇām
āśramāṇām ahaṁ turyo
varṇānāṁ prathamo 'nagha

nāga-indrāṇām—among the best of many-hooded snakes; *anantaḥ*—Anantadeva; *aham*—I am; *mṛga-indraḥ*—the lion; *śṛṅgi-daṁṣṭriṇām*—among animals with sharp horns and teeth; *āśramāṇām*—among the four social orders of life; *aham*—I am; *turyaḥ*—the fourth, *sannyāsa; varṇānām*—among the four occupational orders; *prathamaḥ*—the first, the *brāhmaṇas; anagha*—O sinless one.

TRANSLATION

O sinless Uddhava, among the best of snakes I am Anantadeva, and among those animals with sharp horns and teeth I am the lion. Among the social orders I am the fourth, or the renounced order of life, and among the occupational divisions I am the first, the brāhmaṇas.

TEXT 20

तीर्थानां स्रोतसां गङ्गा समुद्रः सरसामहम् ।
आयुधानां धनुरहं त्रिपुरघ्नो धनुष्मताम् ॥२०॥

tīrthānāṁ srotasāṁ gaṅgā
samudraḥ sarasām aham
āyudhānāṁ dhanur ahaṁ
tripura-ghno dhanuṣmatām

tīrthānām—among holy places; *srotasām*—among flowing things; *gaṅgā*—the sacred Ganges; *samudraḥ*—the ocean; *sarasām*—among steady bodies of water; *aham*—I am; *āyudhānām*—among weapons; *dhanuḥ*—the bow; *aham*—I am; *tri-pura-ghnaḥ*—Lord Śiva; *dhanuḥ-matām*—among those who wield the bow.

TRANSLATION

Among sacred and flowing things I am the holy Ganges, and among steady bodies of water I am the ocean. Among weapons I am the bow, and of the wielders of weapons I am Lord Śiva.

PURPORT

Lord Śiva used his bow to completely cover with arrows the three demoniac cities built by Maya Dānava.

TEXT 21

धिष्ण्यानामस्म्यहं मेरुर्गहनानां हिमालयः ।
वनस्पतीनामश्वत्थ ओषधीनामहं यवः ॥२१॥

dhiṣṇyānām asmy ahaṁ merur
gahanānāṁ himālayaḥ
vanaspatīnām aśvattha
oṣadhīnām ahaṁ yavaḥ

dhiṣṇyānām—residences; *asmi*—am; *aham*—I; *meruḥ*—Mount Sumeru; *gahanānām*—of impervious places; *himālayaḥ*—the Himalayas; *vanaspatīnām*—among trees; *aśvatthaḥ*—banyan tree; *oṣadhīnām*—among plants; *aham*—I; *yavaḥ*—barley.

TRANSLATION

Among residences I am Mount Sumeru, and of impervious places I am the Himalayas. Among trees I am the holy fig tree, and among plants I am those that bear grains.

PURPORT

Oṣadhīnām here indicates those plants that fructify once and then die. Among them, those that give grains, which sustain human life, represent

Kṛṣṇa. Without grains it is not possible to produce milk products, nor can one properly perform Vedic fire sacrifices without offerings of grains.

TEXT 22

पुरोधसां वसिष्ठोऽहं ब्रह्मिष्ठानां बृहस्पतिः ।
स्कन्दोऽहं सर्वसेनान्यामग्रण्यां भगवानजः ॥२२॥

purodhasāṁ vasiṣṭho 'haṁ
brahmiṣṭhānāṁ bṛhaspatiḥ
skando 'haṁ sarva-senānyām
agraṇyāṁ bhagavān ajaḥ

purodhasām—among priests; *vasiṣṭhaḥ*—Vasiṣṭha Muni; *aham*—I am; *brahmiṣṭhānām*—among those fixed in the Vedic conclusion and purpose; *bṛhaspatiḥ*—Bṛhaspati, the spiritual master of the demigods; *skandaḥ*—Kārtikeya; *aham*—I am; *sarva-senānyām*—among all military leaders; *agraṇyām*—among those advancing in pious life; *bhagavān*—the great personality; *ajaḥ*—Lord Brahmā.

TRANSLATION

Among priests I am Vasiṣṭha Muni, and among those highly situated in Vedic culture I am Bṛhaspati. I am Kārtikeya among great military leaders, and among those advancing in superior ways of life I am the great personality Lord Brahmā.

TEXT 23

यज्ञानां ब्रह्मयज्ञोऽहं व्रतानामविहिंसनम् ।
वाय्वग्न्यर्काम्बुवागात्मा शुचीनामप्यहं शुचिः॥२३॥

yajñānāṁ brahma-yajño 'haṁ
vratānām avihiṁsanam
vāyv-agny-arkāmbu-vāg-ātmā
śucīnām apy ahaṁ śuciḥ

yajñānām—of sacrifices; *brahma-yajñaḥ*—study of the *Veda; aham*—I am; *vratānām*—of vows; *avihiṁsanam*—nonviolence; *vāyu*—wind;

agni—fire; *arka*—the sun; *ambu*—water; *vāk*—and speech; *ātmā*—personified; *śucīnām*—of all purifiers; *api*—indeed; *aham*—I am; *śuciḥ*—pure.

TRANSLATION

Among sacrifices I am study of the Veda, and I am nonviolence among vows. Among all things that purify I am the wind, fire, the sun, water and speech.

TEXT 24

योगानामात्मसंरोधो मन्त्रोऽस्मि विजिगीषताम् ।
आन्वीक्षिकी कौशलानां विकल्पः ख्यातिवादिनाम् ॥२४॥

yogānām ātma-saṁrodho
mantro 'smi vijigīṣatām
ānvīkṣikī kauśalānāṁ
vikalpaḥ khyāti-vādinām

yogānām—among the eight stages of *yoga* practice (*aṣṭāṅga*); *ātma-saṁrodhaḥ*—the ultimate stage, *samādhi,* in which the soul is completely separated from illusion; *mantraḥ*—prudent political counsel; *asmi*—I am; *vijigīṣatām*—among those desiring victory; *ānvīkṣikī*—spiritual science, by which one can distinguish between matter and spirit; *kauśalānām*—among all processes of expert discrimination; *vikalpaḥ*—diversity of perception; *khyāti-vādinām*—among the speculative philosophers.

TRANSLATION

Among the eight progressive states of yoga I am the final stage, samādhi, in which the soul is completely separated from illusion. Among those desiring victory I am prudent political counsel, and among processes of expert discrimination I am the science of the soul, by which one distinguishes spirit from matter. Among all speculative philosophers I am diversity of perception.

PURPORT

Any science is based on the faculty of expert discrimination. By skillful definition of isolated and interactive components one becomes expert in any field. Ultimately the most intelligent person can isolate the spirit soul from matter and describe the properties of matter and spirit as both isolated and interactive components of reality. The proliferation of innumerable philosophical speculations is due to differing modes of perception within the material world. As stated in *Bhagavad-gītā* (15.15), *sarvasya cāhaṁ hṛdi sanniviṣṭo mattaḥ smṛtir jñānam apohanaṁ ca:* the Supreme Personality of Godhead is situated in everyone's heart and awards a particular degree of knowledge or ignorance according to one's desire and merit. Thus the Lord Himself is the basis of the mundane process of philosophical speculation, for He creates differing and alternating modes of perception within the conditioned souls. It is to be understood that one can acquire perfect knowledge only by hearing directly from Lord Kṛṣṇa and not by hearing from conditioned philosophers who imperfectly perceive the creation of the Lord through the screen of their personal desires.

TEXT 25

स्त्रीणां तु शतरूपाहं पुंसां स्वायम्भुवो मनुः ।
नारायणो मुनीनां च कुमारो ब्रह्मचारिणाम् ॥२५॥

strīṇāṁ tu śatarūpāhaṁ
puṁsāṁ svāyambhuvo manuḥ
nārāyaṇo munīnāṁ ca
kumāro brahmacāriṇām

strīṇām—among ladies; *tu*—indeed; *śatarūpā*—Śatarūpā; *aham*—I am; *puṁsām*—among male personalities; *svāyambhuvaḥ manuḥ*—the great *prajāpati* Svāyambhuva Manu; *nārāyaṇaḥ*—the sage Nārāyaṇa; *munīnām*—among saintly sages; *ca*—also; *kumāraḥ*—Sanat-kumāra; *brahmacāriṇām*—among *brahmacārīs.*

TRANSLATION

Among ladies I am Śatarūpā, and among male personalities I am her husband, Svāyambhuva Manu. I am Nārāyaṇa among the sages and Sanat-kumāra among brahmacārīs.

TEXT 26

धर्माणामस्मि संन्यासः क्षेमाणामबहिर्मतिः ।
गुह्यानां सुनृतं मौनं मिथुनानामजस्त्वहम् ॥२६॥

dharmāṇām asmi sannyāsaḥ
kṣemāṇām abahir-matiḥ
guhyānāṁ su-nṛtaṁ maunaṁ
mithunānām ajas tv aham

dharmāṇām—among religious principles; *asmi*—I am; *sannyāsaḥ*—renunciation; *kṣemāṇām*—among all types of security; *abahiḥ-matiḥ*—awareness within (of the eternal soul); *guhyānām*—of secrets; *su-nṛtam*—pleasant speech; *maunam*—silence; *mithunānām*—of sexual pairs; *ajaḥ*—Brahmā, the original *prajāpati; tu*—indeed; *aham*—I am.

TRANSLATION

Among religious principles I am renunciation, and of all types of security I am consciousness of the eternal soul within. Of secrets I am pleasant speech and silence, and among sexual pairs I am Brahmā.

PURPORT

One who realizes the eternal soul within no longer fears any material situation and thus is qualified to accept the renounced order of life, *sannyāsa.* Certainly fear is one of the great miseries of material life; therefore the gift of fearlessness is very valuable and represents Lord Kṛṣṇa. Both in ordinary pleasant speech and silence, very few confidential things are revealed, and thus diplomacy and silence are both aids to secrecy. Lord Brahmā is prominent among sexual pairs because the original beautiful couple, Svāyambhuva Manu and Śatarūpā, emerged from Lord Brahmā's body, as explained in Chapter Twelve of the Third Canto of *Śrīmad-Bhāgavatam.*

TEXT 27

संवत्सरोऽस्म्यनिमिषामृतूनां मधुमाधवौ ।
मासानां मार्गशीर्षोऽहं नक्षत्राणां तथाभिजित् ॥२७॥

saṁvatsaro 'smy animiṣām
ṛtūnāṁ madhu-mādhavau
māsānāṁ mārgaśīrṣo 'haṁ
nakṣatrāṇāṁ tathābhijit

saṁvatsaraḥ—the year; *asmi*—I am; *animiṣām*—among the vigilant cycles of time; *ṛtūnām*—among seasons; *madhu-mādhavau*—spring; *māsānām*—among months; *mārgaśīrṣaḥ*—Mārgaśīrṣa (November-December); *aham*—I am; *nakṣatrāṇām*—among asterisms; *tathā*—similarly; *abhijit*—Abhijit.

TRANSLATION

Among the vigilant cycles of time I am the year, and among seasons I am spring. Among months I am Mārgaśīrṣa, and among lunar houses I am the auspicious Abhijit.

TEXT 28

अहं युगानां च कृतं धीराणां देवलोऽसितः ।
द्वैपायनोऽस्मि व्यासानां कवीनां काव्य आत्मवान् ॥२८॥

ahaṁ yugānāṁ ca kṛtaṁ
dhīrāṇāṁ devalo 'sitaḥ
dvaipāyano 'smi vyāsānāṁ
kavīnāṁ kāvya ātmavān

aham—I am; *yugānām*—among ages; *ca*—also; *kṛtam*—Satya-yuga; *dhīrāṇām*—among steady sages; *devalaḥ*—Devala; *asitaḥ*—Asita; *dvaipāyanaḥ*—Kṛṣṇa Dvaipāyana; *asmi*—I am; *vyāsānām*—among the editors of the *Vedas; kavīnām*—among learned scholars; *kāvyaḥ*—Śukrācārya; *ātma-vān*—learned in spiritual science.

TRANSLATION

Among ages I am the Satya-yuga, the age of truth, and among steady sages I am Devala and Asita. Among those who have divided the Vedas I am Kṛṣṇa Dvaipāyana Vedavyāsa, and among learned scholars I am Śukrācārya, the knower of spiritual science.

TEXT 29

वासुदेवो भगवतां त्वं तु भागवतेष्वहम् ।
किंपुरुषाणां हनुमान् विद्याध्राणां सुदर्शनः ॥२९॥

vāsudevo bhagavatāṁ
tvaṁ tu bhāgavateṣv aham
kimpuruṣāṇāṁ hanumān
vidyādhrāṇāṁ sudarśanaḥ

vāsudevaḥ—the Supreme Personality of Godhead; *bhagavatām*—of those entitled to the name Bhagavān; *tvam*—you; *tu*—indeed; *bhāgavateṣu*—among My devotees; *aham*—I am; *kimpuruṣāṇām*—among the Kimpuruṣas; *hanumān*—Hanumān; *vidyādhrāṇām*—among the Vidyādharas; *sudarśanaḥ*—Sudarśana.

TRANSLATION

Among those entitled to the name Bhagavān I am Vāsudeva, and indeed, you, Uddhava, represent Me among the devotees. I am Hanumān among the Kimpuruṣas, and among the Vidyādharas I am Sudarśana.

PURPORT

The Vedic literatures state that one who possesses perfect knowledge of the creation and destruction of all entities and who is completely situated in omniscience is to be known as the Supreme Personality of Godhead, Bhagavān. Although many great personalities are sometimes called Bhagavān, ultimately Bhagavān is the one supreme entity who possesses unlimited opulences. Throughout history, many important personalities have been addressed as "lord," but ultimately there is only one Supreme Lord. In the Lord's *catur-vyūha*, or quadruple expansion, the first manifestation is Vāsudeva, who here represents all of the Lord's expansions in the *viṣṇu-tattva* category.

TEXT 30

रत्नानां पद्मरागोऽस्मि पद्मकोशः सुपेशसाम् ।
कुशोऽस्मि दर्भजातीनां गव्यमाज्यं हविःष्वहम् ॥३०॥

ratnānāṁ padma-rāgo 'smi
padma-kośaḥ su-peśasām
kuśo 'smi darbha-jātīnāṁ
gavyam ājyaṁ haviḥṣv aham

ratnānām—of jewels; *padma-rāgaḥ*—the ruby; *asmi*—I am; *padma-kośaḥ*—the lotus cup; *su-peśasām*—among beautiful things; *kuśaḥ*—the sacred *kuśa* grass; *asmi*—I am; *darbha-jātīnām*—among all types of grass; *gavyam*—cow products; *ājyam*—offering of ghee; *haviḥṣu*—among oblations; *aham*—I am.

TRANSLATION

Among jewels I am the ruby, and among beautiful things I am the lotus cup. Among all types of grass I am the sacred kuśa, and of oblations I am ghee and other ingredients obtained from the cow.

PURPORT

Pañca-gavya refers to five sacrificial ingredients obtained from the cow, namely milk, ghee, yogurt, dung and urine. The cow is so valuable that even its dung and urine are antiseptic and fit for sacrificial offering. *Kuśa* grass is also used for religious occasions. Mahārāja Parīkṣit constructed a sitting place from *kuśa* grass during the last week of his life. Among beautiful things the lotus cup formed by lotus petals represents Lord Kṛṣṇa, and among jewels the ruby, which is similar to Lord Kṛṣṇa's own Kaustubha gem, symbolizes the potency of the Lord.

TEXT 31

व्यवसायिनामहं लक्ष्मीः कितवानां छलग्रहः ।
तितिक्षास्मि तितिक्षूणां सत्त्वं सत्त्ववतामहम् ॥३१॥

vyavasāyinām ahaṁ lakṣmīḥ
kitavānāṁ chala-grahaḥ
titikṣāsmi titikṣūṇāṁ
sattvaṁ sattvavatām aham

vyavasāyinām—of the enterprising; *aham*—I am; *lakṣmīḥ*—fortune; *kitavānām*—of cheaters; *chala-grahaḥ*—the gambling; *titikṣā*—the forgiveness; *asmi*—I am; *titikṣūṇām*—among the tolerant; *sattvam*—the goodness; *sattva-vatām*—among those in the mode of goodness; *aham*—I am.

TRANSLATION

Among the enterprising I am fortune, and among the cheaters I am gambling. I am the forgiveness of the tolerant and the good qualities of those in the mode of goodness.

TEXT 32

ओजः सहो बलवतां कर्माहं विद्धि सात्वताम् ।
सात्वतां नवमूर्तीनामादिमूर्तिरहं परा ॥३२॥

ojaḥ saho balavatāṁ
karmāhaṁ viddhi sātvatām
sātvatāṁ nava-mūrtīnām
ādi-mūrtir ahaṁ parā

ojaḥ—the sensory strength; *sahaḥ*—and mental strength; *bala-vatām*—of the strong; *karma*—the devotional activities; *aham*—I am; *viddhi*—please know; *sātvatām*—among the devotees; *sātvatām*—among those devotees; *nava-mūrtīnām*—who worship Me in nine forms; *ādi-mūrtiḥ*—the original form, Vāsudeva; *aham*—I am; *parā*—the Supreme.

TRANSLATION

Of the powerful I am bodily and mental strength, and I am the devotional activities of My devotees. My devotees worship Me in nine different forms, among which I am the original and primary Vāsudeva.

PURPORT

Generally, the Vaiṣṇavas worship the Personality of Godhead as Vāsudeva, Saṅkarṣaṇa, Pradyumna, Aniruddha, Nārāyaṇa, Hayagrīva, Varāha, Nṛsiṁha and Brahmā. It is understood that when a suitable living entity is not available to fill the post of Brahmā, the Lord Himself assumes the position; therefore Lord Brahmā is mentioned in the list. Lord Viṣṇu sometimes appears as Indra and sometimes as Brahmā, and it is Viṣṇu appearing as Brahmā who is indicated in this connection.

TEXT 33

विश्वावसुः पूर्वचित्तिर्गन्धर्वाप्सरसामहम् ।
भूधराणामहं स्थैर्यं गन्धमात्रमहं भुवः ॥३३॥

viśvāvasuḥ pūrvacittir
gandharvāpsarasām aham
bhūdharāṇām ahaṁ sthairyaṁ
gandha-mātram ahaṁ bhuvaḥ

viśvāvasuḥ—Viśvāvasu; *pūrvacittiḥ*—Pūrvacitti; *gandharva-apsara-asām*—among the Gandharvas and Apsarās; *aham*—I am; *bhū-dharāṇām*—of the mountains; *aham*—I am; *sthairyam*—the steadiness; *gandha-mātram*—the perception of aroma; *aham*—I am; *bhuvaḥ*—of the earth.

TRANSLATION

Among the Gandharvas I am Viśvāvasu, and I am Pūrvacitti among the heavenly Apsarās. I am the steadiness of mountains and the fragrant aroma of the earth.

PURPORT

In *Bhagavad-gītā* (7.9) Lord Kṛṣṇa says, *puṇyo gandhaḥ pṛthivyāṁ ca:* "I am the fragrance of the earth." The original fragrance of the earth is very pleasing and represents Lord Kṛṣṇa. Although unpleasant aromas may be artificially produced, they do not represent the Lord.

TEXT 34

अपां रसश्च परमस्तेजिष्ठानां विभावसुः ।
प्रभा सूर्येन्दुताराणां शब्दोऽहं नभसः परः ॥३४॥

apāṁ rasaś ca paramas
tejiṣṭhānāṁ vibhāvasuḥ
prabhā sūryendu-tārāṇāṁ
śabdo 'haṁ nabhasaḥ paraḥ

apām—of water; *rasaḥ*—the taste; *ca*—also; *paramaḥ*—excellent; *tejiṣṭhānām*—among most brilliant things; *vibhāvasuḥ*—the sun; *prabhā*—the effulgence; *sūrya*—of the sun; *indu*—the moon; *tārāṇām*—and the stars; *śabdaḥ*—the sound vibration; *aham*—I am; *nabhasaḥ*—of the sky; *paraḥ*—transcendental.

TRANSLATION

I am the sweet taste of water, and among brilliant things I am the sun. I am the effulgence of the sun, moon and stars, and I am the transcendental sound that vibrates in the sky.

TEXT 35

ब्रह्मण्यानां बलिरहं वीराणामहमर्जुनः ।
भूतानां स्थितिरुत्पत्तिरहं वै प्रतिसङ्क्रमः ॥३५॥

brahmaṇyānāṁ balir ahaṁ
vīrāṇām aham arjunaḥ
bhūtānāṁ sthitir utpattir
ahaṁ vai pratisaṅkramaḥ

brahmaṇyānām—of those dedicated to brahminical culture; *baliḥ*—Bali Mahārāja, the son of Virocana; *aham*—I am; *vīrāṇām*—of heroes; *aham*—I am; *arjunaḥ*—Arjuna; *bhūtānām*—of all living beings; *sthitiḥ*—the maintenance; *utpattiḥ*—the creation; *aham*—I am; *vai*—indeed; *pratisaṅkramaḥ*—the annihilation.

TRANSLATION

Among those dedicated to brahminical culture I am Bali Mahārāja, the son of Virocana, and I am Arjuna among heroes. Indeed, I am the creation, maintenance and annihilation of all living entities.

TEXT 36

गत्युक्त्युत्सर्गोपादानमानन्दस्पर्शलक्षणम् ।
आस्वादश्रुत्यवघ्राणमहं सर्वेन्द्रियेन्द्रियम् ॥३६॥

gaty-ukty-utsargopādānam
ānanda-sparśa-lakṣaṇam
āsvāda-śruty-avaghrāṇam
ahaṁ sarvendriyendriyam

gati—movement of the legs (walking, running, etc.); *ukti*—speech; *utsarga*—evacuation; *upādānam*—accepting with the hands; *ānanda*—the material pleasure of the sex organs; *sparśa*—touch; *lakṣaṇam*—sight; *āsvāda*—taste; *śruti*—hearing; *avaghrāṇam*—smell; *aham*—I am; *sarva-indriya*—of all the senses; *indriyam*—the potency to experience their objects.

TRANSLATION

I am the functions of the five working senses—the legs, speech, anus, hands and sex organs—as well as those of the five knowledge-acquiring senses—touch, sight, taste, hearing and smell. I am also the potency by which each of the senses experiences its particular sense object.

TEXT 37

पृथिवी वायुराकाश आपो ज्योतिरहं महान् ।
विकारः पुरुषोऽव्यक्तं रजः सत्त्वं तमः परम् ।
अहमेतत्प्रसंख्यानं ज्ञानं तत्त्वविनिश्चयः ॥३७॥

pṛthivī vāyur ākāśa
āpo jyotir ahaṁ mahān
vikāraḥ puruṣo 'vyaktaṁ
rajaḥ sattvaṁ tamaḥ param
aham etat prasaṅkhyānaṁ
jñānaṁ tattva-viniścayaḥ

pṛthivī—the subtle form of earth, aroma; *vāyuḥ*—the subtle form of air, touch; *ākāśaḥ*—the subtle form of sky, sound; *āpaḥ*—the subtle form of water, taste; *jyotiḥ*—the subtle form of fire, form; *aham*—false ego; *mahān*—the *mahat-tattva; vikāraḥ*—the sixteen elements (earth, water, fire, air and sky, the five working senses, the five knowledge-acquiring senses and the mind); *puruṣaḥ*—the living entity; *avyaktam*—material nature, *prakṛti; rajaḥ*—the mode of passion; *sattvam*—the mode of goodness; *tamaḥ*—the mode of ignorance; *param*—the Supreme Lord; *aham*—I am; *etat*—this; *prasaṅkhyānam*—all that has been enumerated; *jñānam*—knowledge of the above-mentioned elements by individual symptoms; *tattva-viniścayaḥ*—steady conviction, which is the fruit of knowledge.

TRANSLATION

I am form, taste, aroma, touch and sound; false ego; the mahat-tattva; earth, water, fire, air and sky; the living entity; material nature; the modes of goodness, passion and ignorance; and the transcendental Lord. All these items, along with knowledge of their individual symptoms and the steady conviction that results from this knowledge, represent Me.

PURPORT

Having given a brief but detailed synopsis of His personal opulences within this world, the Lord now briefly summarizes the opulences that expand from His bodily effulgence. It is stated in *Brahma-saṁhitā* that all of the material universes with their infinite varieties, transformations and opulences rest on the bodily effulgence of the Lord. Śrīla Jīva Gosvāmī has elaborately explained this point in his commentary on this verse.

TEXT 38

मयेश्वरेण जीवेन गुणेन गुणिना विना ।
सर्वात्मनापि सर्वेण न भावो विद्यते क्वचित् ॥३८॥

mayeśvareṇa jīvena
guṇena guṇinā vinā

sarvātmanāpi sarveṇa
na bhāvo vidyate kvacit

mayā—Me; *īśvareṇa*—the Supreme Lord; *jīvena*—the living entity; *guṇena*—the modes of nature; *guṇinā*—the *mahat-tattva; vinā*—without; *sarva-ātmanā*—the soul of all that exists; *api*—indeed; *sarveṇa*—everything; *na*—not; *bhāvaḥ*—existence; *vidyate*—there is; *kvacit*—whatsoever.

TRANSLATION

As the Supreme Lord I am the basis of the living entity, of the modes of nature and of the mahat-tattva. Thus I am everything, and nothing whatsoever can exist without Me.

PURPORT

Without the manifestation of the *mahat-tattva*, or total material existence, and the *jīva*, or living entity, nothing can exist within the material world. Everything we experience is a combination of the living entity and matter, in its various subtle and gross categories. The Supreme Personality of Godhead is the entire basis of the existence of both the living entity and matter. Nothing can possibly exist even for a moment without the mercy of the Supreme Lord. One should not foolishly conclude that the Lord is therefore material. As has been clearly explained in this canto of the *Bhāgavatam*, both the living entity and the Supreme Lord are completely transcendental to material nature. The living entity, however, has the propensity to dream that he is material, whereas the Lord constantly remembers the transcendental position of both Himself and the conditioned dreaming entity. As the Lord is transcendental, His abode is also far beyond the reach of the modes of nature. The actual purpose of life is to understand by mature conviction the transcendental Lord, His transcendental abode, our own transcendental position and the process by which we may go back home, back to Godhead.

TEXT 39

संख्यानं परमाणूनां कालेन क्रियते मया ।
न तथा मे विभूतीनां सृजतोऽण्डानि कोटिशः ॥३९॥

saṅkhyānaṁ paramāṇūnāṁ
kālena kriyate mayā
na tathā me vibhūtīnāṁ
sṛjato 'ṇḍāni koṭiśaḥ

saṅkhyānam—counting; *parama-aṇūnām*—of the atoms; *kālena*—after some time; *kriyate*—is done; *mayā*—by Me; *na*—not; *tathā*—in the same way; *me*—of Me; *vibhūtīnām*—of the opulences; *sṛjataḥ*—who am creating; *aṇḍāni*—universes; *koṭiśaḥ*—by the innumerable millions.

TRANSLATION

Even though over a period of time I might count all the atoms of the universe, I could not count all of My opulences which I manifest within innumerable universes.

PURPORT

The Lord here explains that Uddhava should not expect a complete catalog of the Lord's opulences, since even the Lord Himself finds no limit to such opulences. According to Śrīla Jīva Gosvāmī, *kālena* indicates that the Supreme Personality of Godhead is within every atom and can therefore easily calculate the total number of atoms. However, although the Lord is certainly omniscient, even He Himself cannot supply a finite number for His opulences, because they are infinite.

TEXT 40

तेजः श्रीः कीर्तिरैश्वर्यं ह्रीस्त्यागः सौभगं भगः ।
वीर्यं तितिक्षा विज्ञानं यत्र यत्र स मेंऽशकः ॥४०॥

tejaḥ śrīḥ kīrtir aiśvaryaṁ
hrīs tyāgaḥ saubhagaṁ bhagaḥ
vīryaṁ titikṣā vijñānaṁ
yatra yatra sa me 'ṁśakaḥ

tejaḥ—power; *śrīḥ*—beautiful, valuable things; *kīrtiḥ*—fame; *aiśvaryam*—opulence; *hrīḥ*—humility; *tyāgaḥ*—renunciation; *saubhagam*—that which pleases the mind and senses; *bhagaḥ*—good fortune; *vīr-*

yam—strength; *titikṣā*—tolerance; *vijñānam*—spiritual knowledge; *yatra yatra*—wherever; *saḥ*—this; *me*—My; *aṁśakaḥ*—expansion.

TRANSLATION

Whatever power, beauty, fame, opulence, humility, renunciation, mental pleasure, fortune, strength, tolerance or spiritual knowledge there may be is simply an expansion of My opulence.

PURPORT

Although the Lord stated in the previous verse that His opulences are innumerable, the Lord here gives a specific resumé and demonstration of His opulences.

TEXT 41

एतास्ते कीर्तिताः सर्वाः सङ्क्षेपेण विभूतयः ।
मनोविकारा एवैते यथा वाचाभिधीयते ॥४१॥

etās te kīrtitāḥ sarvāḥ
saṅkṣepeṇa vibhūtayaḥ
mano-vikārā evaite
yathā vācābhidhīyate

etāḥ—these; *te*—to you; *kīrtitāḥ*—described; *sarvāḥ*—all; *saṅkṣepeṇa*—briefly; *vibhūtayaḥ*—spiritual opulences; *manaḥ*—of the mind; *vikārāḥ*—transformations; *eva*—indeed; *ete*—these; *yathā*—accordingly; *vācā*—by words; *abhidhīyate*—each is described.

TRANSLATION

I have briefly described to you all My spiritual opulences and also the extraordinary material features of My creation, which are perceived by the mind and defined in different ways according to circumstances.

PURPORT

According to Sanskrit grammar, and as confirmed by Śrīla Śrīdhara Svāmī, the words *etāḥ* and *ete* describe two distinct sets of the Lord's opulences. The Lord has described His opulent plenary expansions, such as Vāsudeva, Nārāyaṇa, the Supersoul, etc., and further the Lord has described the outstanding features of the material creation, which are also included among the glories of the Personality of Godhead. The plenary manifestations of the Lord, such as Vāsudeva, Nārāyaṇa, etc., are all eternal, unchanging transcendental features of the Lord and are indicated by the term *etāḥ*. The extraordinary aspects of material creation, however, are circumstantial and dependent on individual perception, and they are therefore described here by the words *mano-vikārā evaite yathā vācābhidhīyate*. Śrīla Jīva Gosvāmī explains that by consistent logical application of synonyms, *etāḥ* refers to the Lord's eternal spiritual manifestations, beyond the perception of the material senses, whereas *ete* refers to those opulences that can be perceived by conditioned souls. He gives the example that the paraphernalia and intimate associates of a king are all considered to be part and parcel of the king and are therefore granted royal status. Similarly, the opulent features of material creation are reflected expansions of the Lord's personal opulences and thus may be considered nondifferent from Him. One should not, however, wrongly assume that such insignificant material opulences occupy the same status as the Lord's plenary features as the Personality of Godhead, which are qualitatively and quantitatively equal to the Lord.

Śrīla Viśvanātha Cakravartī Ṭhākura comments as follows on this verse. "The Lord's external opulences are called *mano-vikārāḥ*, or 'related to mental transformation,' because ordinary people perceive extraordinary features of the material world according to their personal state of mind. Thus the word *vācābhidhīyate* indicates that conditioned souls describe the Lord's material creation according to specific material circumstances. Because of the circumstantial relative definitions of material opulence, such opulence is never to be considered a direct plenary manifestation of the Lord's personal form. When one's state of mind is transformed into a favorable or affectionate state, one defines a manifestation of the Lord's energy as 'my son,' 'my father,' 'my husband,' 'my uncle,' 'the son of my brother,' 'my friend,' and so on. One forgets that every living entity is actually part and parcel of the Supreme Personality of Godhead and that whatever opulences, talents or outstanding features one may exhibit are actually the potencies of the Lord. Similarly, when the mind is transformed into a negative or inimical state, one thinks, 'This person will be the ruin of me,' 'This person must be finished by me,' 'He is my enemy' or 'I am his enemy,' 'He is a killer' or 'He should be killed.' The negative state of mind is also expressed when one is attracted to the extraordinary material aspects of particular persons or objects but forgets that they are manifestations of the potency of the Personality of Godhead. Even the demigod Indra, who is quite obviously a manifestation of the Lord's material opulences, is misunderstood by others. For example, Indra's wife, Śacī, thinks that Indra is 'my husband,' whereas Aditi thinks that he is 'my son.' Jayanta thinks that he is 'my father,' Bṛhaspati thinks that he is 'my disciple,' whereas the demons feel that Indra is their personal enemy. Thus different personalities define him according to their mental state. The Lord's material opulences, being relatively perceived, are therefore called *mano-vikāra*, which means they are dependent on mental states. This relative perception is material because it does not recognize the Supreme Personality of Godhead as the actual source of the particular opulence. If one sees Lord Kṛṣṇa as the source of all opulences and gives up all desires to enjoy or possess the Lord's opulences, then one can see the spiritual nature of these opulences. At that time, even though one may continue to perceive the variety and distinctions of the material world, one will become perfect in Kṛṣṇa consciousness. One should not conclude, as do the voidist philosophers, that the Lord's spiritual manifestations in the *viṣṇu-tattva* and liberated *jīva* categories are also products of relative perception and mental states. This useless idea is contrary to the entire body of the Supreme Personality of Godhead's teachings to Śrī Uddhava."

According to Śrīla Jīva Gosvāmī, the word *vācā* also indicates the various Vedic literatures that describe the particular processes by which the Lord manifests His spiritual and material opulences, and in this context *yathā* indicates the specific procedures of manifestation and creation.

TEXT 42

वाचं यच्छ मनो यच्छ प्राणान् यच्छेन्द्रियाणि च।
आत्मानमात्मना यच्छ न भूयः कल्पसेऽध्वने ॥४२॥

vācaṁ yaccha mano yaccha
prāṇān yacchedriyāṇi ca
ātmānam ātmanā yaccha
na bhūyaḥ kalpase 'dhvane

vācam—speech; *yaccha*—control; *manaḥ*—the mind; *yaccha*—control; *prāṇān*—your breathing; *yaccha*—control; *indriyāṇi*—the senses; *ca*—also; *ātmānam*—the intelligence; *ātmanā*—by purified intelligence; *yaccha*—control; *na*—never; *bhūyaḥ*—again; *kalpase*—you will fall; *adhvane*—on the path of material existence.

TRANSLATION

Therefore, control your speaking, subdue the mind, conquer the life air, regulate the senses and through purified intelligence bring your rational faculties under control. In this way you will never again fall onto the path of material existence.

PURPORT

One should see all things as expansions of the Supreme Lord's potency, and thus with speech, mind and words one should offer respect to all things, without minimizing any living entity or material object. Since everything belongs to the Lord, everything ultimately should be engaged in the Lord's service with great care. A self-realized devotee tolerates personal insult and does not become envious of any living entity, nor does he see anyone as his enemy. This is practical enlightenment. Although a pure devotee may criticize those who obstruct the Lord's mission, such criticism is never personally motivated nor is it ever based on enviousness. An advanced devotee of the Lord may chastise his followers or criticize the demoniac, but only to carry out the mission of the Supreme Lord and never out of personal enmity or enviousness. For one who completely gives up the material concept of life there is no possibility of entering again onto the path of birth and death.

TEXT 43

यो वै वाङ्मनसी सम्यगसंयच्छन् धिया यतिः ।
तस्य व्रतं तपो दानं स्रवत्यामघटाम्बुवत् ॥४३॥

yo vai vāṅ-manasī saṁyag
asaṁyacchan dhiyā yatiḥ
tasya vrataṁ tapo dānaṁ
sravaty āma-ghaṭāmbu-vat

yaḥ—one who; *vai*—certainly; *vāk-manasī*—the speech and mind; *saṁyak*—completely; *asaṁyacchan*—not controlling; *dhiyā*—by intelligence; *yatiḥ*—a transcendentalist; *tasya*—his; *vratam*—vows; *tapaḥ*—austerities; *dānam*—charity; *sravati*—run out; *āma*—unbaked; *ghaṭa*—in a pot; *ambu-vat*—like water.

TRANSLATION

A transcendentalist who does not completely control his words and mind by superior intelligence will find that his spiritual vows, austerities and charity flow away just as water flows out of an unbaked clay pot.

PURPORT

When a clay pot is properly baked it holds any liquid substance without leakage. If a clay pot is not properly baked, however, water or any other liquid within it will seep out and be lost. Similarly, a transcendentalist who does not control his speech and mind will find that his spiritual discipline and austerity gradually seep away and are lost. *Dāna*, or "charity," refers to work performed for the welfare of others. Those who are trying to give the highest charity by preaching Kṛṣṇa consciousness should not engage in speaking cleverly for the satisfaction of beautiful women, nor should they attempt to become artificially intellectual simply for the sake of mundane academic prestige. One should not even think of intimate sexual relationships, nor should one daydream of acquiring a prestigious position. Otherwise, one's determination to strictly practice Kṛṣṇa consciousness will be lost, as described here. One must control the mind, senses and speech by higher intelligence so that one's life will be successful.

TEXT 44

तस्माद्वचोमनःप्राणान् नियच्छेन्मत्परायणः ।
मद्भक्तियुक्तया बुद्ध्या ततः परिसमाप्यते ॥४४॥

tasmād vaco manaḥ prāṇān
niyacchen mat-parāyaṇaḥ
mad-bhakti-yuktayā buddhyā
tataḥ parisamāpyate

tasmāt—therefore; *vacaḥ*—words; *manaḥ*—the mind; *prāṇān*—the life airs; *niyacchet*—one should control; *mat-parāyaṇaḥ*—who is devoted to Me; *mat*—unto Me; *bhakti*—with devotion; *yuktayā*—endowed; *buddhyā*—by such intelligence; *tataḥ*—thus; *parisamāpyate*—one fulfills the mission of life.

TRANSLATION

Being surrendered to Me, one should control the speech, mind and life air, and then through loving devotional intelligence one will completely fulfill the mission of life.

PURPORT

One can develop loving devotional intelligence by perfectly chanting the Brahma-gāyatrī *mantra* awarded at the moment of *brāhmaṇa* initiation. By clear intelligence, one becomes naturally and spontaneously disinterested in the rewards offered by mental speculation and fruitive activities and takes full shelter of the Supreme Personality of Godhead.

Thus end the purports of the humble servants of His Divine Grace A. C. Bhaktivedanta Swami Prabhupāda to the Eleventh Canto, Sixteenth Chapter, of the Śrīmad-Bhāgavatam, *entitled "The Lord's Opulence."*

CHAPTER SEVENTEEN

Lord Kṛṣṇa's Description of the Varṇāśrama System

Previously, the Supreme Lord, Śrī Kṛṣṇa, had assumed the form of Haṁsa and glorified the duties of the *brahmacārī* and *gṛhastha* orders. In this present chapter Lord Kṛṣṇa further describes these matters to Uddhava.

After Uddhava inquires from Śrī Kṛṣṇa about the duties of the social and religious orders of the *varṇāśrama* society, the Lord replies that in the first age, Satya-yuga, there was only one social order, called *haṁsa.* In that age men were automatically dedicated to pure devotional service from their very birth, and since everyone was perfect in all respects, the age was called Kṛta-yuga. The *Vedas* were then manifest in the form of the sacred syllable *oṁ*, and the Supreme Lord was perceived within the mind in the form of the four-legged bull of religion. There were no formalized processes of sacrifice, and the sinless people, who were naturally inclined to austerity, simply engaged in meditation on the personal form of the Lord. In the following age, Tretā-yuga, there became manifest from the heart of the Supreme Personality of Godhead the three *Vedas*, and from them the three forms of the sacrificial fire. At that time the system of four *varṇas* and four *āśramas*, which prescribes material and spiritual duties for the different members of society, appeared from the bodily limbs of the Lord. According to how the social divisions took birth from higher and lower features of the Lord's body, they became endowed with higher and lower qualities. After this description, Lord Kṛṣṇa explains the natures of persons in each of the four *varṇas* and of those who are outside the limits of the *varṇas.* He also describes those qualities that pertain to humanity in general.

Members of the higher orders are qualified to accept second birth. After receiving the sacred thread initiation, they should go to live in the *guru-kula*, the home of the spiritual master. With a pacified mind, the student (*brahmacārī*) should absorb himself in study of the *Vedas.* He should keep matted hair and is forbidden to wash his teeth, prepare a nice seat for himself, talk when bathing or evacuating, cut his hair and nails or at any time pass semen. He must regularly perform worship at the three junctures of the day and must render devotional service to his spiritual master in a spirit free from envy. The *brahmacārī* must offer to the *guru* whatever food and other things he obtains by begging. He accepts for his maintenance whatever remnants of the Lord he is granted. He should render menial service to the spiritual master by massaging his feet and worshiping him and should avoid all sense gratification and strictly maintain the vow of celibacy. With his mind, body and words, he should worship the Supreme Lord in the form of the Supersoul in the way prescribed for him. For *brahmacārīs*, seeing or touching women, and conversations or sports in the company of women, are absolutely disallowed. Cleanliness and ritual purification by water should be observed by members of all the spiritual orders of society. Everyone is also advised to always remember that the Supreme Personality of Godhead is the Supreme Soul dwelling within the hearts of all.

After studying all the different aspects of the *Vedas*, a *brāhmaṇa* who has material desires may take permission from his spiritual master and enter family life. Otherwise, if he has no material desire, he may become a *vānaprastha* or *sannyāsī*. The proper order of succession should be followed in changing from one spiritual order to the next. One who wishes to enter the household order should accept a wife who is of the same social class, who is not objectionable, and who is somewhat younger in age than he.

The obligatory duties of the three classes who are twice-born—the *brāhmaṇas*, *kṣatriyas* and *vaiśyas*—are worship of the Lord, study of the *Vedas* and giving charity. The occupational duties of accepting charity, teaching others and performing sacrifice for others are the privilege of the *brāhmaṇas* alone. If a *brāhmaṇa* considers that his consciousness is contaminated by engaging in these occupations, he may sustain his existence by collecting grains from the fields. If he is disturbed by poverty, the *brāhmaṇa* may out of necessity accept the business of a *kṣatriya* or *vaiśya*, but he should never take the occupation of a *śūdra*. In a similar situation, a *kṣatriya* may take the occupation of a *vaiśya*, and a *vaiśya* that of a *śūdra*. But when the emergency has passed, it is not fitting to continue earning one's living by a lower occupation. A *brāhmaṇa* who is properly fixed in his personal duty rejects all insignificant material desires, always serves the Vaiṣṇavas and is under the protection of the Supreme Personality of Godhead. The householder should study the *Vedas* every day and maintain his wards with money honestly earned by his own occupation. As far as possible, he should execute worship of the Lord by ritual sacrifices. Remaining unattached to material life and fixed in devotion to the Supreme Lord, the householder may finally take the order of *vānaprastha,* so that he can fully involve himself in the Lord's worship. If he has a grown son, he may directly take the renounced order of *sannyāsa.* But persons who are excessively lusty after women, who have no proper discrimination, and who are extremely attached to wealth and possessions remain perpetually in anxiety over the welfare of their family members and are doomed to take their next birth in a lower species of life.

TEXTS 1–2

श्रीउद्धव उवाच

यस्त्वयाभिहितः पूर्वं धर्मस्त्वद्भक्तिलक्षणः ।
वर्णाश्रमाचारवतां सर्वेषां द्विपदामपि ॥ १ ॥
यथानुष्ठीयमानेन त्वयि भक्तिर्नृणां भवेत् ।
स्वधर्मेणारविन्दाक्ष तन् ममाख्यातुमर्हसि ॥ २ ॥

śrī-uddhava uvāca
yas tvayābhihitaḥ pūrvaṁ
dharmas tvad-bhakti-lakṣaṇaḥ
varṇāśramācāravatāṁ
sarveṣāṁ dvi-padām api

yathānuṣṭhīyamānena
tvayi bhaktir nṛṇāṁ bhavet
sva-dharmeṇāravindākṣa
tan mamākhyātum arhasi

śrī-uddhavaḥ uvāca—Śrī Uddhava said; *yaḥ*—which; *tvayā*—by You; *abhihitaḥ*—described; *pūrvam*—previously; *dharmaḥ*—religious principles; *tvat-bhakti-lakṣaṇaḥ*—characterized by devotional service to Your Lordship; *varṇa-āśrama*—of the *varṇāśrama* system; *ācāra-vatām*—of the faithful followers; *sarveṣām*—of all; *dvi-padām*—of ordinary human beings (who do not follow the *varṇāśrama* system); *api*—even; *yathā*—according to; *anuṣṭhīyamānena*—the process being executed; *tvayi*—in You; *bhaktiḥ*—loving service; *nṛṇām*—of human beings; *bhavet*—may be; *sva-dharmeṇa*—by one's own occupational duty; *aravinda-akṣa*—O lotus-eyed one; *tat*—that; *mama*—to me; *ākhyātum*—to explain; *arhasi*—You ought.

TRANSLATION

Śrī Uddhava said: My dear Lord, previously You described the principles of devotional service that are to be practiced by followers of the varṇāśrama system and even ordinary, unregulated human beings. My dear lotus-eyed Lord, now please explain to me how all human beings can achieve loving service unto You by the execution of their prescribed duties.

PURPORT

Lord Kṛṣṇa has already elaborately explained the process of *jñāna-yoga, bhakti-yoga* and *aṣṭāṅga-yoga*. Now Uddhava inquires how those inclined toward *karma-yoga* can achieve the perfection of life, Kṛṣṇa consciousness. In *Bhagavad-gītā* (4.13) Lord Kṛṣṇa describes that He is personally the creator of the *varṇāśrama* system. *Cātur-varṇyaṁ mayā sṛṣṭaṁ guṇa-karma-vibhāgaśaḥ*. Therefore the ultimate goal of the *varṇāśrama* system is to please the Supreme Personality of Godhead. In other words, one should become a devotee of the Lord and learn the process of pure devotional service. The easiest method of achieving pure devotional service is by the association of pure devotees of the Lord. If one submissively and faithfully associates with pure devotees, one can immediately achieve the perfection of life. A Kṛṣṇa conscious person is not required to execute all the formalities of the *varṇāśrama* system, because a Kṛṣṇa conscious person, absorbed in love of Godhead, automatically gives up all sense gratification and mental speculation. Those human beings who do not follow the *varṇāśrama* system are here referred to as *dvi-padām*, or two-legged. In other words, one who does not follow the religious path of life is known to be human only by the possession of two legs. Even ordinary animals and insects are eagerly engaged in eating, sleeping, mating and defending; the human being, however, is distinguished from such lower forms of life by his capacity to become religious and, ultimately, to love God in pure Kṛṣṇa consciousness.

TEXTS 3–4

पुरा किल महाबाहो धर्मं परमकं प्रभो ।
यत्तेन हंसरूपेण ब्रह्मणेऽभ्यात्थ माधव ॥ ३ ॥
स इदानीं सुमहता कालेनामित्रकर्शन ।
न प्रायो भविता मर्त्यलोके प्रागनुशासितः ॥ ४ ॥

purā kila mahā-bāho
dharmaṁ paramakaṁ prabho
yat tena haṁsa-rūpeṇa
brahmaṇe 'bhyāttha mādhava

sa idānīṁ su-mahatā
kālenāmitra-karśana
na prāyo bhavitā martya-
loke prāg anuśāsitaḥ

purā—previously; *kila*—indeed; *mahā-bāho*—O mighty-armed one; *dharmam*—religious principles; *paramakam*—bringing the greatest happiness; *prabho*—my Lord; *yat*—which; *tena*—by that; *haṁsa-rūpeṇa*—in the form of Lord Haṁsa; *brahmaṇe*—unto Lord Brahmā; *abhyāttha*—You spoke; *mādhava*—my dear Mādhava; *saḥ*—that (knowledge of religious principles); *idānīm*—presently; *su-mahatā*—after very long; *kālena*—time; *amitra-karśana*—O subduer of the enemy; *na*—not; *prāyaḥ*—generally; *bhavitā*—will exist; *martya-loke*—in human society; *prāk*—previously; *anuśāsitaḥ*—instructed.

TRANSLATION

My dear Lord, O mighty-armed one, previously in Your form of Lord Haṁsa You spoke to Lord Brahmā those religious principles that bring supreme happiness to the practitioner. My dear Mādhava, now much time has passed, and that which You previously instructed will soon practically cease to exist, O subduer of the enemy.

TEXTS 5–6

वक्ता कर्ताविता नान्यो धर्मस्याच्युत ते भुवि ।
सभायामपि वैरिञ्च्यां यत्र मूर्तिधराः कलाः ॥ ५ ॥
कर्त्राविता प्रवक्त्रा च भवता मधुसूदन ।
त्यक्ते महीतले देव विनष्टं कः प्रवक्ष्यति ॥ ६ ॥

vaktā kartāvitā nānyo
dharmasyācyuta te bhuvi
sabhāyām api vairiñcyāṁ
yatra mūrti-dharāḥ kalāḥ

kartrāvitrā pravaktrā ca
bhavatā madhusūdana
tyakte mahī-tale deva
vinaṣṭaṁ kaḥ pravakṣyati

vaktā—speaker; *kartā*—creator; *avitā*—protector; *na*—not; *anyaḥ*—any other; *dharmasya*—of supreme religious principles; *acyuta*—my dear Acyuta; *te*—than You; *bhuvi*—on the earth; *sabhāyām*—in the assembly; *api*—even; *vairiñcyām*—of Lord Brahmā; *yatra*—wherein; *mūrti-dharāḥ*—in the personified form; *kalāḥ*—the *Vedas; kartrā*—by the creator; *avitrā*—by the protector; *pravaktrā*—by the speaker; *ca*—also; *bhavatā*—by Your Lordship; *madhusūdana*—my dear Madhusūdana; *tyakte*—when it is abandoned; *mahī-tale*—the earth; *deva*—my dear Lord; *vinaṣṭam*—those lost principles of religion; *kaḥ*—who; *pravakṣyati*—will speak.

TRANSLATION

My dear Lord Acyuta, there is no other speaker, creator and protector of supreme religious principles other than Your Lordship, either on the earth or even in the assembly of Lord Brahmā, where the personified Vedas reside. Thus, my dear Lord Madhusūdana, when You, who are the very creator, protector and speaker of spiritual knowledge, abandon the earth, who will again speak this lost knowledge?

TEXT 7

तत्त्वं नः सर्वधर्मज्ञ धर्मस्त्वद्भक्तिलक्षणः ।
यथा यस्य विधीयेत तथा वर्णय मे प्रभो ॥ ७ ॥

tat tvaṁ naḥ sarva-dharma-jña
dharmas tvad-bhakti-lakṣaṇaḥ
yathā yasya vidhīyeta
tathā varṇaya me prabho

tat—therefore; *tvam*—You; *naḥ*—among us (human beings); *sarva-dharma-jña*—O supreme knower of religious principles; *dharmaḥ*—the spiritual path; *tvat-bhakti*—by loving service to You; *lakṣaṇaḥ*—characterized; *yathā*—in which way; *yasya*—of whom; *vidhīyeta*—may be executed; *tathā*—in that way; *varṇaya*—please describe; *me*—unto me; *prabho*—my Lord.

TRANSLATION

Therefore, my Lord, since You are the knower of all religious principles, please describe to me the human beings who may execute the path of loving service to You and how such service is to be rendered.

TEXT 8

श्रीशुक उवाच
इत्थं स्वभृत्यमुख्येन पृष्टः स भगवान् हरिः ।
प्रीतः क्षेमाय मर्त्यानां धर्मानाह सनातनान् ॥ ८ ॥

śrī-śuka uvāca
itthaṁ sva-bhṛtya-mukhyena
pṛṣṭaḥ sa bhagavān hariḥ
prītaḥ kṣemāya martyānāṁ
dharmān āha sanātanān

śrī-śukaḥ uvāca—Śrī Śukadeva Gosvāmī said; *ittham*—thus; *sva-bhṛtya-mukhyena*—by the best of His devotees; *pṛṣṭaḥ*—questioned;

saḥ—He; *bhagavān*—the Supreme Personality of Godhead; *hariḥ*—Śrī Kṛṣṇa; *prītaḥ*—being pleased; *kṣemāya*—for the highest welfare; *martyānām*—of all conditioned souls; *dharmān*—religious principles; *āha*—spoke; *sanātanān*—eternal.

TRANSLATION

Śrī Śukadeva Gosvāmī said: Śrī Uddhava, the best of devotees, thus inquired from the Lord. Hearing his question, the Personality of Godhead, Śrī Kṛṣṇa, was pleased and for the welfare of all conditioned souls spoke those religious principles that are eternal.

TEXT 9

श्रीभगवानुवाच

धर्म्य एष तव प्रश्नो नैःश्रेयसकरो नृणाम् ।
वर्णाश्रमाचारवतां तमुद्धव निबोध मे ॥ ९ ॥

śrī-bhagavān uvāca
dharmya eṣa tava praśno
naiḥśreyasa-karo nṛṇām
varṇāśramācāravatāṁ
tam uddhava nibodha me

śrī-bhagavān uvāca—the Supreme Personality of Godhead said; *dharmyaḥ*—faithful to religious principles; *eṣaḥ*—this; *tava*—your; *praśnaḥ*—question; *naiḥśreyasa-karaḥ*—the cause of pure devotional service; *nṛṇām*—for ordinary human beings; *varṇa-āśrama*—the *varṇāśrama* system; *ācāra-vatām*—for those who faithfully follow; *tam*—those highest religious principles; *uddhava*—My dear Uddhava; *nibodha*—please learn; *me*—from Me.

TRANSLATION

The Supreme Personality of Godhead said: My dear Uddhava, your question is faithful to religious principles and thus gives rise to the highest perfection in life, pure devotional service, for both

ordinary human beings and the followers of the varṇāśrama system. Now please learn from Me those supreme religious principles.

PURPORT

The word *naiḥśreyasa-kara* indicates that which awards the highest perfection of life, Kṛṣṇa consciousness, which the Lord is explaining to Śrī Uddhava. When considering religious principles, ordinary human beings remain bogged down in sectarian mundane considerations. The process that awards the highest perfection of life should be considered the most auspicious for human beings. The *varṇāśrama* system is the most scientific presentation of religiosity on the earth, and those who are most perfect in that system come to the point of Kṛṣṇa consciousness, or dedicating everything for the satisfaction of the Supreme Lord.

TEXT 10

आदौ कृतयुगे वर्णो नृणां हंस इति स्मृतः ।
कृतकृत्याः प्रजा जात्या तस्मात् कृतयुगं विदुः ॥१०॥

ādau kṛta-yuge varṇo
nṛṇāṁ haṁsa iti smṛtaḥ
kṛta-kṛtyāḥ prajā jātyā
tasmāt kṛta-yugaṁ viduḥ

ādau—in the beginning (of the millennium); *kṛta-yuge*—in the Satya-yuga, or age of truth; *varṇaḥ*—the social class; *nṛṇām*—of human beings; *haṁsaḥ*—named *haṁsa; iti*—thus; *smṛtaḥ*—well known; *kṛta-kṛtyāḥ*—perfect in the execution of duties by complete surrender to the Supreme Lord; *prajāḥ*—the citizens; *jātyā*—automatically by birth; *tasmāt*—therefore; *kṛta-yugam*—Kṛta-yuga, or the age in which all duties are fulfilled; *viduḥ*—was thus known by the learned.

TRANSLATION

In the beginning, in Satya-yuga, there is only one social class, called haṁsa, to which all human beings belong. In that age all people are unalloyed devotees of the Lord from birth, and thus

learned scholars call this first age Kṛta-yuga, or the age in which all religious duties are perfectly fulfilled.

PURPORT

It is understood from this verse that the supreme religious principle is unalloyed surrender to the Supreme Personality of Godhead. In Satya-yuga there is no influence of the lower modes of nature, and therefore all human beings belong to the highest social order, called *haṁsa,* in which one comes under the direct supervision of the Personality of Godhead. In the modern age people are crying out for social equality, but unless all human beings are situated in the mode of goodness, which is the position of purity and unalloyed devotion, social equality is not possible. As the lower modes of nature become prominent, secondary religious principles arise, by which people may be gradually elevated to the pure stage of unalloyed surrender to God. In Satya-yuga there are no inferior human beings, and thus there is no need of secondary religious principles. Everyone directly takes to the unalloyed service of the Lord, fulfilling perfectly all religious obligations. In Sanskrit, one who perfectly executes all duties is called *kṛta-kṛtya,* as mentioned in this verse. Therefore Satya-yuga is called Kṛta-yuga, or the age of perfect religious action. According to Śrīla Jīva Gosvāmī, the word *ādau* ("in the beginning") refers to the moment of universal creation. In other words, the *varṇāśrama* system is not a recent concoction but naturally arises at the time of creation and should therefore be accepted by all intelligent human beings.

TEXT 11

वेदः प्रणव एवाग्रे धर्मोऽहं वृषरूपधृक् ।
उपासते तपोनिष्ठा हंसं मां मुक्तकिल्बिषाः ॥११॥

vedaḥ praṇava evāgre
dharmo 'haṁ vṛṣa-rūpa-dhṛk
upāsate tapo-niṣṭhā
haṁsaṁ māṁ mukta-kilbiṣāḥ

vedaḥ—the *Veda; praṇavaḥ*—the sacred syllable *oṁ; eva*—indeed; *agre*—in Satya-yuga; *dharmaḥ*—the object of mental activities; *aham*—

I; *vṛṣa-rūpa-dhṛk*—bearing the form of the bull of religion; *upāsate*—they worship; *tapaḥ-niṣṭhāḥ*—fixed in austerity; *haṁsam*—Lord Haṁsa; *mām*—Me; *mukta*—freed from; *kilbiṣāḥ*—all sins.

TRANSLATION

In Satya-yuga the undivided Veda is expressed by the syllable oṁ, and I am the only object of mental activities. I become manifest as the four-legged bull of religion, and thus the inhabitants of Satya-yuga, fixed in austerity and free from all sins, worship Me as Lord Haṁsa.

PURPORT

The bull of religion is described in *Śrīmad-Bhāgavatam* (1.17.24): *tapaḥ śaucaṁ dayā satyam iti pādāḥ kṛte kṛtāḥ.* "In the age of Satya [truthfulness], your four legs were established by the four principles of austerity, cleanliness, mercy and truthfulness." Śrī Vyāsadeva divided the one *Veda* into four—the *Ṛg, Yajur, Sāma* and *Atharva Vedas*— at the end of Dvāpara-yuga, but in Satya-yuga the whole of Vedic knowledge is easily understood by everyone simply by vibrating the syllable *oṁ.* In this age there are no ritualistic or pious activities such as sacrifice, since everyone is sinless, austere and fully engaged in worshiping the Personality of Godhead, Lord Haṁsa, through the process of meditation.

TEXT 12

त्रेतामुखे महाभाग प्राणान्मे हृदयात्त्रयी ।
विद्या प्रादुरभूत्तस्या अहमासं त्रिवृन्मखः ॥१२॥

tretā-mukhe mahā-bhāga
prāṇān me hṛdayāt trayī
vidyā prādurabhūt tasyā
aham āsaṁ tri-vṛn makhaḥ

tretā-mukhe—at the beginning of Tretā-yuga; *mahā-bhāga*—O greatly fortunate one; *prāṇāt*—from the abode of *prāṇa,* or the life air; *me*—My; *hṛdayāt*—from the heart; *trayī*—the threefold; *vidyā*—Vedic knowledge; *prādurabhūt*—appeared; *tasyāḥ*—from that knowledge; *aham*—I; *āsam*—appeared; *tri-vṛt*—in three divisions; *makhaḥ*—sacrifice.

TRANSLATION

O greatly fortunate one, at the beginning of Tretā-yuga Vedic knowledge appeared from My heart, which is the abode of the air of life, in three divisions—as Ṛg, Sāma and Yajur. Then from that knowledge I appeared as threefold sacrifice.

PURPORT

In Tretā-yuga, the bull of religion loses one leg, and only seventy-five percent of religious principles are manifested, represented by the three principal *Vedas*—*Ṛg*, *Sāma* and *Yajur.* The Lord appears in the process of threefold Vedic sacrifice. The three divisions are understood as follows. The *hotā* priest offers oblations into the fire and chants the *Ṛg Veda;* the *udgātā* priest chants the *Sāma Veda;* and the *adhvaryu* priest, who arranges the sacrificial ground, altar, etc., chants the *Yajur Veda.* In Tretā-yuga such sacrifice is the authorized process for spiritual perfection. The word *prāṇāt* in this verse refers to the universal form of the Personality of Godhead. This form is further described in the following verses.

TEXT 13

विप्रक्षत्रियविट्शूद्रा मुखबाहूरुपादजाः ।
वैराजात् पुरुषाज्जाता य आत्माचारलक्षणाः ॥१३॥

vipra-kṣatriya-viṭ-śūdrā
mukha-bāhūru-pāda-jāḥ
vairājāt puruṣāj jātā
ya ātmācāra-lakṣaṇāḥ

vipra—*brāhmaṇas; kṣatriya*—*kṣatriyas,* the martial class; *viṭ*—*vaiśyas,* mercantile men; *śūdrāḥ*—*śūdras,* workers; *mukha*—from the mouth; *bāhu*—arms; *ūru*—thighs; *pāda*—and legs; *jāḥ*—born; *vairājāt*—from the universal form; *puruṣāt*—from the Personality of Godhead; *jātāḥ*—generated; *ye*—who; *ātma*—personal; *ācāra*—by activities; *lakṣaṇāḥ*—recognized.

TRANSLATION

In Tretā-yuga the four social orders are manifested from the universal form of the Personality of Godhead. The brāhmaṇas appear from the Lord's face, the kṣatriyas from the Lord's arms, the vaiśyas from the Lord's thighs and the śūdras from the legs of that mighty form. Each social division is recognized by its particular duties and behavior.

TEXT 14

गृहाश्रमो जघनतो ब्रह्मचर्यं हृदो मम ।
वक्षःस्थलाद् वनेवासः सन्न्यासःशिरसि स्थितः॥१४॥

gṛhāśramo jaghanato
brahmacaryaṁ hṛdo mama
vakṣaḥ-sthalād vane-vāsaḥ
sannyāsaḥ śirasi sthitaḥ

gṛha-āśramaḥ—married life; *jaghanataḥ*—from the loins; *brahmacaryam*—celibate student life; *hṛdaḥ*—from the heart; *mama*—My; *vakṣaḥ-sthalāt*—from the chest; *vane*—in the forest; *vāsaḥ*—dwelling; *sannyāsaḥ*—the renounced order of life; *śirasi*—in the head; *sthitaḥ*—situated.

TRANSLATION

The married order of life appears from the loins of My universal form, and the celibate students come from My heart. The forest-dwelling retired order of life appears from My chest, and the renounced order of life is situated within the head of My universal form.

PURPORT

There are two classes of *brahmacārī* life. The *naiṣṭhiki-brahmacārī* remains celibate throughout life, whereas the *upakurvāṇa-brahmacārī* marries upon finishing his student life. One who remains perpetually celibate is situated within the heart of Lord Kṛṣṇa, but those *brahmacārīs* who eventually marry are situated within the loins of the universal form of the Lord. The word *vane-vāsaḥ* refers to *vānaprastha*, or the retired order of life, which is situated on the chest of the Lord.

TEXT 15

वर्णानामाश्रमाणां च जन्मभूम्यनुसारिणीः ।
आसन् प्रकृतयो नृणां नीचैर्नीचोत्तमोत्तमाः ॥१५॥

varṇānām āśramāṇāṁ ca
janma-bhūmy-anusāriṇīḥ
āsan prakṛtayo nṝṇāṁ
nīcair nīcottamottamāḥ

varṇānām—of the occupational divisions; *āśramāṇām*—of the social divisions; *ca*—also; *janma*—of birth; *bhūmi*—the situation; *anusāriṇīḥ*—according to; *āsan*—appeared; *prakṛtayaḥ*—the natures; *nṝṇām*—of human beings; *nīcaiḥ*—by inferior background; *nīca*—inferior nature; *uttama*—by superior background; *uttamāḥ*—superior natures.

TRANSLATION

The various occupational and social divisions of human society appeared according to inferior and superior natures manifest in the situation of the individual's birth.

PURPORT

According to Śrīla Viśvanātha Cakravartī Ṭhākura, the *brāhmaṇas* and *sannyāsīs*, being situated on the head of the universal form of the Lord, are considered to be the most qualified, whereas the *śūdras* and *gṛhasthas*, being on the legs or loins of the Personality of Godhead, are considered to be in the lowest position. A living entity is born with a certain amount of intelligence, beauty and social opportunity, and he is therefore situated in a particular occupational and social position within the *varṇāśrama* system. Ultimately, such positions are external designations, but since the majority of human beings are conditioned by the external energy of the Lord, they should act according to the scientific *varṇāśrama* divisions until they reach the stage of *jīvan-mukta*, or liberated life.

TEXT 16

शमो दमस्तपः शौचं सन्तोषः क्षान्तिरार्जवम् ।
मद्भक्तिश्च दया सत्यं ब्रह्मप्रकृतयस्त्विमाः ॥१६॥

śamo damas tapaḥ śaucaṁ
santoṣaḥ kṣāntir ārjavam
mad-bhaktiś ca dayā satyaṁ
brahma-prakṛtayas tv imāḥ

śamaḥ—peacefulness; *damaḥ*—sense control; *tapaḥ*—austerity; *śaucam*—cleanliness; *santoṣaḥ*—full satisfaction; *kṣāntiḥ*—forgiveness; *ārjavam*—simplicity and straightforwardness; *mat-bhaktiḥ*—devotional service unto Me; *ca*—also; *dayā*—mercy; *satyam*—truth; *brahma*—of the *brāhmaṇas; prakṛtayaḥ*—the natural qualities; *tu*—indeed; *imāḥ*—these.

TRANSLATION

Peacefulness, self-control, austerity, cleanliness, satisfaction, tolerance, simple straightforwardness, devotion to Me, mercy and truthfulness are the natural qualities of the brāhmaṇas.

TEXT 17

तेजो बलं धृतिः शौर्यं तितिक्षौदार्यमुद्यमः ।
स्थैर्यं ब्रह्मण्यमैश्वर्यं क्षत्रप्रकृतयस्त्विमाः ॥१७॥

tejo balaṁ dhṛtiḥ śauryaṁ
titikṣaudāryam udyamaḥ
sthairyaṁ brahmaṇyam aiśvaryaṁ
kṣatra-prakṛtayas tv imāḥ

tejaḥ—dynamic power; *balam*—bodily strength; *dhṛtiḥ*—determination; *śauryam*—heroism; *titikṣā*—tolerance; *audāryam*—generosity; *udyamaḥ*—endeavor; *sthairyam*—steadiness; *brahmaṇyam*—being always eager to serve the *brāhmaṇas; aiśvaryam*—leadership; *kṣatra*—of the *kṣatriyas; prakṛtayaḥ*—the natural qualities; *tu*—indeed; *imāḥ*—these.

TRANSLATION

Dynamic power, bodily strength, determination, heroism, tolerance, generosity, great endeavor, steadiness, devotion to the brāhmaṇas and leadership are the natural qualities of the kṣatriyas.

TEXT 18

आस्तिक्यं दाननिष्ठा च अदम्भो ब्रह्मसेवनम् ।
अतुष्टिरर्थोपचयैर्वैश्यप्रकृतयस्त्विमाः ॥१८॥

āstikyaṁ dāna-niṣṭhā ca
adambho brahma-sevanam
atuṣṭir arthopacayair
vaiśya-prakṛtayas tv imāḥ

āstikyam—faith in Vedic civilization; *dāna-niṣṭhā*—dedicated to charity; *ca*—also; *adambhaḥ*—being without hypocrisy; *brahma-sevanam*—service to the *brāhmaṇas; atuṣṭiḥ*—remaining dissatisfied; *artha*—of money; *upacayaiḥ*—by the accumulation; *vaiśya*—of the *vaiśyas; prakṛtayaḥ*—the natural qualities; *tu*—indeed; *imāḥ*—these.

TRANSLATION

Faith in Vedic civilization, dedication to charity, freedom from hypocrisy, service to the brāhmaṇas and perpetually desiring to accumulate more money are the natural qualities of the vaiśyas.

PURPORT

Atuṣṭir arthopacayaiḥ indicates that a *vaiśya* is never satisfied with any amount of wealth and always wants to accumulate more. On the other hand, he is *dāna-niṣṭha*, or dedicated to charitable work; *brahma-sevī*, always engaged in assisting the *brāhmaṇas;* and *adambha*, free from hypocrisy. This is due to *āstikyam*, or complete faith in the Vedic way of life, and confidence that one will be rewarded or punished in the next life for one's present activities. The fervent desire of the *vaiśyas* to accumulate wealth is not the same as ordinary material greed, because it is purified and tempered by the superior qualities mentioned in this verse.

TEXT 19

शुश्रूषणं द्विजगवां देवानां चाप्यमायया ।
तत्र लब्धेन सन्तोषः शूद्रप्रकृतयस्त्विमाः ॥१९॥

śuśrūṣaṇaṁ dvija-gavāṁ
devānāṁ cāpy amāyayā
tatra labdhena santoṣaḥ
śūdra-prakṛtayas tv imāḥ

śuśrūṣaṇam—service; *dvija*—of the *brāhmaṇas; gavām*—of the cows; *devānām*—of worshipable personalities such as the demigods and the spiritual master; *ca*—also; *api*—indeed; *amāyayā*—without duplicity; *tatra*—in such service; *labdhena*—with that which is obtained; *santoṣaḥ*—complete satisfaction; *śūdra*—of the *śūdras; prakṛtayaḥ*—the natural qualities; *tu*—indeed; *imāḥ*—these.

TRANSLATION

Service without duplicity to the brāhmaṇas, cows, demigods and other worshipable personalities, and complete satisfaction with whatever income is obtained in such service, are the natural qualities of śūdras.

PURPORT

When the entire social order is functioning properly according to Vedic standards, everyone is happy and satisfied. Although the *śūdras* are to be satisfied with whatever income they obtain through their service, they never lack the necessities of life, because the other orders of society, such as *kṣatriyas* and *vaiśyas,* are required to be abundantly generous, and the *brāhmaṇas* are well known for being the most merciful of all. Therefore, if all social classes obey the Vedic injunctions there will be a new and blissful life for the entire human society under the guidance of Kṛṣṇa consciousness.

TEXT 20

अशौचमनृतं स्तेयं नास्तिक्यं शुष्कविग्रहः ।
कामः क्रोधश्च तर्षश्च सभावोऽन्त्यावसायिनाम् ॥२०॥

aśaucam anṛtaṁ steyaṁ
nāstikyaṁ śuṣka-vigrahaḥ

kāmaḥ krodhaś ca tarṣaś ca
sa bhāvo 'ntyāvasāyinām

aśaucam—dirtiness; *anṛtam*—dishonesty; *steyam*—thievery; *nāstikyam*—faithlessness; *śuṣka-vigrahaḥ*—useless quarreling; *kāmaḥ*—lust; *krodhaḥ*—anger; *ca*—also; *tarṣaḥ*—hankering; *ca*—also; *saḥ*—this; *bhāvaḥ*—the nature; *antya*—in the lowest position; *avasāyinām*—of those residing.

TRANSLATION

Dirtiness, dishonesty, thievery, faithlessness, useless quarrel, lust, anger and hankering constitute the nature of those in the lowest position outside the varṇāśrama system.

PURPORT

Here the Lord describes those who reside outside the scientific social system called *varṇāśrama.* In Europe and America, we have practically observed that the standards of cleanliness are abominable even among so-called educated persons. Going without bathing and the use of indecent language are common. In the modern age people whimsically speak whatever they like, dispensing with all authority, and there is therefore very little truthfulness or true wisdom. Similarly, in both the capitalistic and communistic countries, everyone is busily engaged in stealing and robbing from everyone else in the name of business, taxation or outright crime. People are not confident of the kingdom of God nor of their own eternal nature, and thus their faith is very weak. Moreover, since modern human beings are not very interested in Kṛṣṇa consciousness they constantly quarrel, bicker and fight over completely insignificant issues relating to the material body. Thus at the slightest provocation there are huge wars and massacres. Lust, anger and hankering have become practically unlimited in Kali-yuga. The symptoms and characteristics mentioned here can be abundantly observed throughout the world, wherever people have fallen away from the *varṇāśrama* system. Because of sinful habits such as animal killing, illicit sex, intoxication and gambling, the great majority of human beings have become *caṇḍālas*, or untouchables.

TEXT 21

अहिंसा सत्यमस्तेयमकामक्रोधलोभता ।
भूतप्रियहितेहा च धर्मोऽयं सार्ववर्णिकः ॥२१॥

ahiṁsā satyam asteyam
akāma-krodha-lobhatā
bhūta-priya-hitehā ca
dharmo 'yaṁ sārva-varṇikaḥ

ahiṁsā—nonviolence; *satyam*—truthfulness; *asteyam*—honesty; *a-kāma-krodha-lobhatā*—being free from lust, anger and greed; *bhūta*—of all living entities; *priya*—the happiness; *hita*—and welfare; *īhā*—desiring; *ca*—also; *dharmaḥ*—duty; *ayam*—this; *sārva-varṇikaḥ*—for all members of society.

TRANSLATION

Nonviolence, truthfulness, honesty, desire for the happiness and welfare of all others and freedom from lust, anger and greed constitute duties for all members of society.

PURPORT

The word *sārva-varṇika* indicates that the above-mentioned principles constitute general piety, which should be observed by all members of society, even those outside the *varṇāśrama* system. We practically find that even in societies that have fallen away from the *varṇāśrama* system, the above-mentioned principles are honored and encouraged. Such principles do not constitute a specific path of liberation but are perennial virtues in human society.

TEXT 22

द्वितीयं प्राप्यानुपूर्व्याज्जन्मोपनयनं द्विजः ।
वसन् गुरुकुले दान्तो ब्रह्माधीयीत चाहूतः ॥२२॥

dvitīyaṁ prāpyānupūrvyāj
janmopanayanaṁ dvijaḥ

vasan guru-kule dānto
brahmādhīyīta cāhūtaḥ

dvitīyam—second; *prāpya*—achieving; *ānupūrvyāt*—by the gradual process of purificatory ceremonies; *janma*—birth; *upanayanam*—Gāyatrī initiation; *dvijaḥ*—a twice-born member of society; *vasan*—residing; *guru-kule*—in the *āśrama* of the spiritual master; *dāntaḥ*—self-controlled; *brahma*—the Vedic literatures; *adhīyīta*—should study; *ca*—and also understand; *āhūtaḥ*—being summoned by the spiritual master.

TRANSLATION

The twice-born member of society achieves second birth through the sequence of purificatory ceremonies culminating in Gāyatrī initiation. Being summoned by the spiritual master, he should reside within the guru's āśrama and with a self-controlled mind carefully study the Vedic literature.

PURPORT

The term *dvija*, or "twice-born," here indicates the three superior classes, namely *brāhmaṇas, kṣatriyas* and *vaiśyas*, who all receive the Gāyatrī *mantra*, which signifies their second birth through spiritual initiation. One's first birth is biological, or seminal, and does not necessarily indicate that one is intelligent or enlightened. A young *brāhmaṇa* boy, if qualified, may be initiated with Gāyatrī *mantra* at the age of twelve, and *kṣatriyas* and *vaiśyas* a few years later. In order to become enlightened with spiritual knowledge, the boy resides within the *guru-kula*, or *āśrama* of the spiritual master. The International Society for Krishna Consciousness has established similar *guru-kulas* all over the world and is issuing a great call to civilized human beings to arrange for the proper education of their children. Every young boy and girl should learn to be self-controlled and should become enlightened through study of authorized Vedic literatures. In this way, unlike ordinary animals, insects, fish and birds, etc., an enlightened human being may take birth twice and thus become perfect in the knowledge that leads to ultimate liberation. The word *ānupūrvyāt* in this verse indicates the system of *saṁskāras*, or purificatory rites, beginning with *garbhādhāna-saṁskāra*, or the purification of the sexual act. Generally, *śūdras* and those who do not follow the Vedic system are not attracted to such purificatory ceremonies; therefore they remain ignorant of spiritual life and envious of the bona fide spiritual master. Those whose character has been civilized by a systematic cleansing process give up the tendency to be argumentative and whimsical and instead become submissive and eager to learn in the presence of a bona fide spiritual master.

TEXT 23

मेखलाजिनदण्डाक्षब्रह्मसूत्रकमण्डलून् ।
जटिलोऽधौतदद्वासोऽरक्तपीठः कुशान् दधत् ॥२३॥

mekhalājina-daṇḍākṣa-
brahma-sūtra-kamaṇḍalūn
jaṭilo 'dhauta-dad-vāso
'rakta-pīṭhaḥ kuśān dadhat

mekhalā—belt; *ajina*—deerskin; *daṇḍa*—staff; *akṣa*—bead necklace; *brahma-sūtra*—*brāhmaṇa* thread; *kamaṇḍalūn*—and waterpot; *jaṭilaḥ*—with matted, unruly hair; *adhauta*—without polishing, bleaching or ironing; *dat-vāsaḥ*—the teeth and clothes; *arakta-pīṭhaḥ*—without accepting a luxurious or sensuous seat; *kuśān*—*kuśa* grass; *dadhat*—carrying in his hand.

TRANSLATION

The brahmacārī should regularly dress with a belt of straw and deerskin garments. He should wear matted hair, carry a rod and waterpot and be decorated with akṣa beads and a sacred thread. Carrying pure kuśa grass in his hand, he should never accept a luxurious or sensuous sitting place. He should not unnecessarily polish his teeth, nor should he bleach and iron his clothes.

PURPORT

The word *adhauta-dad-vāsa* indicates that a renounced *brahmacārī* is not concerned with a glistening smile to attract the opposite sex, nor does he pay much attention to his outer garments. *Brahmacārī* life is meant for austerity and obedience to the spiritual master so that later in life, when one becomes a businessman, politician or intellectual *brāhmaṇa*, one will be able to call upon resources of character, discipline, self-control, austerity and humility. Student life, as described here, is far different from the mindless hedonism known as modern education. Of course, in the modern age, Kṛṣṇa conscious *brahmacārīs* cannot artificially adopt the ancient dress and ritualistic duties described here; but the essential values of self-control, purity and obedience to a bona fide spiritual master are just as necessary today as they were in Vedic times.

TEXT 24

स्नानभोजनहोमेषु जपोच्चारे च वाग्यतः ।
न च्छिन्द्यान्नखरोमाणि कक्षोपस्थगतान्यपि ॥२४॥

snāna-bhojana-homeṣu
japoccāre ca vāg-yataḥ
na cchindyān nakha-romāṇi
kakṣopastha-gatāny api

snāna—while bathing; *bhojana*—while eating; *homeṣu*—and while attending sacrificial performances; *japa*—while chanting *mantras* to oneself; *uccāre*—while passing stool or urine; *ca*—also; *vāk-yataḥ*—remaining silent; *na*—not; *chindyāt*—should cut; *nakha*—the nails; *romāṇi*—or hairs; *kakṣa*—in the armpits; *upastha*—pubic; *gatāni*—including; *api*—even.

TRANSLATION

A brahmacārī should always remain silent while bathing, eating, attending sacrificial performances, chanting japa or passing stool and urine. He should not cut his nails and hair, including the armpit and pubic hair.

PURPORT

Nārada Muni gives a similar technical description of Vedic *brahmacārī* life in Canto Seven, Chapter Twelve of *Śrīmad-Bhāgavatam*.

TEXT 25

रेतो नावकिरेज्जातु ब्रह्मव्रतधरः स्वयम् ।
अवकीर्णेऽवगाह्याप्सु यतासुस्त्रिपदां जपेत् ॥२५॥

reto nāvakirej jātu
brahma-vrata-dharaḥ svayam
avakīrṇe 'vagāhyāpsu
yatāsus tri-padāṁ japet

retaḥ—semen; *na*—not; *avakiret*—should spill out; *jātu*—ever; *brahma-vrata-dharaḥ*—one who is maintaining the vow of celibacy, or *brahmacarya; svayam*—by itself; *avakīrṇe*—having flowed out; *avagāhya*—bathing; *apsu*—in water; *yata-asuḥ*—controlling the breathing by *prāṇāyāma; tri-padām*—the Gāyatrī *mantra; japet*—he should chant.

TRANSLATION

One observing the vow of celibate brahmacārī life should never pass semen. If the semen by chance spills out by itself, the brahmacārī should immediately take bath in water, control his breath by prāṇāyāma and chant the Gāyatrī mantra.

TEXT 26

अग्न्यर्काचार्यगोविप्रगुरुवृद्धसुराञ्शुचिः ।
समाहित उपासीत सन्ध्ये च यतवाग् जपन् ॥२६॥

agny-arkācārya-go-vipra-
guru-vṛddha-surāñ śuciḥ
samāhita upāsīta
sandhye dve yata-vāg japan

agni—the fire-god; *arka*—the sun; *ācārya*—the *ācārya; go*—the cows; *vipra*—the *brāhmaṇas; guru*—the spiritual master; *vṛddha*—elder respectable persons; *surān*—the demigods; *śuciḥ*—purified; *samāhitaḥ*—with fixed consciousness; *upāsīta*—he should worship;

sandhye—in the junctions of time; *dve*—two; *yata-vāk*—observing silence; *japan*—silently chanting or murmuring the proper *mantras.*

TRANSLATION

Purified and fixed in consciousness, the brahmacārī should worship the fire-god, sun, ācārya, cows, brāhmaṇas, guru, elderly respectable persons and demigods. He should perform such worship at sunrise and sunset, without speaking but by silently chanting or murmuring the appropriate mantras.

TEXT 27

आचार्यं मां विजानीयान्नावमन्येत कर्हिचित् ।
न मर्त्यबुद्ध्यासूयेत सर्वदेवमयो गुरुः ॥२७॥

ācāryaṁ māṁ vijānīyān
nāvamanyeta karhicit
na martya-buddhyāsūyeta
sarva-deva-mayo guruḥ

ācāryam—the spiritual master; *mām*—Myself; *vijānīyāt*—one should know; *na avamanyeta*—one should never disrespect; *karhicit*—at any time; *na*—never; *martya-buddhyā*—with the idea of his being an ordinary man; *asūyeta*—one should be envious; *sarva-deva*—of all demigods; *mayaḥ*—representative; *guruḥ*—the spiritual master.

TRANSLATION

One should know the ācārya as Myself and never disrespect him in any way. One should not envy him, thinking him an ordinary man, for he is the representative of all the demigods.

PURPORT

This verse appears in *Caitanya-caritāmṛta* (*Ādi* 1.46). His Divine Grace Oṁ Viṣṇupāda Paramahaṁsa Parivrājakācārya Aṣṭottara-śata Śrī Śrīmad A. C. Bhaktivedanta Swami Prabhupāda has commented on this verse as follows.

"This is a verse from *Śrīmad-Bhāgavatam* (11.17.27) spoken by Lord Śrī Kṛṣṇa when He was questioned by Uddhava regarding the four social and spiritual orders of society. He was specifically instructing how a *brahmacārī* should behave under the care of a spiritual master. A spiritual master is not an enjoyer of facilities offered by his disciples. He is like a parent. Without the attentive service of his parents, a child cannot grow to manhood; similarly, without the care of the spiritual master one cannot rise to the plane of transcendental service.

"The spiritual master is also called *ācārya*, or a transcendental professor of spiritual science. *Manu-saṁhitā* (2.140) explains the duties of an *ācārya*, describing that a bona fide spiritual maser accepts charge of disciples, teaches them the Vedic knowledge with all its intricacies, and gives them their second birth. The ceremony performed to initiate a disciple into the study of spiritual science is called *upanīti*, or the function that brings one nearer to the spiritual master. One who cannot be brought nearer to a spiritual master cannot have a sacred thread, and thus he is indicated to be a *śūdra*. The sacred thread worn on the body of a *brāhmaṇa*, *kṣatriya* or *vaiśya* is a symbol of initiation by the spiritual master; it is worth nothing if worn merely to boast of high parentage. The duty of the spiritual master is to initiate a disciple with the sacred thread ceremony, and after this *saṁskāra*, or purificatory process, the spiritual master actually begins to teach the disciple about the *Vedas*. A person born a *śūdra* is not barred from such spiritual initiation, provided he is approved by the spiritual master, who is duly authorized to award a disciple the right to be a *brāhmaṇa* if he finds him perfectly qualified. In the *Vāyu Purāṇa* an *ācārya* is defined as one who knows the import of all Vedic literature, explains the purpose of the *Vedas*, abides by their rules and regulations and teaches his disciples to act in the same way.

"Only out of His immense compassion does the Personality of Godhead reveal Himself as the spiritual master. Therefore in the dealings of an *ācārya* there are no activities but those of transcendental loving service to the Lord. He is the Supreme Personality of Servitor Godhead. It is worthwhile to take shelter of such a steady devotee, who is called *āśraya-vigraha*, or the manifestation or form of the Lord of whom one must take shelter.

"If one poses himself as an *ācārya* but does not have an attitude of servitorship to the Lord, he must be considered an offender, and this offensive attitude disqualifies him from being an *ācārya.* The bona fide spiritual master always engages in unalloyed devotional service to the Supreme Personality of Godhead. By this test he is known to be a direct manifestation of the Lord and a genuine representative of Śrī Nityānanda Prabhu. Such a spiritual master is known as *ācāryadeva.* Influenced by an envious temperament and dissatisfied because of an attitude of sense gratification, mundaners criticize a real *ācārya.* In fact, however, a bona fide *ācārya* is nondifferent from the Personality of Godhead, and therefore to envy such an *ācārya* is to envy the Personality of Godhead Himself. This will produce an effect subversive to transcendental realization.

"As mentioned previously, a disciple should always respect the spiritual master as a manifestation of Śrī Kṛṣṇa, but at the same time one should always remember that a spiritual master is never authorized to imitate the transcendental pastimes of the Lord. False spiritual masters pose themselves as identical with Śrī Kṛṣṇa in every respect, to exploit the sentiments of their disciples, but such impersonalists can only mislead their disciples, for their ultimate aim is to become one with the Lord. This is against the principles of the devotional cult.

"The real Vedic philosophy is *acintya-bhedābheda-tattva,* which establishes everything to be simultaneously one with and different from the Personality of Godhead. Śrīla Raghunātha dāsa Gosvāmī confirms that this is the real position of a bona fide spiritual master and says that one should always think of the spiritual master in terms of his intimate relationship with Mukunda (Śrī Kṛṣṇa). Śrīla Jīva Gosvāmī, in his *Bhakti-sandarbha* (213), has clearly defined that a pure devotee's observation of the spiritual master and Lord Śiva as one with the Personality of Godhead exists in terms of their being very dear to the Lord, not identical with Him in all respects. Following in the footsteps of Śrīla Raghunātha dāsa Gosvāmī and Śrīla Jīva Gosvāmī, later *ācāryas* like Śrīla Viśvanātha Cakravartī Ṭhākura have confirmed the same truths. In his prayers to the spiritual master, Śrīla Viśvanātha Cakravartī Ṭhākura confirms that all the revealed scriptures accept the spiritual master to be identical with the Personality of Godhead because he is a very dear and confidential servant of the Lord. Gauḍīya Vaiṣṇavas therefore worship Śrīla Gurudeva (the spiritual master) in the light of his being the servitor of the Personality of Godhead. In all the ancient literatures of devotional service and in the more recent songs of Śrīla Narottama dāsa Ṭhākura, Śrīla Bhaktivinoda Ṭhākura and other unalloyed Vaiṣṇavas, the spiritual master is always considered to be either one of the confidential associates of Śrīmatī Rādhārāṇī or a manifested representation of Śrīla Nityānanda Prabhu."

TEXT 28

सायं प्रातरुपानीय भैक्ष्यं तस्मै निवेदयेत् ।
यच्चान्यदप्यनुज्ञातमुपयुञ्जीत संयतः ॥२८॥

sāyaṁ prātar upānīya
bhaikṣyaṁ tasmai nivedayet
yac cānyad apy anujñātam
upayuñjīta saṁyataḥ

sāyam—in the evening; *prātaḥ*—in the morning; *upānīya*—bringing; *bhaikṣyam*—food that is collected by begging; *tasmai*—unto him (the *ācārya*); *nivedayet*—one should deliver; *yat*—that which; *ca*—also; *anyat*—other things; *api*—indeed; *anujñātam*—that which is permitted; *upayuñjīta*—one should accept; *saṁyataḥ*—being fully controlled.

TRANSLATION

In the morning and evening one should collect foodstuffs and other articles and deliver them to the spiritual master. Then, being self-contolled, one should accept for oneself that which is allotted by the ācārya.

PURPORT

One who desires to receive the mercy of a bona fide spiritual master should not be eager to accumulate the paraphernalia of sense gratification; rather, whatever one is able to collect one should offer at the lotus feet of the *ācārya.* Being self-controlled, one should humbly accept that which is allotted by the bona fide spiritual master. Every living entity must ultimately be trained to serve the Supreme Personality of Godhead, but until one has become expert in the techniques of spiritual service one should offer everything to the spiritual master, who is completely realized in the process of worshiping the Lord. When the spiritual master sees that the disciple is advanced in Kṛṣṇa consciousness, he then engages the disciple in directly worshiping the Personality of Godhead. A bona fide spiritual master does not use anything for his personal sense gratification and entrusts to his disciple only as much material opulence as the disciple can properly offer to the lotus feet of the Lord. The example may be given that when an ordinary father tries to train his son in business and other material activities, he entrusts to the son only as much wealth as the son can intelligently engage in profitable enterprises without foolishly wasting the father's hard-earned money.

Similarly, the bona fide spiritual master teaches his disciple to worship the Lord, and an immature disciple must simply deliver everything to the lotus feet of the *guru*, just as an immature child does not keep a personal bank account but rather receives his maintenance from the father, who trains the son to be responsible. If one cheats oneself by defying the order of a bona fide spiritual master or Kṛṣṇa, one certainly becomes a nondevotee, or sense enjoyer, and falls from the spiritual path. Therefore, one should be trained to serve a bona fide spiritual master and thus become mature in Kṛṣṇa consciousness.

TEXT 29

शुश्रूषमाण आचार्यं सदोपासीत नीचवत् ।
यानशय्यासनस्थानैर्नातिदूरे कृताञ्जलिः ॥२९॥

śuśrūṣamāṇa ācāryaṁ
sadopāsīta nīca-vat
yāna-śayyāsana-sthānair
nāti-dūre kṛtāñjaliḥ

śuśrūṣamāṇaḥ—engaged in serving; *ācāryam*—the bona fide spiritual master; *sadā*—always; *upāsīta*—one should worship; *nīca-vat*—as a humble servant; *yāna*—by humbly following behind the *guru* when he is walking; *śayyā*—by taking rest with the spiritual master; *āsana*—sitting near the *guru* to render service; *sthānaiḥ*—by standing and humbly waiting upon the *guru; na*—not; *ati*—very; *dūre*—far away; *kṛta-añjaliḥ*—with folded hands.

TRANSLATION

While engaged in serving the spiritual master one should remain as a humble servant, and thus when the guru is walking the servant should humbly walk behind. When the guru lies down to sleep, the servant should also lie down nearby, and when the guru has awakened the servant should sit near him, massaging his lotus feet and rendering other similar services. When the guru is sitting down on his āsana, the servant should stand nearby with folded hands, awaiting the guru's order. In this way one should always worship the spiritual master.

TEXT 30

एवंवृत्तो गुरुकुले वसेद् भोगविवर्जितः ।
विद्या समाप्यते यावद् बिभ्रद् व्रतमखण्डितम् ॥३०॥

evaṁ-vṛtto guru-kule
vased bhoga-vivarjitaḥ
vidyā samāpyate yāvad
bibhrad vratam akhaṇḍitam

evam—thus; *vṛttaḥ*—engaged; *guru-kule*—in the *āśrama* of the spiritual master; *vaset*—he should live; *bhoga*—sense gratification; *vivarjitaḥ*—freed from; *vidyā*—Vedic education; *samāpyate*—is completed; *yāvat*—until; *bibhrat*—maintaining; *vratam*—the vow (of *brahmacarya*); *akhaṇḍitam*—unbroken.

TRANSLATION

Until the student has completed his Vedic education he should remain engaged in the āśrama of the spiritual master, should remain completely free of material sense gratification and should not break his vow of celibacy [brahmacarya].

PURPORT

This verse describes the *upakurvāṇa-brahmacārī*, who enters *gṛhastha-āśrama*, or family life, after completing his Vedic education. The word *evaṁ-vṛttaḥ* indicates that although one may eventually marry and become prominent in society as an intellectual, politician or businessman, during student life one must remain without false prestige as a humble servant of the bona fide spiritual master. The *naiṣṭhiki-brahmacārī*, who never marries, is described in the following verse.

TEXT 31

यद्यसौ छन्दसां लोकमारोक्ष्यन् ब्रह्मविष्टपम् ।
गुरवे विन्यसेद् देहं स्वाध्यायार्थं बृहद्व्रतः ॥३१॥

yady asau chandasāṁ lokam
ārokṣyan brahma-viṣṭapam
gurave vinyased dehaṁ
svādhyāyārthaṁ bṛhad-vrataḥ

yadi—if; *asau*—that student; *chandasām lokam*—the Maharloka planet; *ārokṣyan*—desiring to ascend to; *brahma-viṣṭapam*—Brahmaloka; *gurave*—unto the *guru; vinyaset*—he should offer; *deham*—his body; *sva-adhyāya*—of superior Vedic studies; *artham*—for the purpose; *bṛhat-vrataḥ*—observing the powerful vow of perpetual celibacy.

TRANSLATION

If the brahmacārī student desires to ascend to the Maharloka or Brahmaloka planets, then he should completely surrender his activities to the spiritual master and, observing the powerful vow of perpetual celibacy, dedicate himself to superior Vedic studies.

PURPORT

One who desires the supreme perfection of life must engage his body, mind and words in the service of a bona fide spiritual master. One desiring elevation to superior planets such as Brahmaloka and Maharloka must fully engage in the spiritual master's service. We can thus imagine the sincerity of purpose and service required to achieve the Kṛṣṇaloka planet, which lies far beyond the material universe.

TEXT 32

अग्नौ गुरावात्मनि च सर्वभूतेषु मां परम् ।
अपृथग्धीरुपासीत ब्रह्मवर्चस्व्यकल्मषः ॥३२॥

agnau gurāv ātmani ca
sarva-bhūteṣu māṁ param
apṛthag-dhīr upāsīta
brahma-varcasvy akalmaṣaḥ

agnau—in fire; *gurau*—in the spiritual master; *ātmani*—in oneself; *ca*—also; *sarva-bhūteṣu*—in all living entities; *mām*—Me; *param*—the Supreme; *apṛthak-dhīḥ*—without any concept of duality; *upāsīta*—one should worship; *brahma-varcasvī*—possessing Vedic enlightenment; *akalmaṣaḥ*—sinless.

TRANSLATION

Thus enlightened in Vedic knowledge by service to the spiritual master, freed from all sins and duality, one should worship Me as the Supersoul, as I appear within fire, the spiritual master, one's own self and all living entities.

PURPORT

One becomes glorious and enlightened by faithfully serving a bona fide spiritual master, who is expert in the Vedic way of life. Thus purified, one never engages in sinful activities, which immediately extinguish the fire of spiritual enlightenment; nor does one become foolish and small-minded, trying to exploit material nature for personal sense gratification. A purified human being is *apṛthag-dhī*, or without consciousness of duality, because he has been trained to observe the Supreme Personality of Godhead within all things. Such sublime consciousness should be systematically taught throughout the world so that human society will become peaceful and sublime.

TEXT 33

स्त्रीणां निरीक्षणस्पर्शसंलापक्ष्वेलनादिकम् ।
प्राणिनो मिथुनीभूतानगृहस्थोऽग्रतस्त्यजेत् ॥३३॥

strīṇāṁ nirīkṣaṇa-sparśa-
saṁlāpa-kṣvelanādikam
prāṇino mithunī-bhūtān
agṛhastho 'gratas tyajet

strīṇām—in relation to women; *nirīkṣaṇa*—glancing; *sparśa*—touching; *saṁlāpa*—conversing; *kṣvelana*—joking or sporting; *ādikam*—and so on; *prāṇinaḥ*—living entities; *mithunī-bhūtān*—engaged in sex; *agṛha-sthaḥ*—a *sannyāsī, vānaprastha* or *brahmacārī; agrataḥ*—first of all; *tyajet*—should give up.

TRANSLATION

Those who are not married—sannyāsīs, vānaprasthas and brahmacārīs—should never associate with women by glancing, touching, conversing, joking or sporting. Neither should they ever associate with any living entity engaged in sexual activities.

PURPORT

Prāṇinaḥ indicates all living entities, whether birds, bees or human beings. Among most species of life, sexual intercourse is preceded by diverse mating rituals. In human society, all types of entertainment (books, music, films) and all places of amusement (restaurants, shopping centers, resorts) are designed to stimulate the sexual urge and create an aura of "romance." One who is not married—a *sannyāsī, brahmacārī* or *vānaprastha*— should rigidly avoid anything related to sex and of course should never see any living entity, whether bird, insect or human, engaging in the various phases of sexual intercourse. When a man jokes with a woman, an intimate, sexually-charged atmosphere is immediately created, and this should also be avoided for those aspiring to practice celibacy. Even a householder who becomes attached to such activities will also fall down into the darkness of ignorance.

TEXTS 34–35

शौचमाचमनं स्नानं सन्ध्योपास्तिर्ममार्चनम् ।
तीर्थसेवा जपोऽस्पृश्याभक्ष्यासंभाष्यवर्जनम् ॥३४॥
सर्वाश्रमप्रयुक्तोऽयं नियमः कुलनन्दन ।
मद्भावः सर्वभूतेषु मनोवाक्कायसंयमः ॥३५॥

śaucam ācamanaṁ snānaṁ
sandhyopāstir mamārcanam

tīrtha-sevā japo 'spṛśyā-
bhakṣyāsambhāṣya-varjanam

sarvāśrama-prayukto 'yaṁ
niyamaḥ kula-nandana
mad-bhāvaḥ sarva-bhūteṣu
mano-vāk-kāya-saṁyamaḥ

śaucam—cleanliness; *ācamanam*—purifying the hands with water; *snānam*—bathing; *sandhyā*—at sunrise, noon and sunset; *upāstiḥ*—religious services; *mama*—of Me; *arcanam*—worship; *tīrtha-sevā*—going to holy places; *japaḥ*—chanting the holy names of the Lord; *aspṛśya*—which are untouchable; *abhakṣya*—uneatable; *asambhāṣya*—or not to be discussed; *varjanam*—avoidance of things; *sarva*—for all; *āśrama*—orders of life; *prayuktaḥ*—enjoined; *ayam*—this; *niyamaḥ*—rule; *kula-nandana*—My dear Uddhava; *mat-bhāvaḥ*—perceiving My existence; *sarva-bhūteṣu*—in all living entities; *manaḥ*—of the mind; *vāk*—of words; *kāya*—of the body; *saṁyamaḥ*—regulation.

TRANSLATION

My dear Uddhava, general cleanliness, washing the hands, taking bath, performing religious services at sunrise, noon and sunset, worshiping Me, visiting holy places, chanting japa, avoiding that which is untouchable, uneatable or not to be discussed, and remembering My existence within all living entities as the Supersoul together constitute principles to be followed by all members of society through regulation of the mind, words and body.

TEXT 36

एवं बृहद्व्रतधरो ब्राह्मणोऽग्निरिव ज्वलन् ।
मद्भक्तस्तीव्रतपसा दग्धकर्माशयोऽमलः ॥३६॥

evaṁ bṛhad-vrata-dharo
brāhmaṇo 'gnir iva jvalan
mad-bhaktas tīvra-tapasā
dagdha-karmāśayo 'malaḥ

evam—thus; *bṛhat-vrata*—that great vow of perpetual celibacy; *dharaḥ*—maintaining; *brāhmaṇaḥ*—a *brāhmaṇa; agniḥ*—fire; *iva*—like; *jvalan*—becoming bright; *mat-bhaktaḥ*—My devotee; *tīvra-tapasā*—by intense austerities; *dagdha*—burned; *karma*—of fruitive activities; *āśayaḥ*—the propensity or mentality; *amalaḥ*—without contamination of material desire.

TRANSLATION

A brāhmaṇa observing the great vow of celibacy becomes brilliant like fire and by serious austerity burns to ashes the propensity to perform material activities. Free from the contamination of material desire, he becomes My devotee.

PURPORT

The process of liberation is described in this verse. Once when Śrīla Prabhupāda was traveling by airplane, a fellow passenger, who happened to be a priest, told him that he had seen his disciples and found them "bright-faced." Śrīla Prabhupāda was fond of relating this incident. The spirit soul is more brilliant than the sun, and as the process of spiritual purification gradually takes effect, even the external form of a devotee becomes effulgent. The glowing fire of spiritual knowledge burns to ashes the mentality of sense gratification, and one naturally becomes austere and disinterested in mundane enjoyment. Among all austerities, the best is celibacy, by which the shackles of material life immediately become slackened. One who is *amala*, free from material desire, is known as a pure devotee of the Lord. On the paths of *jñāna, karma* and *yoga* the mind retains the concept of personal interest, but on the path of pure devotion the mind is trained to see only the interests of the Personality of Godhead. Thus a pure devotee of the Lord is *amala*, completely pure.

TEXT 37

अथानन्तरमावेक्ष्यन् यथाजिज्ञासितागमः ।
गुरवे दक्षिणां दत्त्वा स्नायाद् गुर्वनुमोदितः ॥३७॥

athānantaram āvekṣyan
yathā-jijñāsitāgamaḥ
gurave dakṣiṇāṁ dattvā
snāyād gurv-anumoditaḥ

atha—thus; *anantaram*—after that; *āvekṣyan*—desiring to enter family life; *yathā*—properly; *jijñāsita*—having studied; *āgamaḥ*—the Vedic literature; *gurave*—to the spiritual master; *dakṣiṇām*—remuneration; *dattvā*—giving; *snāyāt*—the *brahmacārī* should cleanse himself, comb his hair, put on nice clothes, etc.; *guru*—by the spiritual master; *anumoditaḥ*—permitted.

TRANSLATION

A brahmacārī who has completed his Vedic education and desires to enter household life should offer proper remuneration to the spiritual master, take bath, cut his hair, put on proper clothes, and so on, and, taking permission from the guru, should go back to his home.

PURPORT

This verse describes the process called *samāvartana*, or returning to one's home after finishing Vedic education in the *āśrama* of the spiritual master. One who cannot concentrate all of his desires in the devotional service of the Lord is attracted to householder life, and if this attraction is not regulated, one will fall down. Being covered by the ignorance of fruitive activities and mental speculation, a living entity seeks enjoyment outside the devotional service of the Supreme Lord and becomes a nondevotee. One who takes to family life must rigidly follow the Vedic rules and regulations in order to avoid the collapse of his spiritual determination. One who enjoys intimate sense gratification with women must become duplicitous in his dealings with others and consequently falls down from the platform of simple, pure life. When the mind is disturbed by lust, one begins to resent the principle of submission to the Supreme Personality of Godhead and His pure devotee, and the dark clouds of one's offensive mentality completely cover the light of spiritual knowledge. One should dovetail his propensity to love someone by serving the lotus feet of a pure devotee. As stated in Vedic literature, "One who worships Govinda, Lord Kṛṣṇa, but does not worship His devotees is not to be considered an advanced Vaiṣṇava; rather, he is to be considered a proud hypocrite."

TEXT 38

गृहं वनं वोपविशेत् प्रव्रजेद् वा द्विजोत्तमः ।
आश्रमादाश्रमं गच्छेन्नान्यथामत्परश्चरेत् ॥३८॥

gṛhaṁ vanaṁ vopaviśet
pravrajed vā dvijottamaḥ
āśramād āśramaṁ gacchen
nānyathāmat-paraś caret

gṛham—the family home; *vanam*—the forest; *vā*—either; *upaviśet*—one should enter; *pravrajet*—one should renounce; *vā*—or; *dvija-ut-tamaḥ*—a *brāhmaṇa; āśramāt*—from one authorized status of life; *āśramam*—to another authorized status; *gacchet*—one should go; *na*—not; *anyathā*—otherwise; *amat-paraḥ*—one who is not surrendered to Me; *caret*—should act.

TRANSLATION

A brahmacārī desiring to fulfill his material desires should live at home with his family, and a householder who is eager to purify his consciousness should enter the forest, whereas a purified brāhmaṇa should accept the renounced order of life. One who is not surrendered to Me should move progressively from one āśrama to another, never acting otherwise.

PURPORT

Those who are not surrendered devotees of the Lord must rigidly observe the regulations governing one's authorized social status. There are four social divisions of life, namely *brahmacarya, gṛhastha, vānaprastha* and *sannyāsa*. One who wants to fulfill material desires should become an ordinary householder (*gṛhastha*), establish a comfortable residence and maintain his family. One desiring to accelerate the process of purification may give up his home and business and live in a sacred place with his wife, as indicated here by the word *vanam*, or "forest." There are many sacred forests in India meant for this purpose, such as Vṛndāvana and Māyāpur. The word *dvijottama* indicates the *brāhmaṇas. Brāhmaṇas, kṣatriyas* and *vaiśyas* are all *dvija*, or initiated in the Gāyatrī *mantra*, but the *brāhmaṇa* is *dvijottama*, or the highest among those who have received second birth by spiritual initiation. It is recommended that a purified *brāhmaṇa* take to the renounced order of life (*sannyāsa*), giving up further contact with his so-called wife. The *brāhmaṇa* is specifically mentioned here, since *kṣatriyas* and *vaiśyas* are not to take the renounced order of life. Even so, there are many stories in the *Bhāgavatam* wherein great kings retire with their aristocratic wives to the forest to practice the austerities of *vānaprastha* and thus accelerate the process of purification. The *brāhmaṇas*, however, may directly accept the renounced order of life.

The words *āśramād āśramaṁ gacchet* indicate that one may progressively move from *brahmacārī* life to *gṛhastha* life to *vānaprastha* life and then to *sannyāsa*. The words *āśramād āśramam* emphasize that one should never remain without an authorized social status, nor should one go backward, falling down from a higher position. Those who are not surrendered devotees of the Lord must rigidly observe such injunctions, for otherwise they will quickly become degraded, and their sins will place them outside the bounds of authorized human civilization.

Lord Kṛṣṇa emphasizes here that a nondevotee must rigidly observe the rituals and regulations of Vedic social divisions, whereas the Lord's pure devotee, engaged twenty-four hours a day in Lord Kṛṣṇa's mission, is transcendental to such divisions. If, however, one performs illicit activities on the strength of being transcendental to Vedic social divisions, one is revealed to be a materialistic neophyte and not an advanced devotee of the Lord. An advanced devotee, who remains aloof from material sense gratification, is not bound by the Vedic social divisions; thus even a householder may live very austerely, traveling and preaching Kṛṣṇa consciousness away from home, and even a *sannyāsī* may sometimes engage women in the devotional service of Lord Kṛṣṇa. The most advanced devotees cannot be restricted by the rituals and regulations of the *varṇāśrama* system, and they move freely around the world distributing love of Godhead. *Mat-para* indicates a pure devotee of the Lord who always keeps the Lord fixed in his heart and consciousness. One who falls down to become a victim of sense gratification is not fully established on the platform of *mat-para* and should rigidly observe the social divisions and regulations to remain steady on the platform of pious human life.

TEXT 39

गृहार्थी सदृशीं भार्यामुद्वहेदजुगुप्सिताम् ।
यवीयसीं तु वयसा यां सवर्णामनु क्रमात् ॥३९॥

gṛhārthī sadṛśīṁ bhāryām
udvahed ajugupsitām
yavīyasīṁ tu vayasā
yaṁ sa-varṇām anu kramāt

gṛha—household; *arthī*—one who desires; *sadṛśīm*—possessing similar characteristics; *bhāryām*—a wife; *udvahet*—one should marry; *ajugupsitām*—beyond reproach; *yavīyasīm*—younger; *tu*—indeed; *vayasā*—by age; *yām*—another wife; *sa-varṇām*—the first wife who is of the same caste; *anu*—after; *kramāt*—in succession.

TRANSLATION

One who desires to establish family life should marry a wife of his own caste, who is beyond reproach and younger in age. If one desires to accept many wives he must marry them after the first marriage, and each wife should be of a successively lower caste.

PURPORT

As stated in the Vedic literature,

tisro varṇānupūrvyeṇa
dve tathaikā yathā-kramam
brāhmaṇa-kṣatriya-viśāṁ
bhāryāḥ svāḥ śūdra-janmanaḥ

The purport of this verse is that one's first wife must always be *sadṛśīm*, or similar to oneself. In other words, an intellectual man should marry an intellectual wife, a heroic man should marry a heroic wife, a business-minded man should marry a woman who can encourage him in such activities, and a *śūdra* should marry a less intelligent woman. The wife must be beyond reproach in terms of her background and character and should always be younger than oneself, ideally five to ten years younger. If one desires to marry a second wife, then, as stated in this verse by the word *varṇānupūrvyeṇa* and in the verse spoken by Lord Kṛṣṇa by the word *anukramāt,* one must wait until the first marriage is established and then select a second wife from the next-lower caste. If one marries a third time the wife must be, again, from the next-lower caste. For example, a *brāhmaṇa's* first wife will be a *brāhmaṇī,* his second wife will be from the *kṣatriya* community, his third wife from the *vaiśya* community and fourth wife from the *śūdra* community. A *kṣatriya* may first marry a *kṣatriya* lady and then *vaiśya* and *śūdra* ladies. A *vaiśya* can accept wives from two classes, and a *śūdra* will accept a wife only from the *śūdra* class. By this progression of marriages there will be relative peace in the family. These Vedic marriage injunctions, as mentioned in the previous verse, are especially for those who are not pure devotees of the Lord.

TEXT 40

इज्याध्ययनदानानि सर्वेषां च द्विजन्मनाम् ।
प्रतिग्रहोऽध्यापनं च ब्राह्मणस्यैव याजनम् ॥४०॥

ijyādhyayana-dānāni
sarveṣāṁ ca dvi-janmanām
pratigraho 'dhyāpanaṁ ca
brāhmaṇasyaiva yājanam

ijyā—sacrifice; *adhyayana*—Vedic study; *dānāni*—charity; *sarveṣām*—of all; *ca*—also; *dvi-janmanām*—those who are twice-born; *pratigrahaḥ*—acceptance of charity; *adhyāpanam*—teaching Vedic knowledge; *ca*—also; *brāhmaṇasya*—of the *brāhmaṇa; eva*—only; *yājanam*—performing sacrifices for others.

TRANSLATION

All twice-born men—brāhmaṇas, kṣatriyas and vaiśyas—must perform sacrifice, study the Vedic literature and give charity. Only

the brāhmaṇas, however, accept charity, teach the Vedic knowledge and perform sacrifice on behalf of others.

PURPORT

All civilized men must participate in sacrificial performances, give charity and study the Vedic literature. The best of the twice-born, namely the *brāhmaṇas,* are specifically empowered to lead sacrificial performances on behalf of all members of society, teach everyone Vedic knowledge and receive everyone's charity. Without the assistance or participation of qualified *brāhmaṇas,* the lower classes cannot properly study the Vedic literature, perform sacrifices or give in charity, because they do not have the required intelligence to perfectly execute such functions. When *kṣatriyas* and *vaiśyas* take shelter of bona fide *brāhmaṇas,* they are able to properly execute their respective duties, and society functions smoothly and efficiently.

TEXT 41

प्रतिग्रहं मन्यमानस्तपस्तेजोयशोनुदम् ।
अन्याभ्यामेव जीवेत शिलैर्वा दोषदृक् तयोः ॥४१॥

pratigrahaṁ manyamānas
tapas-tejo-yaśo-nudam
anyābhyām eva jīveta
śilair vā doṣa-dṛk tayoḥ

pratigraham—accepting charity; *manyamānaḥ*—considering; *tapaḥ*—of one's austerity; *tejaḥ*—spiritual influence; *yaśaḥ*—and fame; *nudam*—destruction; *anyābhyām*—by the other two (teaching Vedic knowledge and performing sacrifice); *eva*—indeed; *jīveta*—a *brāhmaṇa* should live; *śilaiḥ*—by collecting rejected grains in the field; *vā*—or; *doṣa*—the discrepancy; *dṛk*—seeing; *tayoḥ*—of those two.

TRANSLATION

A brāhmaṇa who considers that accepting charity from others will destroy his austerity, spiritual influence and fame should maintain himself by the other two brahminical occupations,

namely teaching Vedic knowledge and performing sacrifice. If the brāhmaṇa considers that those two occupations also compromise his spiritual position, then he should collect rejected grains in agricultural fields and live without any dependence on others.

PURPORT

A pure devotee of the Lord should always remember that the Supreme Personality of Godhead will personally take care of him. As the Lord states in *Bhagavad-gītā* (9.22):

ananyāś cintayanto māṁ
ye janāḥ paryupāsate
teṣāṁ nityābhiyuktānāṁ
yoga-kṣemaṁ vahāmy aham

"But those who worship Me with devotion, meditating on My transcendental form—to them I carry what they lack and preserve what they have."

A *brāhmaṇa* should not become a professional beggar for his personal maintenance. In India there are many so-called *brāhmaṇas* who sit at the gates of important temples and beg from everyone who comes and goes. If someone does not give a donation they become angry and chase that person. Similarly, in America there are many big preachers who collect huge amounts of money by begging on television and radio. If a *brāhmaṇa* or Vaiṣṇava considers that being a professional beggar is weakening his austerity, destroying his spiritual influence and giving him a bad reputation, then he should give up that process. One may beg everyone to contribute to the cause of the Supreme Personality of Godhead, but one will be diminished in austerity, influence and reputation by begging for one's personal livelihood. A *brāhmaṇa* may then take up the task of teaching Vedic knowledge and performing sacrifice. But even such occupations do not bring one to the highest platform of trust in God. A *brāhmaṇa* who teaches as a means of livelihood may often be curbed in his teaching, and one who performs sacrifice may be manipulated by materialistic worshipers. In this way, a *brāhmaṇa* may be placed in an embarrassing and compromised position. Therefore a high-class *brāhmaṇa* or Vaiṣṇava ultimately will depend completely on the mercy of the Lord for his maintenance. The Lord promises to maintain His devotee, and an advanced Vaiṣṇava never doubts the word of the Lord.

TEXT 42

ब्राह्मणस्य हि देहोऽयं क्षुद्रकामाय नेष्यते ।
कृच्छ्राय तपसे चेह प्रेत्यानन्तसुखाय च ॥४२॥

brāhmaṇasya hi deho 'yaṁ
kṣudra-kāmāya neṣyate
kṛcchrāya tapase ceha
pretyānanta-sukhāya ca

brāhmaṇasya—of a *brāhmaṇa; hi*—certainly; *dehaḥ*—body; *ayam*—this; *kṣudra*—insignificant; *kāmāya*—for sense gratification; *na*—not; *iṣyate*—is meant; *kṛcchrāya*—for difficult; *tapase*—austerities; *ca*—also; *iha*—in this world; *pretya*—after death; *ananta*—unlimited; *sukhāya*—happiness; *ca*—also.

TRANSLATION

The body of a brāhmaṇa is not intended to enjoy insignificant material sense gratification; rather, by accepting difficult austerities in his life, a brāhmaṇa will enjoy unlimited happiness after death.

PURPORT

One may ask why a *brāhmaṇa* should voluntarily accept inconvenience in keeping his body and soul together. In this verse the Lord explains that advanced human life is meant for serious austerity and not for insignificant sense gratification. By spiritual advancement one is fixed in transcendental bliss on the spiritual platform and gives up useless absorption in the temporary material body. One should remain detached from the material body, accepting only the bare necessities of life. The *brāhmaṇas*, by accepting a troublesome form of livelihood, never forget that the material body is destined to grow old, become diseased and die in misery. Thus remaining alert and transcendental, an advanced *brāhmaṇa*, at the end of this life, goes back home, back to Godhead, where he enjoys unlimited spiritual bliss. Without such higher awareness, how can one be considered a qualified *brāhmaṇa*?

Those devotees engaged twenty-four hours a day in spreading the mission of Lord Kṛṣṇa are beyond the platform of renunciation or sense gratification because they engage everything in Lord Kṛṣṇa's service. A pure devotee of the Lord eats only to get strength for serving the Lord and does not accept either sumptuous or meager food simply for the body's sake. However, everything may be accepted for the Lord, even sumptuous meals. A *brāhmaṇa* who is not working day and night to spread the glories of the Lord should feel embarrassed to eat sumptuously for his personal sense gratification, but a renounced Vaiṣṇava preacher may accept invitations from all classes of pious people, and just to bless their homes he will eat the opulent foods they offer to him. Similarly, he sometimes eats sumptuously to get strength for defeating atheists and impersonalists. As stated in Vedic literature, one cannot be a highly qualified *brāhmaṇa* unless one becomes a devotee of the Lord. And among the devotees, those who are preaching Kṛṣṇa consciousness are the best, as confirmed by the Lord Himself in the Eighteenth Chapter of *Bhagavad-gītā.*

TEXT 43

शिलोञ्छवृत्त्या परितुष्टचित्तो
धर्मं महान्तं विरजं जुषाणः ।
मय्यर्पितात्मा गृह एव तिष्ठ-
न्नातिप्रसक्तः समुपैति शान्तिम् ॥४३॥

śiloñcha-vṛttyā parituṣṭa-citto
dharmaṁ mahāntaṁ virajaṁ juṣāṇaḥ
mayy arpitātmā gṛha eva tiṣṭhan
nāti-prasaktaḥ samupaiti śāntim

śila-uñcha—of gleaning grains; *vṛttyā*—by the occupation; *parituṣṭa*—fully satisfied; *cittaḥ*—whose consciousness; *dharmam*—religious principles; *mahāntam*—magnanimous and hospitable; *virajam*—

purified of material desire; *juṣāṇaḥ*—cultivating; *mayi*—in Me; *arpita*—dedicated; *ātmā*—whose mind; *gṛhe*—at home; *eva*—even; *tiṣṭhan*—remaining; *na*—not; *ati*—very; *prasaktaḥ*—attached; *samupaiti*—achieves; *śāntim*—liberation.

TRANSLATION

A brāhmaṇa householder should remain satisfied in mind by gleaning rejected grains from agricultural fields and marketplaces. Keeping himself free of personal desire, he should practice magnanimous religious principles, with consciousness absorbed in Me. In this way a brāhmaṇa may stay at home as a householder without very much attachment and thus achieve liberation.

PURPORT

Mahāntam refers to magnanimous religious principles such as very hospitably receiving guests, even those who are uninvited and unexpected. Householders must always be magnanimous and charitable to others, being alert to curb unnecessary affection and attachment in family life. In the past, very renounced *brāhmaṇa* householders would collect grains that had fallen on the ground in the marketplace or those that had been left behind in the fields after harvesting. The most important item here is *mayy arpitātmā*, or fixing the mind in Lord Kṛṣṇa. Despite his material situation, anyone who constantly meditates upon the Lord can become a liberated soul. As stated in *Bhakti-rasāmṛta-sindhu* (1.2.187),

īhā yasya harer dāsye
karmaṇā manasā girā
nikhilāsv api avasthāsu
jīvan-muktaḥ sa ucyate

"A person acting in Kṛṣṇa consciousness [or, in other words, in the service of Kṛṣṇa] with his body, mind, intelligence and words is a liberated person, even within the material world, although he may be engaged in many so-called material activities."

TEXT 44

समुद्धरन्ति ये विप्रं सीदन्तं मत्परायणम् ।
तानुद्धरिष्ये नचिरादापद्भ्यो नौरिवार्णवात् ॥४४॥

samuddharanti ye vipraṁ
sīdantaṁ mat-parāyaṇam
tān uddhariṣye na cirād
āpadbhyo naur ivārṇavāt

samuddharanti—uplift; *ye*—those who; *vipram*—a *brāhmaṇa* or devotee; *sīdantam*—suffering (from poverty); *mat-parāyaṇam*—surrendered to Me; *tān*—those who have uplifted; *uddhariṣye*—I will uplift; *na cirāt*—in the near future; *āpadbhyaḥ*—from all miseries; *nauḥ*—a boat; *iva*—like; *arṇavāt*—from the ocean.

TRANSLATION

Just as a ship rescues those who have fallen into the ocean, similarly, I very quickly rescue from all calamities those persons who uplift brāhmaṇas and devotees suffering in a poverty-stricken condition.

PURPORT

The Lord has described how *brāhmaṇas* and devotees achieve the perfection of life, and now a similar perfection is offered to those who utilize their materialistic wealth to relieve the poverty-stricken condition of devotees and *brāhmaṇas.* Although one may neglect the devotional service of the Lord to pursue a material life of sense gratification, one can rectify one's position by dedicating one's hard-earned money to the service of the Lord. Seeing the difficult austerities accepted by saintly persons, a pious person should make arrangements for their comfort. Just as a boat saves hopeless people who have fallen into the ocean, similarly, the Lord uplifts persons who have hopelessly fallen into the ocean of material attachment if they have been charitable to the *brāhmaṇas* and devotees.

TEXT 45

सर्वाः समुद्धरेद् राजा पितेव व्यसनात् प्रजाः ।
आत्मानमात्मना धीरो यथा गजपतिर्गजान् ॥४५॥

sarvāḥ samuddhared rājā
piteva vyasanāt prajāḥ
ātmānam ātmanā dhīro
yathā gaja-patir gajān

sarvāḥ—all; *samuddharet*—must uplift; *rājā*—the king; *pitā*—a father; *iva*—like; *vyasanāt*—from difficulties; *prajāḥ*—the citizens; *ātmānam*—himself; *ātmanā*—by himself; *dhīraḥ*—fearless; *yathā*—just as; *gaja-patiḥ*—a bull elephant; *gajān*—the other elephants.

TRANSLATION

Just as the chief bull elephant protects all other elephants in his herd and defends himself as well, similarly, a fearless king, just like a father, must save all of the citizens from difficulty and also protect himself.

PURPORT

Lord Kṛṣṇa, having concluded His discussion of brahminical duties, now describes the character and activities of a king. Protecting all of the citizens from difficulty is an essential duty for the king.

TEXT 46

एवंविधो नरपतिर्विमानेनार्कवर्चसा ।
विधूयेहाशुभं कृत्स्नमिन्द्रेण सह मोदते ॥४६॥

evaṁ-vidho nara-patir
vimānenārka-varcasā
vidhūyehāśubhaṁ kṛtsnam
indreṇa saha modate

evam-vidhaḥ—thus (protecting himself and the citizens); *nara-patiḥ*—the king; *vimānena*—with an airplane; *arka-varcasā*—as brilliant as the sun; *vidhūya*—removing; *iha*—on the earth; *aśubham*—sins; *kṛtsnam*—all; *indreṇa*—Lord Indra; *saha*—with; *modate*—he enjoys.

TRANSLATION

An earthly king who protects himself and all citizens by removing all sins from his kingdom will certainly enjoy with Lord Indra in airplanes as brilliant as the sun.

TEXT 47

सीदन् विप्रो वणिग्वृत्त्या पण्यैरेवापदं तरेत् ।
खड्गेन वापदाक्रान्तो न श्ववृत्त्या कथञ्चन ॥४७॥

sīdan vipro vaṇig-vṛttyā
paṇyair evāpadaṁ taret
khaḍgena vāpadākrānto
na śva-vṛttyā kathañcana

sīdan—suffering; *vipraḥ*—a *brāhmaṇa; vaṇik*—of a merchant; *vṛttyā*—by the occupation; *paṇyaiḥ*—by doing business; *eva*—indeed; *āpadam*—suffering; *taret*—should overcome; *khaḍgena*—with sword; *vā*—or; *āpadā*—by suffering; *ākrāntaḥ*—afflicted; *na*—not; *śva*—of the dog; *vṛttyā*—by the occupation; *kathañcana*—by any means.

TRANSLATION

If a brāhmaṇa cannot support himself through his regular duties and is thus suffering, he may adopt the occupation of a merchant and overcome his destitute condition by buying and selling material things. If he continues to suffer extreme poverty even as a merchant, then he may adopt the occupation of a kṣatriya, taking sword in hand. But he cannot in any circumstances become like a dog, accepting an ordinary master.

PURPORT

Śva-vṛttyā, or "a dog's profession," refers to the *śūdras*, who cannot live without accepting a master. A destitute *brāhmaṇa* who is suffering intolerably may become a merchant and then a *kṣatriya* but may never take the position of a *śūdra* by working in a company or accepting a master. Although a *kṣatriya* is ordinarily considered more elevated than a *vaiśya*, the Lord here recommends that distressed *brāhmaṇas* first accept the *vaiśya* occupation, since it is not violent.

TEXT 48

वैश्यवृत्त्या तु राजन्यो जीवेन्मृगययापदि ।
चरेद् वा विप्ररूपेण न श्ववृत्त्या कथञ्चन ॥४८॥

vaiśya-vṛttyā tu rājanyo
jīven mṛgayayāpadi
cared vā vipra-rūpeṇa
na śva-vṛttyā kathañcana

vaiśya—of the mercantile class; *vṛttyā*—by the occupation; *tu*—indeed; *rājanyaḥ*—a king; *jīvet*—may maintain himself; *mṛgayayā*—by hunting; *āpadi*—in an emergency or disastrous situation; *caret*—may act; *vā*—or; *vipra-rūpeṇa*—in the form of a *brāhmaṇa; na*—never; *śva*—of the dog; *vṛttyā*—by the profession; *kathañcana*—in any circumstance.

TRANSLATION

A king or other member of the royal order who cannot maintain himself by his normal occupation may act as a vaiśya, may live by hunting or may act as a brāhmaṇa by teaching others Vedic knowledge. But he may not under any circumstances adopt the profession of a śūdra.

TEXT 49

शूद्रवृत्तिं भजेद् वैश्यः शूद्रः कारुकटक्रियाम् ।
कृच्छ्रान्मुक्तो न गर्ह्येण वृत्तिं लिप्सेत कर्मणा ॥४९॥

śūdra-vṛttiṁ bhajed vaiśyaḥ
śūdraḥ kāru-kaṭa-kriyām

kṛcchrān mukto na garhyeṇa
vṛttiṁ lipseta karmaṇā

śūdra—of the *śūdras; vṛttim*—occupation; *bhajet*—may accept; *vaiśyaḥ*—a *vaiśya; śūdraḥ*—a *śūdra; kāru*—of the artisan; *kaṭa*—straw baskets and mats; *kriyām*—making; *kṛcchrāt*—from the difficult situation; *muktaḥ*—freed; *na*—not; *garhyeṇa*—by that which is inferior; *vṛttim*—livelihood; *lipseta*—one should desire; *karmaṇā*—by work.

TRANSLATION

A vaiśya, or mercantile man, who cannot maintain himself may adopt the occupation of a śūdra, and a śūdra who cannot find a master can engage in simple activities like making baskets and mats of straw. However, all members of society who have adopted inferior occupations in emergency situations must give up those substitute occupations when the difficulties have passed.

TEXT 50

वेदाध्यायस्वधास्वाहाबल्यन्नाद्यैर्यथोदयम् ।
देवर्षिपितृभूतानि मद्रूपाण्यन्वहं यजेत् ॥५०॥

vedādhyāya-svadhā-svāhā-
baly-annādyair yathodayam
devarṣi-pitṛ-bhūtāni
mad-rūpāṇy anv-ahaṁ yajet

veda-adhyāya—by study of Vedic knowledge; *svadhā*—by offering the *mantra svadhā; svāhā*—by offering the *mantra svāhā; bali*—by token offerings of food; *anna-ādyaiḥ*—by offering grains, water, etc.; *yathā*—according to; *udayam*—one's prosperity; *deva*—the demigods; *ṛṣi*—sages; *pitṛ*—the forefathers; *bhūtāni*—and all living entities; *mat-rūpāṇi*—manifestations of My potency; *anu-aham*—daily; *yajet*—one should worship.

TRANSLATION

Those in the gṛhastha order of life should daily worship the sages by Vedic study, the forefathers by offering the mantra

svadhā, the demigods by chanting svāhā, all living entities by offering shares of one's meals, and human beings by offering grains and water. Thus considering the demigods, sages, forefathers, living entities and human beings to be manifestations of My potency, one should daily perform these five sacrifices.

PURPORT

The Lord again discusses the duties of those in the household order of life. Obviously, the five ritualistic daily sacrifices mentioned here are meant for those who are not pure devotees of the Lord and who thus have to counteract their exploitation of material nature by the abovementioned sacrifices. The International Society for Krishna Consciousness (ISKCON) is training householders, *sannyāsīs*, *brahmacārīs* and *vānaprasthas* to engage twenty-four hours a day in the loving service of the Lord. Those who are full-time missionary workers in ISKCON have no further obligations or sacrifices to perform, as confirmed in the Eleventh Canto of *Śrīmad-Bhāgavatam* (11.5.41):

devarṣi-bhūtāpta-nṛṇāṁ pitṝṇāṁ
na kiṅkaro nāyam ṛṇī ca rājan
sarvātmanā yaḥ śaraṇaṁ śaraṇyaṁ
gato mukundaṁ parihṛtya kartam

"Anyone who has taken shelter at the lotus feet of Mukunda, the giver of liberation, giving up all kinds of obligation, and has taken to the path in all seriousness, owes neither duties nor obligations to the demigods, sages, general living entities, family members, humankind or forefathers."

TEXT 51

यदृच्छयोपपन्नेन शुक्लेनोपार्जितेन वा ।
धनेनापीडयन् भृत्यान् न्यायेनैवाहरेत् क्रतून् ॥५१॥

yadṛcchayopapannena
śuklenopārjitena vā
dhanenāpīḍayan bhṛtyān
nyāyenaivāharet kratūn

yadṛcchayā—without endeavor; *upapannena*—which is acquired; *śuklena*—by one's honest occupation; *upārjitena*—acquired; *vā*—or; *dhanena*—with money; *apīḍayan*—not subjecting to discomfort; *bhṛtyān*—dependents; *nyāyena*—properly; *eva*—indeed; *āharet*—one should perform; *kratūn*—sacrifices and other religious ceremonies.

TRANSLATION

A householder should comfortably maintain his dependents either with money that comes of its own accord or with that gathered by honest execution of one's duties. According to one's means, one should perform sacrifices and other religious ceremonies.

PURPORT

The Lord here describes the religious duties that are to be performed as far as possible, according to one's means, and when there is opportunity.

TEXT 52

कुटुम्बेषु न सज्जेत न प्रमाद्येत् कुटुम्ब्यपि ।
विपश्चिन्नश्वरं पश्येददृष्टमपि दृष्टवत् ॥५२॥

kuṭumbeṣu na sajjeta
na pramādyet kuṭumby api
vipaścin naśvaraṁ paśyed
adṛṣṭam api dṛṣṭa-vat

kuṭumbeṣu—to the family members; *na*—not; *sajjeta*—one should be attached; *na*—not; *pramādyet*—should become crazy; *kuṭumbī*—having many dependent family members; *api*—although; *vipaścit*—a wise person; *naśvaram*—temporary; *paśyet*—should see; *adṛṣṭam*—future rewards such as residence in heaven; *api*—indeed; *dṛṣṭa-vat*—just like that which is already experienced.

TRANSLATION

A householder taking care of many dependent family members should not become materially attached to them, nor should he become mentally unbalanced, considering himself to be the lord. An

intelligent householder should see that all possible future happiness, just like that which he has already experienced, is temporary.

PURPORT

A family man often acts like a lord, protecting his wife, ordering his children, maintaining servants, grandchildren, domestic animals, and so forth. The words *na pramādyet kuṭumby api* indicate that although one acts like a little lord, surrounded by his family, servants and friends, one should not, through false pride, become mentally unbalanced, considering oneself to be the actual lord. The word *vipaścit* indicates that one should remain sober and intelligent, never forgetting oneself to be the eternal servant of the Supreme Lord.

Householders of the upper, middle and lower classes become attached to different types of sense gratification. In any economic or social class, however, one should remember that all material enjoyment, either here or in the next life, is temporary and ultimately useless. A responsible householder should guide his family members and other dependents back home, back to Godhead, for an eternal life of bliss and knowledge. One should not become a false and puffed-up lord for a brief span of time, for then one will remain bound up, along with his family members, in the cycle of repeated birth and death.

TEXT 53

पुत्रदाराप्तबन्धूनां सङ्गमः पान्थसङ्गमः ।
अनुदेहं वियन्त्येते स्वप्नो निद्रानुगो यथा ॥५३॥

putra-dārāpta-bandhūnāṁ
saṅgamaḥ pāntha-saṅgamaḥ
anu-dehaṁ viyanty ete
svapno nidrānugo yathā

putra—of children; *dāra*—wife; *āpta*—relatives; *bandhūnām*—and friends; *saṅgamaḥ*—the association, living together; *pāntha*—of travelers; *saṅgamaḥ*—association; *anu-deham*—with each change of body; *viyanti*—they are separated; *ete*—all these; *svapnaḥ*—a dream; *nidrā*—in sleep; *anugaḥ*—occurring; *yathā*—just as.

TRANSLATION

The association of children, wife, relatives and friends is just like the brief meeting of travelers. With each change of body one is separated from all such associates, just as one loses the objects one possesses in a dream when the dream is over.

PURPORT

Pāntha-saṅgama indicates the momentary association of travelers at hotels, restaurants, tourist spots or, in more traditional cultures, fresh-water wells and walking paths. We are now associated with many relatives, friends and well-wishers, but as soon as we change our material body we will immediately be separated from all these associates, just as upon awakening we are immediately separated from the imaginary situation of a dream. One becomes attached to the sense gratification of one's dream, and similarly, under the spell of the illusory concepts of "I" and "mine," we become attached to so-called relatives and friends who gratify our sense of false ego. Unfortunately, such fleeting egoistic association covers our real knowledge of the self and the Supreme, and we remain hovering in material illusion, futilely endeavoring for permanent sense gratification. One who remains attached to the bodily concept of family and friends cannot possibly give up the false egoism of "I" and "mine," or "I am everything and everything is mine."

Without giving up material sense gratification we cannot become steady on the transcendental platform of devotional service, and therefore we cannot relish the actual flavor of eternal happiness. Unless one becomes a pure devotee of the Lord, accepting Lord Kṛṣṇa as one's only friend, one cannot give up the hankering for temporary and superficial material relationships. A traveler far away from his home and loved ones may strike up superficial conversations with other travelers, but such relationships have no ultimate meaning. One should therefore revive one's lost relationship with Lord Kṛṣṇa. We are constitutionally part and parcel of Lord Kṛṣṇa, who is the reservoir of all spiritual pleasure, and our original relationship with Him is full of love and happiness. But because of our desire to enjoy independently from Him, we fall down into the confusing, meaningless network of material relationships created by *māyā*. An intelligent person realizes there is no actual pleasure or satisfaction for the soul on either this planet or any other material planet. Therefore, like a weary traveler exhausted from his journey, he should go back home, back to Godhead, for eternal peace as the faithful servant of Lord Śrī Kṛṣṇa.

TEXT 54

इत्थं परिमृशन्मुक्तो गृहेष्वतिथिवद् वसन् ।
न गृहैरनुबध्येत निर्ममो निरहङ्कृतः ॥५४॥

itthaṁ parimṛśan mukto
gṛheṣv atithi-vad vasan
na gṛhair anubadhyeta
nirmamo nirahaṅkṛtaḥ

ittham—thus; *parimṛśan*—deeply considering; *muktaḥ*—a liberated soul; *gṛheṣu*—at home; *atithi-vat*—just like a guest; *vasan*—living; *na*—not; *gṛhaiḥ*—by the domestic situation; *anubadhyeta*—should become bound; *nirmamaḥ*—without any sense of personal proprietorship; *nirahaṅkṛtaḥ*—without false ego.

TRANSLATION

Deeply considering the actual situation, a liberated soul should live at home just like a guest, without any sense of proprietorship or false ego. In this way he will not be bound or entangled by domestic affairs.

PURPORT

The word *mukta*, or "liberated," refers to one freed from all material attachment. In this status, called *mukta-saṅga*, one no longer identifies oneself as a permanent resident of the material world. This liberated status may be attained even by one situated in family life. The only requirement is that one should take up a serious program of *kṛṣṇa-saṅkīrtana*, which includes constant chanting of the holy names of the Lord, worship of the Deity and participation in the Kṛṣṇa consciousness movement. Without a serious program of *kṛṣṇa-saṅkīrtana* it is very difficult to give up the iron shackles of attachment to women and the byproducts of such attachment.

TEXT 55

कर्मभिर्गृहमेधीयैरिष्ट्वा मामेव भक्तिमान् ।
तिष्ठेद् वनं वोपविशेत् प्रजावान् वा परिव्रजेत् ॥५५॥

karmabhir gṛha-medhīyair
iṣṭvā mām eva bhaktimān
tiṣṭhed vanaṁ vopaviśet
prajāvān vā parivrajet

karmabhiḥ—by activities; *gṛha-medhīyaiḥ*—suitable for family life; *iṣṭvā*—worshiping; *mām*—Me; *eva*—indeed; *bhakti-mān*—being a devotee; *tiṣṭhet*—one may remain at home; *vanam*—the forest; *vā*—or; *upaviśet*—may enter; *prajā-vān*—having responsible children; *vā*—or; *parivrajet*—may take *sannyāsa.*

TRANSLATION

A householder devotee who worships Me by execution of his family duties may remain at home, go to a holy place or, having a responsible son, may take sannyāsa.

PURPORT

This verse describes the three alternatives for a householder. He may continue at home, or he may take *vānaprastha*, which involves going to a sacred place with one's wife. Or if he has a responsible son to take over his family duties, he may take *sannyāsa*, the renounced order, for a definitive solution to the problems of life. In all three *āśramas*, ultimate success depends on sincere surrender to the Supreme Lord; therefore, the most important qualification one can have is Kṛṣṇa consciousness.

TEXT 56

यस्त्वासक्तमतिर्गेहे पुत्रवित्तैषणातुरः ।
स्त्रैणः कृपणधीर्मूढो ममाहमिति बध्यते ॥५६॥

yas tv āsakta-matir gehe
putra-vittaiṣaṇāturaḥ

strainaḥ kṛpaṇa-dhīr mūḍho
mamāham iti badhyate

yaḥ—one who; *tu*—however; *āsakta*—attached; *matiḥ*—whose consciousness; *gehe*—to his home; *putra*—for children; *vitta*—and money; *eṣaṇa*—by ardent desire; *āturaḥ*—disturbed; *strainaḥ*—lusty to enjoy women; *kṛpaṇa*—miserly; *dhīḥ*—whose mentality; *mūḍhaḥ*—unintelligent; *mama*—everything is mine; *aham*—I am everything; *iti*—thus thinking; *badhyate*—is bound.

TRANSLATION

But a householder whose mind is attached to his home and who is thus disturbed by ardent desires to enjoy his money and children, who is lusty after women, who is possessed of a miserly mentality and who unintelligently thinks, "Everything is mine and I am everything," is certainly bound in illusion.

PURPORT

Although one may try by various analytical or psychological processes to detach the mind from illusory family attachment, one will inevitably be drawn back into the network of material attachment unless the heart is purified by Kṛṣṇa consciousness. A miserly householder thinks only of his own family or community, without mercy for outsiders. Being egoistic, lusty, attached and always disturbed by ardent desires to enjoy money and children, a materialistic householder is hopelessly bound in a web of anxiety.

TEXT 57

अहो मे पितरौ वृद्धौ भार्या बालात्मजात्मजाः ।
अनाथा मामृते दीनाः कथं जीवन्ति दुःखिताः ॥५७॥

aho me pitarau vṛddhau
bhāryā bālātmajātmajāḥ
anāthā mām ṛte dīnāḥ
kathaṁ jīvanti duḥkhitāḥ

aho—alas; *me*—my; *pitarau*—parents; *vṛddhau*—elderly; *bhāryā*—wife; *bāla-ātma-jā*—having a mere infant in her arms; *ātma-jāḥ*—and my other young children; *anāthāḥ*—with no one to protect them; *mām*—me; *ṛte*—without; *dīnāḥ*—wretched; *katham*—how in the world; *jīvanti*—can they live; *duḥkhitāḥ*—suffering greatly.

TRANSLATION

"O my poor elderly parents, and my wife with a mere infant in her arms, and my other young children! Without me they have absolutely no one to protect them and will suffer unbearably. How can my poor relatives possibly live without me?"

TEXT 58

एवं गृहाशयाक्षिप्तहृदयो मूढधीरयम् ।
अतृप्तस्ताननुध्यायन् मृतोऽन्धं विशते तमः ॥५८॥

evaṁ gṛhāśayākṣipta-
hṛdayo mūḍha-dhīr ayam
atṛptas tān anudhyāyan
mṛto 'ndhaṁ viśate tamaḥ

evam—thus; *gṛha*—in his domestic situation; *āśaya*—by intense desire; *ākṣipta*—overwhelmed; *hṛdayaḥ*—his heart; *mūḍha*—unintelligent; *dhīḥ*—whose point of view; *ayam*—this person; *atṛptaḥ*—unsatisfied; *tān*—them (family members); *anudhyāyan*—constantly thinking of; *mṛtaḥ*—he dies; *andham*—blindness; *viśate*—enters; *tamaḥ*—darkness.

TRANSLATION

Thus, because of his foolish mentality, a householder whose heart is overwhelmed by family attachment is never satisfied. Constantly meditating on his relatives, he dies and enters into the darkness of ignorance.

PURPORT

Andhaṁ viśate tamaḥ indicates that in his next life an attached householder will certainly be degraded because of his primitive mentality of bodily attachment, which is called *mūḍha-dhī*. In other words, after enjoying the sense gratification of considering oneself the center of everything, one enters into a lower species of life. Somehow or other, we must fix our minds on Lord Kṛṣṇa and come out of the darkness of ignorance to our real life in Kṛṣṇa consciousness.

Thus end the purports of the humble servants of His Divine Grace A. C. Bhaktivedanta Swami Prabhupāda to the Eleventh Canto, Seventeenth Chapter, of the Śrīmad-Bhāgavatam, *entitled "Lord Kṛṣṇa's Description of the Varṇāśrama System."*

Appendixes

The Author

His Divine Grace Śrīla Hridayananda dāsa Goswami Ācāryadeva is one of the foremost spiritual leaders of the International Society for Krishna Consciousness. He enjoys the unique status of being among the first Western-born members of the authorized chain of disciplic succession descending from the Supreme Lord, Kṛṣṇa. In modern times, the most essential task of Kṛṣṇa conscious spiritual masters has been to translate the Vedic scriptures of ancient India into modern languages and distribute them widely throughout the world. Śrīla Ācāryadeva has made this mission his life and soul.

Śrīla Ācāryadeva appeared in this world on November 5, 1948, in Los Angeles, California. As an academically gifted student at the University of California, Berkeley, he attended a talk given by His Divine Grace A. C. Bhaktivedanta Swami Prabhupāda, the founder and spiritual master of the Kṛṣṇa consciousness movement. Impressed by Śrīla Prabhupāda's scholarship and saintliness, Śrīla Ācāryadeva became a member of the Kṛṣṇa consciousness community in Berkeley and, shortly thereafter, on February 8, 1970, was initiated as Śrīla Prabhupāda's disciple.

From the beginning, Śrīla Ācāryadeva distinguished himself by his oratorical skills, his spiritual dedication and his devotion to studying the writings of his spiritual master, through which he acquired a deep knowledge of Sanskrit. He quickly gained recognition from Śrīla Prabhupāda himself, who marked him as "a literary man" and in 1970 sent him to Boston to accept responsibilities with ISKCON's publishing activities there. Later, Śrīla Ācāryadeva served as president in ISKCON's center in Gainesville, Florida, and Houston, Texas, and made a significant contribution to the rapid expansion of the Kṛṣṇa consciousness movement there in the early 1970s. In 1972, he adopted the renounced order (*sannyāsa*) in order to fully dedicate himself to serving the mission of his spiritual master: the propagation of the Kṛṣṇa consciousness movement throughout the world. For the next two years he traveled widely, speaking at colleges and universities throughout the United States.

In 1974, Śrīla Ācāryadeva was appointed to the Governing Body Commission of ISKCON and entrusted with the development of the Kṛṣṇa consciousness movement in Latin America. Over the following three years, he established twenty-five centers of the Society and attracted thousands of Latin Americans to the movement, as predicted by Śrīla Prabhupāda himself. In the course of his travels he met with numerous heads of state, government ministers and high religious leaders, conversing with them in fluent Spanish and Portuguese. He also founded the Spanish and Portuguese language divisions of the Bhaktivedanta Book Trust for the translation and publication of Śrīla Prabhupāda's books. At present, more than 20 million books in these two languages have been distributed throughout Latin America and abroad.

Shortly before his departure from this world in November, 1977, His Divine Grace Śrīla Prabhupāda chose Śrīla Ācāryadeva, along with ten other senior disciples, to accept the role of spiritual master and to initiate disciples. Currently, Śrīla Ācāryadeva serves as the Governing Body Commissioner for Brazil and the state of Florida and as one of the initiating spiritual masters for Latin America and the southern United States. His most challenging assignment came, however, in 1979 when the leaders of ISKCON, in recognition of his devotional scholarship, commissioned him to complete Śrīla Prabhupāda's monumental translation of and commentary on the *Śrīmad-Bhāgavatam.* For thousands of years in India, great spiritual masters have presented commentaries on the *Bhāgavatam* to make its urgent message clear to the people of their times. Śrīla Ācāryadeva is the first Westerner to be entrusted with this demanding task, and his success in communicating the essence of India's spiritual heritage to modern readers has already been noted by scholars and religionists around the world.

His Divine Grace
A. C. Bhaktivedanta Swami Prabhupāda

His Divine Grace A. C. Bhaktivedanta Swami Prabhupāda appeared in this world in 1896 in Calcutta, India. He first met his spiritual master, Śrīla Bhaktisiddhānta Sarasvatī Gosvāmī, in Calcutta in 1922. Bhaktisiddhānta Sarasvatī, a prominent religious scholar and the founder of sixty-four Gauḍīya Maṭhas (Vedic institutes), liked this educated young man and convinced him to dedicate his life to teaching Vedic knowledge. Śrīla Prabhupāda became his student, and eleven years later (1933) at Allahabad he became his formally initiated disciple.

At their first meeting, in 1922, Śrīla Bhaktisiddhānta Sarasvatī Ṭhākura requested Śrīla Prabhupāda to broadcast Vedic knowledge through the English language. In the years that followed, Śrīla Prabhupāda wrote a commentary on the *Bhagavad-gītā*, assisted the Gauḍīya Maṭha in its work and, in 1944, without assistance, started *Back to Godhead*, an English fortnightly magazine, edited it, typed the manuscripts and checked the galley proofs. He even distributed the individual copies and struggled to maintain the publication. Once begun, the magazine never stopped; it is now being continued by his disciples in the West and is published in over thirty languages.

Recognizing Śrīla Prabhupāda's philosophical learning and devotion, the Gauḍīya Vaiṣṇava Society honored him in 1947 with the title "Bhaktivedanta." In 1950, at the age of fifty-four, Śrīla Prabhupāda retired from married life, adopting the *vānaprastha* (retired) order to devote more time to his studies and writing. Śrīla Prabhupāda traveled to the holy city of Vṛndāvana, where he lived in very humble circumstances in the historic medieval temple of Rādhā-Dāmodara. There he engaged for several years in deep study and writing. He accepted the renounced order of life (*sannyāsa*) in 1959. At Rādhā-Dāmodara, Śrīla Prabhupāda began work on his life's masterpiece: a multivolume translation of and commentary on the eighteen-thousand-verse *Śrīmad-Bhāgavatam* (*Bhāgavata Purāṇa*). He also wrote *Easy Journey to Other Planets*.

After publishing three volumes of the *Bhāgavatam*, Śrīla Prabhupāda came to the United States, in 1965, to fulfill the mission of his spiritual master. Subsequently, His Divine Grace wrote more than sixty volumes of authoritative translations, commentaries and summary studies of the philosophical and religious classics of India.

In 1965, when he first arrived by freighter in New York City, Śrīla Prabhupāda was practically penniless. It was after almost a year of great difficulty that he established the International Society for Krishna Consciousness in July of 1966. Before his passing away on November 14, 1977, he guided the Society and saw it grow to a worldwide confederation of more than one hundred *āśramas*, schools, temples, institutes and farm communities.

In 1968, Śrīla Prabhupāda created New Vrindaban, an experimental Vedic community in the hills of West Virginia. Inspired by the success of New Vrindaban, now a thriving farm community of more than two thousand acres, his students have since founded several similar communities in the United States and abroad.

In 1972, His Divine Grace introduced the Vedic system of primary and secondary education in the West by founding the Gurukula school in Dallas, Texas. Since then, under his supervision, his disciples have established children's schools throughout the United States and the rest of the world, with the principal educational center now located in Vṛndāvana, India.

Śrīla Prabhupāda also inspired the construction of several large international cultural centers in India. The center at Śrīdhāma Māyāpur in West Bengal is the site for a planned spiritual city, an ambitious project for which construction will extend over the next decade. In Vṛndāvana, India, is the magnificent Kṛṣṇa-Balarāma Temple and International Guesthouse. There is also a major cultural and educational center in Bombay. Other centers are planned in a dozen other important locations on the Indian subcontinent.

Śrīla Prabhupāda's most significant contribution, however, is his books. Highly respected by the academic community for their authoritativeness, depth and clarity, they are used as standard textbooks in numerous college courses. His writings have been translated into over thirty languages. The Bhaktivedanta Book Trust, established in 1972 exclusively to publish the works of His Divine Grace, has thus become the world's largest publisher of books in the field of Indian religion and philosophy.

In just twelve years, in spite of his advanced age, Śrīla Prabhupāda circled the globe fourteen times on lecture tours that took him to six continents. In spite of such a vigorous schedule, Śrīla Prabhupāda continued to write prolifically. His writings constitute a veritable library of Vedic philosophy, religion, literature and culture.

References

The purports of *Śrīmad-Bhāgavatam* are all confirmed by standard Vedic authorities. The following authentic scriptures are specifically cited in this volume. For specific page references, consult the general index.

Bhagavad-gītā

Bhakti-sandarbha

Brahma-saṁhitā

Kāla-saṁhitā

Kṛṣṇa, the Supreme Personality of Godhead

Mahābhārata

Manu-saṁhitā

Nectar of Devotion

Pañcarātra

Prakāśa-saṁhitā

Ṛg Veda

Sāma Veda

Saṅkalpa-kalpadruma

Śrī Gaurāṅga-smaraṇa-maṅgala

Śrī Govinda-līlāmṛta

Śrī Īśopaniṣad

Śrī Kṛṣṇa-bhāvanāmṛta

Śrīmad-Bhāgavatam

Śvetāśvatara Upaniṣad

Tantra-bhāgavata

Upadeśāmṛta

Upaniṣads

Varāha Purāṇa

Vāyu Purāṇa

Viṣṇu Purāṇa

Viveka

Yajur Veda

Glossary

A

Ācārya—a spiritual master who teaches by example.
A. C. Bhaktivedanta Swami Prabhupāda. *See:* Prabhupāda, Śrīla
Aditi—the mother of the demigods.
Agni-hotra sacrifice—fire sacrifice.
Akrūra—an uncle of Lord Kṛṣṇa.
Anantadeva—an incarnation of the Supreme Lord in the form of a many-headed serpent.
Apsarās—beautiful women of the heavenly planets, expert at dancing.
Arjuna—Lord Kṛṣṇa's friend and devotee, to whom He spoke *Bhagavad-gītā.*
Aṣṭāṅga-yoga—the eight-step process of mystic meditation taught by Patañjali.
Avadhūta brāhmaṇa—a spiritually advanced sage who transcends social and religious conventions.

B

Baladeva (Balarāma)—Lord Kṛṣṇa's primary expansion; appears in Kṛṣṇa's eternal pastimes as His brother.
Bhagavad-gītā—the basic directions for spiritual life spoken by the Lord Himself.
Bhagavān—the Lord as the possessor of all opulences.
Bhakti—devotional service to the Supreme Lord, Kṛṣṇa.
Bhaktisiddhānta Sarasvatī Ṭhākura—the spiritual master of His Divine Grace A. C. Bhaktivedanta Swami Prabhupāda.
Bhaktivinoda Ṭhākura—a Vaiṣṇava spiritual master, father of Bhaktisiddhānta Sarasvatī; he started the movement to spread Kṛṣṇa consciousness in the West.
Bhavānanda Goswami—a leading disciple of ISKCON's founder-*ācārya,* Śrīla Prabhupāda; one of the current initiating spiritual masters of ISKCON.
Bhīṣmadeva—a great devotee and senior family member of the Kuru dynasty.
Brahmā, Lord—the first created being; chief of the demigods and creator of the universe.

Brahmaloka—the abode of Lord Brahmā, in the highest planetary system of the material universe.

Brāhma-muhūrta—a period of time just before dawn that is especially favorable for spiritual practices.

Brahman—the all-pervading impersonal aspect of Kṛṣṇa.

Brāhmaṇa—the intelligent class of men, according to the system of social and spiritual orders.

Brahma-saṁhitā—a very ancient Sanskrit scripture recording the prayers of Brahmā to the Supreme Lord, Govinda.

Brahma-sūtra—another name for the *Vedānta-sūtra.*

Bṛhaspati—the spiritual master of the demigods.

C

Caitanya Mahāprabhu—the incarnation of Kṛṣṇa who appeared in India five hundred years ago to propagate the congregational chanting of the Hare Kṛṣṇa *mantra.*

D

Daityas—demons, sons of Diti.

Daśaratha Mahārāja—the father of Kṛṣṇa in His incarnation as Lord Rāmacandra.

Demigods—residents of the heavenly planets.

Diti—the mother of the demons.

E

Ekādaśī—a special fast day for increased remembrance of Kṛṣṇa, which comes on the eleventh day of both the waxing and waning moon.

G

Gandharvas—demigod singers and musicians.

Garbhodaka Ocean—the body of water that fills the bottom part of each material universe.

Garuḍa—the bird-carrier of Lord Viṣṇu.

Gāyatrī mantra—a transcendental vibration chanted by *brāhmaṇas.*

H

Hanumān—the great monkey devotee of Lord Rāmacandra.

Hare Kṛṣṇa mantra—the great chanting for deliverance:
Hare Kṛṣṇa, Hare Kṛṣṇa, Kṛṣṇa Kṛṣṇa, Hare Hare
Hare Rāma, Hare Rāma, Rāma Rāma, Hare Hare.

Heavenly planets—the upper planets in the material universe where the demigods reside.

Hellish planets—the lower planets in the material universe.

I

Indra—the king of the heavenly planets and chief of the administrative demigods.

Īśopaniṣad, Śrī—one of the principal *Upaniṣads.*

Iṣṭā—the performance of public welfare activities such as digging wells or planting trees.

J

Jaimini—an atheistic philosopher who advocated material work as the purpose of life.

Janmāṣṭamī—the celebration of Lord Kṛṣṇa's appearance in the material world.

Jīva Gosvāmī—one of the six Gosvāmīs; author of many authoritative books on the philosophy of Kṛṣṇa consciousness.

K

Kāmadhenu—a cow that gives unlimited quantities of milk.

Kaṁsa—Kṛṣṇa's uncle, who was always trying to kill Him.

Kīrtanānananda Swami—a leading disciple of ISKCON's founder-*ācārya,* Śrīla Prabhupāda; one of the current initiating spiritual masters of ISKCON and the founder of the New Vrindaban spiritual community.

Kṛṣṇa, Lord—the Supreme Personality of Godhead, appearing in His original, two-armed form, which is the origin of all the Lord's other forms and incarnations.

Kṛṣṇa Dvaipāyana Vedavyāsa. *See:* Vyāsadeva

Kṣatriya—the administrative and protective occupation according to the system of social and spiritual orders.

Kurus—the enemies of the Pāṇḍavas.

M

Madhvācārya—a thirteenth-century Vaiṣṇava spiritual master who preached the theistic philosophy of "pure dualism," which maintains that the Lord and the living entities are always distinct from one another.

Mantra—a sound vibration that can deliver the mind from illusion.

N

Nāgas—a race of serpents.

Nārada Muni—a great devotee who travels through space to preach the Lord's glories.

P

Pañcarātra—a class of scriptures that gives instructions for executing devotional service.

Paramātmā—the Supersoul, or localized aspect of the Supreme Lord.

Prabhupāda, Śrīla—founder and spiritual preceptor of the Hare Kṛṣṇa movement.

Prahlāda Mahārāja—a devotee of the Lord who was persecuted by his demoniac father but protected and saved by the Lord.

Pūrtam—performance of sacrifice.

R

Rāmacandra, Lord—an incarnation of the Lord who demonstrated the behavior of a perfect king.

Rūpa Gosvāmī—the chief of the six Vaiṣṇava spiritual masters who directly followed Lord Caitanya Mahāprabhu and systematically presented His teachings.

S

Samādhi—the state of trance in which the mind is fixed on the Supreme.

Saṅkarṣaṇa, Lord—an expansion of Lord Balarāma; assists in the creation, maintenance and destruction of material universes.

Sāṅkhya philosophy—analytical study of the body and the soul.
Sannyāsa order—the renounced order of life.
Satya-yuga—the first of the four ages of a *mahā-yuga*, lasting for 1,728,000 years.
Sītā—the consort of Lord Rāmacandra.
Śiva, Lord—the personality in charge of the mode of ignorance and the destruction of the material universe.
Smṛtis—literatures supplementary to the four *Vedas*, such as the *Purāṇas*, *Bhagavad-gītā* and *Mahābhārata*.
Śrīdhara Svāmī—a great Kṛṣṇa conscious scholar who wrote the original commentary on *Śrīmad-Bhāgavatam*.
Śrīvatsa—the unique curl of hair on the chest of Lord Viṣṇu.
Śrutis—scriptures received directly from God.
Sudarśana disc—a weapon of Lord Kṛṣṇa.
Śūdras—the laborer class of men according to the system of social and spiritual orders.
Śukadeva Gosvāmī—the sage who spoke *Śrīmad-Bhāgavatam* to Parīkṣit Mahārāja.
Supersoul. *See:* Paramātmā
Svāyambhuva Manu—one of the administrative demigods who are the fathers and lawgivers of mankind.
Śvetadvīpa—the only spiritual planet within the material universe; residence of Lord Viṣṇu.

T

Tulasī—a tree sacred to Lord Kṛṣṇa.

U

Uddhava—a great friend and devotee of Lord Viṣṇu.
Upaniṣads—108 philosophical portions of the *Vedas*.

V

Vaiśyas—the class of men engaged in business and farming according to the system of social and spiritual orders.
Vānaprastha—retired life.
Varṇāśrama—the Vedic institution dividing the human population into four social orders (*varṇas*) and four spiritual orders (*āśramas*).

Vedas—the original revealed scriptures first spoken by the Lord Himself.

Vidyādharas—inhabitants of the heavenly planets.

Viṣṇu-tattva—the original Personality of Godhead's primary expansions, each of whom is equally God.

Viśvanātha Cakravartī Ṭhākura—a great Kṛṣṇa conscious spiritual master who wrote a famous commentary on *Śrīmad-Bhāgavatam.*

Vṛndāvana—the village in India where Lord Kṛṣṇa fifty centuries ago displayed His transcendental childhood pastimes.

Vyāsadeva—an incarnation of Viṣṇu who compiled the *Vedas, Purāṇas, Mahābhārata, Vedānta-sūtra,* etc.

Y

Yaśodā—Kṛṣṇa's mother in His Vṛndāvana pastimes.

Yoga—various processes of spiritual realization, all ultimately meant for attaining the Supreme.

Yudhiṣṭhira Mahārāja—the eldest of the Pāṇḍava brothers; Lord Kṛṣṇa established him as king after the Battle of Kurukṣetra.

Sanskrit Pronunciation Guide

Throughout the centuries, the Sanskrit language has been written in a variety of alphabets. The mode of writing most widely used throughout India, however, is called *devanāgarī*, which means, literally, the writing used in "the cities of the demigods." The *devanāgarī* alphabet consists of forty-eight characters: thirteen vowels and thirty-five consonants. Ancient Sanskrit grammarians arranged this alphabet according to practical linguistic principles, and this order has been accepted by all Western scholars. The system of transliteration used in this book conforms to a system that scholars in the last fifty years have accepted to indicate the pronunciation of each Sanskrit sound.

Vowels

अ a आ ā इ i ई ī उ u ऊ ū ऋ ṛ
ॠ ṝ ऌ ḷ ए e ऐ ai ओ o औ au

Consonants

Gutturals:	क ka	ख kha	ग ga	घ gha	ङ ṅa
Palatals:	च ca	छ cha	ज ja	झ jha	ञ ña
Cerebrals:	ट ṭa	ठ ṭha	ड ḍa	ढ ḍha	ण ṇa
Dentals:	त ta	थ tha	द da	ध dha	न na
Labials:	प pa	फ pha	ब ba	भ bha	म ma
Semivowels:	य ya	र ra	ल la	व va	
Sibilants:	श śa	ष ṣa	स sa		
Aspirate:	ह ha	Anusvāra: ं ṁ	Visarga: ः ḥ		

Numerals

०-0 १-1 २-2 ३-3 ४-4 ५-5 ६-6 ७-7 ८-8 ९-9

The vowels are written as follows after a consonant:

ा ā ि i ी ī ु u ू ū ृ ṛ ॄ ṝ े e ै ai ो o ौ au

For example: क ka का kā कि ki की kī कु ku कू kū

कृ kṛ कॄ kṝ के ke कै kai को ko कौ kau

Generally two or more consonants in conjunction are written together in a special form, as for example: क्ष kṣa त्र tra

The vowel "a" is implied after a consonant with no vowel symbol.

The symbol virāma (्) indicates that there is no final vowel: क्

The vowels are pronounced as follows:

a — as in but
ā — as in far but held twice as long as a
ai — as in aisle
au — as in how
e — as in they
i — as in pin
ī — as in pique but held twice as long as i
ḷ — as in lree
o — as in go
ṛ — as in rim
ṝ — as in reed but held twice as long as ṛ
u — as in push
ū — as in rule but held twice as long as u

The consonants are pronounced as follows:

Gutturals
(pronounced from the throat)
k — as in kite
kh — as in Eckhart
g — as in give
gh — as in dig-hard
ṅ — as in sing

Labials
(pronounced with the lips)
p — as in pine
ph — as in up-hill (not f)
b — as in bird
bh — as in rub-hard
m — as in mother

Cerebrals
(pronounced with tip of tongue against roof of mouth)

ṭ — as in **t**ub
ṭh — as in ligh**t-h**eart
ḍ — as in **d**ove
ḍh — as in re**d-h**ot
ṇ — as in si**n**g

Palatals
(pronounced with middle of tongue against palate)

c — as in **ch**air
ch — as in staun**ch-h**eart
j — as in **j**oy
jh — as in he**dgeh**og
ñ — as in ca**ny**on

Dentals
(pronounced as cerebrals but with tongue against teeth)

t — as in **t**ub
th — as in ligh**t-h**eart
d — as in **d**ove
dh — as in re**d-h**ot
n — as in **n**ut

Semivowels

y — as in **y**es
r — as in **r**un
l — as in **l**ight
v — as in **v**ine, except when preceded in the same syllable by a consonant, then like in s**w**an

Sibilants

ś — as in the German word *s***p***rechen*
ṣ — as in **sh**ine
s — as in **s**un

Aspirate

h — as in **h**ome

Anusvāra

ṁ — a resonant nasal sound like in the French word *bo***n**

Visarga

ḥ — a final **h**-sound: **aḥ** is pronounced like **aha**; **iḥ** like **ihi**

There is no strong accentuation of syllables in Sanskrit, or pausing between words in a line, only a flowing of short and long (twice as long as the short) syllables. A long syllable is one whose vowel is long (**ā, ai, au, e, ī, o, ṝ, ū**) or whose short vowel is followed by more than one consonant (including **ḥ** and **ṁ**). Aspirated consonants (consonants followed by an **h**) count as single consonants.

Index of Sanskrit Verses

This index constitutes a complete listing of the first and third lines of each of the Sanskrit poetry verses of this volume of *Śrīmad-Bhāgavatam*, arranged in English alphabetical order. The first column gives the Sanskrit transliteration, and the second and third columns, respectively, list the chapter-verse reference and page number for each verse.

A

N

T

General Index

Numerals in boldface type indicate references to translations of the verses of *Śrīmad-Bhāgavatam.*

A

A as Lord's representation, **293**
Abhibhūyate defined, 224
Abhijit as Lord's representation, **303**
Abhijñam defined, 9
Abja
defined, 150
See also: Universe
Abja-yoni defined, 150
Abode of Lord. *See:* Kṛṣṇa, abode of; Supreme Lord, abode of; *specific abodes of Lord*
Absolute Truth
devotees of. *See:* Devotee(s)
devotional service to. *See:* Devotional service
emanations of, everything as, 17
existence of, in everything, **280, 281**
existence "separate" from, **191**
knowledge about
advice that lacks, 214
via chanting, 115
lacking in *māyā*, 54
Kṛṣṇa as, 5, 14, 36, 71, 78, 104, 138, **284**
kuyogīs' perception of, 279
Lord's words as, 117
loving exchanges with, 79
materialists neglect, 97
part & parcel of, everything as, 14
perceived via hearing & chanting, **232**
perception of, peace via, 71
realization of, via intelligence, 208
"separate" existence from, **191**
as source of everything, 111
speculation about, 117
understanding of, via love for Lord, 82
See also: Kṛṣṇa; Supreme Lord
Ācārya(s)
defined, 343
See also: Spiritual master(s)
A. C. Bhaktivedanta Swami Prabhupāda. *See:* Prabhupāda, Śrīla
Acintya-bhedābheda-tattva philosophy
explanation of, 344
See also: Kṛṣṇa consciousness
Action(s)
fruitive. *See:* Fruitive activities
Lord ultimate performer of, 67
of body. *See:* Body, material, activities of
as offering to Lord, **83–85**, 100
Acyuta, Lord, **324**
See also: Kṛṣṇa; Supreme Lord
Adambha defined, 334
Ādayan defined, 69
Addhā
defined, 171
See also: Meditation, on Lord
Ādhārādi-cakras
defined, 145
See also: Brahmā
Adharma-rataḥ defined, 35
Adhauta-dad-vāsa defined, 339
Adhvaryu priest, 330
Aditi
Indra son of, 315
Viṣṇu son of, **293**, 294
Ādyaḥ defined, 18
Ādye defined, 56
Āgamāpāyino 'nityāḥ
quoted, 30
Age, modern. *See:* Kali-yuga
Aghāsura demon, 226
Agni, Lord, **293**
Agnihotra sacrifice, 124
Agnosticism, **181**–82
Ahaṅkāra-kṛtam defined, 189
Ahaṅkāra-vimūḍhātmā
verse quoted, 38, 68
Aho amī deva-varāmarārcitam
verse quoted, 131

B

Devotional service (*continued*)
vs. *māyā*, 38, 229
meditation on Lord qualification for, 234
meditation on Lord via, **207**
mentality needed for, **108–9**
mental speculation &, 209
methods of
listed, 89
See also: specific methods of service
mind in, **2,** 84, 85, 209, 352
mystic perfections &, **278, 279**
as natural, 209–10, 248
as original position of soul, **231**
peace via, 100
as perfectional stage of welfare work, 98
perfection of life via, 102, **278**
position as devotee understood via, 85
practical, recommended, **83,** 84, 85
Prahlāda's example of, 128
preparatory activities for, 124
pride danger to, 175
pure devotees' association &, 126
pure devotees spread, 91, 93
pure devotional service via, 101–2
purification via, 4, 72, 84, 85, 101–2, **228, 229, 231**
rāja-yoga &, 248
realizations via, 38
recommendation of practical, **83,** 84
regulative duties in, 4
relationship with Lord revived via, 271
as religion's real meaning, 88
religious activities minus, **228**
renunciation in, 74, 371
renunciation of, condemned, 78, 279
secondary activities in, 124–26, **130,** 131, **133,** 145
selfishness absent in, 7, 8
self-realization requires, 237
sense gratification &, 185, 209, 223, 371
via shelter of Lord, 225
sincerity in, 102
spiritual master engages in, 343–44
in spiritual world, 52
spontaneous, 248
spread by mercy of Lord, 93

Devotional service (*continued*)
spread by pure devotees, 93
value judgments (material) &, 190
Vedas recommend, 208–9
Vedic ceremonies &, 125
as welfare work, perfect, 98
worship to Lord &, **115**
yoga's perfection achieved via, **279**
yoga systems &, 248
Yudhiṣṭhira's example of, 125
See also: Pure devotional service; *specific methods of service*
Devotion to Lord
as *brāhmaṇa's* quality, **333**
compared to fire, **225**
compared with *jñāna*, 352
compared with *karma*, 352
compared with *yoga*, 352
devotee protected by, 224
duality ended by, 248
falldown avoided via, 224
pride danger to, 175
purification via, **273**
speculation mixed with, 117
See also: Devotional service
Dharma
defined, 41, 87, 160
See also: Religious principles
Dharmaḥ sv-anuṣṭhitaḥ puṁsām
verse quoted, 133
Dharma-maya defined, 265
Dharmam eke defined, 215
Dharmavyādha, **128,** 129
Dhṛtimān defined, 101
Dhyāna
defined, 237
See also: Meditation
Dīpāvalokaṁ me nopayuñjyān
quoted, 110
Disciple(s)
characteristics of, **10, 11**
compared to business trainee, 346
compared to child, 343, 346
desire of, **10**
false prestige absent in, **10**

G

H

I

Demigod(s) (*continued*)
Lord's representation among, **293, 294**
mystic perfections via birth as, 279
origin of, **211**
perception of, via mystic perfection, **255**
pleasure gardens of, **270**
sacrifices for, **31**
as servants of Lord, 248
spiritual master representative of all, **342**
śūdras servants of, **335**
as universe's managers, 92
worship to. *See:* Worship, to demigods
See also: specific demigods
Demon(s)
compared with devotees, 128
compared with *gopīs*, 128
devotional service &, 128
Indra as perceived by, 315
liberation obtained by, 128
Lord &, 87
Lord's representation among, **295**
midnight hour &, 164
origin of, **211**
See also: specific demons
Designations, material
enmity to Lord increases, 14
freedom from, 14, 55
See also: Bodily concept of life
Desire, material
birth-death cycle via, 35
brahmacārī's fulfilling, **354**
celibacy vow vs., **352**
compared to blow, 224
compared to disease, 224
compared to weeds, 228
creation perceived via, 301
vs. devotees, **224**
in devotional service, 101
enjoying spiritual knowledge as, 84
via family life, **354**
freedom from
via devotional service, 197
via love for Lord, 8
via meditation on Lord, **219**
via perception of material life, **3**, 4
pure devotees possess, 352
Desire, material (*continued*)
fulfillment of all, 264
hearing and chanting about Lord &, 88
via lack of sense control, **169**
material existence via, 154
via meditation on modes of nature, **168**
vs. mental speculation, 229
modes of nature source of, **211**
mystic perfection that facilitates, **253**
vs. mystic *yoga*, 229
philosophies via various, **211–14**
pure devotional service devoid of, 102
saintly person &, **96**
via uncontrolled senses, **169**
of *vaiśyas*, **334**
Desirelessness. *See:* Desire, freedom from
Detachment
from attack, **72**
from body, 98
as desirable, 23
by devotee, 100, 101
via devotional service, 184
as intelligence's symptom, 71
via intelligent observation, 11–12
via knowledge, 101, 184
Kṛṣṇa consciousness necessary for, 374
lack of, **223**
Lord recommends, **11**
materialistic philosophers reject, 22
from mental speculation, 163
via perception of contamination by modes, **170**
via self-realization, 17
by self-realized souls, **70**
via study of scriptures, 163
via spiritual advancement, 360
via understanding Lord, 149
via understanding material world, 196
from worship, **72**
Devakī, Kṛṣṇa son of, 93
Devala, **303**
Devarṣi-bhūtāpta-nṛṇāṁ pitṝṇām
verse quoted, 368

L

M

Materialistic philosophies, **21**, 24–**24**, **212–16**
See also: specific philosophies
Materialistic scriptures, 163–64
Materialistic workers. *See:* Fruitive workers
Materialist(s)
bliss (spiritual) not understood by, 218
compared to animals, 288
defense propensity of, 99
devotee avoids hearing from, 99
devotee not understood by, 100
harmfulness of, 97
intelligence of, **5**
as "killers of the self," 97
Lord's opulences not appreciated by, 288
love for Lord absent in, 218
material life criticized by, 168–67
mentality of, 169
perception by, of enemies, 99
plans of, characteristics of, 169
prayers by, 35
self-realization neglected by, 97
spiritual master criticized by, 344
See also: Conditioned souls
Material life
as artificial imposition, 15
via attachment (material), 152
birth-death cycle via, 167
via bodily concept of life, 152, 189
compared to dream, **53–54**, 65
compared to ocean, 78, 118
compared to tree, **61**–64, **151**–54
compared with Kṛṣṇa consciousness, 26
composition of, **153**
conclusion of, 27
criticism against, by materialists, 168–69
death &, **27–28**, 189
defined, **15**, 51
via desires (material), 154
devotee defeats, 101
devotional service ends, **116**–17
duality of. *See:* Duality
engagement in, requirements for, 28
false ego cause of, **15**
Material life (*continued*)
freedom from
via celibacy, 352
via devotional service, **116**
via knowledge, **15**, 16, 101
via pastimes of Lord, relishing, 118
via shelter of Lord, 118
See also: Liberation
identification with philosophies of, 14
via ignorance, **55**
via illusion, **15**, 40
intelligence lacking in, **168**
knowledge ends, **15**, 16, 101
knowledge lacking in, 54
living entity bound by, **188**, 189
problems of, Lord deliverer from, 141
question about source of, 43
reality lacking in, **54**
as relative, 26
renunciation of desire to enjoy, **188**
results of, **152**
sanity &, 28
suffering via, 152, 167, 189
See also: Conditioned life
Material nature. *See: Māyā;* Nature, material
Material objects
creation of, by Lord, 10
existence of, explained, 55
as expansions of Lord, 77
as happiness' source, 10
See also: Sense objects
Material qualities, six, **96**
Material value judgments, 190
Material variety, 70
Material work. *See:* Fruitive activities
Material world
birth-death cycle in. *See:* Birth-death cycle
bondage to, process of, 51
compared with agricultural field, **150**
conditioned soul's perception of, 314
connection with via imagination, 51
as creation of Lord, 191
dealings in, proper mentality for, **196–97**
as dependent on *mahat-tattva*, 311
detachment from. *See:* Detachment
devotees' perception of, 274

N

O

Q

Questions
by Arjuna, **289, 290**
qualification for answering, 178
by Uddhava. *See:* Uddhava, questions by
Quotations. *See: specific quotes; specific books, quotations from; specific persons quoted*

R

Rabbit, "horns of," illusion &, 191
Rādhārāṇī, 345
Radio, "preachers" on, 359
Raghunātha dāsa Gosvāmī cited on spiritual master, 344
Rāja-dharma defined, 125
Rāja-vidyā defined, 59
Rāja-yoga, 248
Rākṣasas
Lord's representation among, **295**
See also: Demons
Rāmacandra, Lord
as incarnation of Lord, 79, 80
Jaṭāyu &, 129
Vibhīṣaṇa &, 129
Rāmādi-mūrtiṣu kalā-niyamena
verse quoted, 80
Rāma-līla. See: Rāmacandra
Rāsa dance of Kṛṣṇa, 87
See also: Kṛṣṇa, conjugal affairs with
Reality
Lord actual, 199
material life lacks, **54**
of material world, 191
universe as ultimate, illusion of, 82
Recaka exercises, **239**
Regulations, material. *See:* Duties, material
Regulative principles
goodness mode via, 164
See also: Religious principles
Reincarnation. *See:* Birth-death cycle; Transmigration of soul
Religious cult, rejection of, 164
Religious principles
activities in, renunciation of, 102
brāhmaṇa follower of, 362
Religious principles (*continued*)
bull representation of, **329**
devotional service characterizes, **160**
devotional service meaning of, 88
via goodness mode, **160, 161,** 164
Haṁsa teacher of, **323**
for householders, **369**
Lord as goal of, **329**
Lord instructor of, **324**
Lord knower of, **325**
Lord shelter of, **201**
Lord's representation among, **302**
neglect of, **96**
vs. passion, **161**
potency of, minus devotional service, **228**
in Satya-yuga, **327–29**
scientific presentation of, 327
secondary, 328
sectarian, 141
surrender to Lord supreme, 328
in Tretā-yuga, **330**
understood via goodness, **163**
varṇāśrama system scientific presentation of, 327
in Vedic scriptures, **96**
Religious services as principle for society, **351**
Renounced order of life. *See: Sannyāsa* order
Renunciation
artificial platform of, 185
of association with women, **235**
of attachment to women, 372
of bodily concept of life, 316
by *brahmacārī*, **339–49**
defined, 186
of desire to enjoy material life, **188**
by devotee of sense gratification, 101–2
devotee's understanding of, 74
devotee's use of, 100
in devotional service, 74
of devotional service, condemned, 279
of dream of being Lord, 149
as expansion of Lord's opulence, **313**
of false vision of world, **16**
of family life. *See: Sannyāsa* order
of gambling, 9
gradual stages of, 7

S

U

W